Termination of Employment: A Practical Guide for Employers

Second Edition

D1425987

To Orla and Jessica

Termination of Employment: A Practical Guide for Employers

Second Edition

Alastair Purdy
Solicitor

Bloomsbury Professional

Published by
Bloomsbury Professional
Maxwelton House
41–43 Boltro Road
Haywards Heath
West Sussex
RH16 1BJ

Bloomsbury Professional
The Fitzwilliam Business Centre
26 Upper Pembroke Street
Dublin 2

ISBN 978 1 84766 720 5

British Library Cataloguing-in-Publication Data
A catalogue record for this book is available from the British Library

Typeset by Marie Armah-Kwantreng, Dublin, Ireland
Printed and bound in the United Kingdom by CPI Antony Rowe,
Chippenham and Eastbourne

PREFACE

The purpose of the first edition of this book was to produce something that practitioners could 'dip into' and quickly find the solution to the problem they were facing.

I had known from my early days in employment law that whilst learning the law was one thing, putting it into practice properly and professionally took an inordinate amount of time. In fact learning the rudimentaries of the practical aspects of employment law took me at least five years and even at that I am grateful to say that today (some nineteen years on) that I am still learning.

To my great surprise, after I had finished the first edition I found myself 'dipping' into the book on regular occasions. Firstly, I had forgotten most of what I had written and secondly, despite the cringe factor of reading my own book, I found – to my great amazement – that most of it had practical application.

Following the launch of the first edition, I have had many different experiences in the area of employment law. These have arisen by virtue of not only new experiences in the area (as not a day goes past that something new doesn't arise) but also as a result of new legislation and case law that has been effected in the intervening period. The greatest lesson I have learned is that similar to all areas of law it is not possible to dip in and out of employment law. In fact real expertise (as in most areas) only comes from doing something repeatedly.

The legislation in this area is not only substantial: it is also complex. Most importantly, putting it into practice is demanding. This book is primarily concerned with the latter aspect in that it seeks to set out the law as it currently stands but also focuses particularly on the practical aspects that must be considered when a termination of employment either occurs or is contemplated. Specifically, it deals with the notice that must be given, the forms that must be filled out, the various options open to claimants and the penalties for non-compliance. I seek to guide employers through the legal aspects of employment termination in a practical and comprehensible manner. The book is, and should be regarded as, a practical guide for employers who are in the process of dealing with terminations, responding to claims or taking appeals under the legislation.

The text is divided into eleven chapters each of which deals with a particular aspect of the law as it relates to termination of employment. Contained therein are some practical guides pertaining to the issues raised. The text contains only a brief outline of the legislation. A more detailed analysis is beyond the scope of this book.

Alastair Purdy

March 2011

CONTENTS

TABLE OF CASES

TABLE OF STATUTES

TABLE OF STATUTORY INSTRUMENTS

TABLE OF EUROPEAN LEGISLATION

Chapter 1

THE INSTITUTIONAL FRAMEWORK

[1.01] There are numerous statutory bodies that deal with claims brought by claimants under employment legislation. It is essential for practitioners to be able to distinguish between the various bodies, but more importantly to be able to choose the appropriate forum in which to deal with a claim. This applies equally to those representing claimants as well as those defending such proceedings. For those defending proceedings (which this book deals with) it is important to understand the 'end game', ie where the claim is likely to end up and how the particular forum that hears the case is likely to deal with it.

The forum a claimant chooses generally arises as a result of which piece of legislation the claim is being brought under. Increasingly it is a feature of employment law claims that employers are faced with several claims at once under various employment law statutes. It is therefore difficult to predict how a claim will actually be heard. Notwithstanding this, once 'papers' are served employers will know how claimants and their representatives are going to proceed. It is then up to employers to plan a strategy to defend such actions. This demands a proper understanding of the various employment law fora and how they function at a practical level.

RIGHTS COMMISSIONER

[1.02] A Rights Commissioner is an officer appointed under the Industrial Relations Act 1969. Rights Commissioners investigate disputes, grievances and claims that individuals or small groups of workers refer under the following main pieces of legislation:

Acts:

1. Consumer Protection Act 2007;

2. Adoptive Leave Acts 1995 and 2005;

3. Carer's Leave Act 2001;

4. Competition Acts 2002–2006;

5. Employees (Provision of Information & Consultation) Act 2006;

6. Industrial Relations Acts 1969–2004;

7. Maternity Protection Acts 1994 and 2004;

8. National Minimum Wage Act 2000;

9. Organisation of Working Time Act 1997;

10. Parental Leave Act 1998–2006;

11. Payment of Wages Act 1991;

12. Protection of Employees (Fixed-Term Work) Act 2003;

13. Protection of Employees (Part-Time Work) Act 2001;

14. Protection of Young Persons (Employment) Act 1996;

15. Protections for Persons Reporting Child Abuse Act 1998;

16. Safety, Health and Welfare at Work Act 2005;

17. Terms of Employment (Information) Act 1994 and 2001;

18. Unfair Dismissals Acts 1977–2007;

19. Health Act 2007;

20. EU (Transfer of Undertakings) Regulations 2003;

21. Industrial Relations (Miscellaneous Provisions) Act, 2004.

Statutory Instruments:

1. European Communities (Protection of Employment) Regulations 2000;

2. European Communities (Safeguarding of Employees Rights on Transfer of Undertakings) Regulations 2003;

3. European Communities (European PLC) (Employee Involvement) Regulations 2006.

Rights Commissioners issue the findings of their investigations in the form of either non-binding recommendations or decisions, depending on the legislation under which a case is referred.

Regarding the termination of employment, Rights Commissioners may hear a claim under various employment law statues. Whereas claims for unfair dismissal were traditionally the preserve of the 1977 Unfair Dismissals Act (as amended) and the Industrial Relations Act of 1969, in recent years the number of Acts under which claims for the termination of employment are capable of being heard has expanded greatly. Now for instance a claimant can take claims for unfair dismissal under the following:

1. Unfair Dismissals Act 1977–2007;

2. Organisation of Working Time Act 1997;

3. Employment Equality Act 1998–2007;[1]

4. Protection of Employees (Part-Time Work) Act 2001;

5. Protection of Employees (Fixed-Term Work) Act 2003;

6. National Minimum Wage Act 2000;

---

1.   Note these claims are heard by the Equality Tribunal not the Rights Commissioner.

7. Safety, Health and Welfare at Work Act 2005;

8. Protection of Persons Reporting Child Abuse Act 1998;

9. Industrial Relations (Miscellaneous Provisions) Act 2004;

10. Competition Acts 2002–2006;

11. EU (Transfer of Undertakings) Regulations 2003;

12. Maternity Protection Acts 1994 and 2004;

13. Health Act 2007.

The interesting thing about some of these Acts is that, unlike the Unfair Dismissals Act, the one year's continuous service rule may not apply; in other words employees, despite often having less than one year's continuous service, can still qualify to take a claim under legislation.[2]

Referrals

[1.03] A party to a dispute with regard to the termination of employment may object to a Rights Commissioner's investigation where the case has been referred under the Industrial Relations Acts 1969–2004 or under the Unfair Dismissals Acts 1977–2007. Where such an objection is made, the Rights Commissioner cannot investigate the case. If the application is made under the Industrial Relations Acts and same objected to, then that is generally the end of the matter, unless the applicant refers it under s 20 of the 1969 Industrial Relations Act. This, however, is non-binding on employers. Should the applicant have referred the matter under the unfair dismissals legislation and this is objected to, then the matter is automatically referred to the Employment Appeals Tribunal (EAT) to hear the case. A similar right of objection does not apply for referrals under the other Acts. A Rights Commissioner investigates such cases in the first instance.

Referrals under the Industrial Relations Acts generally arise when the claimant does not meet the qualifying criteria under the unfair dismissals legislation or where they are outside the time limits provided for in the other Acts, ie the occurrence of the penalisation or victimisation occurred longer than six to 12 months prior to the referral. They may also arise in unionised companies where the union may wish to strike pursuant to the dismissal.[3] It is highly unusual for employers to agree to attend the Rights Commissioners under the Industrial Relations Acts in a dispute concerning the dismissal of an employee but it can sometimes arise where employers may wish to resolve the matter amicably through a mediated settlement.

---

2. See para **3.09** for definition of continuous service.
3. The Industrial Relations Act 1990, s 9(2) provides that a strike on an individual issue is legal once any locally agreed procedures have been exhausted. It may be argued that if the company objects to the matter being heard under the Industrial Relations Acts that the procedures have been exhausted – this is particularly the case for those claimants that do not meet the qualifying criteria for the Unfair Dismissals Acts.

Appeals

[1.04] It is possible to appeal against a recommendation of the Rights Commissioner provided the appeal is lodged within the time limits set down in the legislation (see Form on time limits at **1.46**). The relevant Acts govern whether the appeal is to the Labour Court or to the EAT. Under the Unfair Dismissals Acts, the EU Transfer of Undertakings Regulations, the Maternity Protection Act 1994 and 2006, the Protection of Persons Reporting Child Abuse Act 1998 and the Competition Acts 2002–2006 the appeal is to the EAT. Under the Industrial Relations Acts, the Protection of Employees (Part-Time Work) Act 2001, the Protection of Employees (Fixed-Term Work) Act 2003, the National Minimum Wage Act 2000, the Organisation of Working Time Act 1997 and the Safety, Health and Welfare at Work Act 2005, the appeal is to the Labour Court.

Having heard the appeal, the court or tribunal will issue a decision which is binding on the parties to the dispute. This is one of the reasons that employers should not agree to have the matter of a dismissal heard under the Industrial Relations Acts as it allows the union (in unionised employments) to strike in pursuit of a binding yet non-enforceable recommendation.

Of importance here is that an appeal to the EAT is a completely new hearing and therefore both sides are free to adduce additional or new evidence at the hearing. However, it must be borne in mind that the appeal form, from the Rights Commissioner to the Employment Appeals Tribunal (form T1–B – see **3.92**), presuming the matter is being heard under the Unfair Dismissal Act, requests that the grounds of appeal be stated and it also provides that a copy of the Rights Commissioner's decision must be forwarded with the form. Therefore, EAT is always aware of the decision of the Rights Commissioner. Consequently this is an issue that might have a bearing on whether a company decides to appeal or not.

Place of hearing

[1.05] Hearings before a Rights Commissioner take place in private, other than claims under the Payment of Wages Act which are held in public. In practice, in relation to the latter it is extremely rare for any member of the public to turn up at such hearing. This is particularly so given that there is no 'public' notice of the hearing so the only people aware of it actually occurring are the parties to it.

Process of hearing

[1.06] The hearings before the Rights Commissioner are formal but not adversarial. Each side is given the chance to fully present their case. Written submissions are not needed but they are requested by the Rights Commissioner and may be helpful to the Rights Commissioner in order to focus on the relevant points. It also assists the Rights Commissioner to have a record of the statements made at the hearing when considering their recommendation or decision following the hearing.

In some cases, it is possible to settle disputes between the parties on the day of a hearing, with the assistance of the Rights Commissioner. This was common practice in previous years but is becoming increasingly less so in present times as many Rights Commissioners are fearful of being sued.

It is entirely a matter for the Rights Commissioner to decide how to conduct a hearing. Rights Commissioners do not allow mobile phones, tape recorders, cameras or other recording equipment to be used at their hearings.

Documents needed

[1.07] The Rights Commissioner's function is to issue decisions or recommendations based on the facts and evidence presented at a hearing. For this reason it must be ensured that relevant information (such as witnesses, pay-slips, correspondence, etc) is available for the hearing.

Representation

[1.08] It is up to the claimant and the employer to decide whether they wish to be represented at a Rights Commissioner's hearing. Traditionally employers were not represented but given the plethora of legislation that now impacts this area it is advisable to bring representation.

Referral of disputes

[1.09] A claimant firstly fills out a complaint form and forwards it to the Secretariat of the Rights Commissioners Service in the Labour Relations Commission (see forms **1.42.** and **1.43.** below for claims regarding the termination of employment). These forms are issued to assist claimants in submitting complaints under each Act. The complaint has to be submitted in writing to the Commission. The Rights Commissioner then sends a note to the employer detailing that the dispute has been referred asking whether the respondant rejects the application and stating that they will be in contact to organise a suitable time and date for the hearing. It is generally not possible at this stage to know which Rights Commissioner will be dealing with the dispute.

Adjournments

[1.10] Similar to the Employment Appeals Tribunal, adjournments must be applied for at the earliest possible opportunity and directed to the Secretariat of the Rights Commissioners Service. Whereas there is no strict rule on this, one adjournment is generally allowed on the basis that the request is genuine, supported by relevant documentation and consented to by the claimant or their representative. However it is not wise to assume that this will always be the case.

EMPLOYMENT APPEALS TRIBUNAL

[1.11] The Employment Appeals Tribunal is an independent body, bound to act judicially. It was set up to provide a speedy, fair, inexpensive and informal means for individuals to seek remedies for alleged infringements of their statutory rights. It is a statutory body and deals with and adjudicates on employment disputes under the following statutes:

- Redundancy Payments Acts 1967 to 2007;

- Minimum Notice and Terms of Employment Acts 1973–2005;

- Unfair Dismissals Acts 1977 to 2007;

- Protection of Employees (Employers' Insolvency) Acts 1984 to 2004;

- Organisation of Working Time Act 1997;

- Payment of Wages Act 1991;

- Terms of Employment (Information) Acts 1994 and 2001;

- Maternity Protection Acts 1994 and 2004;

- Adoptive Leave Acts 1995 and 2005;

- Protection of Young Persons (Employment) Act 1996;

- Parental Leave Acts 1998 and 2006;

- Protections for Persons Reporting Child Abuse Act 1998;

- European Communities (Safeguarding of Employees' Rights on Transfer of Undertakings) Regulations 2003;

- European Communities (Protection of Employment) Regulations 2000;

- Carer's Leave Act 2001;

- Competition Act 2002;

- Consumer Protection Act 2007.

Termination of employment cases

[1.12] In respect of termination of employment cases the Tribunal hears the following statutory claims or appeals:

- **Initial claims** taken under the Unfair Dismissals Acts 1977–2005 or the Minimum Notice and Terms of Employment Acts 1973–2001;

- **Appeals** from a Rights Commissioner's Recommendation are heard under both of the above pieces of legislation along with appeals under the EU Transfer of Undertakings Regulations, the Maternity Protection Act 1994 and 2006, the Protection of Persons Reporting Child Abuse Act 1998 and the Competition Acts 2002–2006. In addition the Tribunal hears appeals under the other employment law statutes, including appeals under the Redundancy Payments Acts 1967–2003 by employees against a decision by an employer or deciding officer or appeals by employers against a decision by the Minister for Enterprise, Trade and Employment or a Deciding Officer;

- **Claims** where an employer has failed to implement a Rights Commissioner's recommendation.

Structure of the Tribunal

[1.13] The tribunal consists of a Chairman, numerous Vice-Chairmen and a panel of members who are nominated by the Irish Congress of Trade Unions and by employers' organisations. A secretariat comprising full-time civil servants seconded from the Department of Enterprise, Trade and Employment, assists the Tribunal in its discharge of administrative duties.

The tribunal sits by division. Each division comprises the Chairperson (or Vice Chairperson), an employee member and an employer member. A secretary from the Department of Enterprise, Trade and Employment is also present. Decisions of the Tribunal may be unanimous or by majority. Where they are by majority the decisions are often accompanied by a dissenting opinion either by the employer or employee member.

Proceedings before the Tribunal

[1.14] Proceedings before the EAT are held in public and governed by the rules of evidence. Whilst these tend not to be as strictly enforced as in the District, Circuit or High Court, legal practitioners are obliged to adhere to them. If there are any documents to be submitted to the Tribunal, the original and at least five copies of the document(s) must be produced at the hearing – three for the Tribunal members, one for the secretary, and one for the other side. It is prudent to exchange these documents with the other side before the hearing and to get agreement on them, otherwise it is likely that they will be objected to or alternatively the Tribunal will ask for an adjournment to allow both parties time to agree on same. Interestingly the Employment Appeals Tribunal, Procedure Revision Groups report published on 23 May 2007 recommended a preliminary hearing at which, amongst other things, such documentation would be exchanged, and that this should be held in camera. To date none of those recommendations have been implemented. If so it would allow a 'two-stage' process which would be somewhat similar to the process in the UK where the initial appeal is to the 'Industrial Tribunal' with appeal to the EAT.

Adjournments

[1.15] Adjournments at the EAT are notoriously difficult to get. The process is that you must appear before the Tribunal and make a formal application. In the 'Notice of Hearing' which is sent to the parties to the appeal it states that:

> A party seeking an adjournment must make a formal application any sitting division of the Tribunal. Good cause must be shown and the consent of the other party sought before any application for an adjournment will be considered by the Tribunal, but the existence of such consent alone is never a sufficient reason for granting an adjournment. Only in the gravest circumstances will the foregoing procedure be departed from.

Further the attached 'Notice for Parties' which each party to a hearing receives states that:

> An application for a postponement should only be made in extremely exceptional circumstances and must be made immediately or within 5 working days of receipt of the Notice of Hearing.

For postponements, this five-day period is most important and should be adhered to at all costs. That said, there are times when other intervening events occur that necessitate late applications and the Tribunal recognises this. Nonetheless, there is no obligation on the Tribunal to grant an adjournment at all, particularly post the five-day period.

It is clear therefore that all applications must be made in a timely manner with the consent of the opposing party. That said, the Tribunal is not consistent in its application of this and I have been at hearings where applications were made on the day and granted because counsel for the claimant failed to turn up, and at others where due to the employer being in another Circuit Court case on the day and despite a previous application being made and rejected for an adjournment the case proceeded in the absence of the employer. Take what you will from this but the lesson is to try and get in as early as possible.

Witness summons?

[1.16] The tribunal has the power to issue witness summonses. However, similar to the above these applications must be made in good time and by way of a formal application to a sitting division of the Tribunal. A brief history of the case should be given along with the reasons as to why the various witnesses are required. If granted the summonses must then be served on the witness.

Joining third parties

[1.17] This generally arises where there is confusion about who the employer is, such as where the employee is an agency worker, or where a transfer of an undertaking has occurred and the claimant has failed to take a claim against one of the parties. In such circumstances the Tribunal will often ask that another party be 'joined' in the proceedings. The tribunal itself actually has no power to join a third party so what generally happens is that the representatives for the claimant make an application to the Tribunal under s 39 of the Organisation of Working Time Act 1997 to have the party 'joined' in the proceedings. Whilst such a direction from the Tribunal is legally suspect, it does occur regularly and the application itself once done correctly under the said section is legally sound. This is dealt with in more detail at **3.12**.

Findings

[1.18] The tribunal issues a written legally binding determination following a hearing. These may be appealed to the Circuit Court if taken under the unfair dismissals legislation and onwards to the High Court on a point of law. Matters taken under the Minimum Notice Acts and Redundancy Acts may only be appealed to the High Court on a point of law.

EQUALITY TRIBUNAL

[1.19] The Equality Tribunal is an independent statutory office which investigates or mediates complaints of unlawful discrimination.

The Equality Tribunal's principal role is the investigation and mediation of complaints of discrimination in relation to employment and in relation to access to goods and services, disposal of property and certain aspects of education. This protection against discrimination applies to all nine grounds on which discrimination is prohibited under the equality legislation.

The tribunal may also investigate complaints of discrimination on the grounds of gender under the Pensions Acts 1990–2008 where an employer has failed to comply with the principle of equal treatment in relation to occupational benefit or pension schemes.

Termination of employment cases

[1.20] Under the Equality Act 2004[4] the Labour Court ceased to have first instance jurisdiction in cases of dismissal where discrimination or victimisation is alleged. Instead the Equality Tribunal now has jurisdiction to deal with all aspects of alleged discrimination and victimisation including discriminatory dismissals with the Labour Court acting exclusively in an appellate capacity.

Procedure

[1.21] A complaint under the Employment Equality Acts 1998–2008 must be made within six months of the last incident of discrimination (except in cases of equal pay). The date on which a complaint is made is taken as the date on which the Tribunal receives a completed complaint form (EE 1) see **11.53** or a complaint made through appropriate alternative arrangements agreed with the Tribunal. The Director of the Tribunal has the power under the Act to extend the time for making a complaint for 'reasonable cause'. This was changed in the 2004 Act from 'exceptional circumstances' which remains the test under the Unfair Dismissals Act. Reasonable cause has been held to be a much less onerous test than 'exceptional circumstances'; however, the complainant must apply for an extension. Should the complainant miss the six-month time limit they must write to the Tribunal giving detailed reasons and including any supporting documents (eg medical certificates) as to why. A copy of their documentation is then sent to the respondent for comment together with a copy of the complaint. The Director or Equality Officer will consider the material presented by both sides and then decide whether to grant the extension for reasonable cause. If either party disagrees with the decision they can appeal this to the Labour Court within 42 days of the decision.

When a complaint is forwarded to the Tribunal it is acknowledged and a copy sent to the employer (the respondent). The tribunal then asks the parties whether they have any objection to the case being referred to mediation. If neither party objects it is referred to

---

4.   Equality Act 2004, s 46.

a mediator who arranges a mutually convenient appointment with both parties. In the event that either party withdraws from the mediation, or the mediator decides that the case cannot be resolved by way of mediation, the mediator issues what is known as a non-resolution notice to both parties. This indicates that the case cannot be resolved by mediation.

The Acts allow for the investigation to be resumed provided that within 28 days of the date of the non–resolution notice the Director receives in writing an application for the investigation to resume.[5]

If either side objects to mediation or the Director deems that the case is not suitable for mediation, then the complainant is asked for a submission/statement.[6] The tribunal will send a copy of the complainant's submission/statement to the respondents and ask for a replying submission. A copy of this is then sent to the complainant for information.

Investigating a complaint

[1.22] An equality officer is assigned to the case. Similar to the EAT there is no automatic right of adjournment. The equality officer arranges a time to meet. The process is one by which the equality officer will ask questions of each party and of any of the witnesses. Opportunity will also be given for the parties to give evidence, make legal submissions, cross-examine and respond to the points raised by the other side.

All claims are held in private. After the hearing the equality officer will issue a written decision which is published on the Equality Tribunal website.

Findings

[1.23] Section 82 of the Employment Equality Acts provides that if a decision of an equality officer is in favour of an employee then any one or more of the following remedies can apply:

    i.   In equal pay cases, equal pay can be provided for from the date of the referral of the claim.

    ii.   Also in equal pay cases any arrears of the shortfall necessary to make up equal pay, for up to a maximum of three years before the date of referral.

    iii.   Compensation for the acts of discrimination or victimisation which occurred.

    iv.   An order for equal treatment in whatever respect is relevant to the case.

    v.   An order that a person or persons take a specified course of action.

    vi.   An order for reinstatement or re-engagement (in dismissal cases), with or without an order for compensation.

---

5.   Section 78.

6.   Note that under Employment Equality Act 1998, s 102 the Tribunal can dismiss the complaint and close the file after a year, if it appears that a complainant has not pursued, or has ceased to pursue, the complaint. A dismissal notice will be sent to the parties. There is no appeal from this decision.

vii.   In cases of dismissal where the equality officer has found no discriminatory dismissal, that the matter be referred to the Employment Appeals Tribunal to determine if there has been an unfair dismissal.

viii.   In cases of gender discrimination, the decision can also order payment of interest under the Courts Act 1981 on all or part of the compensation or the arrears of equal pay.

The tribunal has no general power to award any costs (legal fees, witness or travelling expenses, etc) to any person. However, if the Tribunal considers that a person is obstructing its investigation, it can order that person to pay travelling or other expenses reasonably incurred by another person in connection with the investigation. Equally where the Tribunal deems that a complaint has been made in bad faith or that it is frivolous, vexatious, misconceived or relates to a trivial matter then it can be dismissed without hearing at any stage.[7] If a case is so dismissed under this section it may be appealed to the Labour Court within 42 days.

Appeals

[1.24] Appeals are made to the Labour Court within 42 days of the date of issue of the decision. Presuming no appeal the decision is legally binding and enforcement is through the Circuit Court. (See **1.41** Form No 36E Circuit Court Notice of Motion in the Matter of Section 91 Employment Equality Acts 1998 and 2004.)

LABOUR COURT

[1.25] The Labour Court was established in 1946. The responsibilities and role of the court have been considerably enhanced over the years as a result of the increase in national and European employment legislation.

In the majority of instances the Labour Court operates as an industrial relations forum, hearing both sides in trade disputes and then issuing recommendations setting out its opinion on the dispute and the terms on which it should be settled. While these recommendations are not binding on the parties concerned, the parties are expected to give serious consideration to the court's recommendations.

However, the court's determinations under the Employment Equality, Pensions, Organisation of Working Time, National Minimum Wage, Industrial Relations (Amendment), Protection of Employees (Part-Time Work) and Protection of Employees (Fixed-Term Work) Acts are legally binding.

Role in termination of employment cases

[1.26] There are several ways in which a case involving the termination of employment of an individual can come before the Labour Court:

• Where a Rights Commissioner has dealt with a dispute concerning the dismissal of an employee under the Industrial Relations Act 1969 the court can

---

7.   Employment Equality Acts 1998–2004, s 77A.

hear the appeal of that recommendation. Such appeals are binding when appealed and heard by the court.[8]

- The court can hear appeals of decisions on discriminatory dismissals heard under the Employment Equality Acts 1998–2004. These decisions by the court are binding.

- The court can hear appeals of Rights Commissioners' decisions under the Protection of Employees (Fixed-Term Work) Act 2003. Such determinations by the Labour Court under the Fixed-Term Work Act are also binding but can be appealed on a point of law to the High Court.[9] Section 13 of this Act prohibits penalisation of fixed-term workers and penalisation in this context includes dismissal.

- In addition the Labour Court hears claims on appeal from the Rights Commissioner under the Protection of Employees (Part-Time Work) Act 2001. Such determinations by the Labour Court under the Act are also binding but can be appealed on a point of law to the High Court.[10]

- The Labour Court can hear appeals from the Rights Commissioner under the Organisation of Working Time Act. Such appeals in so far a termination of employment cases are concerned arise out of the penalisation of employees by employers for in good faith opposing any acts which are unlawful under the Act.[11]

- Finally the Labour Court can hear claims under s 20 of the 1969 Industrial Relations Act. Such claims can be heard either under s 20(1) or 20(2). It is more usual for the court to hear claims under s 20(1) as in this instance only the employee has to agree to be bound by the court's recommendation. In the latter both parties have to agree to be bound and hence hearings under this section are rare.

Structure of the Labour Court

[1.27] The Labour Court should consist of nine full-time members, although this varies depending on appointments and retirements, these generally comprise – a Chairman, two Deputy Chairmen and six ordinary members, three of whom are employers' members and three of whom are workers' members. The Chairman and the two Deputy Chairmen are appointed by the Minister for Enterprise, Trade and Employment. The employers' members are nominated by the Irish Business and Employers' Confederation (IBEC) and the workers' members are nominated by the Irish Congress of Trade Unions (ICTU). The Labour Court also has a legal adviser, the Registrar, who is appointed by the Minister for Enterprise, Trade and Employment.

---

8.   Industrial Relations Act 1969, s 13(9).
9.   Protection of Employees (Fixed-Term Work) Act 2003, s 15.
10.   Protection of Employees (Fixed-Term Work) Act 2003, s 15.
11.   Organisation of Working Time Act 1997, s 26.

Operational structure of the Labour Court

[1.28] The court operates in three separate divisions. A division is made up of the Chairman or a Deputy Chairman, an employers' member and a workers' member. Hearings are held in Dublin and at several venues throughout the country.

Investigation method

[1.29] The Labour Court investigates disputes by requiring the parties to a dispute to provide it with written submissions of their positions in relation to the dispute, and subsequently by holding hearings which both parties attend. The hearings are usually held in private, unless one of the parties requests a public hearing.[12] In most instances the Labour Court deals with disputes which are referred to it (this is always the case in termination of employment cases). Occasionally however, the Labour Court will intervene in an industrial relations dispute and invite the parties to a hearing.

Submissions

[1.30] The parties are required to supply the court with written submissions stating their positions in relation to the dispute. A draft structure of a submission is outlined at **1.39** below. The Labour Court may make rules for the regulation of its proceedings.[13]

The rules in relation to the making of submissions are set out in the Notice of Hearing that issues to the parties prior to a hearing. This in effect means that the Labour Court can refuse to hear a case in the event that a party does not comply with the rules as set out. Although generally some leeway is given regarding forwarding submissions within the required timeframe, the court is generally insistent that submissions are in writing and given to it in advance of the hearing.

In industrial relations, working time, national minimum wage, part-time work and fixed-term work cases, six copies of the submissions should be delivered to the court, by post or by hand (but not by fax), no later than three working days prior to the date of the hearing.

In equality cases, separate procedures apply – these are advised to the parties by the court at the time of referral of the case to the court (see **Ch 11**).

Appeals

[1.31] Appeals of a recommendation or a decision of a Rights Commissioner or of a decision or recommendation of the Director of the Equality Tribunal to the Labour Court should be made on the appropriate form (See **1.44** and **1.45** below). If the appeal is made by letter then it should:

- quote the reference number of the Rights Commissioner's/Director of the Equality Tribunal's recommendation or decision;

---

12. Industrial Relations Act 1969, s 8(1).
13. Industrial Relations Act 1946, s 20(5).

- enclose a copy of the Rights Commissioner's/Director of the Equality Tribunal's recommendation or decision; and

- briefly state the grounds for the appeal

An appeal of a recommendation or a decision of a Rights Commissioner or a decision or a recommendation of the Director of the Equality Tribunal must be received by the Labour Court within six weeks of the date of the recommendation or the decision.[14]

NATIONAL EMPLOYMENT RIGHTS AUTHORITY

[1.32] The National Employment Rights Authority (NERA) was established on an interim basis by the Government in February 2007 on foot of a commitment in the social partnership agreement 'Towards 2016'. NERA's aim is to foster and secure compliance with employment rights legislation through five main functions:

1. information;

2. inspection;

3. enforcement;

4. prosecution;

5. protection of young persons.

NERA's headquarters are based in Carlow but there are sub-regional offices located in Dublin, Sligo, Shannon and Cork. There are currently 80 inspectors and they have the powers, given under certain legislation, to:

- enter any premises at a reasonable time;

- demand to see and inspect records;

- take copies of records;

- interview and require information from relevant persons.

After an inspection has occurred, NERA will write to the employer to advise them of the outcome. Where breaches have been identified the inspector may request the employer to rectify the breach. Alternatively the inspector may refer the matter to Legal Services for prosecution or they may undertake a further inspection of the records at the premises in question. Where arrears of payments are due the employer will be expected to put in writing evidence that payment has been made to the employee concerned within one month and confirm compliance going forward.

---

14.   Industrial Relations Act 1969, s 13(9)(a) and Employment Equality Act 1998, s 83(1).

CIRCUIT COURT

[1.33] The Circuit Court is comprised of the President and 27 ordinary judges. The President of the District Court is ex officio, an additional judge of the Circuit Court. The country is divided into eight circuits for the purposes of the Circuit Court with one judge assigned to each circuit except in Dublin where 10 judges may be assigned, and Cork, where there is provision for three judges. There are 26 Circuit Court offices throughout the State with a County Registrar in charge of the work of each office. The Circuit Court is a court of limited and local jurisdiction. The Circuit Court sits in venues in each circuit. Sittings vary in length from one day to three weeks and are generally held every two to four months in each venue in the circuit. Dublin and Cork have continual sittings throughout each legal term. In addition to hearing a wide variety of disputes on diverse civil, criminal and family law issues the Circuit Court has a role in employment disputes. These generally arrive before the Circuit Court by way of appeals of decisions from the Employment Appeals Tribunal but they can also appear before the Circuit Court by way of appeal from the Labour Court under the Employment Equality Legislation. Furthermore the Circuit Court can act as a court of first instance in cases of gender related dismissal.[15] The Circuit Court can also hear cases of wrongful dismissal; see **Ch 8**.

HIGH COURT

[1.34] The High Court is comprised of the President and 25 ordinary judges. The President of the Circuit Court and the Chief Justice are ex officio, additional judges of the High Court. In addition to the High Court having full jurisdiction in and power to determine all matters and questions whether of law or fact, civil or criminal, its jurisdiction also extends to the question of the validity of any law having regard to the provisions of the Constitution. It is in this context that the High Court can hear judicial reviews of decisions made by the Labour Court or by the EAT. The High Court also acts as an appeal court from the Circuit Court in civil matters. In this latter context it could hear appeals of discriminatory dismissal cases on gender grounds that have gone before the Circuit Court.

The High Court sits in Dublin to hear original actions. It also sits in several provincial locations (Cork, Galway, Limerick, Waterford, Sligo, Dundalk, Kilkenny and Ennis) at specified times during the year. In the employment field these are generally constrained to injunctions in respect of dismissal cases.[16]

Matters coming before the High Court are normally heard and determined by one judge but the President of the High Court may decide that any cause or matter or any part thereof may be heard by three judges in what is known as a divisional court.

---

15. In gender discrimination cases only Employment Equality Act 1998, s 77(3) allows a claimant to bypass the Equality Tribunal and the Labour Court and refer the matter directly to the Circuit Court. Employment Equality Act 1998, s 82(3) provides that the award may exceed the normal civil jurisdiction of the Circuit Court (see **Ch 11**).
16. See **Ch 8**.

PRACTICAL ISSUES FOR EMPLOYERS TO CONSIDER IN RESPECT OF EACH FORUM

Rights Commissioner

[1.35] Many employers view the initial step of going to the Rights Commissioner in unfair dismissal cases as an unnecessary step and prefer to proceed directly to the EAT (the rationale being that most employers would prefer not to have to appeal a negative Rights Commissioner's recommendation to the EAT). Although such an appeal is a completely new hearing many feel that a negative recommendation going into the EAT taints the view of the EAT before the off. In this respect the T1–B form (see **1.47** and **3.99**), which is used to appeal such decisions does not help in that it provides that you must state the grounds of appeal and also that you must attach a copy of the Rights Commissioner's recommendation with the form. This greatly taints the view of the Tribunal from the start and it is for this reason that many employers choose to go directly to the EAT.

However, one good reason for letting an unfair dismissal case go before a Rights Commissioner is that many of the Commissioners are experienced ex-trade union officials or employers and as such are skilled negotiators. If one feels the need to settle a case, often it is easier to do so at the Rights Commissioner before proceeding to the EAT. The Rights Commissioners in their own way can act as the 'honest broker' and play a pivotal role in the settlement process. Although, as stated previously, this is becoming less frequent due to the fact that the Rights Commissioners are becoming fearful of being sued. Often therefore it is up to the parties to the hearing to broach the matter of a settlement with the Rights Commissioner rather than waiting for the Rights Commissioner to raise the issue.

Regarding claims heard under the Industrial Relations Acts, one of the mistakes often made by employers and their representatives is to think that these decisions when appealed are not binding. This is not the case. An interesting lacuna exists in the law here. If a Rights Commissioner issues a recommendation under the IR Acts and it is not appealed but the employer fails to implement the recommendation, the recommendation falls into somewhat of a 'black hole' in that the claimant cannot appeal it as they may be outside the time limit and yet it cannot be enforced as it is only a recommendation.

Employment Appeals Tribunal

[1.36] When attending the EAT it is crucial to prepare well beforehand. For employers it is vital to have all documentation ready and in a readable fashion that is easily accessed by the Tribunal. When giving evidence in front of the Tribunal witnesses should be very wary of questions asked by the Tribunal members and it is vital that under no circumstances should such witnesses ever answer hypothetical questions.[17] It may also prove prudent to keep witnesses to a minimum.

---

17.   Details on how to complete the Tribunal forms are dealt with later in **Ch 3**.

The Employment Appeals Tribunal ideally should not be attended by an employer without representation. This unfortunately was not the original intent of the EAT which was set up to hear cases in a prompt and effective manner. Over time the EAT has become increasingly legalistic and whereas a decade or so ago it was attended mainly by those with no legal training such as union officials or officials of the Irish Business and Employers Confederation (IBEC), this is no longer the case. One is governed by the rules of evidence and whilst most Chairs are flexible when hearing cases more leniency tends to be given to the employee (particularly when they are unrepresented) than to the employer. On examination of the unfair dismissal claims appearing before the Tribunal, what is interesting is that generally employers win approximately 50 per cent of the claims.[18] At first, this seems to say that employers have a good chance of winning such claims. That said, employers rarely run cases they believe they are going to lose. What I suspect the statistics really demonstrate is that employers have a 50 per cent chance of winning a case that they believe they should win or should have a good chance of winning. All the more reason to attend well prepared with a good representative.

Equality Tribunal

[1.37] As per the EAT it is advisable for employers to have representation when attending the Equality Tribunal. The Equality Tribunal has significant powers similar to the EAT in respect of dismissal cases and many of the same ground rules apply.

One of the most frequent questions from employers is whether to attend mediation. The answer to this lies in the merits of one's case. If an employer believes in the strength of the case and is confident of winning, then mediation merely slows up the process and is most probably a waste of time. On the other hand, if an employer wishes to keep the matter confidential, or has a weak case, or determines for employee relations reasons or otherwise that it would be more appropriate to deal with the matter amicably, then mediation is the proper route.

Notwithstanding the above, mediation is also extremely useful from the perspective that it allows both parties to hear exactly what the other is going to say at the hearing and for this reason and this reason alone it can be extremely useful.

From details provided by the Equality Tribunal employers win approximately 64 per cent of cases[19] that are heard and some 52 per cent of cases referred to mediation were resolved at mediation.

What is interesting about these numbers is that they are significantly better than the EAT. Why this is so is unclear but it could be speculated that the reason employers are more successful at the Equality Tribunal is either because of the merit of the cases presented or because of the standard of the Equality Tribunal officers who now have considerable experience and who are not subject to change every three years such as the EAT.

---

18.   See annual report from EAT for 2007 and 2008.
19.   See 2009 Annual Report.

Labour Court

[1.38] It should be borne in mind that the Labour Court's determinations under the Employment Equality, Pensions, Organisation of Working Time, National Minimum Wage, Industrial Relations (Amendment), Protection of Employees (Part-Time Work) and Protection of Employees (Fixed-Term Work) Acts are legally binding.

Practitioners used to dealing with the Labour Court in an industrial relations forum often forget this. In respect of these Acts, but more particularly in respect of the equality legislation, the Labour Court's decisions can be wide-ranging. Again it is vital to go prepared and to ensure that all aspects of a case are well thought out. It is furthermore advisable to seek the help of representation when the Labour Court is hearing such cases.

Draft outline of a Labour Court submission

[1.39] (a) The covering page should include the details of the company, the date of the hearing, the venue, the company representative and the issue in dispute.

    (b) There should be a brief introductory paragraph which should set out the issue in dispute. This should begin: 'Chairperson and members of the Court the issue before you today concerns'.

    (c) The next section should outline the background to the case. This should be concise and if necessary in bullet point format.

    (d) The following section should be an outline of the company's arguments, ie the points the company is intent on relying upon in support of its case.

    (e) Finally there should be a summary and a conclusion.

Circuit Court & High Court

[1.40] Clearly it is advisable for employers to have representation before both courts. One of the most interesting questions from employers often arises when they receive an unfavourable determination from the EAT and ask if they should appeal it to the Circuit Court. The answer is, it depends. It depends on many factors, such as what Circuit the appeal will be heard in, what the attitude of the Circuit Court judge is and how strong the case is. It might seem 'odd' to leave the strength of the case to last, however it is my experience that Circuit Court judges do not generally either take the time or have the time to deal with such appeals, consequently the number of successful appeals tends in my opinion to be limited. I should stress that this is an opinion as I have no statistics on which to ground it. If one considers this along with the fact that as an employer you are at risk of costs on appeal then any appeal has to be carefully thought out beforehand.

Forms

[1.41] *Form No 36E Circuit Court Notice of Motion in the Matter of S 91 Employment Equality Acts 1998 and 2004*

Circuit Court Rules

Schedule: B – Forms

Form: 36E Notice of motion in the matter of s. 91 Employment Equality Acts 1998 and 2004

S.I. No. 275 of 2006

FORM 36E

AN CHUIRT CHUARDA

THE CIRCUIT COURT

CIRCUIT

COUNTY OF

NOTICE OF MOTION

IN THE MATTER OF SECTION 91 OF THE EMPLOYMENT EQUALITY ACT, 1998
BETWEEN

A.B.

Plaintiff

AND

C.D.

Defendant

TAKE NOTICE that application will be made to the Court on the .... or the next opportunity thereafter for the following reliefs:

[Here insert details of the relief sought by way of enforcement]

AND FURTHER TAKE NOTICE that the said application will be grounded upon:

1. [here insert grounds upon which the Plaintiff is relying for the reliefs sought and in particular details of the of the failure by the person affected to comply with the determination, decision or mediated settlement, as appropriate and, if appropriate, of the abandonment of an appeal]

2. [here insert the basis of jurisdiction]

3. [here insert the name, address and description of the Plaintiff]

4. [The following documents should, in accordance with Order 57 rule 6(7)(c), be annexed to this Notice of Motion:

(i) a certified copy of the determination of the Labour Court or of the decision of the Director with the date of determination or decision thereon and the original or a certified copy of any letter of the Labour Court or the Director notifying the making of the determination or decision (as the case may be) or, in the case of a mediated settlement pursuant to section 78(5) of the Act, a certified copy of the written record of the settlement together with the date of such written record;

(ii) certified copies of all notices, pleadings, documents and particulars provided by either party to the Labour Court and

(iii) any other relevant documentation].

Dated the .... day of ....

Signed:
Plaintiff/Solicitor for the Plaintiff

To:
Defendant/Solicitor for the Defendant

And

To:

The County Registrar

[1.42] *Application to the Rights Commissioners under the Unfair Dismissals Acts 1977–1993*

APPLICATION TO RIGHTS COMMISSIONER

UNFAIR DISMISSALS ACTS 1977 – 1993

(PLEASE USE BLOCK CAPITALS)

EMPLOYEE'S DETAILS

Name: _____

Address:
_____
_____
_____
_____

Tel: _____

E-Mail: _____

Job Title: _____

COMPANY/EMPLOYER'S DETAILS
(Full legal name: if in doubt consult your P45/P60)

Name: _____

Address:
_____
_____
_____
_____

Tel: _____

E-Mail: _____

N.B.: IS YOUR EMPLOYER AWARE THAT YOU ARE BRINGING THIS DISPUTE TO A RIGHTS COMMISSIONER?   YES__ NO__

Name and Address of your Representative (if any):
_____
_____

DATE ON WHICH THIS EMPLOYMENT BEGAN: ____/____/____

DATE OF DISMISSAL: ____/____/____

PAY PER WEEK (including benefits and regular overtime):

      €_____GROSS
      €_____TAKE HOME

REDRESS SOUGHT (re-instatement, re-engagement, or compensation):
_____
_____
_____

HAVE YOU TAKEN UP NEW EMPLOYMENT SINCE YOUR DISMISSAL?   YES_____NO_____

IF YES, WHEN: ____/____/____

AT WHAT RATE OF PAY?:   € _____per week

THE GROUNDS OF MY CLAIM ARE AS FOLLOWS:
_____
_____
_____
_____

_____

EMPLOYEE'S SIGNATURE: _____   DATE: ____/____/____

PLEASE NOTE THAT A COPY OF THIS FORM WILL BE FORWARDED TO YOUR EMPLOYER.

[1.43] *Application to Rights Commissioner under the Industrial Relations Acts 1969 and 1990*

APPLICATION TO RIGHTS COMMISSIONER

INDUSTRIAL RELATIONS ACTS 1969 AND 1990

(PLEASE USE BLOCK CAPITALS)

NAME:_   NAME OF COMPANY/ EMPLOYER:

_____   _____

ADDRESS:_   ADDRESS:

TEL NO: _____   TEL NO: _____

NAME AND ADDRESS OF YOUR REPRESENTATIVE (IF ANY):   _____

_____

_____

DATE ON WHICH EMPLOYMENT BEGAN: _____

DATE ON WHICH EMPLOYMENT ENDED (*IF APPLICABLE*):_____

PAY (INCLUDING BENEFITS AND REGULAR OVERTIME) PER WEEK

€_____GROSS

€_____TAKE HOME

MY DISPUTE IS THAT:

EMPLOYEE'S SIGNATURE: DATE:

PLEASE NOTE THAT A COPY OF THIS FORM WILL BE FORWARDED TO YOUR EMPLOYER.

[1.44] *Appeal of Rights Commissioner's Recommendation to Labour Court*

THE LABOUR COURT

INDUSTRIAL RELATIONS ACT, 1969
Section 13(9)

Appeal of recommendation of a Rights Commissioner

Rights Commissioner recommendation details:-

Recommendation Reference Number:	Date of recommendation:

Employee Details:-

Name:
Address:

Telephone Number:

Employer Details:-

Name:
Address:

Telephone Number:

Employee Representative Details (if any)

Name:
Address:

Telephone number:

Employer Representative Details (if any)

Name:
Address:

Telephone number:

*Brief summary of grounds on which Appeal of Rights Commissioner recommendation
is being made:-*

Signed: _____Employee/Employer (delete as appropriate)

Date: _____

**Please return completed form and copy of Rights Commissioner's Recommendation
to:**
**Programming Unit, The Labour Court, Tom Johnson House, Haddington Road, Dublin 4
(phone: (01) 6136610, 6136611, 6136650)**

[1.45] *Appeal from Decision of Director of Equality Tribunal to Labour Court*

THE LABOUR COURT

EMPLOYMENT EQUALITY ACTS, 1998 TO 2008
Section 83(1)

<u>**APPEAL FROM DECISION OF THE DIRECTOR OF THE EQUALITY TRIBUNAL**</u>

Director of the Equality Tribunal Decision details:-

Decision Reference Number:	Date of Decision:

Discriminatory Grounds *(please indicate below by X where appropriate):-*

[ ] Age	[ ] Family Status	[ ] Sexual Orientation
[ ] Gender	[ ] Marital Status	[ ] Race, colour, ethnic or national origin
[ ] Disability	[ ] Religious Belief	[ ] Membership of the travelling community

Victimisation [ ] *(please indicate by X where appropriate)*

Appellant details *(see note overleaf):-*

Name:
Address:

Phone number:

Respondent details *(see note overleaf):-*

Name:
Address:

Phone number:

Appellant Representative details (if any):-

Name:
Address:

Phone number:

Respondent Representative details (if any):-

Name:
Address:

Phone number:

Brief summary of grounds on which Appeal from Decision of Director of the Equality Tribunal is being made (you may continue on an additional page if necessary):-

Signed: _____
Date: _____   **Send form to the Labour Court at address overleaf**

Note:-

Appellant means the party who is appealing the decision; Respondent means the other party in the original case. If the employer in the original case is appealing the decision, he or she is the appellant and the employee the original case is the respondent; if the employee in the original case is appealing the decision, he or she is the appellant and the employer is the respondent.

Please send this form to:

Programming Section,
The Labour Court,
Tom Johnson House,
Haddington Road,
Dublin 4.

Telephone: (01) 6136608 or 6136610 or 6136611
Lo-Call (if calling from outside (01) area): 1890 220 228

[1.46] *Time Limits, Appeals and Enforcements*

Acts/Regulations	Time Limit for Claim	Initial Complaint Referred to (Forum)	Appeal to (Forum)	Enforcement
Adoptive Leave Acts 1995 and 2005	Within six months of the date of the alleged contravention and a further 6 in exceptional circumstances	Rights Commissioner	Employment Appeals Tribunal and High Court Point of Law	Employee or Minister for Justice. Equality and Law Reform applies to Circuit Court for Order directing compliance with the Rights Commissioner decision (unless it is appealed) or EAT Determination
Carer's Leave Act 2001	Within six months of the date of the alleged contravention and a further 6 in exceptional circumstances	Rights Commissioner Deciding of Officer of Dept of Social and Family Affairs on certain issues	Employment Appeals Tribunal Department of of Social and Family Affairs Appeals Officer	Party of Minister for Enterprise, Trade and Employment applies to Circuit Court for Order directing compliance with the Rights Commissioner decision (unless appealed) or EAT Determination
Employment Equality Acts 1998 and 2004[a]	Six months from last date of discrimination or up to 12 months for reasonable cause	Mediated settlement Equality Officer's decision Circuit Court	Equality Officer Labour Court High Court	Application to the Circuit Court directing compliance with the mediation settlement, Labour Court determination (unless appealed)
European Communities (Protection of Employees on Transfer of Undertakings) Regulations 2003	Within six months of the date of the alleged contravention and a further 6 in exceptional circumstances	Rights Commissioner	Employment Appeals Tribunal	Employee/representative or Minister for Enterprise, Trade and Employment applies to Circuit Court for Order directing compliance with Rights Commissioner Decision (unless appealed) or EAT determination
Industrial Relations Acts 1946–2004 Trade Disputes – to including Pay, Hours of work & annual leave of a 'Body of Workers'	No time limit	Rights Commissioner	Labour Court	Voluntary Process but Labour Court Decision binding on appeal

Acts/Regulations	Time Limit for Claim	Initial Complaint Referred to (Forum)	Appeal to (Forum)	Enforcement
Trade Disputes of a 'Body of Workers'	No time limit	Labour Relations Commissioner	Labour Court	Voluntary Process
Trade Disputes Section 20 Cases including Dismissals	No time limit	Labour Court	No appeal	Voluntary Process but Labour Court recommendation binding on party who referred it or on both if joint referral
Employment Regulation Orders (ERO's) & Registered Employment Agreements (REA's)	No time limit	Employment Rights Labour Inspectorate (EROs & REA's)	None	Civil/Criminal proceedings
		Labour Court (REA's)	None	Criminal proceedings by Minister
Maternity Protection Acts 1994 and 2004	Within six months of the date of the alleged contravention and a further 6 in exceptional circumstances	Rights Commissioner	Employment Appeals Tribunal	Party or Minister for Justice, Equality and Law Reform applies to Circuit Court for order directing compliance with Rights Commissioner decision (unless appealed) or EAT determination
Minimum Notice and Terms of Employment Acts 1973–2001	6 years (Statute of Limitations 1957–1991 applies)	Employment Appeals Tribunal	None	Employee/Representative or Minister Enterprise Trade and Employment institutes proceedings in District Court for compensation awarded by EAT or alternatively employee sues in relevant court for satisfaction of the debt
National Minimum Wage Act 2000	Within six months of the date of the alleged contravention and a further 6 in exceptional circumstances	Rights Commissioner	Labour Court	Employee/Representative or Minister for Enterprise, Trade and Employment apply to Circuit Court for Order directing compliance with Labour Court Determination (either affirming Rights Commissioners decision or after appeal from Rights Commissioner)
		Employment Rights Labour Inspectorate	None	Civil/Criminal Proceedings by Minister

Acts/Regulations	Time Limit for Claim	Initial Complaint Referred to (Forum)	Appeal to (Forum)	Enforcement
Organisation of Working Time Act 1997	Within six months of the date of the alleged contravention and a further 6 in exceptional circumstances	Rights Commissioner	Labour Court	Employee/Representative or Minister for Enterprise, Trade and Employment apply to Circuit Court for Order directing compliance with Labour Court Determination (either affirming Rights Commissioners decision or after appeal from Rights Commissioner)
Parental Leave Acts 1998 and 2006	Within six months of the occurrence of the dispute	Rights Commissioner	Employment Appeals Tribunal	Employee or Minister for Justice, Equality and Law Reform apply to Circuit Court for Order directing alleged compliance with Rights Commissioners decision (unless appealed) or Employment Appeals Tribunal determination
Payment of Wages Act 1991	Within six months of the date of the alleged contravention and a further 6 in exceptional circumstances	Rights Commissioner	Employment Appeals Tribunal	Rights Commissioner Decision (unless appealed)/ Employment Appeals Tribunal. Determination enforced by employee taking civil proceedings as if it were an order of the Circuit Court in the Circuit Court jurisdiction in which the person normally resides.
		Employment Rights Inspectorate for pay slips only	None	Criminal proceedings by Minister for Enterprise Trade and Employment
Protection of Employees (Fixed Term Work) Act 2003	Within six months of the date of the alleged contravention and a further 6 in exceptional circumstances	Rights Commissioner	Labour Court	Employee/Representative or Minister for Enterprise Trade and Employment apply to Circuit Court for Order directing compliance with Labour Court determination (either affirming the Rights Commissioners decision or on Appeal from the Rights Commissioner)

Acts/Regulations	Time Limit for Claim	Initial Complaint Referred to (Forum)	Appeal to (Forum)	Enforcement
Protection of Employees (Part Time Work) Act 2001	Within six months of the date of the alleged contravention and a further 6 in exceptional circumstances	Rights Commissioner	Labour Court	Employee/Representative or Minister for Enterprise Trade and Employment apply to Circuit Court for Order directing compliance with Labour Court determination (either affirming the Rights Commissioner's decision or on Appeal from the Rights Commissioner)
Protection of Young Persons (Employment) Act 1996	Within six months of the date of the alleged contravention and a further 6 in exceptional circumstances	Rights Commissioner Appeals	Employment Appeals Tribunal	Parent/Guardian of Child or young person or Minister for Enterprise Trade and Employment apply to District Court for Order directing compliance with Employment Appeals Tribunal determination (whether affirming Rights Commissioner's decision or an appeal from the Rights Commissioner)
		Employment Rights Inspectorate	None	Criminal Proceedings by Minister
Protection for Persons Reporting Child Abuse Act 1998	Within six months of the date of the alleged contravention and a further 6 in exceptional circumstances	Rights Commissioner (section 4 of Act only)	Tribunal Appeals Tribunal	Employee/Representative or Minister for Enterprise Trade and Employment apply to Circuit Court for Order directing compliance with Employment Appeals Tribunal determination (either affirming The Rights Commissioner's decision or an appeal from the Rights Commissioner)
Protection of Employment Act 1977	Within six months of the date of the alleged contravention and a further 6 in exceptional circumstances	Redundancy Payments Section of the Department of Enterprise, Trade and Employment	None	Criminal Proceedings by Minister for Enterprise, Trade and Employment

Acts/Regulations	Time Limit for Claim	Initial Complaint Referred to (Forum)	Appeal to (Forum)	Enforcement
European Communities (Protection of Employment) Regulations 2000		Rights Commissioner	Employment Appeals Tribunal	Employee/Representative apply to Circuit Court for Order directing compliance with Employment Appeals Tribunal determination (either affirming the Rights Commissioner's decision or on appeal from the Rights Commissioner)
Redundancy Payments Acts 1967–2005	52 weeks extending to 104 weeks at the discretion of the Employment Appeals Tribunal			
1. Refusal of Employer to pay lump sum		Employment Appeals Tribunal	None	Social Insurance Fund pays award if employer defaults on Employment Appeals Tribunal decision
2. Application to Redundancy Payment Section of DETE by Employer for Rebate		Employer applies to Deciding Officer	Employment Appeals Tribunal	Social Insurance Fund pays rebate to employer if Employment Appeals Tribunal finds in their favour
Terms of Employment (Information) Act 1994–2001	Any time during the employee's employment or within 6 months of termination	Rights Commissioner	Employment Appeals Tribunal	Employee/Representative or Minister for Enterprise Trade and Employment applies to District Court for Order directing compliance with Employment Appeals Tribunal determination (either affirming Rights Commissioner's Recommendation or on appeal from the Rights Commissioner)

Acts/Regulations	Time Limit for Claim	Initial Complaint Referred to (Forum)	Appeal to (Forum)	Enforcement
Unfair Dismissals Acts 1977–2007	Within six months of the date of the alleged contravention and a further 6 in exceptional circumstances	Rights Commissioner Employment Appeals Tribunal	Employment Appeals Tribunal Circuit Court High Court (Point of Law)	Employee/Representative or Minister for Enterprise Trade and Employment apply to District Court for Order directing compliance with Employment Appeals Tribunal determination (either affirming Rights Commissioner's recommendation or on appeal from the Rights Commissioner) or with Circuit Court Order if appealed from Employment Appeals Tribunal
Protection of Employees (Employer's Insolvency) Acts 1984–2005	Within six weeks of the Ministers decision to disallow a claim	Insolvency Section Department of Enterprise, Trade and Employment	Employment Appeals Tribunal if Insolvency Section refuse to pay from Social Insurance fund	Minister for Enterprise, Trade and Employment implements the EAT declaration

a.   As amended by the Equality Act 2004.

31

[1.47] *Forms for Appeal to the EAT*

FORM T1-A   **EMPLOYMENT APPEALS TRIBUNAL**

Please read the notes supplied then complete this form in <u>BLOCK CAPITALS</u>. Please sign and date

FOR OFFICIAL USE ONLY
Case No/s:

1. NOTICE OF CLAIM TO EMPLOYMENT APPEALS TRIBUNAL (Please tick appropriate box or boxes: See II (1) of Notes)

(i) Redundancy Payments Acts 1967 to 2007	☐
(ii) Minimum Notice and Terms of Employment Acts 1973 to 2005	☐
(iii) Unfair Dismissals Acts 1977 to 2007	☐
(iv) Organisation of Working Time Act 1997	☐

2. NAME AND ADDRESS OF PERSON MAKING CLAIM

First Name: ....

Surname: ....

Address: ....

....

....

Phone No: ....

Email Address

Occupation: .... Sex.........

P.P.S. No: ....

3. EMPLOYER'S FULL <u>LEGAL NAME</u> AND ADDRESS (Please see Note 3)

Name: ....

Address: ....

....

....

Phone No: ....

Registered (PAYE) No: ....

Is this a Limited Company? Please indicate
Yes ☐   No ☐

4. WILL YOU HAVE A REPRESENTATIVE AT HEARING? (Trade Union Official, Solicitor, etc.) (Please see Note 4)

Yes ☐   No ☐
If yes, please complete

Name: ....

Address: ....

....

....

Phone No: ....

5. PLEASE ENTER THE FOLLOWING DATES

	Day	Month	Year
Date of Birth			
Employment began			
Dismissal notice received			
Employment ended			

6. NORMAL WEEKLY PAY   €

Basic Weekly Pay	
Regular Bonus or Allowances	
Average Weekly Overtime	
Any other payments including payments in kind – specify	
Weekly Total Gross	
Net	

7. CLAIM UNDER REDUNDANCY PAYMENT ACTS

Has you employer issued you with a Redundancy Certificate?   Yes ☐   No ☐

Have you applied to your employer for a redundancy payment?   Yes ☐   No ☐

Have you applied to the Department of Enterprise, Trade and Innovation for a redundancy payment?   Yes ☐   No ☐

if yes, please attach copy of decision

8. TOWN OF EMPLOYMENT OR NEAREST TOWN

(Please enter below the nearest town to your employment)

PLEASE ADVISE THE TRIBUNAL SECRETARIAT OF ANY CHANGE OF ADDRESS.

---

9. CLAIM UNDER UNFAIR DISMISSALS ACTS

<u>IMPORTANT</u>

THE TRIBUNAL CANNOT HEAR YOUR CLAIM UNDER THE UNFAIR DISMISSALS ACTS UNLESS THERE IS AN OBJECTION TO A RIGHTS COMMISSIONER HEARING IT. (See Notes)

Please Insert "Yes" or "No" in each box below

Do you object? [   ]   Has your employer objec[   ]

If you do not object, you may wish to send this application directly to the Rights Commissioners Service, Labour Relations Commission, Tom Johnson House, Haddington Road, Dublin 4.

---

10. THE REASONS FOR MY CLAIM ARE:
    (you can attach additional sheets of information if necessary)

11. REMEDY SOUGHT (IF APPLICABLE): (Please see Note 11)

IMPORTANT NOTE: INCOMPLETE FORMS WILL BE RETURNED AND MAY DELAY THE PROCESSING OF YOUR APPEAL

---

12. DECISIONS OF THE TRIBUNAL MAY BE PLACED ON THE TRIBUNAL'S WEBSITE
    (Please refer to point (18) of Notes)

SIGNED: _____

DATE: _____

Please note that where the Tribunal processes a claim for hearing, all correspondence (*forms, letter, enclosures* etc.) received in this office will be copied to, and exchanged between, the parties to the claim.

PLEASE ADVISE THE TRIBUNAL SECRETARIAT (01-6313006) IF YOU REQUIRE ANY SPECIAL FACILITIES WHEN ATTENDING A TRIBUNAL HEARING.

Form T1A Notes

NOTICE OF CLAIM TO EMPLOYMENT APPEALS TRIBUNAL UNDER:

(i) REDUNDANCY PAYMENTS ACTS 1967 TO 2007 AND/OR

(ii) MINIMUM NOTICE AND TERMS OF EMPLOYMENT ACTS 1973 TO 2005 AND/OR

(iii) UNFAIR DISMISSALS ACTS 1977 TO 2007 AND

(iv) ORGANISATION OF WORKING TIME ACT 1997

Notes for Persons Making Application

THIS FORM IS TO BE USED BY PERSONS WHO WISH TO MAKE A CLAIM TO THE EMPLOYMENT APPEALS TRIBUNAL UNDER ONE OR MORE OF THE ABOVE ACTS

PART A – TIME LIMITS

I. TIME LIMITS FOR PERSONS BRINGING A CLAIM TO THE TRIBUNAL

A.   **REDUNDANCY PAYMENTS ACTS:**

(i)   A claim for a redundancy lump sum payment must be

         (a) made to the employer
               or
         (b) referred to the Employment Appeals Tribunal

         within 52 weeks from

         (i)   date of dismissal or
         (ii) date of ending of contract of employment.
         (Section 24 of the 1967 Act, as amended by Section 12 of the 1971 Act)

(ii)   In certain cases and for good cause the Tribunal may allow claims made within 104 weeks. (Section 24 of the 1967 Act as amended by Section 12 of the 1971 Act and Section 13 of the 1979 Act).

B.   **UNFAIR DISMISSALS ACTS:**

(i)   **Claims** must be lodged to the Tribunal **within 6 months** of date of dismissal. This time-limit may be extended to 12 months in cases where exceptional circumstances have prevented the lodgement of the claim within the normal time-limit of 6 months.

         (Section 8 of the Unfair Dismissals Act, 1977 as amended by Section 7(2)(b) of the 1993 Act).

(ii)   **Appeals** against a recommendation of a Rights Commissioner must be brought **within 6 weeks** of the date the recommendation is communicated to you. (Section 9(2) of the 1977 Act). For this purpose, use Form T1B to make your application to the Tribunal.

PART B - NOTES

If you wish to have a claim under the Unfair Dismissals Acts heard by the Employment Appeals Tribunal, **either party must first object to the claim being heard by a Rights Commissioner and must so state on the form.**

(1)   Box 1 - TICK APPROPRIATE BOX OR BOXES:
         •   Tick box or boxes representing the act or acts under which you are claiming protection.

         •   If you are bringing a claim under any of the acts mentioned at boxes (i) - (iii) you may also bring a claim under the **Organisation of Working Time Act, 1997 for holiday entitlements due.** In this case, please tick box (iv) and the relevant Act or Acts under which you wish to make a claim.

If you believe you are entitled to payment in lieu of notice remember to tick box (ii). **If unsure, please tick all boxes.**

(2)   **Box 2 - NAME AND ADDRESS OF PERSON MAKING CLAIM:**
If you change your address after lodging this form, be sure to notify the Secretary, Employment Appeals Tribunal, Davitt House, 65A Adelaide Road, Dublin 2 as this may affect the processing and hearing of your appeal. In order to enhance the processing of applications we will use email, where applicable, to all parties at any stage in the processing of an appeal.

(3)   **Box 3 - EMPLOYER'S FULL LEGAL NAME AND ADDRESS:**
It is important that the person making the claim states the correct name of the employer. **Any Order made by the Tribunal may not be enforceable if incorrect information is given.** For assistance, please consult your P45 or where appropriate, the Companies Registration Office (01-8045200 or email info@cro.ie). The employer's Registered (PAYE) No. may be obtained from your P45, P60 and Tax Certificate P.6CL.

(4)   **Box 4 – NAME AND ADDRESS OF REPRESENTATIVE OF PERSON MAKING THIS CLAIM:**
It is not necessary to have representation before the Tribunal. However, if you have arranged for a representative, such as a Trade Union Official, Solicitor etc. to attend on your behalf at the Tribunal, notification of the hearing of your claim will be sent to that person as well as to yourself.

(5)   **Box 5 - DATES:**

Complete all dates

(6)   **Box 6 - NORMAL WEEKLY PAY:**

Basic Weekly Pay:

This means the basic pay before any deductions are made.

Average Weekly Overtime.
In redundancy cases this is normally pay for the average weekly overtime worked during the six months preceding the last three months of employment. In notice and unfair dismissal cases, overtime may be disregarded unless it is a normal feature of work. If it is a normal feature of work inasmuch as you are normally expected to work it, overtime pay is included in your normal weekly pay and overtime is included in normal weekly working hours.

Payments in Kind.

These would include the value of meals or board, health insurance, use of company house or car etc.

(7)   **Box 7 – Appeals under Redundancy Payments Acts.**
If you are submitting a claim under the Redundancy Payments Acts, 1967 to 2007, please indicate if your employer has issued you with a Redundancy Certificate and if you have applied to the Department of Enterprise, Trade and Innovation for your redundancy payment. Please attached copy of the Department's decision.

(8)   **Box 8 –** In this box please give the name of the town where you worked or the nearest town to this.

(9)   **Box 9 –** The Tribunal cannot hear your claim under the Unfair Dismissals Acts unless there is an objection by either party to the claim being heard by a Rights Commissioner.

(10)   **Box 10 - REASON FOR APPLICATION:**
Please give a brief outline of your case in space provided. If you wish to provide further details, please attach any separate sheets to the form.

(11)   **Box 11 - REMEDY SOUGHT:**
Please state what remedy you are seeking. If you are claiming unfair dismissal, you can express a preference for reinstatement, re-engagement or compensation. You can change your mind at a later stage. The Tribunal will take your preference into account but will not be bound by it.

(12)   **ACKNOWLEDGEMENT OF APPLICATION:**
If you do not get an acknowledgement of your application within a reasonable time you should contact the Secretary to the Tribunal by letter, telephone or email (details below).

(13)   **HEARING OF CLAIM:**
Once you have received an acknowledgement, your case will be listed for hearing as soon as possible at the nearest town to your place of employment. You will get at least 2 weeks notice of a date for hearing.

(14)   **ADJOURNMENTS:**
Adjournments may be granted only in **exceptional circumstances.** Otherwise, a case is expected to proceed at the time and place notified to the parties. When applications for adjournments are made, they may be made to any sitting Division of the Tribunal at any venue.

The following conditions should at least be met when applying for an adjournment. However, the existence of any one or all of these conditions should not be considered a guarantee for obtaining an adjournment.

- o   Good cause should be shown as adjournments are only granted for very grave reasons.

- o   The application should be made at the earliest opportunity after receipt of the notice of hearing, save where the Tribunal for just cause dispenses with this requirement.

- o   The application should be made by a party or his representative appearing in person.

- o   Proof of consent from the other party or their representative may be required. The application can be made without consent but the Tribunal may require proof that consent was at least sought.

(15)   WITHDRAWAL OF APPLICATIONS:
If you are seeking to withdraw your application, the Secretary to the Tribunal should be notified in writing as soon as possible.

(16)   COSTS:
Frivolous or vexatious applications may lead to an award of costs against the applicant.

(17)   INFORMATION:
For general information regarding employment rights please contact the National Employment Rights Authority (NERA) at Lo call No: 1890 80 80 90 or submit your query using their eform, which is located in the 'Contact Us' section of their website www.employmentrights.ie

(18)   DATA PROTECTION
The Employment Appeals Tribunal holds data on all applications received. Data Protection is the safeguarding of the privacy rights of individuals in relation to the processing of personal data. The Data Protection Acts 1988 and 2003 confer rights on individuals as well as responsibilities on those persons processing personal data. Personal data, as covered by the Data Protection Acts, relates to the information on individuals and or sole traders only.

The Employment Appeals Tribunal provides copies of its decisions on its website. The decisions do not include the names of the parties (the name/s of the employee/s or the employer/s). The Data Protection Commissioner's web-site *www.dataprotection.ie* offers an explanation of the rights and responsibilities under the Data Protection Acts and information is also available from the Data Protection Commissioner's Office at Canal House, Station Road, Portarlington, Co. Laois; telephone number (057) 8684800.

(19)   USE OF INTERPRETERS
The Tribunal does not provide a language interpreter service. However, if you feel that an interpreter is essential to the hearing of the claim, you can make an application before a sitting Division of the Tribunal. **Please Note: An application must be made at least two weeks in advance of the hearing date.**

NOTE
Please Detach Form from Notes and send to;

Secretary
Employment Appeals Tribunal
Davitt House
65A Adelaide Road
Dublin 2

Telephone: (01) 631 3006
1890 220222 Lo-Call service from outside (01) area
Website: www.eatribunal.ie
Email: eat@deti.ie

FORM T1-B **EMPLOYMENT APPEALS TRIBUNAL**

Please read the notes supplied then complete this form in <u>BLOCK CAPITALS</u>. Please sign and date

FOR OFFICIAL USE ONLY
Case No/s:

1. NOTICE OF APPEAL FROM RIGHTS COMMISSIONER'S RECOMMENDATION UNDER (Tick appropriate box or boxes)

	(i)	Unfair Dismissals Acts 1977 to 2007
	(ii)	Payment of Wages Act 1991
	(iii)	Terms of Employment (Information) Acts 1994 and 2001
	(iv)	Maternity Protection Act 1994 and 2004
	(v)	Adoptive Leave Act 1995
	(vi)	Protection of Young Persons (Employment) Act 1996
	(vii)	Parental Leave Act 1998-2006
	(viii)	Protections for Persons Reporting Child Abuse Act 1998
	(ix)	European Communities (Protection of Employees on Transfer of Undertakings) Regulations 2003
	(x)	European Communities (Protection of Employment) Regulations 2000
	(xi)	Carer's Leave Act 2001
	(xii)	Competition Act 2002
	(xiii)	Consumer Protection Act 2007
	(xiv)	Chemicals Act 2008
		Organisation of Working Time Act 1997 – Appeals as to holiday entitlement can be made to the Employment Appeals Tribunal along with another Act. Otherwise it must be appealed to the Labour Court

PLEASE STATE IF YOU ARE THE <u>EMPLOYEE</u> OR THE <u>EMPLOYER</u>:

2. IF EMPLOYEE:	**2. IF EMPLOYER:**
First Name:	Name/Company: ....
Surname:	Address: ....
Address:	....
....	....
Phone No:	Phone No: ....
Email Address::	Email Address:

3. WILL YOU HAVE A REPRESENTATIVE AT HEARING? (Trade Union Official, Solicitor, etc.) Yes ☐ No ☐	**3. WILL YOU HAVE A REPRESENTATIVE AT HEARING?** (Employer Representative, Solicitor, etc.) Yes ☐ No ☐
If yes, please give:	If yes, please give:
Name:	Name: ....
Address:	Address: ....
....	....
Phone No:	Phone No: ....

4. NAME AND ADDRESS OF PARTY AGAINST WHOM THE APPEAL IS BEING BROUGHT
Name: ....
Address: ....
....
Phone No: ....

PLEASE ADVISE THE TRIBUNAL SECRETARIAT OF ANY CHANGE OF ADDRESS.

5. Please enter the following dates (IF APPLICABLE)	Day	Month	Year
Date of Birth			
Employment Began			
Dismissal Notice Received			
Employment ended			

6. PAY (IF APPLICABLE)	€
Basic Weekly Pay	
Regular Bonus or Allowances	
Average Weekly Overtime	
Any other payments including payments in kind - specify	
Weekly Total Gross	
Net	

7. NAME OF RIGHTS COMMISSIONER

8. DATE AND REF. NO. OF DECISION/RECOMMENDATION TO WHICH THIS APPEAL APPLIES:
(Please enclose a copy of this decision/recommendation with your application)

9. TOWN OF EMPLOYMENT OR NEAREST TOWN:

10 THE REASONS FOR MY APPEAL ARE: (You can attach additional sheets if necessary)

A COPY OF THE RIGHTS COMMISSIONER'S RECOMMENDATION MUST BE FORWARDED WITH THIS FORM.

11. REMEDY SOUGHT (IF APPLICABLE):

IMPORTANT NOTE: INCOMPLETE FORMS WILL BE RETURNED AND MAY DELAY THE PROCESSING OF YOUR APPEAL

12. DECISIONS OF THE TRIBUNAL MAY BE PLACED ON THE TRIBUNAL'S WEBSITE
(Please refer to point (18) of Notes)

SIGNED: _____

DATE: _____

Please note that where the Tribunal processes a claim for hearing, all correspondence (*forms, letters, enclosures etc.*) received in this office will be copied to, and exchanged between, the parties to the claim.

PLEASE ADVISE THE TRIBUNAL SECRETARIAT (01-6313006) IF YOU REQUIRE ANY SPECIAL FACILITIES WHEN ATTENDING A TRIBUNAL HEARING.

Form T1B Notes

NOTICE OF APPEAL TO EMPLOYMENT APPEALS TRIBUNAL UNDER:

(i)	UNFAIR DISMISSALS ACT 1977 TO 2007
(ii)	PAYMENT OF WAGES ACT 1991
(iii)	TERMS OF EMPLOYMENT (INFORMATION) ACT 1994 and 2001
(iv)	MATERNITY PROTECTION ACT 1994 AND 2004
(v)	ADOPTIVE LEAVE ACT 1995
(vi)	PROTECTION OF YOUNG PERSONS (EMPLOYMENT) ACT 1996
(vii)	PARENTAL LEAVE ACT 1998-2006
(viii)	PROTECTIONS FOR PERSONS REPORTING CHILD ABUSE ACT 1998
(ix)	EUROPEAN COMMUNITIES (PROTECTION OF EMPLOYEES ON TRANSFER OF UNDERTAKINGS) REGULATIONS 2003
(x)	EUROPEAN COMMUNITIES (PROTECTION OF EMPLOYMENT) REGULATIONS 2000
(xi)	CARER'S LEAVE ACT 2001
(xii)	COMPETITION ACT 2002
(xiii)	CONSUMER PROTECTION ACT 2007
(xiv)	CHEMICALS ACT 2008

Organisation of Working Time Act 1997 – Appeals as to holiday entitlement can be made to the Employment Appeals Tribunal along with another Act. Otherwise it must be appealed to the Labour Court.

Notes for Persons Making Appeal

THIS FORM IS TO BE USED BY PERSONS WHO WISH TO APPEAL A RECOMMENDATION / DECISION OF A RIGHTS COMMISSIONER TO THE EMPLOYMENT APPEALS TRIBUNAL UNDER ONE OR MORE OF THE ABOVE ACTS

PART A – TIME LIMITS

IMPORTANT: TIME LIMITS FOR PERSONS BRINGING AN APPEAL TO THE TRIBUNAL:

Note:
Appeals against a recommendation or Decision of a Rights Commissioner must be made to the Tribunal within a particular time-limit from the date the recommendation is communicated to you. The time limits for appeals under the various Acts are as follows:

UNFAIR DISMISSALS ACTS 1977 to 2007	Within 6 weeks to the Tribunal.
PAYMENT OF WAGES ACT 1991	Within 6 weeks to the Tribunal AND the other party
TERMS OF EMPLOYMENT (INFORMATION) ACT 1994 and 2001:	Within 6 weeks to the Tribunal.
MATERNITY PROTECTION ACT 1994 and 2004	Within 4 weeks to the Tribunal.
ADOPTIVE LEAVE ACT 1995	Within 4 weeks to the Tribunal.
PROTECTION OF YOUNG PERSONS (EMPLOYMENT) ACT 1996	Within 6 weeks to the Tribunal.
PARENTAL LEAVE ACT 1998-2006	Within 4 weeks to the Tribunal
PROTECTIONS FOR PERSONS REPORTING CHILD ABUSE ACT 1998	Within 6 weeks to the Tribunal
EUROPEAN COMMUNITIES (PROTECTION OF EMPLOYEES ON TRANSFER OF UNDERTAKINGS) REGULATIONS 2003	Within 6 weeks to the Tribunal
EUROPEAN COMMUNITIES (PROTECTION OF EMPLOYMENT) REGULATIONS, 2000	Within 6 weeks to the Tribunal
CARER'S LEAVE ACT 2001	Within 4 weeks to the Tribunal (This time limit may be extended for a further period not exceeding 6 weeks if the Tribunal considers it reasonable to do so having regard to all the circumstances)
COMPETITION ACT 2002	Within 6 weeks to the Tribunal
CONSUMER PROTECTION ACT 2007	Within 6 weeks to the Tribunal
CHEMICALS ACT 2008	Within 6 weeks to the Tribunal

PART B - NOTES

(1) **Box 1 - TICK APPROPRIATE BOX OR BOXES:**
Tick box or boxes representing the Act or Acts under which you are appealing .

(2) **Box 2 - NAME AND ADDRESS OF PARTY MAKING THE APPEAL:**
If you change your address after lodging this form, be sure to notify the Secretary, Employment Appeals Tribunal, Davitt House, 65A Adelaide Road, Dublin 2. In order to enhance the processing of applications we will use email, where applicable, to all parties at any stage in the processing of an appeal.

(3) **EMPLOYER'S FULL LEGAL NAME AND ADDRESS:**
Any Order made by the Tribunal may not be enforceable if incorrect information is given. For assistance, please consult your P45 or where appropriate, the Companies Registration Office (01-804 5200). The employer's Registered (PAYE) No. may be obtained from your P45, P60 and Tax Certificate P.6CL.

(4) **Box 3 - NAME, ADDRESS OF REPRESENTATIVE OF PARTY MAKING THIS APPEAL:**
It is not necessary to have representation before the Tribunal. However, if you have arranged for a representative to attend on your behalf at the Tribunal, notification of the hearing of your appeal will be sent to that person as well as to yourself.

(5) **Box 5 - DATES:**
Insert relevant dates

(6) **Box 6 - PAY:**
Basic Weekly Pay.
This means the basic pay before any deductions are made.

Average Weekly Overtime.
In unfair dismissal cases, overtime may be disregarded unless it is a normal feature of work. If it is a normal feature of work inasmuch as you are normally expected to work it, overtime pay is included in your normal weekly pay and overtime is included in normal weekly working hours.

Payments in Kind.
These would include the value of meals or board, use of company house, car or health insurance etc.

(7) **Box 7 - RIGHTS COMMISSIONER:**
Please fill in the name of the Rights Commissioner that heard your case

(8) **Box 8** – Please include the date the recommendation or decision was issued and the reference no. that appears on the signed decision. **Please enclose a copy of this decision with this form.**

(9) **Box 9** - In this box please give the name of the nearest town where you worked or the nearest town to this.

(10) **Box 10 - REASON FOR APPLICATION:**
Please give an outline of your case in the space provided. If you wish to provide further details, please attach any separate sheets to the form.

(11) **Box 11 – REMEDY SOUGHT**
Please state what remedy you are seeking

(12) **ACKNOWLEDGEMENT OF APPLICATION:**
If you do not get an acknowledgement of your application within a reasonable time you should contact the Secretary to the Tribunal by letter, telephone or email (details below).

(13) **HEARING OF CLAIM:**
Once you have received an acknowledgement, your case will be listed for hearing as soon as possible at the nearest town to your place of employment. You will get at least 2 weeks notice of a date for hearing.

(14) **ADJOURNMENTS:**
Adjournments may be granted only in **exceptional circumstances**. Otherwise, a case is expected to proceed at the time and place notified to the parties. When applications for adjournments are made, they may be made to any sitting Division of the Tribunal at any venue.

The following conditions should at least be met when applying for an adjournment. However, the existence of any one or all of these conditions should not be considered a guarantee for obtaining an adjournment.

    o   Good cause should be shown as adjournments are only granted for very grave reasons.

o The application should be made at the earliest opportunity after receipt of the notice of hearing, save where the Tribunal for just cause dispenses with this requirement.

o The application should be made by a party or his representative appearing in person.

o Proof of consent from the other party or their representative may be required. The application can be made without consent but the Tribunal may require proof that consent was at least sought.

(15) **WITHDRAWAL OF APPLICATIONS:**
If you are seeking to withdraw your application, the Secretary to the Tribunal should be notified in writing as soon as possible.

(16) **COSTS:**
Frivolous or vexatious applications may lead to an award of costs against the applicant.

(17) **INFORMATION:**
For general information regarding employment rights please contact the National Employment Rights Authority (NERA) at Lo call No: 1890 80 80 90 or submit your query using their eform, which is located in the 'Contact Us' section of their website www.employmentrights.ie

(18) **DATA PROTECTION**
The Employment Appeals Tribunal holds data on all applications received. Data Protection is the safeguarding of the privacy rights of individuals in relation to the processing of personal data. The Data Protection Acts 1988 and 2003 confer rights on individuals as well as responsibilities on those persons processing personal data. Personal data, as covered by the Data Protection Acts, relates to the information on individuals and or sole traders only.

The Employment Appeals Tribunal provides copies of its decisions on its website. The decisions do not include the names of the parties (the name/s of the employee/s or the employer/s). The Data Protection Commissioner's web-site www.dataprotection.ie offers an explanation of the rights and responsibilities under the Data Protection Acts and information is also available from the Data Protection Commissioner's Office at Canal House, Station Road, Portarlington, Co. Laois; telephone number (057) 8684800.

(19) **USE OF INTERPRETERS**
The Tribunal does not provide a language interpreter service. However, if you feel that an interpreter is essential to the hearing of the claim, you can make an application before a sitting Division of the Tribunal. **Please Note: An application must be made at least two weeks in advance of the hearing date.**

NOTE
Please Detach Form from Notes and send to;

Secretary
Employment Appeals Tribunal
Davitt House
65A Adelaide Road
Dublin 2

Telephone: (01) 631 3006
1890 220222 Lo-Call service from outside (01) area
Website: www.eatribunal.ie
Email: eat@deti.ie

Form T1-C

<table>
<tr><td colspan="2">**For Official Use:**</td></tr>
<tr><td>Case No:</td></tr>
</table>

NOTICE OF APPEAL TO THE EMPLOYMENT APPEALS TRIBUNAL
UNDER THE PROTECTION OF EMPLOYEES (EMPLOYERS' INSOLVENCY) ACTS, 1984 TO 2001

(THIS FORM MUST BE COMPLETED IN BLOCK CAPITALS)   NOTE: Please read notes overleaf before completing this form

1. EMPLOYEE DETAILS:

Surname:
First Name:
Address:
Telephone No:
Occupation:
R.S.I. No.:

2. NAME AND ADDRESS OF EMPLOYER:

Telephone No:

3. TYPE OF APPEAL:
(Tick ✓ relevant box)

Arrears of Wages	☐
Arrears of Holiday Pay	☐
Arrears of Sick Pay	☐
Pension Contributions	☐

4. APPEAL DETAILS:

PERIOD OVER WHICH CLAIM AROSE							
	Day	Month	Year		Day	Month	Year
From				To			
From				To			
Date of Birth:							
Date of termination of employment:							
Date informed of Minister's decision:							

5. TOWN OR NEAREST TOWN TO PLACE OF EMPLOYMENT:

6. NORMAL WEEKLY PAY:

€

Basic Weekly Pay	
Regular Bonus or Allowance	
Average Weekly Overtime	
Any other payments including: payments in kind - specify	
Weekly Total	

7. NAME AND ADDRESS OF REPRESENTATIVE
(UNION OFFICIAL ETC.) OF PERSON MAKING THE COMPLAINT

Telephone No:

8. THE GROUNDS OF MY APPEAL ARE:
(Please attach copy of Minister's decision)

Signed:
Date:

Send this form to: The Secretary
                     Employment Appeals Tribunal
                     Davitt House,
                     65A, Adelaide Road, Dublin 2
Telephone: **(01) 631 2121**
                     1890 220222 LoCall from outside (01) area

NOTES FOR PERSONS COMPLETING THIS FORM

1.   A Guide to the Acts is available on request from the Information Unit of the Department of Enterprise, Trade and Employment.

2.   Employees and trustees, in the case of pension contributions, may only complete this form if the Minister for Enterprise, Trade and Employment has:

   a)   Refused to pay an amount applied for, or
   b)   Reduced an amount applied for

AND

the claim was in respect of arrears of wages, arrears of sick pay, arrears of holiday pay or unpaid pension contributions.

3.   Complaints to the Tribunal must be made within six weeks from the date on which the Minister's decision on your application was communicated to you.

   The Tribunal has discretion to extend this time limit.

NOTES ON COMPLETING THIS FORM:

BOX 1:   If you change your address after lodging this form, inform the Tribunal immediately.

BOX 3   A trustee of a pension scheme may only make a complaint to the Tribunal in respect of arrears of unpaid contributions.

BOX 4:   The period over which the claim arose is the period over which you were, for example, entitled to holidays and in respect of which you have not been paid.

BOX 6:   A guide to the calculation of normal weekly pay is set out in the Guide to the Acts. Basic pay means gross pay before deductions. Average overtime, bonuses and allowances are calculated by obtaining gross payment for the 26 week period which is immediately prior to 13 weeks before the date of termination of the employee's employment and dividing this figure by 26 to obtain the average.

BOX 7:   Only complete this box if you have consulted the representative beforehand and he/she is willing to attend the Tribunal hearing. Notification of the hearing will be sent to them also.

BOX 8:   If you do not have sufficient space to set out your grounds of appeal, continue them on a sheet of paper and attach to this form.

Caution: The Tribunal may award costs against a party who has acted frivolously or vexatiously in the matter of an appeal.

FORM T1-D   **EMPLOYMENT APPEALS TRIBUNAL**
Please read the notes supplied then complete this form in <u>BLOCK CAPITALS</u>.
Please sign and date

FOR OFFICIAL USE ONLY
Case No:

1. NOTICE OF CLAIM <u>FOR IMPLEMENTATION</u> OF A RIGHTS COMMISSIONER'S RECOMMENDATION (Please tick appropriate box or boxes)

	(i) Unfair Dismissals Acts 1977 to 2007
	(ii) Terms of Employment (Information) Acts 1994 and 2001
	(iii) Protection of Young Persons (Employment) Act 1996
	(iv) Protections for Persons Reporting Child Abuse Act 1998
	(v) European Communities (Protection of Employment) Regulations 2003
	(vi) Competition Act 2002
	(vii) Consumer Protection Act 2007
	(viii) Chemicals Act 2008

2. NAME AND ADDRESS OF PARTY SEEKING THE IMPLEMENTATION:	**3. NAME AND ADDRESS OF PARTY AGAINST WHOM THE CLAIM IS BEING BROUGHT:**
First Name:	Name/Company: ....
Surname:	Address: ....
Address:	....
....	....
....	....
Phone No	Phone No ....
Email Address:	Email Address:

PLEASE ADVISE THE TRIBUNAL SECRETARIAT OF ANY CHANGE OF ADDRESS.

4. WILL YOU HAVE A REPRESENTATIVE AT HEARING? (Trade Union Official, Solicitor, etc.)
Yes ☐   ☐

6. TOWN OF EMPLOYMENT OR NEAREST TOWN:

If yes, please give:
Name: ....
Address: ....
....
Phone No: ....

5. DATES (IF APPLICABLE)

	Day	Month	Year
Date of Birth			
Employment Began			
Dismissal Notice Received			
Employment ended			

7. PAY (IF APPLICABLE)

	€
Basic Weekly Pay	
Regular Bonus or Allowances	
Average Weekly Overtime	
Any other payments including payments in kind - specify	
Weekly Total Gross	
Net	

8. (i) NAME OF RIGHTS COMMISSIONER:
....

8.(ii) DATE AND REF. NO. OF DECISION/RECOMMENDATION TO WHICH THIS CLAIM APPLIES (Please enclose a copy of this decision/recommendation with your application)

9. THE REASONS FOR MY APPEAL ARE: (You can attach additional sheets if necessary)

Important Note: Incomplete forms will be returned and may delay the processing of your appeal

10. DECISIONS OF THE TRIBUNAL MAY BE PLACED ON THE TRIBUNAL'S WEBSITE
(Please refer to point (16) of Notes

SIGNED: _____

DATE: _____

Please note that where the Tribunal processes a claim for hearing, all correspondence (*forms, letters, enclosures etc.*) received in this office will be copied to, and exchanged between, the parties to the claim.

PLEASE ADVISE THE TRIBUNAL SECRETARIAT (01-6313006) IF YOU REQUIRE ANY SPECIAL FACILITIES WHEN ATTENDING A TRIBUNAL HEARING.

Chapter 2

MINIMUM NOTICE AND TERMS OF EMPLOYMENT ACTS 1973–2005

PURPOSE

[2.01] The Minimum Notice Act was originally established with the purpose of encouraging employers to give written contracts of employment to employees. This was done by giving employees the right to ensure that certain terms and conditions of employment be outlined in writing.[1] Its primary purpose was however to establish minimum periods of statutory notice which have to be given by employers and indeed employees prior to the termination of a contract of employment.

APPLICATION

[2.02] The Acts apply to all employers and to most employees. Employees who have worked continuously for the same employer for 13 weeks are covered by the legislation.

Those excluded include:

- the employer's immediate family working in a private dwelling house or on a farm;

- civil servants;

- members of the Defence Forces and the Garda Síochána;

- persons employed under the Merchant Shipping Acts.

NOTICE PERIOD

[2.03] The legislation sets out the minimum periods of notice to be observed by either side on termination of employment. The amount of notice due to an employee depends on the employee's length of service.

Length of Service	Entitlement[2]
13 weeks to 2 years	1 week
2 years to 5 years	2 weeks
5 years to 10 years	4 weeks
10 years to 15 years	6 weeks
15 years+	8 weeks

---

1.   This piece of the legislation has been repealed by the Terms of Employment (Information) Act 1994.

2.   Minimum Notice and Terms of Employment Act 1973, s 4(2).

Notice must be given directly to the employee concerned. It is not sufficient to give it to his/her representative, as this does not discharge the employer's obligations under the minimum notice legislation. Notice must be specific and unequivocal.

CONTINUOUS SERVICE

[2.04] Rights to notice are dependent upon the length of continuous service.[3] An employee's service is deemed to be continuous unless he/she is dismissed or leaves the employment voluntarily. Continuity is not broken by:

- absence due to sickness;

- strikes or lock-outs; lay-off periods; leave granted under protective legislation;

- dismissals followed by immediate re-employment; and

- transfer of the business, unless the employee received and retained a redundancy payment from the transferor at the time of, and by reason of, the transfer.

The Employment Appeals Tribunal will generally deal with the question of continuity of employment in terms as favourable as possible to the employee.

COMPUTABLE SERVICE

[2.05] The 1973 Act establishes rules regarding the computation of an employee's service. When calculating computable service, account is taken of:[4]

- the first 26 weeks of absence due to illness, lay-off or any other absence agreed with the employer (by definition periods of absence due to illness, lay-off or any other absence agreed with the employer are not computable);

- periods of leave granted under protective legislation;

- periods of service with the Defence Forces;

- periods of lock-out; and

- periods of absence due to a trade dispute in another business.

Not taken into account are:

- periods of absence while on strike.

It should be noted that the periods of employment may be continuous but not computable.

---

3.   Minimum Notice and Terms of Employment Act 1973, Sch 1.
4.   Minimum Notice and Terms of Employment Act 1973, Sch 1.

WHAT CONSTITUTES PAY?

[2.06] Pay for notice purposes is defined by the Second Schedule of the 1973 Act. The Schedule sets out two methods of calculating pay:

i.   In employments where there are normal working hours. In this instance pay is calculated by reference to the average rate of pay earned by the employee in respect of any time worked during the 13 weeks next preceding the giving of notice.[5]

ii.   In employments for which there are no normal working hours pay is calculated as the sum not less than the average weekly earnings of the employee in the thirteen weeks next preceding the giving of notice.

In both instances above pay includes such overtime as is usually worked.[6]

Importantly, however, pay is only due if the employee is ready and willing to work.[7] This often arises when employees are absent on long-term illness and a decision is taken to terminate their employment. In this instance, although entitled to notice, the employee because they are not willing and/or able to work will not receive any pay for that notice. (See also **2.16**.)

NOTICE TO EMPLOYERS

[2.07] An employee who has greater than 13 weeks' service with their employer and who wishes to terminate their contract of employment must give at least one week's notice of termination.[8] The required period of notice may be longer than this if provided for in the contract of employment. If this is the case, then the greater contractual period of notice prevails over the lesser statutory one in respect of both parties. It is therefore the longer period – be it contractual or statutory – that is binding. (See also **2.13**.)

WAIVER AND PAYMENT IN LIEU OF NOTICE

[2.08] Either side may voluntarily waive their right to notice.[9] The 1973 Act also allows employees to accept payment in lieu of notice.[10]

Where payment in lieu of notice is given by the employer and is accepted by the employee, or where there is provision for payment in lieu of notice in the employee's contract of employment, then the date of termination of the contract of employment is the date upon which the employee physically leaves the employment. This is so as the contract will have been determined in accordance with the terms of the contract. In the alternative if there is no right to give pay in lieu of notice in the contract, the EAT will

---

5.   Minimum Notice and Terms of Employment Act 1973, Sch 2, para 2(b).
6.   Minimum Notice and Terms of Employment Act 1973, s 2(a)(ii) and Sch 2.
7.   Minimum Notice and Terms of Employment Act 1973, s 2(a)(ii) and Sch 2 and Minimum Notice and Terms of Employment Act 1973, Sch 2, para 4.
8.   Minimum Notice and Terms of Employment Act 1973, s 6.
9.   Minimum Notice and Terms of Employment Act 1973, s 7(1).
10.   Minimum Notice and Terms of Employment Act 1973, s 7(1).

treat the case as a 'no notice' one and will determine the date of termination by adding on the contractual or statutory notice period, whichever is the greater [11] (see also **3.14**)

For statutory redundancy purposes, the date of termination of employment is the date on which notice, if given, would have expired.[12]

The legislation provides that an employee may only 'accept' payment in lieu of notice. The Minimum Notice Act 1973 gives no guidance as to what should occur in a situation where payment in lieu of notice is not provided for in the contract of employment and/or if the employee concerned is unwilling to accept payment in lieu of notice and wishes 'to work' the notice period. Some experts[13] suggest that failing agreement to such an arrangement the employee is entitled to stay on and work their notice period. The practicalities of this may make the arrangement inoperable such as if there is no work for the employee and/or if relationships have broken down. In any event it is usually more beneficial for the employee to receive payment in lieu of notice as notice monies may be paid as part of any severance arrangement and are subject to generous tax allowances.[14] If, however, there is provision for payment in lieu of notice in the contract of employment, the notice pay albeit that it is paid in lieu is subject to taxation in the normal way (see **Ch 7**).

Calculation of pay in lieu of notice

[2.09] Most people when they think of pay automatically think of basic pay. However, as discussed previously (see **2.06**) pay for the purpose of payment in lieu of notice must include overtime. When agreeing pay in lieu of notice with an employee it may be intended to include in the calculation such additional other benefits such as pension payments, car allowances etc. The contract of employment may provide some assistance in this regard. Typically pay in lieu of notice clauses provide that 'nothing in this contract shall prohibit the employer from paying the employee in lieu of notice' or in the alternative they might say 'nothing shall prohibit the employer from making a payment in lieu of notice'. In the latter case it can be construed that the employer has the right to make a payment in lieu of notice whereas in the former it could be construed that 'paying' the employee means taking into account their total remuneration.

This is an important distinction; where a contract provides for an employer to elect to give a payment in lieu of notice it will be difficult for an employee to insist on their salary during the notice period.

NO ENTITLEMENT TO NOTICE

[2.10] There are certain circumstances when an employer is not obliged to give notice.

---

11.   See *O'Reilly v Pulmann Kellogg Ltd* UD 340/1979.
12.   Minimum Notice and Terms of Employment Act 1973, s 7(2).
13.   See Meenan, *Working within the Law – A practical guide for employers and employees* (2nd edn, Oak Tree Press, 1999).
14.   See chapter on Taxation of Termination Payments.

Misconduct

[2.11] Where an employee is dismissed for misconduct no notice pay is due.[15] However, the Act does not define 'misconduct' but the EAT has held that this applies only where the misconduct is of a gross/serious nature.[16] Thus it is not always possible to define or determine what will be sufficient to justify summary dismissal on the grounds of gross misconduct. The High Court in *Carvill v Irish Industrial Bank Ltd,*[17] expressed the view that the grounds relied on to justify a dismissal without notice of an employee must be actions or omissions by the employee which are inconsistent with the performance of the express or implied terms of its contract of service.

Constructive dismissal

[2.12] An employee who is constructively dismissed is not entitled to notice or payment in lieu of notice as the employee, and not the employer, ended the contract of employment. The tribunal has consistently upheld this in such cases.[18]

Resignation

[2.13] If an employee voluntarily leaves their job there is no obligation on the employer to pay notice.

Under the Acts, although an employee is obliged to give one week's notice of resignation,[19] this period is usually more extensive in written contracts. If an employee leaves employment immediately without giving any notice, the employer has the legal right to sue the employee. However, this is moot point as the practical position often outweighs the reality. Not the least the cost of issuing proceedings against the employee could exceed the amount due. (See also **2.07**.)

Fixed-term/specified purpose contracts

[2.14] No notice has to be given on the expiry of a fixed term/specified purpose contract drawn up in accordance with the terms of the Unfair Dismissals Acts 1977–2005 (that is, when the contract is in writing and expressly provides that the terms of the Unfair Dismissals Acts will not apply to the termination of the contract by reason only of the expiry of the fixed term/specified purpose and where it is signed by both parties).[20]

However, such contracts should always include a general notice/termination clause to provide for the contract to be terminated prior to the expiry of the fixed term/

---

15. Minimum Notice and Terms of Employment Act 1973, s 8.
16. See *Kelly v Sanser Ltd* M1343/1983 and *Brewster v Burke and Minister for Labour* (1985) 4 JISLL 98.
17. *Carvill v Irish Industrial Bank Ltd* (1986) IR 325.
18. *Halal Meat Packers (Ballyhaunis) Ltd v Employment Appeals Tribunal* (1990) ELR 49 and *Stamp v Mc Grath UD* 1243/1983.
19. Minimum Notice and Terms of Employment Act 1973, s 6.
20. Minimum Notice and Terms of Employment Act 1973, s 2(2)(a).

specified purpose, otherwise the employee may be entitled to payment of the total balance of monies due under the contract.

Note that it was confirmed in *O'Mahony v College of the Most Holy Trinity*[21] that a notice period in a fixed-term contract does not exclude the fact that it is a genuine fixed-term contract. (Prior to this there was some doubt as to whether the inclusion of a notice period in a fixed term contract invalidated the fixed term nature of that contract. See also **2.15** below for fixed-term contracts and retirement.)

Retirement

[2.15] Notice does not have to be given nor payment made in lieu when terminating the employment contract of an employee who has reached retirement age, as stated in the contract of employment, or the normal retirement age in the employment concerned, or the general state retirement age of 66.[22] However, best practice would be to give notice well in excess of what would otherwise be required under the Minimum Notice Acts (say, three to six months). This is especially important in employments where the normal retirement age may be in doubt and in such cases the notice required under the Minimum Notice Acts should at least be given.

Of note here also is s 6(3)(a)(c) of the Employment Equality Act 1998 which provides that 'offering a fixed term contract to a person over the compulsory retirement age for that employment or to a particular class or description of employee in that employment shall not be taken as constituting discrimination on the age ground'.

This, however, given a number of recent cases[23] may not be as clear cut. (See also **Ch 11**.)

Incapability and notice

[2.16] Whilst an employer is obliged to give the appropriate period of notice to the employee on terminating employment on the grounds of incapability[24] (either under the minimum notice legislation or the contract of employment), employers are not obliged to pay the employee for the notice period as pay is only due if the employee is ready and willing to work[25] see also para **2.08**). This also negates any right to payment in lieu of notice.

Lay-off/short-time

[2.17] An employee who claims and receives a statutory redundancy payment in respect of lay-off or short-time working is deemed to have voluntarily left their employment and therefore not to be entitled to notice. This is not the case where the employer terminates

---

21. *O'Mahony v College of the Most Holy Trinity* (1998) ELR 159.
22. Minimum Notice and Terms of Employment Act 1973, s 2(1)(b).
23. *Félix Palacios de la Villa v Cortefiel Servicios SA* (Case C–411/05).
24. This generally arises in the context of long-term absenteeism.
25. Minimum Notice and Terms of Employment Act 1973, s 2(a)(ii) and Sch 2; Minimum Notice and Terms of Employment Act 1973, Sch 2, para 4.

the employee's contract during a period of lay-off or short-time working – see *Irish Leathers v Minister for Labour*.[26] Also see Form RP9 (see **6.81**) which states:

> An employee who claims and receives a redundancy payment in respect of lay off or short time is deemed to have voluntarily left his/her employment and therefore not entitled to notice under the Minimum Notice and Terms of Employment Acts, 1973 to 2001.

Minimum notice and civil servants

[2.18] Civil Servants do not have an entitlement to statutory minimum notice. However, the Civil Service Disciplinary Code (circular 14/2006) which was issued on 4 July 2006 regulates notice for civil cervants. The Code replaces the disciplinary code circular 1/92 and it applies to all new disciplinary cases after the effective date.[27] Paragraph 64 of the Code provides that where termination is proposed, the personnel officer makes a recommendation to the appropriate authority and provides him with a written report on the circumstances of the case. In accordance with s 9(1) of the Public Services Management Act 1997, a decision to dismiss an officer must be made by the appropriate authority. Where a decision to dismiss is taken in cases other than gross misconduct, notice of termination will be given in accordance with the officer's terms of employment.

In essence this means that when a dismissal occurs (other than in gross misconduct cases, where no notice is due) the contract of employment will determine the notice period.

MINIMUM NOTICE AND THE PAYMENT OF WAGES ACT 1991

[2.19] The Payment of Wages Act 1991 governs the payment of wages to an employee by an employer. Wages are defined under s 1 as:

> 'wages', in relation to an employee, means any sums payable to the employee by the employer in connection with his employment, including:
>
> (a)   any fee, bonus or commission, or any holiday, sick or maternity pay, or any other emolument, referable to his employment, whether payable under his contract of employment or otherwise, and
>
> (b)   any sum payable to the employee upon the termination by the employer of his contract of employment without his having given to the employee the appropriate prior notice of the termination, being a sum paid in lieu of the giving of such notice:

As such, any payments under the Minimum Notice and Terms of Employment Act and/ or contractual notice are deemed to be 'wages' for the purposes of 1991 Act and employees can pursue claims for unpaid notice under this act.

---

26.   *Irish Leathers v Minister for Labour* (1986) 5 JISLL 211.
27.   4 July 2006.

In so far as what actually constitutes wages for the purposes of notice and the Payment of Wages Act, this was dealt with in the case of *Sullivan v Department of Education*.[28] Here the Tribunal took the word 'payable' to mean 'properly payable'; consequently it was not simply a matter of what may have been paid from the outset but all sums to which an employee is properly entitled.

LEAVE AND MINIMUM NOTICE

Annual leave

[2.20] Annual leave may run concurrently with notice, if the employee is still in employment. Under the Organisation of Working Time Act 1997 it is at the employer's discretion to decipher the time annual leave may be taken.[29]

Protective leave/adoptive leave

[2.21] Protective leave is regulated by the Maternity Protection Acts 1994–2004 and includes:

• maternity leave;

• additional maternity leave;

• leave to which the father is entitled upon the death of the mother (s 16 leave);

• health and safety leave.

Adoptive leave is regulated by the Adoptive Leave Acts 1995–2005. Both the Maternity Protection Acts 1994–2004 and the Adoptive Leave Acts 1995–2005 provide that any notice of termination of employment given on the notification of or during protective leave/adoptive leave is void. A resignation by an employee with notice given during protective or adoptive leave is also void and cannot take effect until after the leave period.[30] The operative word here is 'void'.

EXTENDING THE NOTICE PERIOD

[2.22] In 1987 the Supreme Court, in the case of *Bolands Ltd v Ward*,[31] found that an employer would have satisfied the requirements of the Act where the notice is extended from week to week and it would not be necessary to serve notice afresh giving the full statutory requirement.

Waterford Multiport v Fagan[32] upheld this decision and the court went on to state that the notices given were not invalidated by virtue of the employer not ensuring that the

---

28. *Sullivan v Department of Education* [1998] ELR 217.
29. Organisation of Working Time Act 1997, s 20.
30. Maternity Protection Acts 1994, s 23.
31. *Bolands Ltd (In Receivership) v Ward* [1987] IESC 1; [1988] ILRM 392 (30 October 1987).
32. *Waterford Multiport v Fagan* [1999] IEHC 158 (13 May 1999).

employees left on the due date, being a certain date, for the purposes of the Act on the expiry of that notice. Best practice is therefore to agree any extension of the notice period in writing with the effected employee(s).

RIGHTS AND DUTIES OF EMPLOYEES DURING THE NOTICE PERIOD

[2.23] Employees working out a notice period are still employed and are entitled to the same rights during the notice period as were enjoyed prior to the notice period.[33] They are entitled to all benefits including holiday leave, sick leave, pension contributions, and company car. Also if they are given notice in a redundancy situation they are entitled to reasonable time off to look for work.

NOTICE MUST BE SPECIFIC

[2.24] There is no legal requirement that notice should be in writing. However, it must be specific with regard to the minimum notice period. The High Court has confirmed this point in *Bolands Ltd (in receivership) v Josephine Ward*.[34]

Even if notice is given verbally, it should be confirmed in writing. Similarly, if an employee informs an employer verbally that he/she is resigning, he/she should be asked to put it in writing.

Payment in lieu of notice must also be specific. A sum of money paid to an employee on termination of employment should be accompanied by a clear statement indicating the individual components of the lump sum. The employee should be asked to sign one copy of the statement (see also point **2.30** below).

WITHDRAWAL OF NOTICE

[2.25] Notice, once given, cannot be withdrawn without the consent of the other party.

DISPUTES AND REDRESS

Disputes

[2.26] Under the 1973–2005 Acts, any dispute regarding notice may be referred to the Employment Appeals Tribunal. No time limit is laid down by the Acts for such claims so they fall under the statute of limitations for contract disputes, which is six years. This is very unlike most other employment law statutes which generally only allow claimant six months to a year to take a claim.

---

33. Minimum Notice and Terms of Employment Act 1973, Sch 2.
34. *Waterford Multiport v Fagan* [1998] ILRM 382.

Redress

[2.27] In assessing loss with regard to notice, the Tribunal will take into account not merely salary/wages but also all other remuneration such as: commission earnings, regular and rostered overtime and other fringe benefits. The tribunal will only award an employee compensation for any loss they sustained due to their employer's default in failing to give proper notice. However, if the employee was sick during the notice period or was on strike, no compensation is payable.[35] (See also **2.13** and **2.07**.)

It is important to note that the only matter that the Tribunal can deal with is the statutory notice period. It is not within the Tribunal's remit to deal with contractual notice periods greater than those provided for under the Act. These, if they arise must be litigated upon as a breach of contract claim in the civil courts.

A determination of the Tribunal in notice cases may be appealed to the High Court on a point of law only, by way of special summons within 21 days of the date of receipt of the Tribunal's decision. However, an application to the High Court for an extension of time for appeal may be made provided that reasonable cause can be shown for the delay.

WRONGFUL DISMISSAL AND NOTICE

[2.28] An employee who pursues a claim of unlawful dismissal at common law (wrongful dismissal) is asking the court for damages for breach of contract. By definition this materialises into a claim for contractual notice and the claim is limited to this (see **Ch 8**).

MINIMUM NOTICE AND REDUNDANCY

[2.29] Notice periods under the Minimum Notice and Terms of Employment Acts 1973–2005, the Redundancy Payments Acts 1967–2007, the Protection of Employment Act 1977 and contractual notice run concurrently. This is somewhat different if it is a collective redundancy.

Example

Company A wishes to make 200 staff redundant. The following notice must be given:

1. Statutory notice due under the Minimum Notice and Terms of Employment Acts 1973–2005.

2. As this constitutes a collective redundancy (see **Ch 6**) notice must be given to the Minister for Enterprise, Trade and Employment in accordance with the Protection of Employment Act 1977, ie 30 days prior to the first notice of redundancy.

---

35.   Minimum Notice and Terms of Employment Act 1973, Sch 2 provides that the employee must be 'ready and willing to work'.

3. Contractual notice in accordance with the various employees' contracts of employment.

4. Notice in accordance with the Redundancy Payments Acts 1967–2007.

All these 'notice periods' can run concurrently after the 30-day consultation period required for a collective redundancy expires. Therefore an employee with 16 years' service would be entitled to eight week's notice (presuming their contractual notice did not exceed this) and this eight-week period would begin to run after the 30-day 'consultation period' given to the Minister.

Presuming there was no collective redundancy, the statutory notice, contractual notice and notice in accordance with the Redundancy Payment Acts 1967–2007 would run concurrently.

MINIMUM NOTICE IN PRACTICE

Always be specific about the notice period

[2.30] This is one of the main mistakes that employers make. Every employee should be given a letter outlining what their notice period is and what exactly is to happen during the notice period. It is also necessary to be specific about the amount of notice pay due and to ensure that the employee accepts that the sum is in 'full and final settlement' and acknowledges that the document has been read over and explained to them and that they understand and accept the contents (see **Ch 6** for draft severance letters).

Payment in lieu of notice as a bargaining tool

[2.31] It is often beneficial for the employee to take payment in lieu of notice. This is something to bargain with during the termination of an employee where things are going badly and the employee insists on working their notice even though there may be no work for them or the relationship has broken down. If the employee agrees to payment in lieu of notice and presuming this is not provided for in the contract of employment then this forms part of the severance pay and as such is eligible for the usual tax relief.

Remember not all employees are entitled to a notice period

[2.32] (See **2.10–2.15**.)

Chapter 3

UNFAIR DISMISSAL

[3.01] The Unfair Dismissals Act was enacted in 1977 and was significantly amended in 1993. The 1977 Act brought into force for the first time in Irish law a process whereby an employee could take a claim before a tribunal – the Employment Appeals Tribunal (EAT) – to pursue a claim for unfair dismissal. The Act was far-reaching in its inception in that it introduced into Irish law a method whereby employers could legitimately dismiss an employee providing they did so fairly as defined within the Act.[1] Claims by employees can be brought before a rights commissioner or the Employment Appeals Tribunal (EAT) within six months of the date of dismissal (see **3.11**) or in exceptional circumstances this can be extended to 12 months (see **3.13**). The main advantages of a claim for unfair dismissal over that of wrongful dismissal (see **Ch 8**) generally lie in time and expense. One of the main aims of those drafting the legislation was to provide an informal forum to address such matters; this has largely been forgotten as the EAT now operates in a very legal and process driven fashion in accordance with the rules of evidence.

PRELIMINARY REQUIREMENTS

[3.02] There are certain minimum requirements that employees bringing a claim before the EAT must satisfy before the claim can be heard.

It is often the case that a hearing will involve consideration of not only the substantive issues but of preliminary points such as whether the claim was brought within the six-month time limit. The general tendency of the EAT is to hear all issues, both preliminary and substantive, before making a determination. This speaks to the general principle that all litigation should be disposed of in one set of proceedings and also prevents the EAT being judicially reviewed. Nonetheless there are circumstances where a preliminary point should be determined separately from the remainder of the case. In *Bus Éireann v SIPTU*[2] the Labour Court indicated that this would normally be done where it could lead to 'considerable savings in both time and expense' and where the point was a 'a question of pure law where no evidence was needed and no further information is required'. In practice this is very rarely the position adopted by the EAT.

Contract of employment

[3.03] In order to qualify for protection under the Unfair Dismissal Act, the worker in question must be an 'employee' employed under a 'contract of employment'.

---

1.   Unfair Dismissals Act 1977, s 15.
2.   *Bus Éireann v SIPTU* PTD 8/2004 citing O'Higgins CJ in *Tara Exploration and Development Co Ltd v Minister for Industry and Commerce* [1975] IR 242, 256

A contract of employment is defined in the Act as 'a contract of service or of apprenticeship, whether it is express or implied and (if it is express) whether it is oral or in writing'.

Therefore the claimant must be employed under a contract of employment whether it be oral or in writing.

The claimant must be an employee

[3.04] An employee is defined under the Act as:

> an individual who has entered into or works under (or, where the employment has ceased, worked under) a contract of employment and, in relation to redress for a dismissal under this Act, includes, in the case of the death of the employee concerned at any time following the dismissal, his personal representative.

In the majority of cases it will be readily evident who the employer is but confusion may arise where, for example, the employee is working for an agency or where they may appear to be an independent contractor.

Employee or agency worker

[3.05] The Employment Agency Act 1971 regulates employment agencies in this jurisdiction. It does not deal at all with the rights or status of agency workers. Previously agency workers were regarded as neither having a contract of employment with the agency nor the end user; however, more recently the courts have been willing to find that the agency worker was an employee of the end user or client.

For unfair dismissal purposes the 1993 Act extended the scope of who may be considered an employee for the purpose of the Act to include 'agency temps'.[3] This class of employees are now considered employees of the hiring company once they are placed by an employment agency. In *Bourton v Narcea and Anglo Irish Beef Processors (AIBP)*[4] it was held that Narcea, was an agency that provided boners to AIBP and the employee, although employed by Narcea, was deemed to be an employee of AIBP for the purposes of the Unfair Dismissals Act.

Employee or independent contractor?

[3.06] The tests which are applied by the Tribunal to establish the status of a claimant are based on the general legal rules which were developed by the courts to distinguish between 'employees' and 'independent contractors'. The question that the Tribunal has to consider is whether the employee is truly working for himself or for someone else. The contract itself will be examined to determine whether this is the case. In *O'Coindealbhain (Inspector of Taxes) v Mooney*,[5] the High Court, in holding that the claimant was not an employee, noted the facts that the respondent was (a) in business on his own account; (b) that the profit he made was dependent on how he decided to

---

3.   Unfair Dismissal (Amendment) Act 1993, s 13.
4.   *Bourton v Narcea and Anglo Irish Beef Processors (AIBP)* UD 186/1994.
5.   *O'Coindealbhain (Inspector of Taxes) v Mooney* (1990) 1 IR 422.

perform the work; and (c) that he was not obliged to provide his own work or skill, which were all factors that were inconsistent with a contract of service.

In *Readymix Concrete v Minister of Pensions and National Insurance*[6] the court held that a contract of service exists if:

- 'A worker provides his own work or skill for payment in performing some service for the employer.'

- 'He agrees to be sufficiently subject to the other party's control to make that other party his employer.' This is sometimes known as the 'control test' which, whilst still important, has become less so.[7]

- The other terms of the contract are consistent with it being a contract of service. This is often known as the 'economic test'. This aspect is the one which in particular has led to a widening of the test in recent years. Employees today have more perks and benefits associated with their employment than heretofore and these will be examined to determine whether they are consistent with being an employee or otherwise.

In addition to the above the test for what constitutes an independent contractor has become the subject of significant litigation and clarity has been given in this area in several cases. The case of *Hogan v United Beverages*[8] is one such case. Mr Hogan was employed as a driver for United Beverages. He transferred from being an employed driver in 1989, having agreed to a redundancy package. He then bought his own lorry and became an independent contractor for the company. In 2003 the company informed Mr Hogan that his services were no longer required. The case came before Smyth J in the Circuit Court on appeal from the EAT. Smyth J made the following observations:

1. Each case has to be examined on its own particular facts.

2. Irrespective of the wording of the contract the court would scrutinise the way the contract was actually performed and the fact that the contract described a person as an independent contractor would not conclusively decide the issue.

3. The issue of control was potentially crucial as traditionally the power to control a worker was considered by the courts to be indicative of a contract of service rather than a contract for services. Smyth J referred however to the different approach taken in *Henry Denny*[9] where the court went on to say that the control test 'does not always provide satisfactory guidance'. Smyth J, in finding that the degree of direction and control exercised by the respondent in this instance was no more than would be normal in a customer-driven business, referred to the fact that the appellant had purchased his own lorry and the accounts kept by him since 1989 were profit and loss accounts which listed expenses such as wages, printing, light, heat etc. Also in this regard Smyth J referred to the fact that

---

6.   *Readymix Concrete v Minister of Pensions and National Insurance* (1968) 2OB 497.
7.   See the decision in *Re The Sunday Tribune* [1984] IR 50.
8.   *Michael Hogan v United Beverages Sales Ltd* (14 October 2005, unreported), Circuit Court.
9.   *Henry Denny and Sons (Ireland) Ltd v Minister for Social Welfare* [1989] IR 34, 49.

the appellant was not personally obliged to perform the work and could sub-contract it if he so wished

4. Fair procedures are not relevant where the contract for services has come to an end. Smyth J distinguished this from the *Tierney* case[10] where the Supreme Court had to consider whether a contract for services should be construed as containing an implied term that the respondent was obliged to conduct disciplinary action provided for in the contract in accordance with fair procedures. Smyth J held that in that case the court considered the termination of an existing contract, whereas in *Hogan* the appellant's contract had run its full course and it was the failure to renew the contract that was in dispute.

It is clear from the above that the control test has been significantly weakened recently and the broader 'business on your own account' as outlined in *Hogan* and *Denny* is now seen as more appropriate.

Additionally, in respect of whether an employee is an independent contractor or not, regard needs to be had to the Code of Practice for determining Employment or Self-Employment Status of Individuals. This code of practice was drawn up by the Employment Status group set up under the National Agreement – Programme for Prosperity and Fairness, because of a concern by the social partners, in particular the trade union movement, that there may be increasing numbers of workers categorised as self-employed when it would be more appropriate for them to have employee status. The code refers to the 'control test' and other factors as being relevant. Whilst it is not legally binding it is a useful reference point.

The Revenue Commissioners also show an interest in this area and in this regard have their own informal checklist, broadly similar to this:

Criteria on whether an individual is *an employee*		Criteria on whether an individual is *self employed*	
1	Is under the control of another person who directs as to *how*, *when* and *where* the work is to be carried out.	Y/N	1	Owns his or her own business.	Y/N
2	Supplies labour only		2	Is exposed to financial risk, by having to bear the cost of making good faulty or substandard work carried out under the contract.	
3	Receives a fixed hourly/weekly/monthly wage.		3	Assumes responsibility for investment and management in the enterprise.	
4	Cannot sub-contract the work. If the work can be subcontracted and paid on by the person subcontracting the work, the employer/ employee relationship may simply be transferred on.		4	Has the opportunity to profit from sound management in the scheduling and performance of engagements and tasks.	

10. *Tierney v An Post* [2000] 1 IR 536.

Criteria on whether an individual is *an employee*		Criteria on whether an individual is *self employed*	
Criteria on whether an individual is *an employee*		Criteria on whether an individual is *self employed*	
5	Does not supply materials for the job.	5	Has control over what is done, how it is done, when and where it is done and whether he or she does it personally.
6	Does not provide equipment other than the small tools of the trade. The provision of tools or equipment might not have a significant bearing on coming to a conclusion that employment status may be appropriate having regard to all the circumstances of a particular case.	6	Is free to hire other people, on his or her terms, to do the work, which has been agreed to be undertaken.
7	Is not exposed to personal financial risk in carrying out of the work.	7	Can provide the same services to more than one person or business at the same time.
8	Does not assume any responsibility for investment and management in the business.	8	Provides the material for the job.
9	Does not have the opportunity to profit from sound management in the scheduling of engagements or in the performance of tasks arising from the engagements.	9	Provides equipment and machinery necessary for the job, other than the small tools of the trade or equipment which in an overall context would not be an indicator of a person in business on their own account.
10	Works set hours or a given number of hours per week or month.	10	Has a fixed place of business where materials/equipment can be stored.
11	Works for one person or for one business.	11	Costs and agrees a price for the job.
12	Receives expenses payments to cover subsistence and/or travel costs.	12	Provides his or her own insurance cover eg public liability cover, etc.
13	Is entitled to extra pay or time off for overtime	13	Controls the hours of work in fulfilling the job obligations.
14		14	Is the business subject to a tender.

Score:

Generally an individual should satisfy the self employed guidelines above, otherwise, he or she will normally be an employee.

It should be noted that a person who is a self employed contractor in one job is not necessarily self employed in the next job. It is also possible to be employed and self employed at the same time in different jobs.

Casual workers?

[3.07] The law in this area is complex. Under common law there has to be 'mutuality of obligation' for an employment relationship to exist, ie the employer must have an obligation to provide work and the worker must have an obligation to carry it out. What may start out as a casual working relationship with no mutuality of obligation may evolve into a formal employee/employer relationship over time. This may arise where there is a clear pattern of work, where there is a limited pool of people to choose from, where there are repercussions when the employee refuses work, or where the employee is entitled to staff benefits such as sick pay or subject to the employer's policies and procedures.

Casual workers are specifically dealt with under the Protection of Employees (Part-Time Work) Act 2001.

Before deciding though that a worker has automatic protection under the Unfair Dismissals or Part-Time Work Acts, determine first if there is 'mutuality of obligation' or in the alternative whether they are 'employed under a contract of employment' in which case the Act applies in any event.

The contract must be enforceable

[3.08] The next issue that will fall to be considered is whether the contract is enforceable or not. In general, illegal contracts are unenforceable at law.[11] As such, contracts which are tainted by illegality cannot be relied upon to support an unfair dismissal claim. This position, however, was altered by s 7(d) of the Unfair Dismissal (Amendment) Act 1993 which provides that an unfairly dismissed claimant shall be entitled to redress under the Unfair Dismissal Acts even if the evidence shows that a term or condition of the contract of employment contravenes the Income Tax or Social Welfare Acts. (Where such illegalities are shown to have occurred, the Rights Commissioner, EAT or Circuit Court is obliged to notify the Revenue Commissioners or the Minister for Social Welfare as appropriate.)[12]

Continuous service

[3.09] Continuous service for the purposes of the unfair dismissals legislation is defined in a number of different pieces of legislation.

Section 2(4) of the 1977 Act provides that 'the First Schedule to the Minimum Notice and Terms of Employment Act 1973 as amended by s 20 of this Act shall apply for the purpose of ascertaining for the purposes of this Act the period of service of an employee and whether that service has been continuous.'

The first schedule to the Minimum Notice and Terms of Employment Acts 1973 to 2001 therefore contains most of the rules for determining continuity of service. It provides that service is continuous unless an employee is dismissed by their employer or voluntarily leaves their employment. It also provides that continuity is not broken by:

- sickness;

- strikes or lock-outs;

---

11.   See *Hayden v Sean Quinn Properties Ltd* [1994] ELR 45 and *Lewis v Squash Ireland Ltd* [1983] ILRM 363.

12.   Unfair Dismissals Act 1977, s 8(11) as inserted by Unfair Dismissal (Amendment) Act 1993, s 7.

- lay-offs;

- the dismissal of an employee followed by their immediate re-employment;

- the dismissal of an employee followed by their re-employment within 26 weeks if the dismissal was wholly or partly for or was connected with the purpose of avoidance of liability under the Act;[13]

- the transfer of a business from one person to another unless the employee received and retained a redundancy payment from the transferor at the time of and by reason of the transfer.[14]

The Redundancy Payments Acts, the Maternity Protection Act 1994 and the Adoptive Leave Acts 1995 and 2005 also provide that continuity is not broken by:

- service in the reserve defence forces of the State;[15]

- a period of adoptive leave;[16]

- a period of protective leave, natal care or for breastfeeding;[17]

- a period parental leave or *force majeure* leave;

- a period of carer's leave within the meaning of the Carer's Leave Act 2001.

How continuity of service is broken

[3.10] Continuity of service is broken by the employee either being dismissed or voluntarily leaving their employment. Once an employee receives a redundancy lump sum payment their continuity of employment is broken (unless redress by way of reinstatement or re-engagement under the Unfair Dismissals Act has been ordered).[18] However, if an employee is dismissed for redundancy before attaining 104 weeks' continuous service and resumes employment with the same employer within 26 weeks, such employment will be treated as continuous.[19]

Also the Unfair Dismissals Act provides that the dismissal of an employee followed by their re-employment by the same employer within 26 weeks will not break their

---

13. Unfair Dismissals Act 1977, s 2(5) as inserted by Unfair Dismissal (Amendment) Act 1993, s 3.
14. Minimum Notice Acts 1973–2001, Sch 1 as amended by Unfair Dismissal (Amendment) Act 1993, s 15.
15. Redundancy Payments Act 1967, Sch 3, para 5(iv).
16. Redundancy Payments Act 1967, Sch 3, para 5(b) as substituted by the Adoptive Leave Act 1995, s 28 (as substituted by the Adoptive Leave Act 2005, s 20).
17. Redundancy Payments Act 1967, Sch 3, para 5(c) as substituted by the Maternity Protection (Amendment) Act 2004, s 24.
18. Redundancy Payments Act 1967, Sch 3, para 4.
19. Redundancy Payments Act 1967, s 5(A) as inserted by the Redundancy Payments Act 1971, s 19(1).

continuity of service if the dismissal was connected with the avoidance of liability under the Act.[20]

Part-timers are protected in the same way as full-time employees, as provided for in the Protection of Employees (Part-Time Work) Act 2001.

Six-month/12-month time limit

[3.11] A claim to be valid must be brought before the Rights Commissioner or EAT within six months of the date of dismissal. The Act provides that the time limit may be extended up to 12 months from the date of dismissal as long as the Rights Commissioner or tribunal is satisfied that there were 'exceptional circumstances' preventing the service of the claim within the first six months of the date of dismissal.[21] 'Exceptional' has been defined in *Byrne v PJ Quigley Ltd*[22] as 'something out of the ordinary'. The tribunal must therefore be satisfied that the exceptional circumstances prevented the lodging of the claim within the six-month time frame and that the exceptional circumstances actually occurred within the six months. See also *Quinn v HSS Ltd.*[23]

In *Murphy v Citizens Information Call Centre*,[24] illness, supported by a medical certificate, entitled the employee to an extension. On the other hand, in *Leonard v Hunt t/a Willie's Restaurant*[25] the EAT refused to grant an extension of time where the claimant erroneously posted her claim to premises the EAT had vacated 10 years previously. *Byrne* is important as it indicates that the death of a close family member constitutes exceptional circumstances for the purposes of s 8 of the Act and will most likely mean that the employee will be allowed an extension of time within which to make a claim.

The test of 'exceptional circumstances' should not be confused with the test of 'reasonable cause' which applies to most other employment rights, including the Employment Equality Legislation. Here, the Labour Court and the EAT have quite divergent views: notwithstanding the fact that 'reasonable cause' is a much lower bar for claimants to cross than 'exceptional circumstances', the Labour Court has ruled that even where a claimant proves 'reasonable cause', they still should consider whether in the circumstances it is correct to grant an extension[26] whereas the EAT has held that once a claimant demonstrates 'exceptional circumstances', the extension of time is mandatory but the length of the extension is discretionary, subject to the limits of the statute.

---

20. Unfair Dismissals Act 1977, s 2(5) as inserted by Unfair Dismissal (Amendment) Act 1993, s 3(c).
21. Unfair Dismissals Act 1977, s 8(2)(b) as inserted by Unfair Dismissal (Amendment) Act 1993, s 7.
22. *Byrne v PJ Quigley Ltd* [1995] ELR 205.
23. *Quinn v HSS Ltd* UD 11344/2005.
24. *Murphy v Citizens Information Call Centre* UD 59/2005.
25. *Leonard v Hunt t/a Willie's Restaurant* [2004] ELR 14.
26. See *Cementation Skanska v Carroll* DWT 30/2003.

Extension by application to or leave of the Tribunal (s 39 of the Organisation of Working Time Act 1997)

[3.12] Section 39 of the Organisation of Working Time Act allows a 'relevant authority', which includes a Rights Commissioner, the Employment Appeals Tribunal and the Labour Court to amend any application for unfair dismissal if the name of the employer on the application is incorrect.

Equally, and more controversially, s 39(4) appears to give the Tribunal the power to 'join' a party to the proceedings on application by the employee in the event that the name of the employer was 'inadvertently' incorrectly stated or there was any other particular (missing) which could identify the respondent and this holds regardless of the time limits having expired. Therefore in such circumstances the six-month and/or 12-month time limits do not appear to apply.

Exceptions to six-month/12-month time limit

[3.13] It is well settled that an employee who does not have one year's continuous service cannot fall within the scope of the Act. If, however, an employee is dismissed by reason of pregnancy and has less than one year's service they can pursue a claim under both the unfair dismissals legislation and the equality legislation, but in the former case the burden of proof shifts to the employee to prove that she was dismissed by reason of her pregnancy. (Note, however that if she is incapable of performing her job the burden of proof rests with the employer.)

There are therefore three significant exceptions to the rule that dismissed employees are precluded from bringing a claim if they have less than one year's continuous service with the employer who dismissed them:

1. Employees dismissed for trade union membership or activity (s 14 of the 1993 Amendment Act);

2. Employees dismissed for pregnancy or matters connected therewith, including breastfeeding, giving birth, invoking various statutory rights (including maternity, adoptive, force majeure and carer's leave), (s 6(2A) inserted by s 38(5) of the Maternity Protection Act 1994);

3. Employees dismissed for exercising their rights under the National Minimum Wage Act 2000;

It used to be considered that those employees pursuing cases under s 27 of the Health, Safety and Welfare at Work Act 2005 also had an exception to the one year rule, but this was settled by the High Court in the case of *Sharma & Anor v Employment Appeals Tribunal*.[27] The claimants alleged that they had been penalised and dismissed within the meaning of s 27 of the Health, Safety and Welfare at Work Act 2005. The issue was whether one years' continuous service was necessary in order to bring a claim of penalisation under the Unfair Dismissal Acts. The Court said that it could not read into

---

27. *Sharma & Anor v Employment Appeals Tribunal* [2010] IEHC 178.

the Unfair Dismissal Act 1977 a specific provision lifting the service requirement in the circumstances where the 2005 Act was silent on the point. It was up to the legislature to do this. Accordingly, the Court held that the one year service rule applies for penalisation claims under the Health and Safety legislation alleging unfair dismissal.

Employers need to be particularly mindful of this rule as the Tribunal tends to exercise its discretion 'to the full' when it comes to claims made by employees in this regard. A case in point is *Mulholland v Currabeg Developments Limited*.[28] The claimant was dismissed by the respondent less than two weeks after he had submitted a union membership form to the respondent. The claimant had been employed by the respondent as a 'scaffolder' for just over three months when he was dismissed. Albeit that the respondents site manager gave evidence that the claimant had been dismissed because there was no more work for him, the Tribunal stated that the onus was on the respondent to show that the dismissal was fair in all the circumstances. In the absence of any evidence to the contrary, the Tribunal held that the respondent did not have a union-tolerant workplace and awarded him €20,000 which was significantly reduced because he had failed to mitigate his loss.

Date of dismissal

[3.14] In order to determine an employee's service the EAT must first of all establish the date of dismissal. The date is important to establish whether the employee has the requisite continuous service such that the Act applies; it is also important to determine whether the employee has taken the claim within the six-month time limit. For the purposes of the time limit the date of dismissal, will be one of the following:[29]

- if the employee is dismissed for gross misconduct and no notice is given the date will be the date of dismissal, ie the day the employee leaves the premises;

- if notice is given, the date of dismissal will be the date that notice runs out;

- if a contract provides for a notice period, it will be in breach of that contract to pay in lieu of notice unless the employer reserves the right to do so. If there is a payment in lieu of notice clause and the employee accepts same, the date of dismissal will be the date on which the termination takes effect, probably the day in which the employee leaves the premises.

If there is no right to pay in lieu of notice the EAT will simply add on the contractual or statutory notice whichever is the greater and the date of dismissal will be date the notice if given would have expired.

One important point that often raises 'its head' in the Tribunal, both regarding the six- and 12-month time limit is what part an employee's annual leave entitlement has to play when calculating the six or 12 months. It is now well settled that an employee's

---

28.   *Mulholland v Currabeg Developments Limited* MN 729/2006 & UD 1105/2006.
29.   Minimum Notice and Terms of Employment Acts 1973–2001.

holiday entitlement cannot be added to a period of service in order to qualify for statutory unfair dismissal.[30]

EXCLUSIONS

[3.15] To be able to pursue a claim under the Act an employee must not fall within any of the restricted categories.[31] The categories of employees who are excluded and/or to whom the Act does not apply are:

- Persons who have reached normal retirement age

    The employee must be under the normal retirement age for employees of 'the same employer', otherwise they are excluded.[32] In order to prove normal retirement age regard should be had firstly to the contract of employment. If the contract provides for a specific retirement age this will then be the 'normal retirement age' for the purposes of the Act and any deviation from this will be difficult (although not impossible to argue). Regard should then be had to the actual practice in the employment concerned. If, for example, the contract provided for retirement at age 60, yet the practice was that everyone retired at age 65, then this may be deemed the 'normal retirement age'. In *Waite v Government Communications Headquarters*[33] it was held that simply because a few people were kept on beyond the normal retirement date this was not sufficient to alter what was set down in the contract of employment. However, in the High Court case of the *County of Donegal v Neil Porter*[34] the High Court went on to say that forcing employees to retire at age 55 would unilaterally alter the contract of employment unless it could be justified lawfully in another way.

    Also note that s 14 of the 1993 Act provides that the exclusion for normal retirement age does not apply to dismissal for trade union membership or activity.

- Persons employed by a close relative in a private house or on a farm where both reside. Close relative is defined as; spouse, father, mother, grandfather, grandmother, step-father, step-mother, son daughter, grandson, granddaughter, step-son, step-daughter, brother, sister, half-brother or half-sister;[35]

- Members of the defence forces and Garda Síochána;[36]

- FÁS trainees and apprentices;[37]

---

30. *Maher v B & I Line* UD 271/1978.
31. Unfair Dismissals Act 1977, s 2(1).
32. Unfair Dismissals Act 1977, s 2(1)(b).
33. *Waite v Government Communications Headquarters* (1983) IRLR 341.
34. *County of Donegal v Neil Porter* (1993) ELR 101.
35. Unfair Dismissals Act 1977, s 2(1)(c).
36. Unfair Dismissals Act 1977, s 2(1)(d) and (e).
37. Unfair Dismissals Act 1977, s 2(1)(f).

- Employees dismissed during a period of probation or training if the contract is in writing and the duration of the probation or training is one year or less and this is stated in the contract;[38]

- Persons employed by or under the State who are dismissed by Government;[39]

- Manager of a local authority for the purposes of the Local Government Act 2001, s 144; [40]

- Officers of a vocational education committee established by the Vocational Education Act 1930;[41]

- The Chief Executive Officer of the Health Service Executive for the purposes of the Health Act 2004, s 17;[42]

- Employees dismissed whilst undergoing training for the purpose of becoming qualified or registered as a nurse, pharmacist, health inspector, medical laboratory technician, occupational therapist, physiotherapist, speech therapist, radiographer or social worker.[43]

- Persons on fixed-term/specified purpose contracts – see also **3.62**

A fixed-term contract is one where at the date it is entered into, the date of commencement and termination are clear. A contract for a specified purpose is one where at the time it was entered into the duration of the contract was not capable of being ascertained; an example may be where a person is required to fill in for a leave of absence which might be extended or where the person is hired to complete a particular job such as building a road or a bridge.

Where either a fixed-term contract expires because its term has come to an end or a specified purpose contract expires because the task is complete, the Unfair Dismissals Act shall not apply if:[44]

1. the contract is in writing;

2. the contract is signed by both parties;

3. the contract contains a statement that the Act shall not apply to a dismissal consisting only of the expiry of the fixed term or cesser of the aforesaid;

---

38. Unfair Dismissals Act 1977, s 3(1).
39. Unfair Dismissals Act 1977, s 2(1)(h) as substituted by the Civil Service Regulation (Amendment) Act 2005, s 22.
40. Unfair Dismissals Act 1977, s 2(1)(i) as substituted by the Local Government Act 2001, s 164.
41. Unfair Dismissals Act 1977, s 2(1)(j) as substituted by the Health Act 2004, s 75.
42. Unfair Dismissals Act 1977, s 2(1)(k) as inserted by the Health Act 2004, s 75.
43. Unfair Dismissals Act 1977, s 3(2).
44. Unfair Dismissals Act 1977, s 2(2)(b).

- Persons covering for persons on protective leave or natal care

  This is specifically excluded under s 2(2)(c) as amended, once the employer informs the 'covering' employee at the commencement of the contract, in writing, that the employment will terminate on the return to work of the other employee who is on protective leave or natal care absence. Protective leave in this instance includes maternity leave, additional maternity leave, fathers' leave under s 16(1) and so-called s 18 leave on health and safety grounds;

- Persons covering for persons on adoptive leave

  Section 2(2)(d) provides a further exclusion for employees hired specifically to cover for someone on adoptive leave, again once the employer informs the person in writing at the commencement of the contract that the contract will terminate on the return of the adopting parent:[45]

- Employees dismissed who, under the relevant contract of employment, ordinarily worked outside the State unless–

  (i) they were ordinarily resident in the State during the term of the contract, or

  (ii) they were domiciled in the State during the term of the contract, and the employer–

      (a) in case the employee was an individual, was ordinarily resident in the State, during the term of the contract, or

      (b) in case the employer was a body corporate or an unincorporated body of persons, had its principal place of business in the State during the term of the contract;[46]

  In the current world we live in this section may soon become a thing of the past and the EAT have certainly made comment in this regard:[47]

- Employees dismissed whilst working for foreign embassies in Ireland. This was established in the Supreme Court case of *Government of Canada v Employment Appeals Tribunal and Brian Burke*[48] where the Supreme Court held that the employment of an embassy chauffeur was within the sphere of governmental or sovereign activity, that the doctrine of restrictive immunity applied and as such the employee had no cause of action against his employer;

- Employees dismissed whilst employed under a statutory apprenticeship (under the Industrial Training Act 1967) if the dismissal takes place during the first six

---

45. Unfair Dismissals Act 1977, s 2(2)(d) was substituted for the original version (which in itself was inserted by the Adoptive Leave Act 1995, s 23 and amended by the Carer's Leave Act 2001, s 27(1)) by the Adoptive Leave Act 1995, s 23 (as substituted by the Adoptive Leave Act 2005, s 18). The full stop at the end of the subparagraph appears to be an error.

46. Unfair Dismissals Act 1977, s 2(3).

47. See *Buckly v Overlay Partners Ltd* UD 1509/2003.

48. *Government of Canada v Employment Appeals Tribunal and Brian Burke* [1992] ELR 29.

months of the apprenticeship or within one month after the completion of the apprenticeship.[49]

ONUS OF PROOF

[3.16] The Act provides[50] that all dismissals are deemed 'unfair' unless there were substantial grounds justifying the dismissal. In effect this means that the onus of proving that the dismissal was fair rests with the employer. Consequently at a hearing of the Rights Commissioner or EAT the employer presents their evidence first. This will not be the case where the fact of dismissal is in dispute or where the claimant is alleging constructive dismissal. In such instances the employee must establish that a dismissal occurred or that the employer's actions were so severe as to justify the employee terminating their employment. (See also **3.63**.)

UNFAIR DISMISSALS

[3.17] As stated, the Act presumes all dismissals are unfair unless there are substantial grounds that justify them. More specifically the Act provides for various circumstances where dismissals are actually unfair regardless of the circumstances.[51]

Membership of a trade union or involvement in trade union activities

[3.18] An employee cannot be dismissed because of trade union membership or because of a proposal that they or another employee become a member of a trade union. However, this only applies where the times at which they engage in such activities are outside their hours of work or times during their hours of work in which they are permitted, pursuant to the contract of employment between them and their employer, so to engage. That said, the Tribunal is very conscious of the constitutional right to join a trade union and employers would be well advised to be extra cautious if there is any suggestion of trade union activity.[52]

Lock-out or strike

Strike

[3.19] Strike is defined in s 1 of the 1977 Act as:

> the cessation of work by any number or body of employees acting in combination or a concerted refusal or a refusal under a common understanding of any number of employees to continue to work for an employer, in consequence of a dispute, done as a means of compelling their employer or any employee or body of employees, or to aid other employees in compelling their

---

49.   Unfair Dismissals Act 1977, s 4.
50.   Unfair Dismissals Act 1977, s 6.
51.   Unfair Dismissals Act 1977, s 6(2).
52.   See *White v Simon Betson* [1992] ELR 120.

employer or any employee or body of employees, to accept or not to accept terms
or conditions of or affecting employment;

What the reason for the strike is or how the strike came about whether lawfully or not is
irrelevant. Nor does it matter what type of strike it is. For example it could be a 'go
slow', a work to rule, the 'blue flu', a one-day stoppage or a traditional indefinite work
stoppage. All definitions of strike are therefore included.

Technically if no notice of strike or the intention to strike is given and it is not
provided for in the contract of employment a breach of contract occurs. In practice it is
highly improbable that a clause allowing strike would be expressly provided for in the
contract although an implied right to strike could arise as a result of custom and practice.
The question therefore arises as to what is the status of an employee on strike? In this
jurisdiction (following the UK lead) in the case *Becton Dickinson v Lee*[53] the Supreme
Court endorsed the doctrine of suspension as expressed by Lord Denning in the case of
Morgan v Fry.[54] This in effect provides that once an employee who is intending to strike
gives notice of at least the length of notice to terminate their contract, their employment
rights and obligations are suspended for the period of the strike. This case occurred
before the enactment of the 1990 Industrial Relations Act which provided for a period of
seven days' notice to be given to employers before a strike could lawfully occur. It is
unclear whether this seven-day notice period 'replaces' the contractual notice period as
provided for in the *Becton Dickinson* case.

Notwithstanding this, the concept itself is a difficult one to grasp! What happens
during a strike should the employer wish to dismiss all employees for going on strike or
if they wish to impose some form of disciplinary action short of dismissal for an act of
misconduct whilst on strike or alternatively should they wish to suspend an employee
pending investigation of an incident whilst on strike. Does this mean that no sanction
can be taken against striking employees? The answer is no. As the employment
relationship must continue during any suspension then equally so must the range of
obligations attaching to the employment contractual relationship. Equally it is difficult
to fathom how this doctrine of suspension could override the common law right of either
an employer or employee to terminate the contract of employment.

Section 5(2) of the Act goes on to provide that:

> (2) The dismissal of an employee for taking part in a strike or other industrial
> action shall be deemed, for the purposes of this Act, to be an unfair dismissal, if–
>
> (a)   one or more employees of the same employer who took part in the strike
>   or other industrial action were not dismissed for so taking part, or
>
> (b)   one or more of such employees who were dismissed for so taking part
>   were subsequently permitted to resume their employment on terms and
>   conditions at least as favourable to the employees as those specified in the
>   said paragraph (a) or (b) and the employee was not.[55]

---

53.   *Becton Dickinson v Lee* [1973] IR 1.
54.   *Morgan v Fry* [1968] QB 710.
55.   Unfair Dismissals Act 1977, s 5(2) was substituted in its entirety by Unfair Dismissal
        (Amendment) Act 1993, s 4.

This does not mean that if you dismiss all people for taking part in the strike those dismissals will be deemed to be fair. Such dismissals are subject to the general presumption in s 6(1) that all dismissals are unfair. This was also clarified by s 62(A) of the 1977 Act which was inserted by s 26 of the Protection of Employment (Exceptional Collective Redundancies and Related Matters) Act 2007 which goes on to provide:

> (2A) Without prejudice to the applicability of any of the provisions of section 6 to the case, where–
>
> (a)   an employee–
>
>   (i)   is deemed by subsection (1) to have been dismissed by reason of a lock-out, or
>
>   (ii)   is dismissed for taking part in a strike or other industrial action,
>
>   and
>
> (b)   none of those who were locked out, or took part in the strike or industrial action, were re-engaged,
>
> in determining whether, in those circumstances, the dismissal is an unfair dismissal, the rights commissioner, the Tribunal or the Circuit Court, as the case may be, shall have regard, for that purpose only, to–
>
> (i)   the reasonableness or otherwise of the conduct (whether by act or omission) of the employer or employee in relation to the dismissal
>
> (ii)   the extent (if any) of the compliance or failure to comply by the employer with the procedure referred to in section 14(1),
>
> (iii)   the extent (if any) of the compliance or failure to comply by the employer or the employee with provisions of any code of practice referred to in section 7(2)(d), and
>
> (iv)   whether the parties have adhered to any agreed grievance procedures applicable to the employment in question at the time of the lock-out, strike or industrial action.

Subsection (2)(A)[56] therefore makes it conclusive that selective dismissals for taking part in a strike or other industrial action are unfair. The wording in this section is interesting in so far as it specifically says those who 'took part'. This could mean that employees who took part and then returned to work before the strike was finished or the striking employees were dismissed would also have to be dismissed.

Notwithstanding this, it is now clear from s 62(A) that the reasonableness of the employers' actions will be scrutinised by the Tribunal in the event that such a dismissal occurred. In *Power v National Corrugated Products*[57] the employer dismissed 128 employees for participating in a strike (a sit-in). The EAT held that the dismissals were unfair within the legislation. No further clarification is provided on this point and their determination would seem to run contrary to s 5(2). However, what seems probable is that the Tribunal interpreted the reasonableness of the employers' dismissal in the same

---

56.   Subsection (2)(A) was inserted by the Protection of Employment (Exceptional Collective Redundancies and Related Matters) Act 2007, s 26.
57.   *Power v National Corrugated Products* UD 336/1980.

way as they would an individual being dismissed and is as now provided for under sub-s (2)(A). Notably this was prior to the 1993 Amendment Act and the 2007 Exceptional Collective Redundancies Act, which clearly strengthened this whole area. In this case the EAT considered that management had made no serious attempts to contact the union during the sit-in and issued the termination notices prior to having a union meeting. It would be interesting nonetheless to see what the attitude of the Tribunal would be in the event that all procedures were exhausted (including the Labour Court), where this was rejected and warning letters were provided to employees beforehand. In such an instance the employers' behaviour could hardly be deemed unreasonable.[58]

Lock-out

[3.20] Section 5(5) of 1977 Act defines a lock-out:

> '[L]ock-out' means an action which, in contemplation or furtherance of a trade dispute (within the meaning of the Industrial Relations Act, 1946),[59] is taken by one or more employers, whether parties to the dispute or not, and which consists of the exclusion of one or more employees from one or more factories, offices or other places of work or of the suspension of work in one or more such places or of the collective, simultaneous or otherwise connected termination or suspension of employment of a group of employees;

> 'the original employer' means, in relation to the employee, the employer who dismissed the employee.

Section 5(1) of the Act goes on the state that:

> For the purposes of this Act (other than section 2(4)), the lock-out of an employee shall be deemed to be a dismissal and the dismissal shall be deemed to be an unfair dismissal if, after the termination of the lock-out–

> (a)   the employee was not permitted to resume his employment on terms and conditions at least as favourable to the employee as those specified in paragraph (a) or (b) of subsection (1) of section 7 of this Act, and

> (b)   one or more other employees in the same employment were so permitted.

Therefore, this section deems the lock-out of an employee to be a dismissal and deems the dismissal unfair if after the lock-out the employee was not allowed to resume his position on terms and conditions at least as favourable as those of others who were reinstated or re-engaged. This section was significantly amended by the 1993 Act which replaced in its entirety the previous s 5(1) which did not deem a lock-out to be a

---

58.   At the time of writing Aer Lingus are currently involved in this process.

59.   Under the Industrial Relations Act 1969, s 24(1), the 1969 Act is to be construed as one with the 1946 Act. Under the Industrial Relations Act 1976, s 12(1), that Act is to be construed as one with the 1946 Act. Under the Industrial Relations Act 1990, s 2(1) the 1990 Act (other than Part II thereof) and the Industrial Relations Acts of 1946, 1969 and 1976 are to be construed together as one Act. Under the Industrial Relations (Amendment) Act 2001, s 13(1), that Act and the previous Acts as set out may be cited as the Industrial Relations Acts 1946 to 2001 and shall be construed together as one.

dismissal. It has now been further amended by sub-s (2)(A) which provides that the Tribunal in considering whether it was an unfair dismissal has to have regard to the reasonableness or otherwise of the conduct (whether by act or omission) of the employer or employee to the dismissal, the extent of compliance with any code of practice etc.

Therefore unless you comply with the code of practice, adhere to the grievance procedure if same exists, adhere to the disciplinary and dismissal procedure and then behave reasonably, it will be an unfair dismissal. It is respectfully suggested that in the event of a strike or lock-out adhering to all of the above, dismissing is not only difficult but inconsistent. It is hard to imagine how an employer dealing with striking workers can possibly afford them the full rights of natural justice. This is particularly so when the issue of trade union recognition is the subject matter of the dispute.

All told, dismissals for participating in a strike or lock-out are fraught with legal difficulties.

Religious or political opinions

[3.21] It will be deemed unfair if a person is dismissed for religious or political reasons. In the case of *Merriman v St James's Hospital*[60] the claimant was dismissed for refusing to bring a crucifix and a candle to a dying patient. Despite this being the practice in the hospital, Clarke J ordered her re-engagement and ordered that she did not have to participate in the practice going forward, essentially allowing the claimant's terms and conditions to be different from her colleagues. Claims under this heading can also be heard under the Employment Equality Acts 1998–2004.

Race, colour or sexual orientation

[3.22] Initially the 1977 Act provided that an employee could not be dismissed because of their race or colour. This was extended under the 1993 Act to include sexual orientation. Claims under this heading can also be heard under the Employment Equality Acts 1998–2004.

Age

[3.23] The Act provides that an employee cannot be dismissed because of their age. This provision does not affect the qualifying criteria that an employee must be between 16 years and normal retirement age.[61] In *Kerrigan v Peter Owens Advertising and Marketing Ltd*[62] the Tribunal held that a redundancy based on a number of factors including age was an unfair dismissal. Claims under this heading can in addition be heard under the Employment Equality Acts 1998–2004.

---

60. *Merriman v St James's Hospital* (24 November 1986, unreported), Circuit Court, Clarke J.
61. The Equality Act 2004, s 4(c)(d) amended Unfair Dismissals Act 1977, s 2 by inserting the lower age of 16
62. *Kerrigan v Peter Owens Advertising and Marketing Ltd* UD 31/97.

In the case of *William O'Mara v College Freight Limited T/A Target Express Ireland*,[63] two claimants successfully argued that there was no normal retirement age in the company. This was despite the fact that the respondents' HR manager gave evidence that the custom and practice in the company was for employees to retire at 65 and it was because of a 'glitch' in the computerised HR system that the employees the subject of the claim were overlooked and worked beyond 65.

The Tribunal, having heard all the evidence, concluded that there was no retirement clause in either claimants' terms and conditions of employment. No policy document was produced to the Tribunal nor was it given to the claimants. Furthermore, in examining the open drive insurance policy which the employer alleged did not permit anyone to drive beyond their 65th birthday, the Tribunal adduced evidence from an email dated 17 June 2010 stating that there was, in fact, an option to extend the age limit on the policy, subject to an increase in the premium. The Tribunal held that it was not satisfied that the company had a retirement policy or even a comprehensive custom and practice in relation to retirement. The tribunal found both to be unfairly dismissed and awarded €33,500 and €19,500 to the respective claimants.

In *Michael Kavanagh v Kilkenny County Council*,[64] the claimant was a part-time fire fighter. When he commenced his employment in 1967 there was no age condition in the general terms of employment, but he claimed he would be 'in the job' until age 65. Evidence was given that the claimant's union entered into negotiations which culminated in an agreement in 1990 to reduce the retirement age to 60. The Tribunal held that the claimant had been aware of the 1990 agreement and had consented to it: therefore there was no unfair dismissal.

In conclusion: in considering 'normal retiring age' the Tribunal will firstly examine what is agreed contractually between the parties and then examine the custom and practice of an employer and more particularly whether this is enforced fairly across the company. In the event that employees are allowed work past their contractual retirement age, such contractual terms will be ignored by the Tribunal. Therefore, it is vital that employers implement their compulsory retirement policies otherwise they will create a new policy by custom and practice which employees can rely on to retire at a greater age than that specified in the contract of employment. (See also **11.12**.)

Pregnancy or connected matters

[3.24] An employee cannot be dismissed by reason of pregnancy or related matters.[65] The employee must discharge the onus of proof that she was dismissed by reason of pregnancy. It will be for the employer then to establish that the real reason for dismissal was not pregnancy related.

There is a significant amount of law at EU level regarding pregnancy. One of the most important is the case of *Webb v EMO Air Cargo (UK) Ltd*.[66] Here the European

---

63.   *William O'Mara v College Freight Limited T/A Target Express Ireland* UD 1371/2009.
64.   *Michael Kavanagh v Kilkenny County Council* (2008) ELR.
65.   Unfair Dismissals Act 1977, s 6(2)(f).
66.   *Webb v EMO Air Cargo (UK) Ltd* C–32/93 (1994) IRLR 482.

Court of Justice (the ECJ) held that the dismissal of a pregnant woman could not be justified on the basis that because she was pregnant she was not capable of carrying out the job for which she was hired, which was in fact to replace another pregnant employee. This decision was bolstered in the case of *Brown v Rentokil Ltd*,[67] where the ECJ held that dismissal of a woman at any time during her pregnancy for absences due to incapacity for work due to an illness relating to her pregnancy constituted direct discrimination on grounds of sex. This will often arise during a pregnancy where a woman becomes ill or incapacitated as a result of her pregnancy. Following the *Brown* decision any such dismissals will be deemed unfair. This, along with the Equal Treatment Directive,[68] led to a significant overhaul of s 6(2)(f) of the Unfair Dismissals Act 1977. The original provided that an employer could justify the dismissal of a pregnant worker on the basis of her performance.

Pregnancy and related matters must be read in conjunction with the Employment Equality Acts 1998–2004 and the Maternity Protection Acts 1994–2004. Claims can be taken under both the unfair dismissals legislation and the Employment Equality Acts 1998–2004. Furthermore, there is a possibility that such a claim could also be brought straight to the Circuit Court on a 'gender-based dismissal' basis with the prospect of unlimited compensation.

Dismissal and the Maternity Protection Acts 1994–2004

[3.25] In addition to protection as a result of pregnancy, a dismissal for pursuing maternity entitlements is also unfair as is dismissal for exercising a right to any form of protective leave or natal care absence, or to time off from work or a reduction in hours of work for breastfeeding. Employees' statutory and contractual rights are protected by the Maternity Protection Acts 1994–2004. The Act gives very wide protection against the imposition of certain disciplinary measures and against termination of employment during a period of statutory maternity leave or 'protective leave'.

An employee cannot be in receipt of a disciplinary suspension when she is on maternity leave or 'protective leave'.[69] Notices of termination of employment given during maternity and to take effect during leave or after the end of maternity leave are void. The wording in the Act is quite specific. It does not refer to notice of dismissal but to notice of termination of employment. In other words this includes notice given either by the employer or by the employee. As such, any notice of resignation given by an employee during maternity leave is void and may not be relied upon.[70] The normal obligation to have one year's continuous employment before coming within the scope of the Unfair Dismissals Acts does not apply where it can be shown that the dismissal is due to the employee's pregnancy, giving birth or breastfeeding, or any matter connected therewith. The Maternity Protection Act is enforced through the Unfair Dismissals Act.

---

67.   *Brown v Rentokil Ltd* 1998 IRLR 445.

68.   Equal Treatment Directive 76/207/EEC.

69.   Protective leave is defined under the Maternity Protection Act 1994, s 21(1) as maternity leave, additional maternity leave, leave for fathers on the death of the mother (s 16 leave) and health and safety leave.

70.   Maternity Protection Act 1994, s 23.

In this regard the Unfair Dismissals Act is extended to provide for the determination of disputes over entitlements under the Maternity Act as well as alleged unfair dismissal for exercising rights under the Act.

DISMISSAL/FIXED-TERM CONTRACTS AND MATERNITY

[3.26] It may sometimes arise that a person temporarily replacing another on maternity leave becomes pregnant herself and requires maternity leave prior to the return of the first employee. In such circumstances the *Webb* case[71] applies and employers cannot dismiss or cut short the contract merely as a result of the pregnancy. (See **3.24**.)

DISPUTE RESOLUTION UNDER THE MATERNITY PROTECTION ACTS 1994–2004

[3.27] Disputes under the 1994 Act go initially to a Rights Commissioner and only on appeal to the Employment Appeals Tribunal (EAT)[72] and may be appealed to the High Court only on a point of law.

Dismissals contrary to the Adoptive Leave Acts 1995 and 2005

[3.28] Dismissal as a result of the exercise or contemplated exercise by an adoptive parent of rights under the Adoptive Leave Acts 1995 and 2005 to adoptive leave or additional adoptive leave or to a period of time off to attend certain pre-adoption classes or meetings is automatically unfair.

Membership of the Travelling Community

[3.29] The 1993 Act introduced the provision that an employee cannot be dismissed for being a member of the travelling community. Again claims can be brought under the unfair dismissals legislation or the employment equality legislation.[73]

Civil or criminal proceedings

[3.30] If an employee is dismissed because they actually issue or threaten to issue civil or criminal proceedings against their employer such dismissals will be deemed unfair.[74] This will also be the case where the employee has made any complaint or statement to the prosecuting authority connected with the case. One should note in this respect the protection afforded to 'whistle blowers' by the Competition Authority under their 'leniency' programme. (See **4.13**.)

---

71. *Webb v EMO Air Cargo (UK) Ltd* C–32/93 (1994) IRLR 482.
72. Maternity Protection Act 1994, s 33(1).
73. Unfair Dismissals Act 1977, s 6(2)(e) as inserted by Unfair Dismissal (Amendment) Act 1993, s 5.
74. Unfair Dismissals Act 1977, s 6(2)(c).

DISMISSALS IN ACCORDANCE WITH ACTS OTHER THAN THE UNFAIR DISMISSALS ACT

Persons reporting child abuse

[3.31] The Protections for Persons reporting Child Abuse Act 1998, which came into force on 23 January 1999 provides protection from civil liability to people who report child abuse 'reasonably and in good faith' to designated officers of the Health Board or to the Garda Síochána.

The main provisions are:

- the provision of protection to persons who report child abuse from penalisation by their employers;

- the creation of an offence of false reporting of child abuse.

The avenue of redress for such employees who have been discriminated against or dismissed is by way of complaint to a Rights Commissioner with provision for appeal to the EAT. Such employees may not however be granted relief both under this Act and under the Unfair Dismissals Act.

Dismissals and the Employees (Provision of Information and Consultation) Act 2006

[3.32] Section 13 of the Employees (Provision of Information and Consultation) Act 2006 provides protection for the employees' representative against penalisation which may include dismissal.

Dismissals and the Health, Safety and Welfare at Work Act 2005

[3.33] Section 27 of the Health, Safety and Welfare at Work Act 2005 was enacted with a view to protecting employees from any 'penalisation' from their employers on foot of them making a complaint regarding health and safety concerns. Penalisation includes dismissal within the meaning of the Unfair Dismissals Acts. Claims under this section are made to a Rights Commissioner within six months of the date of the alleged contravention and the appeal is to the Labour Court. A Rights Commissioner, should they find that the complaint is well-founded, may instruct the employer to take a specific course of action or award the employee a sum of money that is deemed just and equitable, having regard to the circumstances. This is particularly interesting in that the limit on compensation under the Unfair Dismissals Acts does not seem to apply to dismissals under this Act.

Following the initial enactment of this section of the Act, claims made under it were mostly successful without, so it seems, having due regard to the actual wording of the legislation.

In order to succeed under this section three elements must be satisfied:

1. An employee must have acted in accordance with one of the protected activities set out in s 27(3)(a)–(f) of the 2005 Act. These are as follows:

Section 27(3):

An employer shall not penalise or threaten penalisation against an employee for–

(a)   acting in compliance with the relevant statutory provisions,

(b)   performing any duty or exercising any right under the relevant statutory provisions,

(c)   making a complaint or representation to his or her safety representative or employer or the Authority as regards any matter relating to safety, health or welfare at work,

(d)   giving evidence in proceedings in respect of the enforcement of the relevant statutory provisions,

(e)   bringing a safety representative or an employee designated under section 11 or appointed under section 18 to perform functions under this Act,

(f)   subject to subsection (6) in circumstances of danger which the employee reasonably believes to be serious and imminent in which he or she could not reasonably have been expected to avert, leaving (or proposing to leave) or while the danger persisted, refusing to return to his or her place of work or any dangerous part of his or her place of work or taking (or proposing to take) appropriate steps to protect himself or herself or other persons from the danger.

2.   He/she must have suffered detriment within the meaning of s 27(1) or s 27(2) of the 2005 Act:

Section 27(1):

Penalisation includes any act or omission by an employer or a person acting on behalf of an employer that affects, to his or her detriment, an employee with respect to any term or condition of his or her employment.

Section 27(2):

Without prejudice to the generality of subsection (1) penalisation includes–

(i)   suspension, lay off or dismissal (including a dismissal within the meaning of the Unfair Dismissal Acts 1977 to 2001) or the threat of suspension, lay off or dismissals,

(ii)   demotion or loss of opportunity for promotion,

(iii)   transfer of duties, change of location of place of work, reduction in wages or change in working hours,

(iv)   imposition of any discipline, reprimand or other penalty (including a financial penalty),

(v)   coercion or intimidation.

3.   The reason the employer imposed the detriment must have been as a result of the protected activity.

A case which succeeded under this section is that of *LW Associates and Lisa Lacey*.[75] In this case, the employee informed her employer that she was pregnant and requested that a risk assessment be carried out. Such an assessment duly took place: however, due to the employer's delay in acting on same, the employee lodged an official grievance. The employer then decided that there was a medium to low risk to the employee and she was placed on health and safety leave. The employee initiated her claim under s 27 and contended that the employer had not properly considered suitable alternative employment or assisting her by the use of certain equipment. It was confirmed that being on health and safety leave was detrimental to the employee both financially and in relation to her career. The Labour Court agreed and duly awarded the employee the sum of €1,000.

In *Citizens Information Board and John Curtis*,[76] the employee spoke to management over some minor health and safety issues such as overhead lighting and an air vent. The employer immediately dealt with all the concerns. The employee then spoke with his manager about undertaking what he considered inappropriate work. On foot of this, he alleged that his duties had been changed and he had lost the facility to work flexitime. The employer claimed that the discussion with the manager which preceded the amendment of the duties did not relate to health and safety matters and, in any event, he did not suffer any detriment. The Rights Commissioner did not uphold the employee's complaint and on appeal to the Labour Court under s 29 of the Act, held that the discussions with the employee's manager were not of a health and safety nature and thus anything that flowed from that could not be dealt with under this section. For the sake of completeness, the Court went on to state that the employee did not suffer any detriment under the terms of that section of the Act.

A further action, *Margaret Bailey T/a Finesse Beauty Salon and Lisa Farrell*,[77] was appealed from the Rights Commissioner to the Labour Court by both the employee and the employer. The Rights Commissioner had found in favour of the employee and awarded the sum of €5,000. In this case, the employee informed her employer in May 2008 that she was pregnant. It was disputed between the parties as to whether shorter working hours were sought by the employee at that juncture. In any event, no medical certificate was forwarded to the employer supporting a claim for reduced hours until 16 June 2008 and on 17 June the employer stated that they were not agreeing to reduced hours. The Court considered whether or not the refusal of the employer to accommodate the employee constituted penalisation under s 27. It found that in some circumstances this could be penalisation but, in this case, reduced hours were not agreed due to business and economic reasons. The Court found that on the facts before it, it could not hold that the employer's refusal to accommodate the employee with reduced hours primarily resulted from a complaint or representation made by the employee about a health and safety issue. It further stated that to be in breach of the section, the employer would have had to have reached such a conclusion because the employee had made a

---

75.   *LW Associates and Lisa Lacey* HSC/08/2, Determination No HSD085.
76.   *Citizens Information Board and John Curtis* (HSD101).
77.   *Margaret Bailey T/a Finesse Beauty Salon and Lisa Farrell* HSC/09/23, Determination No HSD/104.

complaint on matters of health and safety at work and this was not the case. The Labour Court showed a similar attitude in *St John's National School v Akduman*.[78]

The above shows that succeeding in a claim of penalisation under s 27 of the 2005 will warrant an employee being in a position to adequately prove all three elements are present and fully fall within the definitions as laid down by the Act.

Dismissals and the Parental Leave Act 1998 and 2006 and the Carers Leave Act 2001

[3.34] Section 16(A)(4) of the Parental Leave Act 1998[79] provides that an employee who is entitled to return to work following a period of parental leave but is not permitted to do so shall be deemed to have been dismissed and the dismissal for the purposes of the Unfair Dismissals Act shall be deemed to be an unfair dismissal.

There is a similar provision in s 16(4) of the Carer's Leave Act 2001.

Dismissals contrary to the National Minimum Wage Act 2000

[3.35] Section 36 of the National Minimum Wage Act 2000 provides that an employer shall not dismiss an employee for having exercised his right under the Act, opposed by any lawful means an act unlawful under the Act or becoming entitled in the future to any remuneration greater than the provisions of the Act and that for the purposes of the Unfair Dismissals Act any such dismissal will be deemed to be unfair.

Dismissals contrary to the Standards in Public Office Act 2001

[3.36] Under s 5(3) of the Standards in Public Office Act 2001, where an employer dismisses an employee to whom the Unfair Dismissals Act applies and the dismissal constitutes disciplinary action in contravention of s 5(1) of the 2001 Act in relation to the employee, the dismissal is a dismissal for the purposes of the 1977 Act by virtue of s 6(2)(f) of that Act is deemed to be an unfair dismissal.[80]

Dismissals for whistleblowing

[3.37] (see **4.14**).

---

78.   *St John's National School v Akduman* HSC/07/03, Determination No HSD102.
79.   Parental Leave Act 1998, s 16(A) 4 was inserted by the Parental Leave (Amendment) Act 2006, s 11.
80.   Please note the reference to sub-s (f) seems to be an error as that subsection relates to matters concerning the maternity protection legislation.

FAIR DISMISSALS

[3.38] Dismissal is deemed not to be unfair if the employer can show that it arose principally from any one of the following:[81]

Capability, competence or qualifications of the employee

[3.39] None of these words are defined in the 1977 Act and they are often used interchangeably by the Tribunal and practitioners. Despite this they have significantly different meanings.

Capability

[3.40] Dismissal for capability is deemed not to be unfair where it results 'wholly or mainly' from an employee's capability to perform the work of the kind which he was employed by the employer to do'.[82] Capability is generally defined as the inability of the person to fulfil the terms of their contract of employment arising out of the long-term illness of the person. Incapability has been defined by the EAT in the case of *Reardon v St Vincent's Hospital*[83] as 'long term illness'.

That said, incapability can take many guises. It may be that the person is a mere malingerer or it may be that the person has suffered an injury at work, or the person may be absent for a long period of time but as a result of a plethora of different ailments. The belief amongst employers that they cannot dismiss someone once they continue to hand in medical certificates is incorrect and an employee's employment may be terminated fairly once their ill health prevents them from performing in their role or attending work on a regular basis.

LONG-TERM ABSENCE

[3.41] For prolonged periods of absence employers may be justified in dismissal once:

- the absence poses actual or potential problems for the employer; and

- there is no reasonable prospect of an early return to work.

It is the second issue which is the most challenging. There is nothing to prevent an employer dismissing an employee for long-term absenteeism once it has been established that there is no reasonable date of return to work. Of course the employer has to be satisfied that expert medical opinion verifies this and where there is a conflict between medical advisers, an independent third party expert should be called upon.[84]

---

81.   Unfair Dismissals Act 1977, s 6(4).
82.   Unfair Dismissals Act 1977, s 6(4).
83.   *Reardon v St Vincent's Hospital* UD 74/1979.
84.   *Lawless v Dublin City Council* UD 335/1989.

The onus of proof lies with the employer so it will be for the employer to show that he honestly believed that the employee was incapable of fulfilling his duties. As stated, before he can do this he must get independent medical advice. He must then prove that:

(i)   it was the illness that was both the reason and the substantial reason for the dismissal;

(ii) that the employee received fair notice that the question of his capability was being considered; and that

(iii) he received an opportunity to put forward his own case.

What this will mean in practice is that in the event of an employer receiving a definitive medical report stating that the employee is not fit to work, notwithstanding this, the employee must be put on notice that his dismissal for incapability is being considered, that further he has an opportunity to be heard and lastly that there is a right of appeal of any decision to dismiss.

Every case should be examined on its own merits and the Tribunal will demand extra patience from employers where there is an added complication such as drug or alcohol addiction.

(For surveillance of employees on long-term absence or monitoring in general see **3.67**.)

SHORT-TERM OR SPORADIC ABSENCE

[3.42] This to some extent is more difficult to deal with for employers. To justify a dismissal for short-term absence employers will generally have to show that:

1.   the employee had a continuing pattern of absence over a long period of time;

2.   it was reasonable to conclude that this continued period of absence would not improve;

3.   the continuation of the pattern of absence was unacceptable; and

4.   adequate warnings had been given to the employee as to the consequences of the continuing absence.[85]

LIGHT DUTIES

[3.43] Another additional complication arises when there is a request by the employee and/or their doctor to return to work for 'light duties'. Before the 2004 Employment Equality Act was introduced it was well established that there was no obligation on employers to provide 'light work' or alternative duties.[86] With the enactment of the 2004 Employment Equality Act, discrimination on the basis of disability was introduced for the first time. Whilst it is clear that the ground of disability does not apply where the

---

85.   *Mooney v Rowntree Mackintosh Ltd* UD 473, 474, 475 and 478/1980.
86.   *Gurr v Office of Public Works* [1990] ELR 42.

person is not willing to perform the work or is fully capable of doing the work, if that capability arises out of a disability then the issue of providing light duties has to be examined with that in mind (see **11.20** and **11.21** for further discussion on this topic).

This topic was given an extensive examination in the case of *Carroll v Bus Atha Cliath/Dublin Bus*.[87] Here the plaintiff was seeking an order requiring that he be permitted to return to work on a route that would facilitate him taking regular breaks given that he had injured his back. In the course of the case counsel for the defendant sought to rely on the case of *Rogers v Dublin Corporation*[88] where it was held that an employer is not under any legal obligation to provide alternative work to an employee who is no longer medically fit to perform the duties for which he was originally employed. Clarke J agreed with this proposition but went on to make it subject to two caveats:

1. The first caveat distinguished between the work which the employee was originally employed to do and that which they may now be able to do. Clarke J held that the employee must be reasonably fit to carry out the work for which he was employed but that an overly technical objection to an employee's fitness to carry out such duties may disentitle the employer to treat the employee as being unable to do so. What in essence this means is that if an employee was able to convince the court that the work they were originally employed to do was little different from the work they were now capable of doing the employer may not be justified in terminating their employment by reason of incapacity.

2. Secondly, whilst recognising that no term would be implied into a contract to the effect that an employer is under a duty to provide 'light duties' to an otherwise incapacitated employee, this rule may be displaced by an express term in the contract of employment or by custom and practice.

What employers can take from all of this is:

*   there is no obligation to provide light work;

*   this presumption may be displaced by an express term in the contract or well-established custom and practice;

*   if the employee can prove that the work they were employed to do is not radically different from that which they are now capable of doing (despite what they are now being asked to do) this may render the termination of employment on the basis of incapacity unfair.

To some extent the matter has moved on since *Carroll*, the EAT takes a view that the employer needs to explore all alternatives to the dismissal prior to termination and that this is in keeping with the right of employees to fair procedures and natural justice.

---

87.   *Carroll v Bus Atha Cliath/Dublin Bus* [1997] ELR 208.
88.   *Rogers v Dublin Corporation* (1998) ELR 59.

Competence

[3.44] Whilst there has always been some difficulty distinguishing between capability and competence (again the words are not defined in the Act) the Tribunal has generally proceeded on the basis that competence deals with the employee's ability to do the work. In cases of dismissal for incompetence the test of whether such dismissal will be regarded as not being unfair has a number of aspects:

- Did the employer honestly believe that the employee was incompetent or unsuitable for the job?

- Were the grounds for this belief reasonable?[89]

- Before a decision to dismiss is taken an employer should have an up-to-date assessment of the employee's performance.[90]

Competence or rather incompetence is notoriously difficult to prove, involving as it does significant judgement on behalf of managers. The EAT has stressed that incompetence is a very serious charge.[91]

Dealing with incompetence demands a detailed plan from employers. Rather than proceeding straight away through the disciplinary procedure, it is demanded that employers first set out a detailed Performance Improvement Plan (sometimes referred to as a PIP). This PIP should have structured targets and a detailed review mechanism. It should also allow for some independent review outside of the employee's immediate manager in order to afford added objectivity. Only when the employee misses or fails to achieve the agreed targets should the disciplinary procedure be implemented and only then at the first stage with the process being repeated until the employee is dismissed.

One of the major dilemmas faced by employers is that implementing this process generally falls to middle or senior managers and often once it is put in train there is no way back. Equally the process often leads to counter claims of bullying which may have to be investigated, adding not insignificantly to the time involved. A more recent trend is for the PIP to be countered by a personal injury claim for stress-related illness. Ironically what started out as a well-meaning way to protect employees has evolved into a process that employers deem too time-consuming and costly and thus it often leads to the premature dismissal of employees by employers in the knowledge that whilst they may lose an unfair dismissal claim it is 'cheaper' than the alternative.

Qualifications

[3.45] Similar to 'capability' and 'competence', the word 'qualifications' is not defined in the Act. However, per s 6(4)(a) qualifications are defined as being 'wholly or mainly ... for performing work of the kind which he was employed by the employer to do'. Clearly they cover technical and professional qualifications. They do not however cover

---

89.   See *McDonnell v Rooney* UD 504/1991.
90.   *O'Brien v Professional Contract Cleaners* UD/184 1990.
91.   See *McGrath and Restrick v Fisher Field Construction and Farm Machines Ltd* UD 927 and 928/ 1982.

such matters as work permits as a permit is necessary to carry out the job but it is not a qualification. In the case of *Ojierathi v An Post*[92] the claimant was a foreign national employed by An Post. Having read an article in the weekend paper the company commenced an investigation into whether the claimant had a proper work permit such that he was entitled to work in the country. Despite the company asking for this on numerous occasions the claimant did not produce it and ultimately he was dismissed. Ultimately the claimant (during the course of the hearing at the EAT) received confirmation that he had been granted the right to work in Ireland. However, the Tribunal said that the only matters they could take into account were those up to the date of his dismissal in October 2007 and as the employee did not have a valid work permit at that point and the matter having been fairly investigated, the claim failed.

Conduct

[3.46] Section 6(4)(b) of the Act provides that dismissals for 'conduct' are deemed not to be unfair. The use of the word conduct can be distinguished here from the use of the word 'misconduct' in the Minimum Notice and Terms of Employment Act 1973, s 8 of which allows an employer to dismiss an employee without notice for 'misconduct'. In interpreting the word misconduct the Tribunal has restricted it to serious misconduct or matters such as violence, theft etc at work.[93] Thus the range of conduct envisaged by the 1977 Act is much broader than that envisaged by the 1973 Act. There is no definitive list of the types of conduct which will be adjudged as being so serious as to warrant dismissal. Significant weight will be given to such matters as the level of responsibility, the nature of the work, the experience of the individual, the training provided, the company policies and procedures and the reasonableness of the decision. Much will turn on the procedural aspects. Given the concentration on this and the reasonableness of the conclusion this matter is dealt with separately in **Ch 4**.

Dishonesty

[3.47] Dishonesty is as broad a category as conduct or misconduct, encompassing as it does such minor infractions as a lack of integrity to such major ones such as theft and fraud.

The employer and indeed the EAT need not prove beyond reasonable doubt the allegations of dishonesty; what both the EAT and employer must do is establish a genuine belief in the guilt of the employee, based on reasonable grounds following a fair and impartial investigation (see **Ch 4**). This matter has been dealt with extensively by the Tribunal in the cases of *Looney & Co Ltd*,[94] *Thompson v Powers Supermarkets Ltd*[95]

---

92.   *Ojierathi v An Post* UD 1113 (2007).
93.   *Lennon v Bredin* M160/1978.
94.   *Looney & Co Ltd* UD 843/1984.
95.   *Thompson v Powers Supermarkets Ltd* UD 531/1998.

and *Martin v Audio Video Services Centre Ltd*.[96] What emerges from this are a general set of guidelines as follows:

1. A blemish-free record, even if this is coupled with long service, is unlikely to render an otherwise fair dismissal unfair as dishonesty is seen as a serious offence.

2. It is not necessarily relevant that the employee themselves did not gain from the offence.[97]

3. The value of the goods themselves or the extent of the goods stolen is not necessarily relevant. In *Carolan v Smith & Nephew Southalls (Ireland) Ltd*[98] the claimant was dismissed for taking an 'ophthalmic torch' and albeit that he returned it, it was still held to be sufficient to warrant dismissal. The tribunal in this instance took particular notice of the 'strict rule' in the company handbook which said that in the case of theft employees would be 'liable to instant dismissal'. Therefore, whilst the value of the goods themselves should not be relevant the dismissal must still comply with the terms of the company disciplinary procedure.

4. The offence may not necessarily be against the employer himself. It could be perpetrated against a supplier or another third party, eg where an employee stole four loaves of bread from a delivery van.[99]

5. Even if an employee is acquitted of a criminal offence this does not mean that the same offence cannot be relied upon to dismiss an employee fairly. In *Mooney v An Post*[100] Keane J stated that 'the acquittal by the plaintiff in the criminal proceedings did not preclude the defendants from considering whether the circumstances which gave rise to the criminal proceedings were such as to necessitate the plaintiff's dismissal'.

Conduct and Criminal Proceedings and the Gardaí

[3.48] One issue that often arises for employers is what to do if criminal proceedings have been instituted prior to or in the middle of an investigation into the employment law aspects of the matter or whether prior to completing an investigation into an employment law matter which is also a criminal offence whether the employer should inform the Gardaí?

Invariably the employee may refuse to participate in the employers' investigation pending the outcome of the criminal investigation and indeed they may be justified in this. Also an employee may be acquitted of a criminal offence given the standard of proof required but may be perfectly fairly dismissed for the same offence. If an employer waits until after the criminal trial they will invariably leave themselves open to the accusation that the court acquitted and therefore they should too. Also once a criminal investigation begins invariably the employee will be advised by his solicitor not

96. *Martin v Audio Video Services Centre Ltd* UD 617/1991.
97. *Hardyside v Tesco Stores (Irl) Ltd* UD 256/1984.
98. *Carolan v Smith & Nephew Southalls (Ireland) Ltd* UD 542 (1984).
99. *Handyside v Tesco Stores Ireland Ltd* UD 256/1984.
100. *Mooney v An Post* [1994] ELR 103, 117.

to say anything that will incriminate him and will claim privilege against self-incrimination.[101] Finally, if the Gardaí are investigating they will not be able to offer any evidence to the EAT if there are pending criminal proceedings and they may be the only party able to adduce evidence.

In the case of *Brock v An Post*[102] the EAT made it clear that where a conviction was handed down the company was entitled to rely on it notwithstanding claims as 'to its authenticity'.

In light of all of the above, and given the length of time such criminal investigations and proceedings take, it is more practical, presuming it is possible, to conclude any internal investigation first and deal with the employment law aspects prior to involving the Gardaí. If this is not possible employers are not precluded from relying on the record of the proceedings and the employee will be expected to offer an explanation if they wish to dispute it.[103]

DISHONESTY AND GROUPS OF EMPLOYEES

[3.49] Often it will be difficult to pinpoint exactly who amongst a number of employees committed an offence. This is not like school where the teacher can decide to punish all. In such circumstances employers will be have to be seen to go to considerable lengths prior to disciplining or dismissing a group of employees. It will be necessary for the employer to call all of them together to outline concerns and to ask the perpetrators to desist and to further explain that in the event that they cannot identify the specific perpetrator or perpetrators that they will be left with no alternative but to dismiss all of them.

Even with that the employer must then establish with certainty that the dishonesty occurred and that it was committed by one or all of the group, even though it was not possible to identify which. A very extensive investigation will have to occur prior to coming to any conclusions. In *Hubbard v McMullen and Gillen*[104] it was necessary to dismiss three barmen in a public house to stem losses as a result of pilferage and this was held to be fair. Arising out of this there seem to be a number of rules:

1. that the offence itself if attributable to one person has to be sufficient to justify dismissal;

2. that the employees concerned were first warned as a group and individually as to the consequences of the matter continuing;

3. that there was a thorough investigation;

4. that as a result of the investigation the employer was satisfied and reasonably believed that one or more were responsible for the dishonesty. Note that it does not seem sufficient that the employer believed that the loss or dishonesty was down to one person;

---

101. See *Cousins v Brookes Thomas Ltd* UD 45/1988.
102. *Brock v An Post* UD 57/1987.
103. See *Brock v An Post* UD 57/1987 and *Mahon v Cummins Graphics Supplies Ltd* UD 673/1989.
104. *Hubbard v McMullen and Gillen* UD 580, 670 and 721/1983.

5.   that as between the members of the group the employer could not distinguish who was responsible.

Fighting and general horseplay

[3.50] Practically all company handbooks and contracts of employment that contain a discipline and dismissal procedure provide that violence towards others constitutes gross misconduct, the penalty for which is dismissal without notice.

In general the Tribunal takes a strong stance on violence in the workplace; however, whether dismissal will be held to be fair will be determined by the nature of the offence, the time at which it occurred, the state of mind of the person who is alleged to carry out the offence and whether it was effected on or off the premises. Equally the nature of the investigation and the reasonableness of the conclusion are paramount. The following are some guidelines:

1.   If the offence occurred off the premises the employer will be required to show that it was work-related. In *Keane v Westinghouse Electric Ireland Ltd*[105] the employee was dismissed following a scuffle between the claimant and his supervisor over the fact that the claimant had been suspended as a result of his supervisor reporting him. The tribunal took the view that this was 'work-related'. Contrast this with the decision in *Murray v LFS & P Enterprises*[106] where it was held that the dismissal of an employee following an altercation at 5.30am was not the right climate to make 'an appraisal of the employee's conduct'.

2.   Dismissal as a result of assault on a junior employee by a person in authority will generally be held to be fair.[107]

3.   Similarly, where the incident involves an alleged assault on a person of diminished capacity the dismissal is likely to be deemed fair.[108]

4.   The capacity of the person committing the offence has to be considered. Thus in *Bergin v Bus Atha Cliath*[109] the claimant had committed an assault on a fellow employee as a result of a medical problem and his having asked to be relieved from duty five times during the day was taken into account.

5.   Horseplay, which although dangerous does not injure another, is generally given a higher tolerance level by the Tribunal.[110] That said, in light of the Safety, Health and Welfare at Work Act 2005 and the onus on employers to provide proper protective equipment (PPE) in addition to training employees in

105.   *Keane v Westinghouse Electric Ireland Ltd* UD 63/1986.
106.   *Murray v LFS & P Enterprises* UD 11/1986.
107.   *Dublin Corporation v Hardy* UD 571/1983.
108.   *Mc Gee v Peamount Hospital* UD 136/1984.
109.   *Bergin v Bus Atha Cliath* UD 61/1987.
110.   See *Brennan v St Lukes Home Incorporated* UD 643/1988.

health and safety coupled with the need for Safety Statements, the tolerance of
the Tribunal to such matters may wane.

(See also **3.53**.)

Attending work under the influence of drink and drugs

[3.51] This is one of the more difficult matters to deal with and in general a very lenient
view is taken by the Tribunal on such matters. This is particularly so where alcohol
abuse has been a problem over time. Again, many collective agreements, company
handbooks and contracts of employment provide that attending work under the influence
of drugs or alcohol will constitute gross misconduct the penalty for which is dismissal
without notice.

This topic has developed significantly in recent years with the passing of the Safety,
Health and Welfare at Work Act 2005. Section 13 sets out the general duties of an
employee with regard to health and safety. It includes an obligation to ensure that they
are not under the influence of an intoxicant to the extent that they are in 'such a state as
to endanger [their] own safety, health or welfare at work or that of any other person'.
'Any person' is not defined and is extremely broad. It can mean a fellow employee or a
customer or indeed a member of the public. The section goes on to provide that if
'reasonably requested by his or her employer' an employee must submit to 'any
appropriate, reasonable and proportionate tests for intoxicants by, or under the
supervision of, a registered medical practitioner who is a competent person, as may be
prescribed'. The section also compels the employee to cooperate with their employer to
comply with any 'relevant statutory provisions'.

In the case of *Trevor Kennedy v Veolia Transport Ireland*[111] the EAT upheld a
dismissal for gross misconduct after Mr Kennedy failed a random workplace alcohol
test on a Sunday morning shift. There had been a drug and alcohol policy in place and it
had been agreed with the union although Mr Kennedy never received a copy. The
Labour Court took a slightly different view in the case of *Alstom Ireland Ltd v A
Worker*.[112] This came before the Labour Court on appeal from the Rights Commissioner
under s 13(9) of the Industrial Relations Act 1969. Here the worker had failed a random
drugs test even though the quantity of intoxicant found was very low (described as a
residue). His union argued that it was of such a low percentage that the test should
properly be classified as negative. The company, however, operated a zero-tolerance
policy. The court went on to state:

> The Court is satisfied that the Company acted honestly and reasonably in dealing
> with what was reported to it as a positive result for a prohibited drug. The worker
> has at all times denied that he used the drug in question. In the Court's view, in
> all the circumstances of this case, there is room for some doubt as to whether the
> particular result in issue should have been reported as positive or negative. In the
> light of the conclusion reached earlier in this Decision on the necessity for
> agreement on the modalities of these tests, and the recommendation that agreed

---

111. *Trevor Kennedy v Veolia Transport Ireland* UD 240/2006.
112. *Alstom Ireland Ltd v A Worker* Decision No AD 0765.

guidelines be now put in place about which there can be no dubiety, the Court is of the view that the worker should be given the benefit of the doubt.

What can be determined from all of the above is:

1. Dismissal is not automatically appropriate for alcohol- or drug-related offences.

2. A proper policy regarding drugs and alcohol has to be in place, the employees have to be aware of it and if this extends to random drug and alcohol testing they should be reminded about it on regular occasions. If there is a union representing the workforce it should be agreed with them.

3. Each case has to be judged on its own merits and factors such as risks to health and safety, the level of responsibility of the employee, the risks involved, contact with members of the public and the company policies will all be taken into account.[113]

4. Where alcohol abuse has been a consistent problem, dismissal will only be deemed to be fair once the procedures have been exhausted, once the person has been given the opportunity for treatment and once they have been put on clear notice that any further offences will result in the termination of their employment.[114]

Gross insubordination/refusal to obey instructions

[3.52] It is reasonable to expect as an employer that employees would obey reasonable and lawful instructions. The High Court in *Brewster v Burke*[115] stated that:

> It has long been part of our law that a person repudiates the contract of service if he wilfully disobeys the lawful and reasonable orders of his master. Such a refusal justifies an employer in dismissing an employee summarily.

It is respectfully suggested that whereas the general thrust of this decision is correct, the EAT might take an entirely different view on the summary dismissal aspect of this. In particular since the 1993 Amendment Act there is a substantial focus on fair procedures and it is probable that the Tribunal would demand that an opportunity be given for the employee to consider their refusal prior to being summarily dismissed.

It must also be borne in mind that the instruction has to be lawful and reasonable and notwithstanding this the Tribunal will also consider whether the employee was justified in refusing to obey the instruction.

Also one has to consider s 27 of the Safety, Health, and Welfare at Work Act 2005 which provides protection to employees who are penalised as a result of raising issue of a health and safety nature or leaving their place of work in order to protect themselves.

What can therefore be determined from this is:

1. The refusal by the employee must be unreasonable.

---

113. See *Chadwick v Power Supermarkets* UD 340/1983.
114. *Griffin v Beamish and Crawford* UD 90/1983.
115. *Brewster v Burke* (1978, unreported), HC.

2.   If the refusal is in breach of a term of the contract and the employee is afforded the opportunity to consider their refusal prior to a decision to dismiss being taken and they are fully warned as to the consequences of their continued refusal the dismissal is likely to be upheld.[116]

3.   The refusal to carry out an illegal act will not be held to be unfair[117] nor will the refusal to carry out an instruction which is in breach of health and safety legislation.[118]

Crimes outside the workplace

[3.53] It often arises that an employee may commit a crime outside the workplace which may in some instances result in the incarceration of the employee. In such circumstances is it reasonable for an employer to dismiss the employee with or without notice or do they have to hold their job open and if so for how long? Similar to other aspects of employment law it depends on various factors such as whether the claimant's criminal conduct renders him unsuitable for employment. In the case of *O'Leary v Crosbie,*[119] where the claimant was convicted of indecent assault and received a 12-month sentence which was reduced on appeal to a suspended sentence and fine, the Tribunal stated that the critical factor is 'whether or not the claimant's criminal record was such as to render him unsuitable for his employment with the respondent or unacceptable to other employees'. In this case the Tribunal was of the opinion that the onus was not fully discharged. Equally, however, in *Barry and French v Irish Linen Service Ltd*[120] where the claimants were involved in an attempted robbery in which one of the company's vehicles was involved there was deemed to be a clear nexus between the criminal behaviour and the place of work.

Clearly a large factor in such dismissals is the position held by the claimant and the greater the responsibility attaching to that position then the more likely the 'bond of trust' between the employer and employee will have broken down and the greater the probability that dismissal will be held to be fair.

Thus in *Noonan v Dunnes Stores*[121] where an employee was dismissed following a late night assault on a garda who she allegedly hit with her umbrella, dismissal was held to be unfair and re-engagement was ordered. In contrast, in another case involving Dunnes Stores the same year an employee who burgled an adjoining premises was held to have been fairly dismissed as the Tribunal felt he had breached the bond of trust.[122]

The case of *Graham v Portroe Stevedores*[123] illustrates the danger for employers in this area. Here the EAT awarded the maximum compensation possible of €154,772 after

---

116.   *Rankin v Peamount Hospital* UD 107/1982.
117.   *Brown v McNamara Freight Ltd* UD 745/1987.
118.   Health, Safety and Welfare at Work Act 2005, s 27.
119.   *O'Leary v Crosbie* UD 1118/1983.
120.   *Barry and French v Irish Linen Service Ltd* UD 905 and 906/1986.
121.   *Noonan v Dunnes Stores* UD 1068/1998.
122.   *Martin v Dunnes Stores (Enniscorthy) Ltd* UD 571/1988.
123.   *Graham v Portroe Stevedores* UD 574/2006.

a late night fracas. The main reason for this seemed to be not the fracas itself, but the fact that the HR manager who had witnessed the incident himself carried out the investigation.

In the case of *Pearce v David Flynn*[124] the Claimant a general operative was convicted for driving away without paying from a petrol station on ten occasions. The Respondent was carrying out 'snagging work' at the petrol station at the time. The conviction was reported in the press and a number of senior managers read about it. The matter was discussed between the Managing Director (MD) and the head of HR. Both said they had lost trust in the claimant. There was however no formal investigation into it and despite the Claimant trying to call the MD the MD refused to take his calls. Whilst the EAT found that the Respondent 'had substantial grounds for dismissing the Claimant', the dismissal was found to be procedurally unfair.

What can be taken from all of the above is:

1. The crime itself must be sufficiently serious, and most probably it must be an indictable offence.

2. There must be a clear connection between the crime and the place of work.

3. The crime itself must be sufficient to warrant that the bond of trust between the company and the individual is broken.

4. The crime must render the person unsuitable for working with the remaining employees.

INCARCERATION OF EMPLOYEES

[3.54] Notwithstanding all of the above what happens when a person is convicted and incarcerated? Do employers have to hold open the job until the person is released? Again it depends on the nature of the offence and the duration of the sentence. Clearly, the longer the sentence the less onus there is on an employer to hold open the job. Equally, however, a short sentence for a very senior employee could result in dismissal if the bond of trust had broken down.

Equally where the crime makes it impossible for the person to do their job, such as in *O'Connor v Astra Pumps Ltd*[125] where the claimant's driving licence was suspended, the dismissal was found not to be unfair as the claimant was unable to carry out the job for which he was employed.

INVOLVEMENT OF THE GARDAÍ

[3.55] In a crime committed outside the workplace the employer will have no control over the pace of the criminal investigation. That does not mean that an employer has to cease any internal investigation until such time as the criminal one is concluded (see **3.48**).

---

124. *Pearce v David Flynn* UD 833/2006.
125. *O'Connor v Astra Pumps Ltd* UD 486/1986.

Bullying and/or harassment

[3.56] This area is probably one of the most difficult for employers to deal with. Often such cases are coupled with personal injury cases for injury and stress. Harassment is also an offence under the Employment Equality Act. Because claims of bullying and harassment generally involve intra-employee disputes, such issues more often than not give rise to constructive dismissal claims (see **3.63**) as distinct from unfair dismissal claims. However, where such claims are raised and subsequent to proper investigation are deemed to be well-founded, it can give rise to the imposition of disciplinary action up to and including dismissal.

Loyalty

[3.57] A breach of loyalty generally occurs in three instances:

1. Where an employee directly or indirectly competes against his employer.

   An example of indirect competition is the case of *Fairbrother v Steifel Laboratories (Ireland)*[126] where the employee was dismissed following his wife's actions in promoting the launch of a competitive product. As the employee had been made aware of the likely consequences of his wife's actions the dismissal was deemed not to be unfair.[127] In *Higgins v Aer Lingus*[128] the employee was dismissed for involvement as managing director in a new Irish airline. The general principles of this were laid down in *McDermott v Kemek Ltd/Irish Industrial Explosives Ltd*[129] where the EAT went on to state:

   (a) It is legitimate for an employee to aspire to set up their own business.

   (b) A person would consider it normal to work in the industry in which he is familiar.

   (c) It would be contrary to public policy to prevent someone setting up in competition.

   (d) However, an employee's duty of fidelity continues so long as he remains in employment and there may be a point where the preparations for the new business become incompatible with continuing to serve the existing employer.

   (e) If an employer believes that an employee's actions in pursuit of his ambition have become incompatible he owes the same duty not to dismiss unfairly as he would in any other type of case.

2. Where an employee 'double jobs'.

---

126. *Fairbrother v Steifel Laboratories (Ireland)* UD 665/1985.
127. It is respectfully suggested that with the passing of the Employment Equality Acts 1989–2004 that this may not be the decision today.
128. *Higgins v Aer Lingus* UD 410/1986.
129. *McDermott v KemekLtd/Irish Industrial Explosives Ltd* [1996] ELR 233.

In today's economy it is not untypical for some employees to hold separate jobs;[130] however, this may impinge on the working relationship particularly if the employee is working for a competitor. In such circumstances the employer would need to give a clear warning to the employee. Regard must also be had to the Organisation of Working Time Act 1997 provisions on double employment.

3. Where an employee breaches confidentiality.

Often contracts of employment contain non-disclosure and confidentiality clauses. Nonetheless, accessing confidential information or files may be a breach of loyalty. In *Mullins v Digital Equipment International*[131] the employee was dismissed for allegedly trying to gain access to the company's computer control system. The tribunal held that the employee knew at all times what he was doing and deemed the dismissal fair.

Breach of internet and email usage

[3.58] Facebook, Twitter and Linkedin are just some of the many social networking websites which have grown in popularity. If employees abuse or misuse the internet and email facilities in the workplace, it has the potential to not only to damage the reputation of the company but also to significantly impact on the productivity levels of the business. The critical issue here is that all employers must have detailed internet and email policies and these must be applied consistently and fairly to avoid claims for discrimination and unfair dismissal and due process must be afforded to the employee against whom a breach is alleged.

Thus in the case of *Colum O'Leary v Eagle Star Life and Pensions*[132] the plaintiff was dismissed for sending emails around the workplace describing colleagues in derogatory and intimidating terms. The Employment Appeals Tribunal awarded him €21,000 for unfair dismissal, noting that Eagle Star had a policy on emails but had never indicated that sending an abusive email would be considered gross misconduct leading directly to dismissal. It also criticised the company for neither accepting the plaintiff's apology nor granting him a right of appeal. In *James Mehigan v Dyflin Publications Ltd*[133] the plaintiff was fired after pornographic images were found on his computer. The EAT awarded the plaintiff €2,000 on the grounds that the company had no policy or code of practice in place which explained the consequences of misuse of email/internet. The plaintiff's dismissal was therefore unfair.

What we can learn from the above is:

1. It is legitimate for an employer to dismiss for a breach the of internet or email usage policy.

---

130. Note the Organisation of Working Time Act 1997, s 33 which prohibits double employment if it exceeds the period for which an employee can lawfully work.
131. *Mullins v Digital Equipment International* UD 329/1989.
132. *Colum O'Leary v Eagle Star Life and Pensions* UD 2002.
133. *Mehigan v Dyflin Publications Ltd* UD/582/2001.

2. It is not only necessary to have a detailed policy but this must be explained to staff.

3. Regardless as to the breach of policy due process must be followed.

MONITORING EMAIL AND INTERNET USE

[3.59] Where employers monitor employees' internet and email use, regard should be had to the EU Article 29 Working Group document on the surveillance of electronic communications in the workplace, as it is likely that this will be raised as defence. This document offers guidelines and examples about what constitutes legitimate monitoring of employees and the acceptable limits of worker surveillance by the employer. The Irish Data Protection Commissioner and the Working Group accept that companies have a right to protect their legitimate business interests. However, the monitoring of employees involves the processing of personal data. Accordingly the Working Group found that in balancing the rights of the employer and employee the following principles should apply:

1. The monitoring must be *transparent*;

2. It must be *necessary*;

3. The processing of personal data must be *fair*.

Working whilst on sick leave

[3.60] Some employees who work whilst on sick leave or otherwise abuse sick leave could be liable to dismissal; this is particularly so where the employee is in receipt of sick pay where an additional ground of dishonesty arises. However, and critically, it must be proven that the activities that the employee partook in were incompatible with the employee being fit for normal duties. There is significant case law in this area and it can be summarised as follows:

1. The tribunal will take into consideration the previous sick record and any warnings to the employee. Also this is a matter for consideration by the employer when determining the penalty.[134]

2. If the employee is in receipt of pay from the employer this may add to the offence.[135]

3. If the employee whilst on sick leave either takes holidays or plays sport, it is likely that it will be held to be a fair dismissal, so in the case of *Murphy v Tesco Stores (Ireland) Ltd*[136] where the employee was out of the country on holidays or in *Mulraney v Group 4 Securitas (Ireland) Ltd*[137] where the claimant had

---

134. *McGowran v Laura Ashley Ltd* UD 741/1988.
135. *Roy v Wavin Pipes Ltd* UD 119/1983.
136. *Murphy v Tesco Stores (Ireland) Ltd* UD 1241/1983.
137. *Mulraney v Group 4 Securitas (Ireland) Ltd* UD 841/1985.

been absent for a back strain but played a football match the dismissals were deemed fair.

Redundancy

See also **6.49–6.66**)

[3.61][138] The Act provides that the dismissal of an employee by reason of redundancy is not unfair once it results 'wholly or mainly' from the redundancy of the employee. This does not necessarily mean that every redundancy is fair. It merely means that redundancy can be an absolute defence to a claim for unfair dismissal but a number of requirements are needed:

1. It must be a genuine redundancy within the meaning of the Act. Thus in *Hurley v Royal Cork Yacht Club*[139] the Tribunal held that a redundancy did not exist.

2. The employer must behave reasonably. This is where the High Court and the EAT diverge greatly in their approach. The High Court takes the view that as a redundancy is a so-called 'no fault' termination, as a consequence the issue of fair procedures and natural justice does not arise[140] and necessarily the matter of reasonableness of the employer's actions and decision need not be examined. The EAT, however, is constrained by the 1993 amendment Act, which provides that the reasonableness of an employer's conduct is now an essential factor to be considered for all dismissals, including redundancy dismissals. Section 6(7) of the 1997 Act provides that 'in determining if a dismissal is an unfair dismissal, regard may be had' to the reasonableness or otherwise of the conduct (whether by act or omission) of the employer in relation to the dismissal'. Thus in the case of *Beaumont v Muintir na Tíre*[141] the Tribunal stated that 'as a basic principle of natural justice and fairness items as important as redundancy should be clearly discussed with the employee'. Whereas one might question the rationale of the Tribunal's reference to fairness and natural justice given the approach of the High Court, the fact remains that the Tribunal noted the lack of consultation and deemed the dismissal unfair. Also, in the case of *Roche v Richmond Earthworks Ltd*,[142] the Tribunal held that the 'failure to hold any selection process or consultation with the claimant rendered the dismissal unfair'.

3. The employer must have a fair and transparent selection process. This requirement has to be distinguished from the fact of redundancy where the matter of the job is in question. When selecting someone the process 'moves'

---

138. Note a much more comprehensive discussion on this is to be found in Ch 6 at **6.49** onwards.
139. *Hurley v Royal Cork Yacht Club* 1999 ELR 7.
140. See *Minnock v Irish Casing* [2007] ELR 229, where Clarke J confirmed that 'an investigation which does not involve any findings is not a matter to which the rules of natural justice apply and is not a matter with which the Court should interfere'.
141. *Beaumont v Muintir na Tíre* UD 668/2004.
142. *Roche v Richmon Earthworks Ltd* UD 329/97.

from one of the job to the person or persons involved. Section 6(3) of the Act provides that where an employee is selected for redundancy but their selection for dismissal resulted 'wholly or mainly' from:

(a)   their membership of a trade union or engaging in industrial action;

(b)   their religious beliefs;

(c)   threatened or actual civil or criminal proceedings against the employer;

(d)   the race or colour of the employee;

(e)   the age of the employee;

(f)   their membership of the travelling community;

(g)   their pregnancy; or

(h)   where they were selected in contravention of an agreed procedure;

then the dismissal shall be deemed to be an unfair dismissal. Accordingly if there is no agreed procedure or custom and practice for selecting employees for redundancy and if the redundancy does not result wholly or mainly from of the above, (a–h), then the Tribunal will consider whether the employer has acted reasonably in all the circumstances. Where there is no agreed procedure there is nothing to prevent employers 'constructing' a so-called 'redundancy matrix' against which employees will be measured. Such a matrix might include such things as length of service, attendance record, disciplinary record, performance ratings etc. However, this needs to be shared with the employees beforehand and they must get an opportunity to comment on it.[143] All other things being equal the Tribunal will expect the employer to apply Last In First Out (LIFO).[144]

Expiry of a fixed-term or specified purpose contract

(See also **3.15.**)

[3.62] Dismissal of an employee by reason only of the expiry of a fixed-term or specified purpose contract will not be unfair provided the contract is in writing, it is signed by both parties and it contains a clause to the effect that the terms of the Unfair Dismissals Acts 1977–2001 do not apply to it. Therefore the Act does not apply once three conditions are met:

1.   The fixed-term contract is in writing.

2.   It is signed by both parties.

---

143.   See *Boucher v Irish Productivity Centre* [1990] ELR 205.
144.   It should be noted that LIFO could be deemed to be discriminatory and contrary to the Employment Equality Act 1998 and 2005. This has already been found to be the case in the UK.

3. The contract contains a specific cause stating that the Act shall not apply to a dismissal consisting only of the expiry of the fixed term.

An important word in this is 'only', ie the dismissal must be as a result only of the expiry of the fixed term. Thus in the case of *Nwosu v Banta Global Turnkey*,[145] even though the fixed-term contract was in compliance with s 2 of the Act and this was noted by the Tribunal and the contract came to an end at its natural time, the Tribunal in holding for the claimant determined that the reason the contract terminated was not due to its expiry but rather other reasons – here the claimant had been 'in trouble' with the company before and had made an appeal to the Rights Commissioner.

An interesting issue which was raised in *O'Cuinnegain v Guardian Angels National School*[146] was whether the Tribunal had jurisdiction to hear the case where the clause containing the 'waiver', in accordance with s 2(2)(b) of the Act, was provided some time after the contract was agreed. The tribunal held that:

> The Claimant submits that to have any effect the waiver 'must' be in place 'when the contract is entered into'. This is not stated in the Act. The Claimant refers to Redmond's Dismissal Law in Ireland, however Dr Redmond does not state that the waiver 'must be in place when the contract is entered into'. She in fact states that the conditions 'should' be satisfied 'at the time the contract is made'. Clearly there is no requirement at law that a written contract be in place at the time of commencement of the term of the contract of employment. Dr Redmond in her discussion on the waiver clearly states that 'any provisions excluding employment rights will be strictly construed' Section 2(2)(b) of the Unfair Dismissals Act, 1977, as amended, clearly applies to the instant case in that the three criteria established therein are met'.

CONSTRUCTIVE DISMISSAL

[3.63] In cases of constructive dismissal, because the fact of dismissal is in dispute the employee goes into evidence first and the onus of proof then lies with them.

Section 1 of the 1977 Act defines constructive dismissal as:

> the termination by the employee of his contract of employment with his employer whether prior notice of the termination was or was not given to the employer in circumstances in which, because of the conduct of the employer the employee was or would have been entitled or it was or would have been reasonable for the employee to terminate the contract of employment with out giving prior notice of the termination to the employer.

In examining the definition of constructive dismissal under the Act it becomes clear that there are two circumstances which constitute constructive dismissal:

1. where 'because of the conduct of the employer the employee was or would have been entitled', to terminate the contract; and/or ('the contract test')

---

145. *Nwosu v Banta Global Turnkey* UD 10/2008.
146. *O'Cuinnegain v Guardian Angels National School* UD 1008/2006.

2. where it would have 'been reasonable' for the employee to terminate the contract ie the employer may have acted within the terms of the contract but the conduct may have been unreasonable.[147] ('the reasonableness test')

These have become known as the 'two tests'. Whereas it is easy to define these neatly when considering the wording of the Act, the EAT does not approach the matter as distinctly and either test may be applied. Again upon examination of the wording it is clear that the 'contract test' is more stringent, as the breach must go to the root of the contract.

The contract test

[3.64] For an employee to rely on the breach of contract test they must prove that the breach went to the root of the contract or in the alternative that the employer no longer intended to be bound by the main terms of the contract.[148] As the latter is somewhat hypothetical the majority of cases rest on the former. Thus in *Cosgrave v Kavanagh Meat Products Ltd*,[149] even though the claimant was able to prove that he worked excessive hours and that he was exploited in being paid less than the recommended rate for a person of his 'training and experience', that was not deemed sufficient for the employee to terminate the contract of employment. This case illustrates the high burden of proof on employees in such cases.

The tribunal generally stresses the necessity for ongoing respect and mutual trust in the employer/employee relationship, not only in constructive dismissal cases, thus in *Brady v Newman*[150] it went on to state that 'as an employer is entitled to expect his employee to behave in a manner which would preserve his employer's reasonable trust and confidence in him, so also must the employer behave'.

The reasonableness test

[3.65] As stated above even where the employee may not be legally entitled to terminate the contract, where the employer has acted unreasonably the Tribunal may still find a constructive dismissal. In such cases the Tribunal will examine the conduct of both the employee and the employer. In the case of *Kane v Willstan Racing (Ireland) Limited*[151] the claimant had informed three senior managers that she felt intimidated and bullied by her new manager. The EAT found that no serious consideration was given to these matters by any of these persons and the claimant was entitled to terminate her contract. In finding for the claimant the Tribunal considered the matter of reasonableness and went on to say that 'this must be considered with reference to all of the circumstances of the case and especially where there have been changes to the terms, conditions or personality of a workplace which the employee may find difficult to accept'.

---

147. Note in the UK the 'reasonableness test' does not exist in law.
148. See *Byrne v R H M Foods (Ireland) Ltd* UD 69/1979.
149. *Cosgrave v Kavanagh Meat Products Ltd* UD 6/1988.
150. *Brady v Newman* UD 330/1979.
151. *Kane v Willstan Racing (Ireland) Group* UD 1263/2008, MN 1168/2008 and WT.

So in *Melligan v Karmarton Limited*[152] the Tribunal, in finding for the employee, a sales executive who pleaded constructive dismissal after his sales targets were trebled before any bonus became payable, the Tribunal said that it was 'bound to find that the contract of employment and the terms and conditions of his employment were being interfered with to such an extent that he could no longer continue in the workplace.'

Thus what we can take from all of the above is:

1. The 'reasonableness test is somewhat easier to 'attain' than the contract test.

2. The tribunal will examine all the circumstances of the case.

3. Where there is a unilateral change in terms and conditions of employment the Tribunal takes a very strict view.

Obligation to utilise the grievance procedure

[3.66] Whilst employees are generally expected to invoke or to try to invoke the employer's grievance procedure in an effort to resolve their grievance before resigning, this may not be so where the case is sufficiently serious. However, in *Feely v Fresenius Medical Care*[153] the EAT found that there had not been a breach of a significant term of the claimant's contract (the contract test). The EAT went on to find that the failure to invoke an employer's grievance procedure or speak to a trusted manager about her concerns were fatal to the constructive dismissal claim. In addition, the EAT found that the employee had not allowed enough time to pass to firmly establish whether her superior's behaviour towards her was as detrimental to her employment future as she believed. Equally in *Donovan v Dunnes Stores*[154] the EAT noted that, while a failure to use the grievance procedure is not necessarily fatal in a constructive dismissal case, the omission by the claimant to do this had greatly damaged her case. Added to that, the EAT noted the absence of medical evidence to support her contention that she suffered from work-related stress. Finally in *Garry Keogh v JTM Jumpstarters Limited,*[155] the employee failed on the basis that he had not brought his grievance to the respondent in spite of the fact that there was no grievance procedure in place. The EAT found that this did not outweigh the claimant's duty to have attempted all reasonable means within the company to resolve his grievances before resigning.

SURVEILLANCE OF EMPLOYEES/USE OF PRIVATE INVESTIGATORS

[3.67] Surveillance of employees is generally used where employers suspect something untoward; this may range from misuse of internet/email to suspicions of theft. Equally private investigators are usually used in situations of suspected dishonesty, but they may

---

152. *Melligan v Karmarton Limited* UD 101/2008, MN 105/2008.
153. *Feely v Fresenius Medical Care* UD 758/2008, MN 697/2008.
154. *Donovan v Dunnes Stores* UD 1163/2007.
155. *Garry Keogh v JTM Jumpstarters Limited* UD 1090/2008, MN 1000/2008.

also be used where an employee is absent due to sickness or where they are suspected of working elsewhere.

However, if an employer decides to dismiss an employee following the monitoring of the employee or the use of the private investigator, it is not sufficient to rely solely on the surveillance of either the monitoring equipment or the investigator's report. The decision must take account of all the circumstances. Thus in *Murphy v Galway City Council*[156] a private investigator was hired to observe an employee who was allegedly working elsewhere whilst on sick leave. The tribunal found that the claimant had been unfairly dismissed as the employer relied solely on the evidence of the private investigator.

Equally whilst employers may monitor employees, proper procedures must be observed. This by necessity involves putting all the evidence before the employee and allowing them a right of response.

In instances where an employee is accused of abusing the sick pay scheme or being absent while being able to work it is not sufficient for employers to simply rely on video or other evidence showing the employee either engaged in other work or involved in some activity which on the surface appears to be contradictory to their illness. Employers must be fully satisfied as to whether the employee is medically capable of performing their duties. Thus in *Malone v Burlington Industries (Ireland) Ltd*,[157] where the employee was seen on a farm while medically certified ill, the Tribunal held the dismissal unfair as there was a difference between being fit for industrial work for an eight-hour shift and 'doing a bit' around a farm or household.

Covert Cameras

[3.68] The use of covert cameras in the workplace is a difficult subject. Aside from the privacy issues raised, the European Convention on Human Rights Act[158] protects the right to private and family life.[159] As yet, the Act has not been pleaded before the Tribunal: however it does seem that if it were, the Tribunal would be obliged to interpret the Act[160] to comply with the Convention.[161]

In the EAT case of *James Caren v Celuplast & Conservatory Roofs Limited*,[162] the company had installed video cameras covertly in the storeroom. Subsequently, the Managing Director viewed video footage which showed the claimant, along with another loading pallets of panelling into the back of his delivery truck. The EAT held that the dismissal was fair. The EAT placed significant importance on the procedures undertaken by the employer. Specifically, it referred to the fact that the allegations were put to the employee and a thorough investigation was conducted. Of note however is that there was no challenge by the claimant as to the admissibility of the video tape evidence.

---

156. *Murphy v Galway City Council* UD1446/2005.
157. *Malone v Burlington Industries (Ireland) Ltd* UD 947/82.
158. European Convention on Human Rights Act 2003.
159. European Convention on Human Rights Act 2003, art 8.
160. The Unfair Dismissals Act 1977–2005.
161. The Convention for the Protection of Human Rights and Fundamental Freedoms Rome, 4.XI.1950. See the UK case of *Pay v Lancashire Probation Service* (2004) IRLR 129 EAT.
162. *James Caren v Celuplast & Conservatory Roofs Limited* UD 653/2003.

Against a background where the Convention on Human Rights Act is now law, the EAT may be more challenged in such cases.

Aside from the employment law aspects of this, the use of surveillance can give rise to difficult industrial relations issues. In 2001, management at the Procter & Gamble Plant in Nenagh, County Tipperary was forced to admit that a micro camera had been placed covertly in a smoke alarm. The decision to install the camera was taken without any staff consultation. Arising out of this, the company apologised and paid money to a charity nominated by the employees' Union (SIPTU). In 2004, notice of strike action was served by the SIPTU and AGEMOU trade unions on the National Car Testing Service allegedly due to the fact that Management began to use private detectives and hidden cameras to monitor employees. The Labour Court dealt with this issue in the case of *Crown Equipment v Amicus/AEEU*.[163] In this case, the Court recommended that the cameras which were to be used for process improvement should be deemed part of normal ongoing change, however they did also recommend that there should consultation with the union on a draft code of practice on the matter.

Use of private investigators for employment law and 'cross over' with personal injury litigation

[3.69] An interesting case in this regard is *Fogarty v Lufthansa Technik Turbine Shannon Limited*.[164] The claimant/employee began his employment as a welder in the employer's aircraft facility in 1993.

In or around July 2005, the employee claimed that he sustained a neck injury whilst at work. From August 2005 he went on sick leave and availed of the company sick pay scheme. He also subsequently took a personal injury claim for the injury sustained in this incident. The company had concerns about the injuries being reported and out of that concern put the employee under surveillance. The employee returned to work in September 2005 but as he did not present himself with a fitness to return to work cert he was sent home. As part of the surveillance of the employee the company medical officer concluded that the employee was clearly able to do heavy physical work without any restriction of neck movement and that this was contrary to what the employee told him during his examination. As a result of this the employer wrote to the employee in December 2005, providing him with various medical reports along with the relevant surveillance information. The employee was called to a disciplinary meeting. The employer felt that the employee was guilty of gross misconduct and subsequently dismissed him, as the video evidence had confirmed the employee's ability to work while he claimed he was unfit to work and benefited from the sick pay scheme at the time.

The EAT determined that the employer had taken advantage of its investigation of the personal injury claim to effect the dismissal in circumstances where enquiries from the employee were not adequately answered. The EAT specifically referred to s 6(2)(C) of the Acts which outlines that a dismissal shall be unfair if it 'results wholly or mainly'

---

163. *Crown Equipment v Amicus/AEEU* CD/03/571, Recommendation Number 17568.
164. *Fogarty v Lufthansa Technik Turbine Shannon Limited* UD 394/2006.

from 'civil proceedings whether actual, threatened or proposed against the employer to which the employee is or will be a party ...' As a result the Tribunal determined that the employee was unfairly dismissed. The Data Protection Commissioners Annual Report in 2009 contains a case study on surveillance. In summary the company, the subject of the complaint, asked a private investigator to survey an employee (a sales representative) without warning him beforehand. The Commission found this to be a breach of the terms and not justified. The Commission went on to state that covert surveillance is difficult to reconcile under the terms of the Act and at a minimum there must be strong evidence-based justification for it in the first instance. What can be taken from this is that if you have suspicions as to the activities of an employee, these must be dealt with separately to any personal injury claim. Also employees should be warned beforehand of the fact that surveillance may be used and that fair practices, including providing all the data to the employee, before taking a decision, must be used. It is submitted that this may not be that easy and the approach of the Tribunal in this instance seems to place unnecessary burden and expense on employers.

IMPORTANCE OF PROCEDURES

[3.70] The original Act did not lay down procedures for employers to follow in proceeding to dismiss an employee. Nonetheless, the Tribunal and the courts over the years have provided that the basic rules of fairness and natural justice should apply to every dismissal. These include:

- the right of the employee to a fair hearing;

- the right of the employee to be informed that a problem exists;

- the right of the employee to representation;

- the right of the employee to state their case;

- the right of the employee to be presented with the evidence before them and to have an opportunity to examine same and refute same.

The Industrial Relations Act 1990 allowed for the first time for the setting down of codes of practice. The first of these codes – the Industrial Relations Act 1990 (Code of Practice on Grievance and Disciplinary Procedures) (Declaration) Order 2000 (SI 146/ 2000) provides a template to employers on how to handle disciplinary issues in the workplace. Whilst not legally binding it is considered by the Tribunal to be best practice and employers need to be mindful of it.

Also s 7(2) as amended by the 1993 Act provides that the Tribunal in determining the amount of compensation is required to have regard to:

1.   the extent (if any) to which the financial loss is attributable to an act, omission or conduct by or on behalf of the employer;

2.   the extent (if any) of the compliance or failure to comply by the employer with an agreed or established disciplinary procedure.

In relation to the latter the code of practice established under SI 146/2000 is of particular importance (also see **Ch 4**).

REASONABLENESS OF THE EMPLOYER'S DECISION

[3.71] The first question that arises from the Tribunal's perspective in assessing the fairness or otherwise of a dismissal, is the reason for the dismissal, or the reasons, if there is more than one. The reason for dismissal must have existed at the date of dismissal.[165] Section 6(6) of the Act provides that the employer must demonstrate that the dismissal 'resulted wholly or mainly from one or more of the matters specified in subsection 4 of this section or that there were other substantial grounds justifying the dismissal'.

Whilst the words 'wholly or mainly' are not defined in the Act, it may be inferred from the above wording that there must be at least one reason for the dismissal.

Equally, s 14(4) of the Act states that an employer, if requested, must:

> ... furnish to the employee within 14 days of the request, particulars in writing of the grounds for the dismissal, but in determining for the purposes of this Act whether the dismissal was unfair there may be taken into account any other grounds which are substantial grounds and which would have justified the dismissal.

Therefore, there is an additional inference in s 14 that there must be grounds for the dismissal.

This is not necessarily the case when it comes to the Tribunal considering what redress to order. Here the Tribunal can take into account 'post dismissal' events. Thus in *Loughran v Bellwood Ltd*[166] the Tribunal recognised the employer's right to introduce evidence after the dismissal to verify an act of misconduct which formed part of the reason to dismiss.

It is vitally important that the person who took the decision to dismiss is present at the Tribunal hearing. Thus in *Byrne v Telecom Éireann*[167] the Tribunal held that in the absence of evidence from the persons who took the decision to dismiss,[168] the employer had failed to discharge the onus of proof.

RESIGNATION FOLLOWED BY UNILATERAL WITHDRAWAL

[3.72] Workplaces, by their very nature, are contentious places: often disagreements will arise and employees and employers will do things on the spur of the moment that they regret subsequently. Some of these disagreements may not be so serious as to go to the root of the contract but some may. Often it arises that during heated discussions

---

165. See *Madden v Brown Thomas & Co Ltd* UD 263/1992.
166. *Loughran v Bellwood Ltd* UD 206/1978.
167. *Byrne v Telecom Éireann* UD 24/1990.
168. In this instance it was the Board of Directors – this case highlights the difficulties where there is collective responsibility.

employees resign and upon reflection withdraw their resignation. How does the Tribunal treat this?

Generally, an employee does not have the right to withdraw their resignation. However, the Tribunal has been flexible in its approach to this matter and will consider the context in which such resignations occur.

Thus, in the case of *McManus v Brian McCarthy Contractors*[169] the withdrawal of a resignation by an employee after her manager had allegedly verbally abused her was held to be an unfair dismissal.

Equally, in the case of *Kieran McHugh v The Sign and Graphic Centre Ltd t/a O'Reilly Signs*[170] the Tribunal found that following a disagreement between the employer and employee where the employee allegedly stated that 'he was fed up of this place and I am out of here', which was taken to be a resignation by the employer and was independently verified by another employee, was still an unfair dismissal.

The Labour Court case of *Charles Shinkwin and Donna Millett*[171] (relying on the UK case of *Kwik-Fit (GB) Limited v Lineham*)[172] was an application under the Employment Equality legislation: In this case it was held that an employee may withdraw a notice of resignation where special circumstances exist relating to the context in which the decision to resign was taken. The Labour Court stated that: 'The resignation must be withdrawn within a reasonable time which will probably be quite short. The test of reasonableness is an objective one decided in the circumstances of the case'. It was held that the refusal of the respondent to allow the complainant to continue in her employment amounted to a dismissal.

What we can take from all of the above is:

1. If an employee resigns in the heat of the moment it is not sufficient for the employer to merely accept that resignation as final;

2. If the words of resignation used are ambiguous they will generally be construed in favour of the employee;

3. Employers should allow a reasonable cooling off period.

REMEDIES

[3.73] Section 7 of the Act sets out the remedies open to the Rights Commissioner, the Tribunal and the civil courts following a finding of unfair dismissal:

*   section 7(a) provides for **reinstatement** of the employee in his previous position with effect from the date of dismissal and with the same terms and conditions of employment as before;

---

169. *McManus v Brian McCarthy Contractors* UD 946/2007.
170. *McHugh v The Sign and Graphic Centre Ltd t/a O'Reilly Signs* UD 334/2008.
171. *Charles Shinkwin and Donna Millett* [ED/03/33].
172. *Kwik-Fit (GB) Limited v Lineham* [1992] IRLR 156.

- section 7(b) provides for **re-engagement** of the employee in his previous position or in another reasonably suitable position on conditions (including pay) specified by the Rights Commissioner, tribunal or court; or

- section 7(c) provides for **compensation** of up to a maximum of 104 weeks' remuneration in respect of any financial loss caused to the employee by the unfair dismissal. Where an employee is found to have contributed to his own dismissal this amount may be reduced to take account of that percentage contribution.[173]

COMPENSATION

[3.74] Whilst the remedies of re-instatement and re-engagement are possible in practice, the majority of successful claims by employees fall to be dealt with under the compensation heading.

In general, the Employment Appeals Tribunal picks a broad approach and requires employers to compensate employees fully if the employer cannot prove the reason for dismissal and that they acted fairly. In this regard, the awards from the Employment Appeals Tribunal, whilst they tend to be small, are increasing somewhat. In particular over the last number of years there have been a significant number of large awards. In *Foley v Calview Investments Limited*[174] the employee was re-instated from the date of dismissal and the employer was ordered that wages be paid accordingly. The claimant was awarded over €300,000.00 but this payment constituted back pay and not compensation. Similarly, in *Basnet v Elan Pharma*[175] an award of €195,000.00 was made.[176] Equally, the value applicable to share options by an employee was accepted by the Employment Appeals Tribunal.[177]

Definition of Financial Loss

[3.75] The Unfair Dismissals Act 1977 gives no power to award exemplary damages. Financial loss is defined by s 7(3) of the 1977 Act to include:

1. Any actual loss, and

2. Any estimated prospective loss of income attributable to the dismissal and

---

173. For a definition of what is defined as remuneration see *Bunyan v United Dominions Trust Ltd* UD 66/1980. See also Purdy, 'employers beware! Stock options could be considered remuneration when defining compensation in an unfair dismissal case' Irish Employment Law Journal Volume II Spring 2005, 17.
174. *Foley v Calview Investments Limited* UD 1228/2003.
175. *Basnet v Elan Pharma* UD 737/2005.
176. See also *Ponisi v JVC Europe Ltd* UD 949/2008.
177. For a further discussion on share options see Purdy 'Employers beware! Stock options could be considered remuneration when defining compensation in an unfair dismissal case' Irish Employment Law Journal (Thompson – Roundhall Volume II No 1 Spring 2005). .

3. The value of any loss or diminution, attributable to the dismissal, of the rights of the employee under the Redundancy Payments Acts 1967 to 2003, or the value of any loss or diminution in relation to superannuation.

Therefore, remuneration includes allowances in the nature of pay and benefits in lieu of or in addition to pay. It is clear also that the objective of compensation is to make reparation to the claimant/ employee to fully compensate them for the loss suffered. Whereas it is for the claimant to prove loss, the Tribunal does not deem it necessary that the precise and detailed proof of every item of loss is actually produced.

Notwithstanding this, s 7(2) of the Unfair Dismissals Act 1977, as amended by s 6(b) of the 1993 Act clarifies the issue of compensation and goes on to state that regard shall be had to:

(a) the extent (if any to which the financial loss referred to in that sub-section was attributable to an act, omission or conduct by or on behalf of the employer;

(b) the extent (if any to which the said financial loss was attributable to an act, omission or conduct by or on behalf of the employee;

(c) the measures (if any) adopted by the employee or, as the case may be, his failure to adopt measures, to mitigate the loss aforesaid;[178]

(d) the extent (if any) of the compliance or failure to comply by the employer, in relation to the employee, with the procedure referred to in the sub-section (1) of Section 14 of this Act or with the provisions of any code of practice relating to the procedures regarding dismissal approved of by the Minister; [179]

(e) the extent (if any) of the compliance or failure to comply by the employer, in relation to the employee, with the said Section 14, and[180]

(f) the extent (if any) to which the conduct of the employee (whether by act or omission) contributed to the dismissal.[181]

Section 7(2)(A) deals with the calculation of financial loss and states that 'for the purpose of calculating financial loss, payments to the employee under (the Social Welfare Acts) in respect of any period following the dismissal concerned, or under the Income Tax Acts arising by reason of dismissal shall be disregarded'. This changed the position that prevailed prior to 1993 when payments under the Social Welfare Acts were deducted in respect of actual loss.

Section 7(3) then deals with financial loss in relation to the employee. Financial loss is defined in relation to the dismissal of an employee as including any 'actual loss' and any estimated prospective loss of income attributed to dismissal. It is clear in this regard

---

178. The word 'and' was deleted from the end of s 7(2)(c) by the Unfair Dismissal's (Amendment) Act 1993, s 6.
179. Section 7(2)(d) was inserted by the Unfair Dismissal's (Amendment) Act of 1993, s 6.
180. Section 7(2)(e) was inserted by the Unfair Dismissal's (Amendment) Act of 1993, s 6.
181. Section 7(2)(f) was inserted by the Unfair Dismissal's (Amendment) Act of 1993, s 6.

that the actual loss must be based on the net figures and it is the net figures, therefore, that the Tribunal must be concerned with in considering the loss. Also, in completing the loss, the EAT computes to that net loss taking into account basic pay, average bonuses, average overtime and prospective loss of income including any reduction in future net earnings and any loss of fringe benefits. Also of note are; loss of statutory protection, expenses, pension rights and stock options. All of these are, of course, limited to a maximum of 104 weeks' loss. The EAT decisions of *Bunyan v United Dominions Trust (Ireland) Limited*[182] and *Healy v Cormeen Construction Limited*[183] are both instructive in this regard.

Ability to Mitigate Loss

[3.76] An employee who is ill for the relevant period may face the prospects of winning their case but failing in respect of compensation as their loss of earnings would be assessed at zero. This is because in such circumstances the assessment of compensation is based on the claimant's availability to work.[184] Thus, in the case of *O'Meara v AIBP (Nenagh) Limited*[185] the claimant declared himself at the Hearing unable to return to his normal work because of his medical condition. He also stated that had been left with some disability in the long term. The Tribunal determined that it followed that he had suffered no loss and accordingly he was awarded the minimum four weeks' remuneration under the Amendment Act. This case also clarified the figure to be taken for calculating compensation when an employee is working short time. In this regard it is not the net figure being received by the employee whilst on short time but the figure he receives on normal working hours. The EAT determined this having considered the Unfair Dismissals (Calculation of Weekly Remuneration) Regulations 1977, reg 4 (Appendix E) which goes on to state:

> 'The weekly remuneration in respect of the relevant employment shall be his earnings in respect of that employment (including any regular bonus or allowance which does not vary having regard to the amount of work done and any payment in kind) in the latest week before the date o'.

Illness Resulting from Dismissal

[3.77] It has always been reasonably clear that if you cannot mitigate your loss because of an illness then there is no loss: it is somewhat less clear if that illness arises out of an act of the employer.

In *Maryland v City West Golf and Country Club*,[186] the EAT, in giving consideration to the cases such as *Eastwood v Magnox*[187] and *Johnson v Unisys*,[188] concluded that a

---

182. *Bunyan v United Dominions Trust (Ireland) Limited* 1982 ILRM 404.
183. *Healy v Cormeen Construction Limited* M263; UD 98/1978.
184. See *Murray v Reilly* UD 3/1978.
185. *O'Meara v AIBP (Nenagh) Limited* UD 1099/1993.
186. *Maryland v City West Golf and Country Club* UD 1438/2004.
187. *Eastwood v Magnox* [2004] IRLR 733.
188. *Johnson v Unisy* [2001] IRLR 279.

claim for psychological injuries resulting in financial loss constituted a claim for personal injuries at common law and it was not properly within its jurisdiction to consider financial loss in such instances. However, in the case of *Liz Allen v Independent Newspapers*,[189] Ms Allen had been unfit for work by reason of illness since her employment had ended. Ms Allen argued successfully at the Tribunal that her illness was attributable to the fact that it made her resign from her employment and claim constructive dismissal. As a consequence, she also argued successfully that her illness had led to a financial loss. Significant medical evidence was adduced by both parties and there was a dispute between both parties' medical experts both in relation to the duration of the illness and the nature of it. On balance, the Tribunal accepted the evidence of the claimant's medical witness as to the diagnosis and prognosis. The Tribunal ultimately held that the claimant's financial loss was contributed to by the conduct of the employer and awarded her 78 weeks' remuneration.

As you can see from the above, this issue is a matter of some debate but there have been several UK cases similar to this.[190]

UNFAIR DISMISSAL IN PRACTICE

[3.78] This section is designed to aid employers and assist them through the process when a former employee (a claimant) decides to pursue a case for unfair dismissal. Due to the very nature of our society today many employers will be faced with a barrage of letters and correspondence prior to the dismissal occurring. Advice during this stage of the process is absolutely vital. Unfortunately due to the varying nature of 'pre-dismissal' correspondence there is no clear process or procedure for dealing with such issues. Consequently this section begins after the dismissal.

Bringing a claim

[3.79] A former employee (the claimant) has a number of options in bringing a claim for unfair dismissal.

Their first option is to bring the claim to the Rights Commissioner who will hear the case and issue a recommendation.[191] An employer can object to the claim being heard and if this is so, the case is then referred to the EAT.

Rights Commissioner

[3.80] A claim will be investigated by the Rights Commissioner once it has been referred to him by the claimant and the employer has consented or failed to object to the hearing of the matter before the Commissioner.

---

189. *Liz Allen v Independent Newspapers* [2002] 13 ELR 84.
190. See Decision in *Devaney v Designer Wholesale Flowers Sundries Limited* [1993] IR LR.
191. See para **1.02**.

Claims

[3.81] To refer a case, the claimant has to fill out a complaint form and send it to the Secretariat of the Rights Commissioners Service in the Labour Relations Commission. The Unfair Dismissals (Claims and Appeals) Regulations 1977[192] provide that certain information must be contained in the Notice of Claim:

- name and address of the claimant;
- name and address of the employer;
- date of commencement of employment;
- date of dismissal;
- claimant's weekly remuneration.

The actual format of the claim does not matter once it complies with the above. In practice though, most claims are made on the official claims form.

The claim form should be studied in detail once received. In particular the following items should be checked:

- Is the proper name of the employer on the form?
- Are the commencement and dismissal dates correct?
- Is the figure for weekly remuneration the gross or the net figure? (The net weekly figure is the relevant one.)
- Is this figure accurate?

If the employer wishes to dispute any of this information it can be done on the day of the hearing by bringing all the relevant accurate data and presenting it. This may include such things as the employee's P45, pay slips, letter of offer, including commencement date etc.

Preliminary issues

[3.82] Once the employee has made the claim the employer will be contacted and asked whether he is prepared to allow the Rights Commissioner to investigate the claim.

At this juncture the employer should seek the advice of a representative. Some employers decide not to proceed to the Rights Commissioner on the basis that it is an unnecessary step that will ultimately lead in any event to one party appealing to the EAT. Furthermore, many employers do not want to have a negative recommendation on file and then have to appeal that to the EAT. It should be noted that in two thirds of cases (depending on the legislation) Rights Commissioners have found in favour of the claimants.[193] This fact alone is enough to 'scare' most employers off. Despite the fact that the EAT is a complete re-hearing of the case 'de nova', many take the view that it is still on record and will form the basis for any decision of the Tribunal. That said, there

---

192.   Unfair Dismissals (Claims and Appeals) Regulations 1977 (SI 286/1977), reg 3.
193.   Labour Relations Commission website.

are circumstances where the Rights Commissioner can be of more use than the EAT. Speaking from experience, these generally arise when there is scope for the case to be settled. There is more opportunity for 'side sessions' and negotiations at a Rights Commissioner Hearing than at the EAT, so some employers wishing to settle may prefer to take this route. This is where dealing with a representative who spends most of their time in this forum can prove invaluable.

Employers may object to a Rights Commissioner's investigation within 21 days of the giving to the employer of the notice of claim (where the case has been referred under the Industrial Relations Acts 1969–1990 or under the Unfair Dismissals Acts 1977–2001). Where such an objection is made, the Rights Commissioner cannot investigate the case. The applicant can instead request the Labour Court, if referred under the IR Acts, or the EAT, if referred under the Unfair Dismissals Acts, to hear the case.

Despite the fact that the Rights Commissioners generally ask employers to state their grounds of defence they are not required to do so. Indeed it may be prudent in some instances to 'keep your powder dry' so to speak until the actual date of the hearing.

A claimant must notify the Rights Commissioner of his claim within six months of the date of dismissal or in exceptional circumstances this may be extended up to a year.[194]

It should also be noted that s 8(10) of the Act, as substituted by s 7(d) of the Amendment Act, provides that:

- A dispute in relation to a dismissal as respects which a recommendation has been made by a Rights Commissioner or a hearing has commenced by the Tribunal shall not be referred under the Industrial Relations Acts 1946 to 1990 to a Rights Commissioner or the Labour Court.

- Where, in relation to a dismissal, a recommendation has been made by a Rights Commissioner or a hearing has commenced by the Labour Court under the Industrial Relations Acts, the employee concerned shall not be entitled to redress under the Unfair Dismissals Acts in respect of the dismissal.

This effectively bars claimants from having 'two bites of the cherry'.

The investigation

[3.83] A hearing by a Rights Commissioner is very informal. Hearings before a Rights Commissioner take place in private.[195] The employer's representative generally gives an outline of their case first, although this may vary at the discretion of the Rights Commissioner as no strict procedure is adopted. The claimant then generally gives their side of the case and invariably the Commissioner will thereafter seek to question both parties. Written submissions can be made. Employers need to consider tactically beforehand whether a written submission is appropriate. Generally it is but there may be

---

194.   Unfair Dismissals Act 1977, s 8(3) as amended.
195.   Except where the dispute has been referred under the Payment of Wages Act 1991. Hearings under that Act are generally held in public

instances where the opposite can be the case. Taking legal advice on this beforehand is again crucial. Invariably the Rights Commissioner will seek to talk to both parties separately to determine whether some agreement can be reached on the dispute. However, this may not always be the case. This generally occurs where it is evident to the Commissioner that the case of neither party is particularly strong.

Appeals

[3.84] If no agreement can be reached by the Commissioner he will proceed to issue a recommendation which is binding on the parties unless an appeal to the EAT is taken. If no appeal is taken within the prescribed time limit (six weeks)[196] the employer will be bound by the recommendation and if he fails to implement it a claimant may apply to the EAT to seek implementation of it (Form T1–D is used for this purpose, see **3.95**).

Form T1–B is used for appeals from the Rights Commissioner to the EAT. Note this is more suited to appeals by employees and care should be taken in completing same. It is reproduced at **3.96**. Employers are not specifically required to state their grounds of appeal but the Tribunal may request it, in which case it should be provided.

The Employment Appeals Tribunal

Claims

[3.85] Once a claim has been forwarded to the EAT the Tribunal will send notification to the employer. A copy of the claim form (either form T1–A (see **3.97**) which is used for direct claims to the Tribunal or form T1–B (see **3.96**) which is used for appeals to the Rights Commissioners recommendations) will accompany such notification. Once this is received the employer has 14 days to enter an appearance. This is done by way of a notice of appearance form known as a T 2 (see **3.96**).

Procedural issues

[3.86] The Redundancy (Redundancy Appeals Tribunal) Regulations 1968 (SI 24/ 1968) govern the 'order' of matters for unfair dismissal claims before the Employment Appeals Tribunal.

The tribunal is defined in reg 2 as the Employment Appeals Tribunal.[197] Regulation 4 provides that the notice of appeal shall be given on the form provided by the Minister and this is the basis for the form T1A.

Regulations 10 and 11 provide that the Chairman of the Tribunal shall from time to time fix dates, times and places for the hearing of appeals by the Tribunal and that the

---

196. Unfair Dismissals Act 1977, s 9(2).
197. The Redundancy (Redundancy Appeals Tribunal) Regulations 1968 (SI 24/1968), reg 2 originally referred to the Redundancy Appeals Tribunal. However, the Unfair Dismissals Act 1977, s 18 provided that this tribunal should be known as the Employment Appeals Tribunal and that references in the Redundancy Payments Act 1967 and any other Act of the Oireachtas and any instrument made under any Act of the Oireachtas to the Redundancy Appeals Tribunal should be construed as references to the Employment Appeals Tribunal.

hearing of an appeal shall be in public unless otherwise decided by the Tribunal at the request of either party.

Regulation 13 determines the procedure at hearings and provides that:

> A party to an appeal heard by the Tribunal may–
>
> (a)   make an opening statement,
>
> (b)   call witnesses,
>
> (c)   cross-examine any witnesses called by any other party,
>
> (d)   give evidence on his own behalf, and
>
> (e)   address the Tribunal at the close of the evidence.

Whereas the Tribunal has no jurisdiction in general to award costs against either party to an appeal[198] in certain circumstances, where in the opinion of the Tribunal a party to the proceedings had acted 'frivolously or vexatiously' the Tribunal can make an order that that party 'shall pay' a 'specified amount in respect of travelling expenses and any other costs or expenses reasonably incurred by that other party in connection with the hearing'.

Strictly speaking the rules of evidence apply before the Tribunal and more often than not solicitors and barristers will be asked to adhere to them. In contrast, significant leeway is often given, notably to non-legally qualified persons and in particular to claimants who do not have a representative present. The procedure before the Tribunal generally runs as follows:

- In Dublin the venue is Davitt House, 65(A) Adelaide Road, Dublin 2. Outside Dublin hearings are generally held in either the local court house or at a hotel.

- Both parties sit opposite each other.

- Everyone present rises when the Tribunal members enter and leave the room.

- The tribunal will generally check the details as set out in the T1–B form and ask both sides for submission on any points of contention. As stated above this is a vitally important part of the proceedings for employers and it is necessary to ensure that the Tribunal is made aware of the exact conditions of employment of the claimant. There may then be some opening submissions on points raised in the T1–B, eg if dismissal as a fact is in dispute or if the length of service of the claimant is in dispute or whether the claimant was in fact employed. Such issues should be raised at this juncture and an oral submission made to the Tribunal prior to introducing any witnesses to deal with same.

- If none of the above arises the next step is to make an opening submission outlining the background to your case. Sometimes the Tribunal will not entertain this but experience has shown that it is important for employers to do this and some insistence may be necessary on this point.

- Once this is done it is necessary to introduce your first witness. There is no guidance on the sequence of witnesses but it is usually prudent to introduce the

---

198.   Redundancy (Redundancy Appeals Tribunal) Regulations 1968 (SI 24/1968), reg 19(1).

person who actually dismissed the claimant first as this may negate the need for others to spend a lot of time in the stand. Generally, given the nature of such hearings, they tend to run over. This is not a positive point from an employer's perspective as by the time the second or even third day has come around the employer's point may have been 'watered down' or at worst lost completely on the Tribunal. Therefore, it is recommended to try and finish the hearing in one sitting (which is becoming less and less frequent) rather than allowing it to carry over.

- The main points in respect of witnesses is firstly to ensure that at no time do you lead them but vitally to ensure that at no time do they answer hypothetical questions either posed by the Tribunal itself or by the claimant's representative. Aside from this the other advice is to try and keep the examination as brief and to the point as possible. Most chairmen will not tolerate an examination that goes into periphery areas and wanders off the point. A tip here is to choose the core topics that you intend to explore and to base your questions succinctly around them.

- The next step is that the witness will be cross-examined by the claimant or their representative. As above, the tip here is to ensure that all answers are brief and to the point. There may be room for a small further examination of your witness at the end of the cross-examination but you need to ask the Tribunal's permission and you should not rely on this happening from the outset.

- Once all the employer's witnesses have been heard and cross-examined the employee and witnesses (if any) will also take the stand. Similarly they will be first of all examined by their own representative or in the absence of one the Tribunal will generally assist. The opportunity will arise for cross-examination. Styles obviously vary in respect of cross-examination but experience has shown that being aggressive with a witness (particularly the claimant) is often not in the best interests of the employer's case as it is frowned upon by the Tribunal. Occasionally if the claimant is being difficult and obtuse the Tribunal will intervene and this is more often than not more preferable than getting aggressive with a witness.

- When all witnesses have been heard the Tribunal will invariably give the opportunity to both sides to sum up. It is wise to remember this and to insist politely that you get the opportunity to summarise your points. Either after this or shortly before the Tribunal will deal with the remedy sought and loss sustained – **3.73**.

Form T1–A or form T1–B?

[3.87] Before replying by way of the T2 careful scrutiny should be given to the T1–A or T1–B form to ensure that the claimant has completed it correctly:

- In particular it is important to check under which Act the claim is being pursued.

- Employers should also ensure that the correct information including the company's registered office is provided. There have been cases in the past where the Tribunal has refused to hear cases because the name of the employer was incorrectly stated.[199] (More often than not the Tribunal will allow amendments to this on the day, but this cannot be guaranteed.)

- Employers should also give careful consideration to the dates. This is crucial for the various time limits such as the necessity to have one year's continuous service under the Unfair Dismissals Acts and to take the claim within six months of the termination of employment.

- Close regard should also be given to the normal weekly pay details provided by the claimant. In unfair dismissal cases the net figures are the appropriate ones and the rate of pay at the date of dismissal is the relevant figure. It will be necessary to also assess any benefits that the employee may have received to determine the actual loss to the employee. The most common of these are the provision of an occupational pension scheme and a company car. All details in respect of these benefits need to be brought to the Tribunal for the hearing. If there is a difference in the figures set out in the form as opposed to those actually received, the employer will have to provide evidence to dispute this on the day. Hence such items as pay slips, copy of pension details, returns made for BIK purposes etc should be made available where it is likely that any issue or dispute will arise.

- The grounds of application should also be studied carefully as these may provide useful information on the claimant's case. Further particulars can be sought if the grounds stated are vague. In some instances it may be vital, such as in a case where the claimant is alleging discriminatory dismissal or unfair selection for redundancy. In these instances it would be extremely useful to know who the comparators are so that the case can be prepared properly. In such cases it is good practice to request the Tribunal to seek these additional facts as a claimant is not obliged to respond unless the Tribunal asks for the information.

- Lastly it is useful to see what redress the claimant is seeking. Whilst the ultimate decision on this rests with the Tribunal a clear answer has to be given to the Tribunal at the end of the proceedings as to which form of redress an employer would prefer if the claim succeeded. Any hesitation at this point could lead the Tribunal to believe that reinstatement or re-engagement might be acceptable when the opposite may in fact be the case.

Form T 2 (Employer's Response)

[3.88] This form is a notice of appearance and in order to be represented at and attend the hearing it must be completed by the employer. It is a fairly minimalist form and only

---

199. See *Delaney v De La Rue Smurfit Ltd* UD/182/1983.

basic information is required. That said, it is vitally important to take time over its completion. The main part of the form that necessitates detailed thought is the section that requires employers to set out their grounds of defence. Over the years it has become apparent that the less employers put in to this section the better for them. Given the varied reasons for dismissal it is hard to say what exactly should be put in every T2 but experience suggests it is better to be brief, as further grounds can be added at the date of the hearing. Some suggestions are:

- The claimant was dismissed for gross misconduct in accordance with the company's disciplinary procedure.

- The claimant was dismissed following a long absence because he/she was incapable of fulfilling his/her contract of employment.

- The claimant was dismissed for repeated and sustained intermittent absence in accordance with the company's disciplinary procedure.

- The claimant was dismissed by reason of redundancy having been fairly selected for same.

Obviously every dismissal is different and requires different claims. It is also wise to place a general 'indemnity clause' at the end of the grounds of defence to the effect that additional grounds of defence may be added at the date of hearing. I would generally suggest phrases along the following lines:

> The respondent company reserves the right to adduce any further or other grounds of appeal at the hearing herein.

Whilst this may sometimes not be accepted by the Tribunal and notably whilst the Tribunal under reg 24 of SI 24/1968 has the power to 'require a party to an appeal to furnish in writing further particulars with regard to the facts and contentions contained in the notice of appearance' this is very rarely utilised. However, if the notice of appearance is not disputed beforehand, it puts both parties on notice that such additional grounds may indeed be raised. Whilst the Tribunal can ask for additional information the claimant is not entitled to seek such information. Finally you should try and respond to the T2 within the 14-day period as this is provided for in the regulations.[200] However, it is clear from the Supreme Court decision in *Halal Meat Packers (Ballyhaunis) Ltd v Employment Appeals Tribunal*[201] that, if the Tribunal takes a rigid view, that regardless of the merits of the case the employer is automatically barred by virtue of the non-entering of an appearance, its determination will be quashed by way of judicial review.

Adjournments

[3.89] In order to get an adjournment of an EAT hearing a party to a claim may appeal to any division of the Tribunal, sitting at any venue, to have the hearing adjourned. Regulation 14[202] provides that 'the Tribunal may postpone or adjourn the hearing of an

---

200. Redundancy (Redundancy Appeals Tribunal) Regulations 1968 (SI 24/1968), reg 9(1).
201. *Halal Meat Packers (Ballyhaunis) Ltd v Employment Appeals Tribunal* (1990) ILRM 293.
202. Redundancy (Redundancy Appeals Tribunal) Regulations 1968 (SI 24/1968).

appeal from time to time'. The procedure used by the Tribunal for appeals is that once an application is lodged they first send out an acknowledgement letter to the claimant, and they at the same time forward a copy of the notice of appeal (T1A) to the employer and ask him to complete the response form (T2). Once this is lodged the employer and the employee receive official notification of the date of hearing. This document will contain a clause stating inter alia that any adjournments are to be made before the Tribunal within five working days. The statutory basis for this is somewhat unclear but seems to be grounded in SI 24/1968, reg 14 which in effect provides a 'carte blanche' for the Tribunal to do as they wish in so far as adjournments are concerned. Also of note in this regard is reg 10 of SI 24/1968 which allows the chairman of the Tribunal to fix dates, times and places for the hearing of appeals and to provide notice of same. This would also seem to provide a statutory basis for the 'notice for hearing' in which the five-day time limit is set out. Regardless as to the statutory basis for this in practice, in order to have a chance of succeeding applications should:

- be made as soon as possible after the notification to appear has been received;

- be made by a party to the dispute or their representative appearing in person. A substitute representative will often be 'balked at' by the Tribunal;

- be made with the written consent of the other party or their representative;

- only be made in grave circumstances. Excuses such as one of the parties being on annual leave for example will generally be dismissed by the Tribunal.

It should be noted that even if these conditions are complied with, the Tribunal is loath to grant adjournments.

Witness summons

[3.90] Either party to a case may summon witnesses to appear at the hearing. This is done by way of application to the Tribunal to have a witness summons issued requiring the party to attend. Such applications need to be made well in advance of the hearing. The summons should be sent by registered post to the affected person, once received.

Production of documents/discovery

[3.91] There is no basis for the discovery of documents in the EAT. That said it is open to a party to a hearing to make an application before the Tribunal to ask the Tribunal to compel the production of any documents under a person's control which relate to the claim at issue.

Appeals

[3.92] Section 11(1) of the 1993 Act provides that:

> a party concerned may appeal to the Circuit Court from a determination of the Tribunal in relation to a claim for redress under the Principal Act within 6 weeks from the date on which the determination is communicated to the parties.

The Circuit Court has no jurisdiction to extend this time limit.[203] This time limit begins to run from the date that the written determination is communicated to the parties and not from the date that the decision was verbally communicated. The Circuit Court on appeal from the EAT will conduct a complete rehearing of the case and in this instance, unlike at the EAT, costs may be awarded.

If an employer fails to carry out a determination within six weeks, s 11(3) of the Amendment Act provides that the employee or the Minister for Enterprise, Trade and Employment, where he thinks it appropriate, may apply to the Circuit Court for an order directing the employer to implement the determination. The Circuit Court will only take evidence in relation to the non-implementation of the determination, ie they will not rehear the case in such instances. In addition the Circuit Court is empowered under s 11 to change the nature of the award from reinstatement or re-engagement to financial compensation. They may also award interest on an award of compensation from the date of expiry of the appeal and may make an order to pay the employee loss of wages in respect of the period during which the employer failed to implement an order of re-instatement or re-engagement.

The rules governing appeals to the Circuit Court are set out in Circuit Court Rules Order 57, Rule 1 – Unfair Dismissals Acts 1977–1993 (No 10 of 1977, No 5 of 1991 and No 22 of 1993). (This form (36A) is reproduced at **3.99**). There are a number of requirements:

> 1. All applications under s 10 of the 1977 Act or under s 11 of the 1993 Act whether by way of claim for redress by the Minister or by way of claim for enforcement or by way of appeal from the Tribunal have to be made by way of Notice of Motion and this has to set out the grounds upon which the plaintiff is relying for the reliefs sought. All such applications have to be in accordance with form 36A.

> 2. Applications shall be brought in the county where the employer concerned ordinarily resides or carries on any profession, business or occupation.

> 3. All applications must be served no later than 10 days prior to the return date set out in the motion either in accordance with the provisions as to service of civil bills and other documents contained in order 11 of the rules or by being delivered to or served upon the solicitor who is on record before the Tribunal as acting for the person named as the defendant before the court. Service of an application or any other document upon such solicitor, or delivery of the same at his office, or sending the same to him by prepaid post to such office shall be deemed to be good service upon the party for whom such solicitor acts upon the day when the same is so delivered or served, or upon which in the ordinary course of postage it would be delivered. The motion shall be listed for mention only on the return date set out therein at which time a date for hearing shall be fixed by the court.

> 4. Notice of every application must be given to the Tribunal. Such notice must be effected before the filing of the application by the delivery of a copy of the

---

203. *McIlwraith v Fawsitt* [1990] ILRM 1.

application at, or by sending same by prepaid registered post to, the office of the secretary of the Tribunal.

5. The following documents have to be filed with the application:

(a)   a copy of the original notice to appeal to the Tribunal;

(b)   a copy of the notice of appearance;

(c)   a copy of the determination of the Tribunal;

(d)   the original letter from the Tribunal notifying the making of communication of the said determination;

(e)   a copy of any particulars provided by either party to the Tribunal.

6. Every application made by way of an appeal from a determination of the Tribunal must contain a statement of the grounds upon which the applicant intends to rely. If the plaintiff wishes to appeal against part only of a determination of the Tribunal, the application has to clearly identify that part against which it is intended to appeal.

7. All applications shall be dated and bear the name, address and description of the plaintiff and shall be signed by his solicitor, if any, or if none, by himself.

8. Upon the application on notice of any party the judge may order any other party to deliver full and better particulars of any matters stated in the application, or to deliver copies of any documents referred to therein.

9. Save by special leave of the court or save as otherwise provided for by the Acts, all applications under the Acts are heard upon oral evidence.

10. The court may make such order as to costs as may be appropriate, having regard to the provisions of s 10 of the 1977 Act, including an order measuring the costs. This is dissimilar to the Tribunal where no costs are awardable.

11. The secretary of the Tribunal shall have the right of access to all the information contained on the file kept in the office of the county registrar in respect of each application and shall be entitled, upon request, to receive a copy of any written judgment delivered by the judge relating thereto.

It is noteworthy that the determination may be appealed in whole or in part. Therefore an appeal could be taken against the redress awarded without appealing the substantive finding. The application must, however, state the grounds of appeal. Thus if only part of the determination is being appealed that part must be clearly identified.

High Court

[3.93] The Act does not specifically provide for an appeal to the High Court but it has been accepted that an appeal under the Act is a 'civil action or matter' within the meaning of s 38 of the Courts of Justice Acts 1936 and that a full appeal does lie to the High Court.[204] The ordinary rules for appeals from the Circuit Court to the High Court apply (Order No 61) and such appeals must be lodged within 10 days of the Circuit Court decision.

---

204.   *McCabe v Lisney & Sons* (1981) ILRM 239.

FORMS

Official Form for Application to the Rights Commissioner under the Unfair Dismissals Acts

[3.94]

APPLICATION TO RIGHTS COMMISSIONER

UNFAIR DISMISSALS ACTS 1977 –1993

(PLEASE USE BLOCK CAPITALS)

EMPLOYEE'S DETAILS

Name: _____

Address:

_____
_____
_____
_____

Tel: _____

E-Mail: _____

Job Title: _____

COMPANY/EMPLOYER'S DETAILS
(Full legal name: if in doubt consult your P45/P60)

Name: _____

Address:

_____
_____
_____
_____

Tel: _____

E-Mail: _____

N.B.: IS YOUR EMPLOYER AWARE THAT YOU ARE BRINGING   YES__ NO__
THIS DISPUTE TO A RIGHTS COMMISSIONER?

Name and Address of your Representative (if any):

_____
_____

DATE ON WHICH THIS EMPLOYMENT BEGAN: ___/___/___
DATE OF DISMISSAL: ___/___/___
PAY PER WEEK (including benefits and regular overtime):

€_____GROSS

€_____TAKE HOME
REDRESS SOUGHT (reinstatement, re-engagement, or compensation):

_____
_____

HAVE YOU TAKEN UP NEW EMPLOYMENT SINCE YOUR
DISMISSAL?

YES_____ NO_____

IF YES, WHEN: ____/____/____

AT WHAT RATE OF PAY?:   € _____ per week

THE GROUNDS OF MY CLAIM ARE AS FOLLOWS:

_____

_____

_____

_____

_____

_____

EMPLOYEE'S SIGNATURE: DATE: ___/___/___

_____

PLEASE NOTE THAT A COPY OF THIS FORM WILL BE FORWARDED TO YOUR EMPLOYER.

Form T1–D

[3.95]

FORM T1-D **EMPLOYMENT APPEALS TRIBUNAL** Please read the notes supplied then complete this form in <u>BLOCK CAPITALS</u>. Please sign and date	**FOR OFFICIAL USE ONLY** Case No:

1. NOTICE OF CLAIM <u>FOR IMPLEMENTATION</u> OF A RIGHTS COMMISSIONER'S RECOMMENDATION (Please tick appropriate box or boxes)

☐	(i)	Unfair Dismissals Acts 1977 to 2007
☐	(ii)	Terms of Employment (Information) Acts 1994 and 2001
☐	(iii)	Protection of Young Persons (Employment) Act 1996
☐	(iv)	Protections for Persons Reporting Child Abuse Act 1998
☐	(v)	European Communities (Protection of Employment) Regulations 2003
☐	(vi)	Competition Act 2002
☐	(vii)	Consumer Protection Act 2007
☐	(viii)	Chemicals Act 2008

2. NAME AND ADDRESS OF PARTY SEEKING THE IMPLEMENTATION:	**3. NAME AND ADDRESS OF PARTY AGAINST WHOM THE CLAIM IS BEING BROUGHT:**
First Name: .... Surname: .... Address: .... Phone No .... Email Address:	Name/Company: .... Address: .... Phone No .... Email Address:

PLEASE ADVISE THE TRIBUNAL SECRETARIAT OF ANY CHANGE OF ADDRESS.

4. WILL YOU HAVE A REPRESENTATIVE AT HEARING? (Trade Union Official, Solicitor, etc.)
Yes   ☐   ☐

6. TOWN OF EMPLOYMENT OR NEAREST TOWN:

If yes, please give:
Name: ....
Address: ....
....
Phone No: ....

5. DATES (IF APPLICABLE)

	Day	Month	Year
Date of Birth			
Employment Began			
Dismissal Notice Received			
Employment ended			

7. PAY (IF APPLICABLE)

	€
Basic Weekly Pay	
Regular Bonus or Allowances	
Average Weekly Overtime	
Any other payments including payments in kind - specify	
Weekly Total Gross	
Net	

8. (i) NAME OF RIGHTS COMMISSIONER:
....

8.(ii) DATE AND REF. NO. OF DECISION/RECOMMENDATION TO WHICH THIS CLAIM APPLIES (Please enclose a copy of this decision/recommendation with your application)

9. THE REASONS FOR MY APPEAL ARE: (You can attach additional sheets if necessary)

Important Note: Incomplete forms will be returned and may delay the processing of your appeal

10. DECISIONS OF THE TRIBUNAL MAY BE PLACED ON THE TRIBUNAL'S WEBSITE
(Please refer to point (16) of Notes

SIGNED: _____ DATE: _____	Please note that where the Tribunal processes a claim for hearing, all correspondence (*forms, letters, enclosures etc.*) received in this office will be copied to, and exchanged between, the parties to the claim.

PLEASE ADVISE THE TRIBUNAL SECRETARIAT (01-6313006) IF YOU REQUIRE ANY SPECIAL FACILITIES WHEN ATTENDING A TRIBUNAL HEARING.

Form T1–B

[3.96]

FORM T1-B   **EMPLOYMENT APPEALS TRIBUNAL**
Please read the notes supplied then complete this form in <u>BLOCK CAPITALS</u>. Please sign and date

	FOR OFFICIAL USE ONLY
	Case No/s:

1. NOTICE OF APPEAL FROM RIGHTS COMMISSIONER'S RECOMMENDATION UNDER (Tick appropriate box or boxes)

	(i)	Unfair Dismissals Acts 1977 to 2007
	(ii)	Payment of Wages Act 1991
	(iii)	Terms of Employment (Information) Acts 1994 and 2001
	(iv)	Maternity Protection Act 1994 and 2004
	(v)	Adoptive Leave Act 1995
	(vi)	Protection of Young Persons (Employment) Act 1996
	(vii)	Parental Leave Act 1998-2006
	(viii)	Protections for Persons Reporting Child Abuse Act 1998
	(ix)	European Communities (Protection of Employees on Transfer of Undertakings) Regulations 2003
	(x)	European Communities (Protection of Employment) Regulations 2000
	(xi)	Carer's Leave Act 2001
	(xii)	Competition Act 2002
	(xiii)	Consumer Protection Act 2007
	(xiv)	Chemicals Act 2008

Organisation of Working Time Act 1997 – Appeals as to holiday entitlement can be made to the Employment Appeals Tribunal along with another Act. Otherwise it must be appealed to the Labour Court

PLEASE STATE IF YOU ARE THE <u>EMPLOYEE</u> OR THE <u>EMPLOYER</u>:

2. IF EMPLOYEE:

First Name: ....

Surname: ... .

Address: ....

....

Phone No: ....

Email Address::

2. IF EMPLOYER:

Name/Company: ....

Address: ....

....

....

Phone No: ....

Email Address:

3. WILL YOU HAVE A REPRESENTATIVE AT HEARING? (Trade Union Official, Solicitor, etc.)
Yes ☐   No ☐

If yes, please give:

Name: ....

Address: ....

....

Phone No: ....

3. WILL YOU HAVE A REPRESENTATIVE AT HEARING? (Employer Representative, Solicitor, etc.)
Yes ☐   No ☐

If yes, please give:

Name: ....

Address: ....

....

Phone No: ....

4. NAME AND ADDRESS OF PARTY AGAINST WHOM THE APPEAL IS BEING BROUGHT

Name: ....

Address: ....

....

Phone No: ....

PLEASE ADVISE THE TRIBUNAL SECRETARIAT OF ANY CHANGE OF ADDRESS.

5. Please enter the following dates (IF APPLICABLE)	Day	Month	Year
Date of Birth			
Employment Began			
Dismissal Notice Received			
Employment ended			

6. PAY (IF APPLICABLE)	€
Basic Weekly Pay	
Regular Bonus or Allowances	
Average Weekly Overtime	
Any other payments including payments in kind - specify	
Weekly Total Gross	
Net	

7. NAME OF RIGHTS COMMISSIONER

8. DATE AND REF. NO. OF DECISION/RECOMMENDATION TO WHICH THIS APPEAL APPLIES:
(Please enclose a copy of this decision/recommendation with your application)

9. TOWN OF EMPLOYMENT OR NEAREST TOWN:

10 THE REASONS FOR MY APPEAL ARE: (You can attach additional sheets if necessary)

A COPY OF THE RIGHTS COMMISSIONER'S RECOMMENDATION MUST BE FORWARDED WITH THIS FORM.

11. REMEDY SOUGHT (IF APPLICABLE):

IMPORTANT NOTE: INCOMPLETE FORMS WILL BE RETURNED AND MAY DELAY THE PROCESSING OF YOUR APPEAL

12. DECISIONS OF THE TRIBUNAL MAY BE PLACED ON THE TRIBUNAL'S WEBSITE
(Please refer to point (18) of Notes)

SIGNED: _____

DATE: _____

Please note that where the Tribunal processes a claim for hearing, all correspondence (*forms, letters, enclosures etc.*) received in this office will be copied to, and exchanged between, the parties to the claim.

PLEASE ADVISE THE TRIBUNAL SECRETARIAT (01-6313006) IF YOU REQUIRE ANY SPECIAL FACILITIES WHEN ATTENDING A TRIBUNAL HEARING.

Form T1B Notes

NOTICE OF APPEAL TO EMPLOYMENT APPEALS TRIBUNAL UNDER:

(i)   UNFAIR DISMISSALS ACT 1977 TO 2007
(ii)   PAYMENT OF WAGES ACT 1991
(iii)   TERMS OF EMPLOYMENT (INFORMATION) ACT 1994 and 2001
(iv)   MATERNITY PROTECTION ACT 1994 AND 2004
(v)   ADOPTIVE LEAVE ACT 1995
(vi)   PROTECTION OF YOUNG PERSONS (EMPLOYMENT) ACT 1996
(vii)   PARENTAL LEAVE ACT 1998-2006
(viii) PROTECTIONS FOR PERSONS REPORTING CHILD ABUSE ACT 1998
(ix)   EUROPEAN COMMUNITIES (PROTECTION OF EMPLOYEES ON TRANSFER OF
        UNDERTAKINGS) REGULATIONS 2003
(x)   EUROPEAN COMMUNITIES (PROTECTION OF EMPLOYMENT) REGULATIONS 2000
(xi)   CARER'S LEAVE ACT 2001
(xii)   COMPETITION ACT 2002
(xiii) CONSUMER PROTECTION ACT 2007
(xiv)   CHEMICALS ACT 2008

Organisation of Working Time Act 1997 – Appeals as to holiday entitlement can be made to the Employment Appeal: Tribunal along with another Act. Otherwise it must be appealed to the Labour Court.

Notes for Persons Making Appeal

THIS FORM IS TO BE USED BY PERSONS WHO WISH TO APPEAL A RECOMMENDATION / DECISION OF A RIGHTS COMMISSIONER TO THE EMPLOYMENT APPEALS TRIBUNAL UNDER ONE OR MORE OF THE ABOVE ACTS

PART A – TIME LIMITS

IMPORTANT: TIME LIMITS FOR PERSONS BRINGING AN APPEAL TO THE TRIBUNAL:

Note:
Appeals against a recommendation or Decision of a Rights Commissioner must be made to the Tribunal within a particular time-limit from the date the recommendation is communicated to you. The time limits for appeals under the various Acts are as follows:

UNFAIR DISMISSALS ACTS 1977 to 2007	Within 6 weeks to the Tribunal.
PAYMENT OF WAGES ACT 1991	Within 6 weeks to the Tribunal AND the other party
TERMS OF EMPLOYMENT (INFORMATION) ACT 1994 and 2001:	Within 6 weeks to the Tribunal.
MATERNITY PROTECTION ACT 1994 and 2004	Within 4 weeks to the Tribunal.
ADOPTIVE LEAVE ACT 1995	Within 4 weeks to the Tribunal.
PROTECTION OF YOUNG PERSONS (EMPLOYMENT) ACT 1996	Within 6 weeks to the Tribunal.
PARENTAL LEAVE ACT 1998-2006	Within 4 weeks to the Tribunal
PROTECTIONS FOR PERSONS REPORTING CHILD ABUSE ACT 1998	Within 6 weeks to the Tribunal
EUROPEAN COMMUNITIES (PROTECTION OF EMPLOYEES ON TRANSFER OF UNDERTAKINGS) REGULATIONS 2003	Within 6 weeks to the Tribunal
EUROPEAN COMMUNITIES (PROTECTION OF EMPLOYMENT) REGULATIONS, 2000	Within 6 weeks to the Tribunal
CARER'S LEAVE ACT 2001	Within 4 weeks to the Tribunal (This time limit may be extended for a further period not exceeding 6 weeks if the Tribunal considers it reasonable to do so having regard to all the circumstances)
COMPETITION ACT 2002	Within 6 weeks to the Tribunal
CONSUMER PROTECTION ACT 2007	Within 6 weeks to the Tribunal
CHEMICALS ACT 2008	Within 6 weeks to the Tribunal

PART B - NOTES

(1)   **Box 1 - TICK APPROPRIATE BOX OR BOXES:**
Tick box or boxes representing the Act or Acts under which you are appealing .

(2)   **Box 2 - NAME AND ADDRESS OF PARTY MAKING THE APPEAL:**
If you change your address after lodging this form, be sure to notify the Secretary, Employment Appeals Tribunal, Davitt House, 65A Adelaide Road, Dublin 2. In order to enhance the processing of applications we will use email, where applicable, to all parties at any stage in the processing of an appeal.

(3)   **EMPLOYER'S FULL LEGAL NAME AND ADDRESS:**
Any Order made by the Tribunal may not be enforceable if incorrect information is given. For assistance, please consult your P45 or where appropriate, the Companies Registration Office (01-804 5200). The employer's Registered (PAYE) No. may be obtained from your P45, P60 and Tax Certificate P.6CL.

(4)   **Box 3 - NAME, ADDRESS OF REPRESENTATIVE OF PARTY MAKING THIS APPEAL:**
It is not necessary to have representation before the Tribunal. However, if you have arranged for a representative to attend on your behalf at the Tribunal, notification of the hearing of your appeal will be sent to that person as well as to yourself.

(5)   **Box 5 - DATES:**
Insert relevant dates

(6)   **Box 6 - PAY:**
Basic Weekly Pay.
This means the basic pay before any deductions are made.

Average Weekly Overtime.
In unfair dismissal cases, overtime may be disregarded unless it is a normal feature of work. If it is a normal feature of work inasmuch as you are normally expected to work it, overtime pay is included in your normal weekly pay and overtime is included in normal weekly working hours.

Payments in Kind.
These would include the value of meals or board, use of company house, car or health insurance etc.

(7)   **Box 7 - RIGHTS COMMISSIONER:**
Please fill in the name of the Rights Commissioner that heard your case

(8)   **Box 8** – Please include the date the recommendation or decision was issued and the reference no. that appears on the signed decision. **Please enclose a copy of this decision with this form.**

(9)   **Box 9** - In this box please give the name of the nearest town where you worked or the nearest town to this.

(10)   **Box 10 - REASON FOR APPLICATION:**
Please give an outline of your case in the space provided. If you wish to provide further details, please attach any separate sheets to the form.

(11)   **Box 11 – REMEDY SOUGHT**
Please state what remedy you are seeking

(12)   **ACKNOWLEDGEMENT OF APPLICATION:**
If you do not get an acknowledgement of your application within a reasonable time you should contact the Secretary to the Tribunal by letter, telephone or email (details below).

(13)   **HEARING OF CLAIM:**
Once you have received an acknowledgement, your case will be listed for hearing as soon as possible at the nearest town to your place of employment. You will get at least 2 weeks notice of a date for hearing.

(14)   **ADJOURNMENTS:**
Adjournments may be granted only in **exceptional circumstances**. Otherwise, a case is expected to proceed at the time and place notified to the parties. When applications for adjournments are made, they may be made to any sitting Division of the Tribunal at any venue.

The following conditions should at least be met when applying for an adjournment. However, the existence of any one or all of these conditions should not be considered a guarantee for obtaining an adjournment.

      o   Good cause should be shown as adjournments are only granted for very grave reasons.

o   The application should be made at the earliest opportunity after receipt of the notice of hearing, save where the Tribunal for just cause dispenses with this requirement.

o   The application should be made by a party or his representative appearing in person.

o   Proof of consent from the other party or their representative may be required. The application can be made without consent but the Tribunal may require proof that consent was at least sought.

(15)   WITHDRAWAL OF APPLICATIONS:
If you are seeking to withdraw your application, the Secretary to the Tribunal should be notified in writing as soon as possible.

(16)   COSTS:
Frivolous or vexatious applications may lead to an award of costs against the applicant.

(17)   INFORMATION:
For general information regarding employment rights please contact the National Employment Rights Authority (NERA) at Lo call No: 1890 80 80 90 or submit your query using their eform, which is located in the 'Contact Us' section of their website www.employmentrights.ie

(18)   DATA PROTECTION
The Employment Appeals Tribunal holds data on all applications received. Data Protection is the safeguarding of the privacy rights of individuals in relation to the processing of personal data. The Data Protection Acts 1988 and 2003 confer rights on individuals as well as responsibilities on those persons processing personal data. Personal data, as covered by the Data Protection Acts, relates to the information on individuals and or sole traders only.

The Employment Appeals Tribunal provides copies of its decisions on its website. The decisions do not include the names of the parties (the name/s of the employee/s or the employer/s). The Data Protection Commissioner's web-site *www.dataprotection.ie* offers an explanation of the rights and responsibilities under the Data Protection Acts and information is also available from the Data Protection Commissioner's Office at Canal House, Station Road, Portarlington, Co. Laois; telephone number (057) 8684800.

(19)   USE OF INTERPRETERS
The Tribunal does not provide a language interpreter service. However, if you feel that an interpreter is essential to the hearing of the claim, you can make an application before a sitting Division of the Tribunal. **Please Note: An application must be made at least two weeks in advance of the hearing date.**

NOTE
Please Detach Form from Notes and send to;

Secretary
Employment Appeals Tribunal
Davitt House
65A Adelaide Road
Dublin 2

Telephone: (01) 631 3006
1890 220222 Lo-Call service from outside (01) area
Website: www.eatribunal.ie
Email: eat@deti.ie

Form T1–A

[3.97]

FORM T1-A   **EMPLOYMENT APPEALS TRIBUNAL**

Please read the notes supplied then complete this form in <u>BLOCK CAPITALS</u>. Please sign and date

FOR OFFICIAL USE ONLY
Case No/s:

1. NOTICE OF CLAIM TO EMPLOYMENT APPEALS TRIBUNAL (Please tick appropriate box or boxes: See II (1) of Notes)

(i) Redundancy Payments Acts 1967 to 2007 ☐

(ii) Minimum Notice and Terms of Employment Acts 1973 to 2005 ☐

(iii) Unfair Dismissals Acts 1977 to 2007 ☐

(iv) Organisation of Working Time Act 1997 ☐

2. NAME AND ADDRESS OF PERSON MAKING CLAIM

First Name: ....

Surname: ....

Address: ....

Phone No: ....

Email Address

Occupation: .... Sex........

P.P.S. No: ....

3. EMPLOYER'S FULL <u>LEGAL NAME</u> AND ADDRESS (Please see Note 3)

Name: ....

Address: ....

Phone No: ....

Registered (PAYE) No: ....

Is this a Limited Company? Please indicate
Yes ☐   No ☐

4. WILL YOU HAVE A REPRESENTATIVE AT HEARING? (Trade Union Official, Solicitor, etc.) (Please see Note 4)

Yes ☐   No ☐
If yes, please complete

Name: ....

Address: ....

Phone No: ....

5. PLEASE ENTER THE FOLLOWING DATES

	Day	Month	Year
Date of Birth			
Employment began			
Dismissal notice received			
Employment ended			

6. NORMAL WEEKLY PAY   €

Basic Weekly Pay	
Regular Bonus or Allowances	
Average Weekly Overtime	
Any other payments including payments in kind – specify	
Weekly Total Gross	
Net	

7. CLAIM UNDER REDUNDANCY PAYMENT ACTS

Has you employer issued you with a Redundancy Certificate?   Yes ☐   No ☐

Have you applied to your employer for a redundancy payment?   Yes ☐   No ☐

Have you applied to the Department of Enterprise, Trade and Innovation for a redundancy payment?   Yes ☐   No ☐

If yes, please attach copy of decision

8. TOWN OF EMPLOYMENT OR NEAREST TOWN

(Please enter below the nearest town to your employment)

PLEASE ADVISE THE TRIBUNAL SECRETARIAT OF ANY CHANGE OF ADDRESS.

9. CLAIM UNDER UNFAIR DISMISSALS ACTS

<u>IMPORTANT</u>

THE TRIBUNAL CANNOT HEAR YOUR CLAIM UNDER THE UNFAIR DISMISSALS ACTS UNLESS THERE IS AN OBJECTION TO A RIGHTS COMMISSIONER HEARING IT. (See Notes)

Please Insert "Yes" or "No" in each box below

Do you object? [   ]   Has your employer object[   ]

If you do not object, you may wish to send this application directly to the Rights Commissioners Service, Labour Relations Commission, Tom Johnson House, Haddington Road, Dublin 4.

---

10. THE REASONS FOR MY CLAIM ARE:
   (you can attach additional sheets of information if necessary)

11. REMEDY SOUGHT (IF APPLICABLE): (Please see Note 11)

IMPORTANT NOTE: INCOMPLETE FORMS WILL BE RETURNED AND MAY DELAY THE PROCESSING OF YOUR APPEAL

---

12. DECISIONS OF THE TRIBUNAL MAY BE PLACED ON THE TRIBUNAL'S WEBSITE
   (Please refer to point (18) of Notes)

SIGNED: _____

DATE: _____

<u>Please note</u> that where the Tribunal processes a claim for hearing, all correspondence (*forms, letter, enclosures etc.*) received in this office will be copied to, and exchanged between, the parties to the claim.

PLEASE ADVISE THE TRIBUNAL SECRETARIAT (01-6313006) IF YOU REQUIRE ANY SPECIAL FACILITIES WHEN ATTENDING A TRIBUNAL HEARING.

Form T1A Notes

NOTICE OF CLAIM TO EMPLOYMENT APPEALS TRIBUNAL UNDER:

(i) REDUNDANCY PAYMENTS ACTS 1967 TO 2007 AND/OR

(ii) MINIMUM NOTICE AND TERMS OF EMPLOYMENT ACTS 1973 TO 2005 AND/OR

(iii) UNFAIR DISMISSALS ACTS 1977 TO 2007 AND

(iv) ORGANISATION OF WORKING TIME ACT 1997

Notes for Persons Making Application

THIS FORM IS TO BE USED BY PERSONS WHO WISH TO MAKE A CLAIM TO THE EMPLOYMENT APPEALS TRIBUNAL UNDER ONE OR MORE OF THE ABOVE ACTS

PART A – TIME LIMITS

I. TIME LIMITS FOR PERSONS BRINGING A CLAIM TO THE TRIBUNAL

A.   **REDUNDANCY PAYMENTS ACTS:**

(i)   A claim for a redundancy lump sum payment must be

     (a) made to the employer
           or
     (b) referred to the Employment Appeals Tribunal

     within 52 weeks from

     (i) date of dismissal or
     (ii) date of ending of contract of employment.
     (Section 24 of the 1967 Act, as amended by Section 12 of the 1971 Act)

(ii)   In certain cases and for good cause the Tribunal may allow claims made within 104 weeks. (Section 24 of the 1967 Act as amended by Section 12 of the 1971 Act and Section 13 of the 1979 Act).

B.   **UNFAIR DISMISSALS ACTS:**

(i)   **Claims** must be lodged to the Tribunal **within 6 months** of date of dismissal. This time-limit may be extended to 12 months in cases where exceptional circumstances have prevented the lodgement of the claim within the normal time-limit of 6 months.

     (Section 8 of the Unfair Dismissals Act, 1977 as amended by Section 7(2)(b) of the 1993 Act).

(ii)   **Appeals** against a recommendation of a Rights Commissioner must be brought **within 6 weeks** of the date the recommendation is communicated to you. (Section 9(2) of the 1977 Act). For this purpose, use Form T1B to make your application to the Tribunal.

PART B - NOTES

If you wish to have a claim under the Unfair Dismissals Acts heard by the Employment Appeals Tribunal, **either party must first object to the claim being heard by a Rights Commissioner and must so state on the form.**

(1)   **Box 1 - TICK APPROPRIATE BOX OR BOXES:**
     •   Tick box or boxes representing the act or acts under which you are claiming protection.

     •   If you are bringing a claim under any of the acts mentioned at boxes (i) - (iii) you may also bring a claim under the **Organisation of Working Time Act, 1997 for holiday entitlements due.** In this case, please tick box (iv) and the relevant Act or Acts under which you wish to make a claim.

If you believe you are entitled to payment in lieu of notice remember to tick box (ii). **If unsure, please tick all boxes.**

(2) **Box 2 - NAME AND ADDRESS OF PERSON MAKING CLAIM:**
If you change your address after lodging this form, be sure to notify the Secretary, Employment Appeals Tribunal, Davitt House, 65A Adelaide Road, Dublin 2 as this may affect the processing and hearing of your appeal. In order to enhance the processing of applications we will use email, where applicable, to all parties at any stage in the processing of an appeal.

(3) **Box 3 - EMPLOYER'S FULL LEGAL NAME AND ADDRESS:**
It is important that the person making the claim states the correct name of the employer. **Any Order made by the Tribunal may not be enforceable if incorrect information is given.** For assistance, please consult your P45 or where appropriate, the Companies Registration Office (01-8045200 or email info@cro.ie). The employer's Registered (PAYE) No. may be obtained from your P45, P60 and Tax Certificate P.6CL.

(4) **Box 4 – NAME AND ADDRESS OF REPRESENTATIVE OF PERSON MAKING THIS CLAIM:**
It is not necessary to have representation before the Tribunal. However, if you have arranged for a representative, such as a Trade Union Official, Solicitor etc. to attend on your behalf at the Tribunal, notification of the hearing of your claim will be sent to that person as well as to yourself.

(5) **Box 5 - DATES:**

Complete all dates

(6) **Box 6 - NORMAL WEEKLY PAY:**

Basic Weekly Pay:

This means the basic pay before any deductions are made.

Average Weekly Overtime.
In redundancy cases this is normally pay for the average weekly overtime worked during the six months preceding the last three months of employment. In notice and unfair dismissal cases, overtime may be disregarded unless it is a normal feature of work. If it is a normal feature of work inasmuch as you are normally expected to work it, overtime pay is included in your normal weekly pay and overtime is included in normal weekly working hours.

Payments in Kind.

These would include the value of meals or board, health insurance, use of company house or car etc.

(7) **Box 7 – Appeals under Redundancy Payments Acts.**
If you are submitting a claim under the Redundancy Payments Acts, 1967 to 2007, please indicate if your employer has issued you with a Redundancy Certificate and if you have applied to the Department of Enterprise, Trade and Innovation for your redundancy payment. Please attached copy of the Department's decision.

(8) **Box 8 –** In this box please give the name of the town where you worked or the nearest town to this.

(9) **Box 9 –** The Tribunal cannot hear your claim under the Unfair Dismissals Acts unless there is an objection by either party to the claim being heard by a Rights Commissioner.

(10) **Box 10 - REASON FOR APPLICATION:**
Please give a brief outline of your case in space provided. If you wish to provide further details, please attach any separate sheets to the form.

(11) **Box 11 - REMEDY SOUGHT:**
Please state what remedy you are seeking. If you are claiming unfair dismissal, you can express a preference for reinstatement, re-engagement or compensation. You can change your mind at a later stage. The Tribunal will take your preference into account but will not be bound by it.

(12) **ACKNOWLEDGEMENT OF APPLICATION:**
If you do not get an acknowledgement of your application within a reasonable time you should contact the Secretary to the Tribunal by letter, telephone or email (details below).

(13) **HEARING OF CLAIM:**
Once you have received an acknowledgement, your case will be listed for hearing as soon as possible at the nearest town to your place of employment. You will get at least 2 weeks notice of a date for hearing.

(14) **ADJOURNMENTS:**
Adjournments may be granted only in **exceptional circumstances.** Otherwise, a case is expected to proceed at the time and place notified to the parties. When applications for adjournments are made, they may be made to any sitting Division of the Tribunal at any venue.

The following conditions should at least be met when applying for an adjournment. However, the existence of any one or all of these conditions should not be considered a guarantee for obtaining an adjournment.

- o   Good cause should be shown as adjournments are only granted for very grave reasons.

- o   The application should be made at the earliest opportunity after receipt of the notice of hearing, save where the Tribunal for just cause dispenses with this requirement.

- o   The application should be made by a party or his representative appearing in person.

- o   Proof of consent from the other party or their representative may be required. The application can be made without consent but the Tribunal may require proof that consent was at least sought.

(15)   WITHDRAWAL OF APPLICATIONS:
If you are seeking to withdraw your application, the Secretary to the Tribunal should be notified in writing as soon as possible.

(16)   COSTS:
Frivolous or vexatious applications may lead to an award of costs against the applicant.

(17)   INFORMATION:
For general information regarding employment rights please contact the National Employment Rights Authority (NERA) at Lo call No: 1890 80 80 90 or submit your query using their eform, which is located in the 'Contact Us' section of their website www.employmentrights.ie

(18)   DATA PROTECTION
The Employment Appeals Tribunal holds data on all applications received. Data Protection is the safeguarding of the privacy rights of individuals in relation to the processing of personal data. The Data Protection Acts 1988 and 2003 confer rights on individuals as well as responsibilities on those persons processing personal data. Personal data, as covered by the Data Protection Acts, relates to the information on individuals and or sole traders only.

The Employment Appeals Tribunal provides copies of its decisions on its website. The decisions do not include the names of the parties (the name/s of the employee/s or the employer/s). The Data Protection Commissioner's web-site *www.dataprotection.ie* offers an explanation of the rights and responsibilities under the Data Protection Acts and information is also available from the Data Protection Commissioner's Office at Canal House, Station Road, Portarlington, Co. Laois; telephone number (057) 8684800.

(19)   USE OF INTERPRETERS
The Tribunal does not provide a language interpreter service. However, if you feel that an interpreter is essential to the hearing of the claim, you can make an application before a sitting Division of the Tribunal. **Please Note: An application must be made at least two weeks in advance of the hearing date.**

NOTE
Please Detach Form from Notes and send to;

Secretary
Employment Appeals Tribunal
Davitt House
65A Adelaide Road
Dublin 2

Telephone: (01) 631 3006
1890 220222 Lo-Call service from outside (01) area
Website: www.eatribunal.ie
Email: eat@deti.ie

Form 36A (Circuit Court Appeal Form)

[3.98]

FORM 36A

AN CHUIRT CHUARDA

THE CIRCUIT COURT

CIRCUIT COUNTY OF

IN THE MATTER OF THE UNFAIR DISMISSALS ACTS, 1977–1993

NOTICE OF MOTION FOR RELIEF UNDER SECTION 10 OF THE UNFAIR DISMISSALS ACT, 1973 OR SECTION 11 OF THE UNFAIR DISMISSALS (AMENDMENT) ACT, 1993

BETWEEN

.... Plaintiff

AND

.... Defendant

Take notice that application will be made to the Court on the

or the next opportunity thereafter for the following reliefs:

[Here insert details of the relief sought whether by way of redress by the Minister, enforcement or appeal.]

And further take notice that the said application will be grounded upon:

1. [here insert grounds upon which the Applicant is relying for the reliefs sought]

2. [here insert basis of jurisdiction]

3. [here insert name, address and description of the Plaintiff]

FORM 36A (continued)

4. [The following documents must be annexed to this Notice of Motion namely a copy of the original Notice to Appeal to the Tribunal; a copy of the Notice of Appearance; a copy of the determination of the Tribunal; the original letter from the Tribunal notifying the making of communication of the said determination; a copy of any particulars provided by either party to the Tribunal.]

Dated the day of

Signed ....

Plaintiff/Solicitor for the Plaintiff

To: ....

The Defendant/Solicitor for the Defendant

And

To: The Employment Appeals Tribunal

And

To: The County Registrar

Form T2

[3.99]

> IN ORDER TO ACKNOWLEDGE RETURN RECEIPT OF THIS FORM YOU ARE
> ASKED TO SUPPLY, IF POSSIBLE, A DEDICATED EMAIL ADDRESS.

EMAIL ADDRESS:

FORM T2 | Case No: |

EMPLOYMENT APPEALS TRIBUNAL

- ☐ (i) Redundancy Payments Acts, 1967 to 2003
- ☐ (ii) Minimum Notice and Terms of Employment Acts, 1973 to 2001
- ☐ (iii) Unfair Dismissals Acts, 1977 to 2001
- ☐ (iv) Protection of Employees (Employers' Insolvency) Acts, 1984 to 2001
- ☐ (v) Organisation of Working Time Act, 1997

NOTICE OF APPEARANCE

by a party against whom a claim has been lodged under the legislation ticked above

by _____

against _____

N.B. If employer's name is different from above, please give employer's correct legal name.

Do you have a representative acting for   Yes _____   No _____
you?

If yes, please give name and address:

Do you dispute the claim/s being made?   Yes _____   No _____

If yes, please state the claim/s at no.'s (i) to (v) above being disputed:

P.T.O

139

Please set out the reasons in the space provided below:

(Note: While you should try to set out your case as fully as possible, you will not be necessarily confined to what is given on this form at the hearing.)

DECISIONS OF THE TRIBUNAL MAY BE PLACED ON THE TRIBUNAL'S WEBSITE
(Please refer to point (7) of Notes)

Signed: _____

Date: _____

Chapter 4

FAIR PROCEDURES AND NATURAL JUSTICE: INVESTIGATIONS AND DISCIPLINARY HEARINGS IN THE WORKPLACE

PROCEDURAL FAIRNESS

[4.01] The Unfair Dismissals Act, when it was passed in 1977, came in for stern criticism from some members of the trade union movement allowing as it did (and still does) a mechanism by which employers can fairly dismiss employees. This, of course, is within a particular context, ie that it is done fairly. Fairness in employment law rests on a number of factors:

1. Whether the employee's 'behaviour' falls within one of the fair reasons for dismissal as outlined in the Act.

2. Whether the employer's behaviour was reasonable. Reasonableness is somewhat subjective (see **3.71**) and whereas it is an important factor for the Tribunal in determining whether a dismissal was fair or unfair and indeed this is enshrined in the Act,[1] it is not a procedural issue per se although it can be deemed to be unreasonable to breach procedure or natural justice.

3. Whether the employer followed fair procedures and natural justice. This can 'neatly' be further divided in three, ie:

   (a) whether the employer followed the disciplinary procedure as outlined in the contract of employment and/or company handbook;

   (b) whether the employer afforded the employee his rights to natural and constitutional justice;

   (c) whether the employer breached any code of practice.

The company's disciplinary procedure

[4.02] Under s 6(7) of the Unfair Dismissals Act 1977, as amended, in determining whether a dismissal is unfair, the EAT can have regard to:

(a) the reasonableness or otherwise of the conduct of the employer in relation to the dismissal; and

(b) the extent of the compliance or failure to comply with the employer's dismissal procedure or with the provisions of any code of practice by the employer.

Section 6(7)(b) is the operative section in so far as compliance with procedures is concerned. Notably the section does not provide that a breach of procedure is unfair: it

---

1. See Unfair Dismissals Act 1977, s 6(7)(a).

merely says that the Tribunal can have regard to the failure to comply with such procedures when reaching a determination.

The inference, of course, is that in dismissing an employee, employers will be expected to follow their own procedures. Typically in this jurisdiction, disciplinary procedures follow a corrective path, ie they generally start with counselling, then move to verbal, written, final written warning and ultimately dismissal. This system, albeit common in Ireland, has significant downsides:

1.   It deals with employees whose performance is not improving by imposing increasingly greater sanction on them. This is hardly corrective.

2.   It (in experience) rarely if ever works and often leads to counter claims by employees that they are being bullied, harassed or stressed by their employer.

3.   Equally the procedure takes so long to finalise that both employers and employees get stressed about it.[2]

Regardless as to the merits of this system, once it is inserted in the contract of employment and/or company handbook, it must be adhered to by employers if they are to sustain a case for fair dismissal.

Fairness of disciplinary procedures

[4.03] It may seem logical but even if an employer has detailed disciplinary procedures those procedures in themselves must be fair. The Code of Practice on Grievance and Disciplinary Procedures[3] provides a guide in this respect. Whilst the Code is admissible in evidence, it is not binding:

> Equally employers need to be mindful of s 14(1) of the Act which provides that employers must give an employee notice in writing not later than 28 days after he enters a contract of employment of the; 'procedure which the employer will observe before and for the purpose of dismissing the employee' and under s 14(2) any change in that policy must be notified to the employee within 28 days.

Universal and consistent application of disciplinary procedures

[4.04] Not only must there be a detailed disciplinary policy, but also there is an onus on employers to apply that policy consistently. Difficulties in this area often arise where certain behaviour has been tolerated by employers: this may include such things as employees 'clocking in or swiping in' for one another, or where there is laxity around break times. In such circumstances it is incumbent upon employers to specifically bring it to employees' attention that their policy has been changed and that such behaviour will not be tolerated in future.[4]

---

2.   Best practice in this area would suggest a more constructive approach. For a discussion on this see Redmond, *Dismissal Law in Ireland* (Bloomsbury Professional, 2007).

3.   Code of Practice on Grievance and Disciplinary Procedures (SI 146/2000).

4.   See *O'Neill v RSL (Ireland) Ltd* [1990] ELR 31.

Rights to natural and constitutional justice

[4.05] Natural justice embodies two basic elements: *audi alteram partem*, which translated literally means 'hear the other side', and *nemo iudex in causa sua*, which translated means 'no one should be a judge in their own cause'. Constitutional justice embodies natural justice but goes beyond it to include other guarantees such as the right to sue for damages and the right to an administrative decision within a reasonable time.[5] Over time, the rights to natural and constitutional justice have become intertwined in use in the EAT and can now be loosely collated into a number of rules applied by the Tribunal (albeit again loosely) as follows:

1. The employee must be aware of what is expected from them and the consequences of shortcomings. This is stressed in the Code of Practice on Grievance and Disciplinary Procedures from the Labour Relations Commission which goes on to state that 'It is important procedures of this kind exist and the purpose, function and terms of such procedures are clearly understood by all concerned'. Thus, in *Harris v PV Doyle Hotels*[6] where the claimant was dismissed for drinking on the premises it was held to be an unfair dismissal as the company had not made employees sufficiently aware that this would result in summary dismissal.

2. The employer must primarily determine all allegations against the employee before commencing disciplinary action. Whilst having clear rules and procedures is necessary it is vital that those rules are applied to the facts prior to the employer takes disciplinary action[7] (see **4.06** below on investigations).

3. The employee must be informed of all of the allegations against them. This does not mean that the employer must inform the employee in advance of the first meeting the purpose of same.[8] The employee must also be provided with all relevant documentation and be given an opportunity to defend himself or provide an explanation.[9] Thus, in *Gearon v Dunnes Stores Ltd*,[10] the Tribunal stated:

> 'the right to defend herself and have her arguments and submissions listened to and evaluated by the respondent in relation to the threat to her employment is a right of the claimant and is not the gift of the respondent or this Tribunal ... As the right is a fundamental one under natural and constitutional justice; it is not open to this Tribunal to forgive its breach'.

4. The employee is entitled to representation. This does not necessarily mean legal representation, although if dismissal is contemplated it generally does. This was the

---

5. See *McCormack v Garda Complaints Board* [1997] 2 IR 489, see also Hogan and Whyte, *JM Kelly the Irish Constitution* (4th edn, Bloomsbury Professional, 2003).

6. *Harris v PV Doyle Hotels* UD 150/1978.

7. See *Vanfleet Transport Ltd v Mark Murphy* (25 Nov 1988, unreported), HC.

8. See *Eanna Dowling v Cumann na Daoine Aontaithe Teo* (UD 545/2007) where the EAT held that as suspension was not a disciplinary action, the principles of natural justice did not apply.

9. See *Moran v Bailey Gibson Ltd* UD 69/1977; *McCarthy v Irish Shipping* US 100/1978; *McGarrigle v Donegal Sports and Golf Centre Ltd* UD 680/2002.

10. *Gearon v Dunnes Stores Ltd* UD 367/1988.

principle set down by the High Court in *Stoskus v Goode Concrete Limited*[11] and the Supreme Court decision in *Alan Burns and Another v The Governor of Castlerea Prison*.[12] This entitlement does, however, always amount to the right to have a trade union official or fellow employee present. (See also **4.11**.)

5. The investigation must be carried out in an impartial manner. Thus, in the case of *Eanna Dowling v Cumann na Daoine Aontaithe Teo*,[13] where the decision to dismiss was taken by the employer's management committee which consisted of eight members, two of whom had been involved in the investigatory and disciplinary stages of the process, this was held to be unfair and 'contrary to the concepts of reasonableness and fairness'. The case mentioned at **3.53**, *Graham v Portroe Stevedores,*[14] is also instructive in this regard. In this case, the employee was given the maximum compensation available to the Tribunal following a late night altercation which was investigated by the HR manager who himself was a witness to the incident.

6. The employee is entitled to question the facts and examine all relevant witnesses. This is probably one of the most difficult issues for employers. In certain circumstances such as in cases of alleged sexual harassment, allowing one employee to cross-examine another may not be practical, possible or advisable. Also some witnesses may wish to provide information in confidence. In all of this there are some basic guidelines:

     i.   The employee, if it is practical, should be offered the opportunity to have all witnesses brought to the disciplinary meeting, the complainants and/or accusers should be named and the employee should be afforded the right to meet them face to face. This is best practice and preferable.

     ii.   Only in certain very limited circumstances is it appropriate to deny an employee the right to cross-examine witnesses. This will generally arise where there is a need to protect those witnesses either from a medical perspective or from some other threat such as violence. At all times this decision has to be balanced against the risk of a serious injustice to the employee. In only the most serious of cases should this arise![15]

     iii.   It is generally mistaken for employers to proceed to dismiss someone based on confidential information. In the case of *McNamara v Lannit (Ireland) Ltd*[16] the Tribunal went on to say: 'It is most unusual for a tribunal to accept the word of an employer as to the reliability of its informants when the Tribunal itself has no other evidence of it'. (See also the use of private investigators at **3.67**.)

7. Finally, employees have the right to be treated as individuals. All individuals have different personalities and characteristics. In some instances it will be necessary, and

---

11.   *Stoskus v Goode Concrete Limited* (2007) IEHC 432.
12.   *Alan Burns v The Governor of Castlerea Prison* [2009] IESC 33.
13.   *Eanna Dowling v Cumann na Daoine Aontaithe Teo* UD 545/2007.
14.   *Graham v Portroe Stevedores* UD 574/2006.
15.   See *A Worker v A Hospital* (1997) ELR 214.
16.   *McNamara v Lannit (Ireland) Ltd* UD 910/1984.

indeed desirable, to take account of such characteristics. An employee who is blind will require extra facilities, similarly an employee who has a disability will need extra time and consideration to explain themselves adequately. Consideration needs also to be shown to foreign nationals who may require an interpreter in order to make them fully understand the process and the allegations being levelled at them.

INVESTIGATIONS

[4.06] Workplace investigations can arise in many instances: most of these concern complaints of bullying or harassment or disciplinary investigations. The law in relation to this area is detailed, complex and often misleading. In general, the High Court takes the view that it will not interfere in the internal workings of a company[17] (which clearly includes investigations) yet there are numerous examples of where it has done just that.[18] At the end of the day, the effect of these decisions on employers is a lack of clearly defined 'dos and don'ts', leading to the most basic investigations becoming bogged down with claims from lawyers for procedural fairness, oral hearings coupled with stenographers, demands for lists of witnesses beforehand and the ability to cross-examine such witnesses, a process further complicated when there is a need for confidentiality and speedy resolution. All of which inevitably culminates in a breakdown of the disciplinary process and the matter being compromised by both parties.

The fundamental issue, that the courts wrestle with and that employers must consider, is the applicability of the right to fair procedures and natural justice to the investigation process.

Also, it is sometimes difficult to ascertain when an investigation ends and when a formal disciplinary hearing commences, as often one naturally evolves into the other. At one end of the scale it is clear that employers are entitled to ask their employees reasonable questions and to expect to be provided with reasonable answers. At the other end it is clear that employees are entitled to be fully protected during a formal disciplinary investigation.

Therefore, if I ask one of my employees where they were yesterday, with the purpose of ascertaining whether the expense sheet that they submitted yesterday was correct and they reply 'Cork', is this a formal investigation that requires the employee to be put on full notice of her rights to fair procedures and natural justice? Clearly not! If, however, once the employee answers 'Cork' and I then say 'I saw you in Dublin, yet you have claimed travelling expenses to and from Cork for the day', and failing no reasonable explanation from the employee, I then say 'I have to suspend you with pay pending a formal investigation of this matter'! Have I now strayed into a formal investigation which requires me to afford the employee full rights of natural and constitutional justice? The answer is yes.

---

17.   See *Turner v O'Reilly* [2006] IEHC 92, Hedigan J.
18.   See *Boland v Phoenix Shannon plc* [1997] ELR 113.

DISTINCTION BETWEEN INFORMAL AND FORMAL INVESTIGATION

[4.07] In the case of *O'Sullivan v Mercy Hospital Cork*,[19] Clarke J made the distinction between an entirely informal investigation carried out by an employer for the purposes of ascertaining whether there might be a basis for initiating disciplinary procedures which do not purport to reach conclusions other than perhaps to determine that disciplinary proceedings should be instigated, and on the other hand statutory schemes which require a decision of a particular body as to the existence of a prima facie case as a prerequisite to formal disciplinary proceedings.

Clearly, in the former there is no right to fair procedures and natural justice whereas in the latter there is. Whilst this clarification is welcome, the lines are more than often not that distinct, particularly in private sector employment.

What we can take from the above is:

1. Where it is merely an informal investigation there is no requirement to afford the full rights to natural justice.

2. When commencing an investigation it is best to make it clear that the initial investigation is merely that, that no conclusions will be reached other than to determine whether disciplinary proceedings should be instigated.

3. Once the investigation is finalised and if it is concluded that disciplinary proceedings should be initiated, then the employee should be put on notice of their right to representation, fair procedures etc.

INDEPENDENT INVESTIGATORS

[4.08] Quite an industry has grown up around independent investigations. This is so because in particular the Code of Practice on Sexual Harassment and Harassment at Work from the Equality Authority, provides that in investigating a complaint the:

> '... investigation should be, and be perceived to be, independent and objective. The purpose of the investigation is to investigate the allegations and will focus on the complaint. Those carrying out the investigation should not be connected with the allegation in any way'.

In practically every organisation, small or large, the only way to ensure absolute independence and to ensure no connection with the allegation in an investigation is to appoint an external person. This has obvious advantages but often these are met with substantial, generally financial, disadvantages as these investigations take considerable time.

Whilst in general it is not necessary to appoint an outside investigator, in some circumstances it will be inevitable.

The question of whether the employee the subject matter of the investigation can object to the person appointed by the company was the subject matter of an application

---

19.   *O'Sullivan v Mercy Hospital Cork* (3 June 2005, unreported), HC, Clarke J.

for interlocutory relief in the case of *Harrington v Irish Nationwide Building Society*.[20] Here, Mr Harrington had been suspended by the building society for alleged irregularities. The society appointed the author to carry out the investigation. Mr Harrington objected on the basis that he should have an input into the choice of investigator. The court found against him.

It is clear from this that unless it can be shown that the investigator his/herself is biased (which in itself could give rise to a claim for defamation if proven incorrect), there is no basis for an employee insisting that they have an input into the choice of investigator.

This should however be contrasted with the situation that prevails for Health Service Executive (HSE) workers. The Disciplinary Procedure for Employees of the HSE agreed in January 2007 specifically provides that an 'investigation will be conducted by person(s) who are acceptable to both sides' (see **Ch 5**).

DISCIPLINARY HEARINGS

[4.09] Disciplinary hearings are to some extent more straightforward than investigations as it is clear that the employee concerned is entitled to the full rights to natural justice. Generally, the only matter for consideration for employers is whether to allow either a trade union official in non-union companies or a legal representative to attend.

Representation

[4.10] It is a fundamental right of all employees to be afforded representation during the disciplinary process. Any denial of this right will lead to a finding of unfair dismissal. (See also **4.05**.)

Legal representation

[4.11] The issue of legal representation is complicated. Whereas the disciplinary code makes it clear that it does not contemplate legal representation, many employers are inclined to proceed on that basis regardless. Certainly, where employers are carrying out workplace investigations where there may be serious consequences, the standard does seem to be somewhat higher and now appears to contemplate legal representation coupled with full oral hearings, the right to cross examine witnesses etc.

Many companies fear that allowing solicitors to attend on behalf of employees is a 'bad thing', but to that I would make a number of observations:

1. Should you allow a solicitor to attend then it is very difficult for the employee to subsequently argue procedural defects.

2. It must always be remembered that whatever representative attends they are there merely to represent. They cannot answer questions on the employee's

---

20. *Harrington v Irish Nationwide Building Society* (2008, unreported), HC.

behalf, therefore to some extent it does not matter who the representative is. This in itself therefore does not necessarily mean that full oral hearings, cross examination etc also have to apply.

3.   Lastly there is a grave risk to solicitors (which many fail to recognise) in attending such hearings and it is that, if there is a debate over any matters that arise, then they themselves become a witness and are liable to be called before the EAT or court as applicable.

Trade union representation

[4.12] A somewhat more difficult decision in non-union companies is whether to allow an official from a trade union to represent an employee. The problem to this lies in Industrial Relations Act 1990 Code of Practice on Grievance and Disciplinary Procedures.[21] Paragraph 5 of the Code provides that 'for the purposes of this Code of Practice, "employee representative" includes a colleague of the employee's choice and a registered trade union but not any other person or body unconnected with the enterprise.' You will note the wording of this section in that it states '*and* a registered trade union', it does not say may, it is quite specific. Paragraph 6 of the Code provides that the employee concerned must be 'given the opportunity to avail of the right to be represented during the procedure'. Therefore, if the employee wishes to be represented by a trade union official and the company is non-union, on a strict reading of the Code of Practice to deny the employee the right to be so represented would amount to a breach of the Code. Whereas the Code is non-binding, it must be remembered that s 6(7)(b) of the 1977 Act provides that when the Tribunal is determining whether the dismissal of an employee is fair or unfair they may have regard to 'the extent (if any)' to which the employer has complied with any Code of Practice.

Generally, as a compromise in non-union companies such representation is allowed but all meetings occur off the premises.

Whistleblowers

[4.13] Protection for employees against being penalised by their employers for informing on them is to be found in several pieces of legislation.

Section 50 of the 2002 Competition Act prohibits penalisation of employees who report breaches by the employer under s 6 or 7 of that Act. The Protection for Person Reporting Child Abuse Act 1998 protects employees for penalisation for having reported child abuse.[22] For a significant number of companies operating in Ireland who are listed on the US stock exchange, employees are protected from reporting concerns

---

21.   Industrial Relations Act 1990 Code of Practice on Grievance and Disciplinary Procedures (SI 146/2000)
22.   Protection For Persons Reporting Child Abuse Act 1998, s 4(3).

regarding questionable auditing or accounting matters under the US Sarbannes-Oxley Act,[23] which was the Act that effectively emerged from the so-called 'Enron scandal'.

In so far as either an initial investigation hearing into the complaints is being dealt with or a disciplinary hearing arising out of such complaints is being held, a distinction may need to be made between such an investigation and an 'ordinary' pre-disciplinary investigation. In the latter it is probable that the person the subject matter of the complaint will be suspended on full pay pending investigation. In the former it is more likely that a fellow employee is making the complaint, probably against a senior member of management. In such circumstances it may be appropriate to place both parties on paid leave. This is so because if the 'whistleblower'/informant turns out to have wronged the other party maliciously or recklessly it may be necessary to discipline them and it will be necessary to show absolute impartiality.

Also the Prevention of Corruption (Amendment) Act 2010 contains specific protection for employees who disclose wrong doing in the context of their employment. This includes protection against penalisation by their employer (or threats of penalisation). Protection includes any act or omission by an employer that affects an employee to his or her detriment.

Expert witnesses

[4.14] It may arise from time to time that during an investigation it is necessary to introduce expert witnesses. Such instances may be where, for example, a technical expert is required to assess a person's handwriting. In such circumstances the employee the subject of the investigation should be given full access to the expert and their report and allowed to comment on it. A difficulty often arises in such circumstances where the employee engages their own alternative expert. This is often the case in long-term absence cases where two doctors often disagree as to the long-term prognosis of a patient. Whereas in such cases the opinion of a third medical expert is generally required, this may not be the case for other expert witnesses. Thus in the case of *Cleary v TSB Bank*[24] where there was some disagreement between two handwriting experts the Tribunal upheld the bank's decision to dismiss.

Probationary employees

[4.15] A question that often arises is whether employers have to show equal deference, in so far as natural justice and fair procedures applies, to employees on probation? The

---

23. The Sarbanes-Oxley Act of 2002 (Pub L 107–204, 116 Stat 745, enacted 30 July 2002) is also known as the Public Company Accounting Reform and Investor Protection Act (in the US Senate) and Corporate and Auditing Accountability and Responsibility Act' (in the US House of Representatives) and commonly called Sarbanes–Oxley, Sarbox or SOX. The law set new or enhanced standards for all US public company boards, management and public accounting firms. It is named after sponsors US Senator Paul Sarbanes (D-MD) and US Representative Michael G Oxley (R-OH).

24. *Cleary v TSB Bank* 754/1995.

answer to this lies in the clause in the contract on probation. Either of two scenarios therefore apply:

> 1. There is a probationary clause. In such circumstances the employer must adhere to that.
>
> 2. There is no probationary clause. In such circumstances the terms of the disciplinary procedure apply.

In either case, should the employer move to dismiss contrary to the probationary clause or disciplinary procedure then a breach of contract will arise. Technically the employee may seek to injunct the employer. For this reason the terms of both the probationary clause and indeed the contract are vital. At all times there should be a 'no fault' termination clause in the contract which allows employers to terminate the contract with notice or pay in lieu thereof. This is critical, particularly for probationary employees as it may not always be practical to conduct a long drawn out investigation which might in itself bring the employee over the one-year threshold necessary to pursue a claim for unfair dismissal.

Appeals

[4.16] The Code of Practice on Grievance and Disciplinary Procedures[25] provides that there is an obligation on employers to make available 'an internal appeals mechanism'. The problem for employers generally arises in setting the appeal hearing. Clearly, the person hearing the appeal should not have been party to the previous disciplinary action or dismissal. For most employers, this poses a great difficulty as invariably the only person authorised to dismiss an employee is either the managing director, chief executive, head of HR or some other senior executive. Even in large companies it would be highly unusual for the chief executive or the senior management team not to know or hear about, even informally, the circumstances surrounding the dismissal of an employee. The fact is therefore that the insistence on someone impartial hearing an appeal in most companies is farcical. That said, employers are left with a dilemma. If they don't allow an appeal it can be technically argued that they are not affording the right to fair procedures and natural justice: equally if they do they run the risk of being accused of exactly that.

A case which illustrates the pitfalls for employers in this is *Maliuk v Shellfish De La Mer Limited*.[26] Here the claimant, who was employed with the respondent since 2003, received a verbal warning regarding his performance in May 2006. There was no disciplinary hearing and when he asked if he could appeal it he was told he could not. On 10 November 2006, the claimant was suspended with pay pending the outcome of an investigation after a meeting with the respondent. He was given a final written warning on 15 November. He was not informed of a right of appeal. Following this, the claimant was notified on 16 and 21 November of two complaints made by two female employees. This was so even though the complaints had been made the previous October and no

---

25. Code of Practice on Grievance and Disciplinary Procedures (SI 146/2000).
26. *Maliuk v Shellfish De La Mer Limited* UD 211/2007.

reference to them was made at the previous meeting on 10 November. The claimant, as a result, was suspended with pay and dismissed by way of letter on 28 of November. Again, he was not informed of a right of appeal against the dismissal. The Tribunal, in finding the dismissal unfair, said it was satisfied that fair procedures 'were not invoked by the Respondent'.[27]

Practically, the best advice would seem to be:

1.   If there is no possible person internally who can hear the appeal, afford the employee an independent external person to hear it.

2.   If there is someone internally who can hear the appeal, ensure that they have had no dealing whatsoever previously in the matter. If necessary and if possible appoint someone from another division, plant or location to hear it.

---

27.   See also *Pearce v David Flynn Limited* UD 833/2006.

Chapter 5

CIVIL SERVANTS

[5.01] Prior to 2006, the remedy for a dismissed civil servant lay in public law and as such their remedy lay in judicial review. However, since 4 July 2006, dismissed civil servants (other than those dismissed by Government) are now able to claim under the Unfair Dismissals Act. A new s 2A was inserted into the Act[1] to provide:

> For the purposes of this Act, as respects the dismissal of a person who prior to such dismissal was a civil servant a reference in this Act to an 'employee' shall be construed as including a civil servant who held office in the Civil Service of the Government or in the Civil Service of the State.

The insertion of this section into the Act had the effect of applying the statutory code of unfair dismissal to countless thousands of civil servants, whilst at the same preserving the status of those employees as 'officers'[2] of the State, ie that they continue to hold office at the will and pleasure of the Government.[3]

DEFINITION OF CIVIL SERVANT

[5.02] A civil servant is defined under s 1 of the Civil Service Regulation Act 1956 as a person holding a position in the civil service, including a member of the staff of the Oireachtas or an officer of the Attorney General. The 1956 Act defines the Civil Service as the 'civil service of the government and the civil service of the state'.

The consequences of this were that civil servants held office at the will of the Government and as such a Government decision was required to dismiss them. This was unsatisfactory from a number of perspectives: first, it extended a much greater security of tenure to civil servants than others. Secondly it removed the 'day to day' management of civil servants from managers in the civil service, leading to poor performance management practices.

APPLICABILITY OF UNFAIR DISMISSALS ACT

[5.03] Section 7 of the Act amends s 5 of the 1956 Act. Whilst it restates[4] that every established civil servant shall hold office at the will and pleasure of the Government, the amended section provides that the powers and functions of the Government may be exercised where the Government so authorises by a relevant Minister or by 'the appropriate authority' depending on the category of civil servant.

Section 6 of the Act amends s 2 of the 1956 Act which defines 'appropriate authority'. Thus civil servants up to the position of principal officer may be dismissed

---

1.   The entirety of Unfair Dismissals Act 1977, s 2A was inserted in the Act by the Civil Service Regulation (Amendment) Act 2005, s 22.
2.   Unfair Dismissals Act 1977, s 2A(6).
3.   Civil Service Regulation Act 1956, s 5.
4.   Civil Service Regulation Act 1956, s 5(1).

by the Secretary General.[5] Persons holding the grade of principal officer and above[6] can only be dismissed by the appropriate Minister on recommendation of the secretary general.

The Act continues to afford protection for those civil servants appointed directly by the Government who can only be dismissed by the Government.

An anomaly seems to have arisen as regards the dismissal of a person at or beyond principal officer grade. As can be seen from the Act, they can only be dismissed by the Minister on the recommendation of the Secretary General. Technically therefore it is the Minister who ultimately dismisses, not the Secretary General. This is in reality the same as the 1956 Act. It seems an unnecessary and needless step to have inserted in the process and will inevitably lead to significant legal argument about who took the decision to dismiss and who should attend the EAT on the day. From strict reading of the section, it would appear to be the Minister and as such the Minister will have to appear before the EAT to defend his or her decision. The practicalities do not appear to make much sense.

Section 22 of the Act deals with the remedies available to dismissed employees. Similar to the Unfair Dismissals Act, the primary remedies of reinstatement and re-engagement are available: however, unlike the Unfair Dismissals Act where reinstatement is actually to the position held before dismissal, reinstatement of civil servant can be 'in the grade or rank held by the civil servant prior to his dismissal'.[7] This seems to contemplate a scenario where a civil servant need not necessarily get the same job but may be placed elsewhere in the service once they get the same grade or rank previously held.

THE CIVIL SERVICE DISCIPLINARY CODE

[5.04] The Civil Service Disciplinary Code ('the Code')[8] was issued on 4 July 2006 (the same day the Act came into effect). The Code applies to all new disciplinary cases of Principal Officer and below beginning after that date. Agreement on the Code was required by the national agreement at the time ie '*Sustaining Progress*'.

The Code replaced the Disciplinary Code[9] and made significant changes to it, not least:

- The Secretary General/Head of Scheduled Office became the 'appropriate authority' to make disciplinary decisions including dismissal for all grades below Principal Officer. He may assign these powers to another officer.[10]

---

5. Unfair Dismissals Act 1977, s 62(1)(c).
6. Unfair Dismissals Act 1977, s 62(1)(b).
7. Unfair Dismissals Act 1977, s 2A(5).
8. Civil Service Disciplinary Code ('the Code') circular 14/2006.
9. Disciplinary Code circular 1/92.
10. Clauses 3 & 4.

- It extended the application of the Unfair Dismissals Acts, the Minimum Notice and Terms of Employment Acts to civil servants and allowed them a route of appeal previously unknown to the Rights Commissioner Service, the Employment Appeals Tribunal and potentially the courts.

- The grounds on which disciplinary action may be taken were widened as were the range of penalties.[11]

- Before any disciplinary action can be taken on performance grounds the Performance Management Development Scheme (PMDS)[12] procedures must be fully applied in terms of provision of training and staff development. The Civil Service Regulation (Amendment) Act 2005[13] provides that disciplinary action in relation to underperformance on the part of an officer should not be taken unless 'the appropriate authority is satisfied that measures aimed at improving the performance of the civil servant through training or development:

  (a) have in relation to that civil servant been introduced and applied, and have failed to result in specified improvement in performance of the civil servant; or

  (b) have in relation to that civil servant no reasonable prospect of resulting in an improvement in performance on the part of the civil servant.

- The new Code provides for several stages similar to the normal disciplinary process typical in most private sector employments, ie:

  (a) Stage 1 – Verbal Warning;[14]

  (b) Stage 2 – Written Warning;[15]

  (c) Stage 3 – Final Written Warning.[16]

- Only more senior officers can carry out the investigation at Stage 3. They have the power to overturn any earlier decisions and to issue a verbal or written warning.[17]

- Serious misconduct or alleged failure by an officer to meet the requirements of a Stage 3 Final Written Warning may lead to Stage 4 Disciplinary Action.[18]

---

11. Clauses 5 & 15.
12. The first Civil Service-wide Evaluation of the PMDS began in September 2003, using a framework agreed by a sub-committee of General Council (General Council is a forum for discussion on industrial relations issues between civil service trade unions and management representatives).
13. Civil Service Regulation (Amendment) Act 2005, s 10(4).
14. Clauses 24 & 25.
15. Clauses 25 & 27.
16. Clauses 28 & 29.
17. Clauses 30 & 31.
18. Clauses 34–41.

In addition to the significant changes in managerial responsibility, the Code marked a significant change in HR practice. This included not least that:

   (i)   disciplinary action could be taken in cases of underperformance as well as in cases of misconduct, irregularity, neglect or unsatisfactory behaviour;

   (ii)   whereas disciplinary action in cases of underperformance could be taken it could only be taken when the staff member had been warned and given the opportunity to improve his or her performance and where appropriate training and development measures have been taken;

   (iii) suspension without pay could now be used as a disciplinary measure;

   (iv) any suspension pending the conclusion of disciplinary proceedings will be suspension on 'ordinary remuneration' in accordance with s 9 of the Civil Service Regulation (Amendment) Act 2005;[19]

   (v)   a person may be appointed to be an established civil servant on the basis of a probationary contract.

Definition of disciplinary action under the Code

[5.05] For the purposes of the Code, the term 'disciplinary action' is defined as any action taken by the 'appropriate authority' under the Civil Service Regulation Act by reason of, or as a direct consequence of, a finding that the officer concerned has, in the opinion of the appropriate authority, failed to perform his or her duties to an adequate or appropriate standard, or has been guilty of misconduct, irregularity, neglect or unsatisfactory behaviour. 'Disciplinary action' shall be taken to comprise:

   (i)   formal written notes placed on the officer's personnel file;

   (ii)   deferral of an increment;

   (iii)   debarment from competitions or from specified competitions or from promotion for a specified period of time;

   (iv)   transfer to another office or division or geographical location;

   (v)   withdrawal of concessions or allowances;

   (vi)   placing the civil servant on a lower rate of remuneration (including the withholding of an increment);

   (vii) reducing the civil servant to a specified lower grade or rank;

   (viii) suspending the civil servant without pay; or

   (ix)   dismissal.

---

19.   This amended Civil Service Regulation Act, 1956, s 14 which provided that staff could be suspended without pay pending the outcome of a disciplinary investigation.

Appeals under the Code

[5.06] A decision to take disciplinary action against an officer under the Code may be appealed within 10 days to the Civil Service Disciplinary Code Appeal Board (the 'Board'). The composition of this Board is set out in clauses 43–48 of the Code. The Board is only empowered to issue a recommendation. It is therefore not definitive. Its only task is to ascertain whether:

(i)   the provisions of this code were not adhered to;

(ii) all the relevant facts were not ascertained;

(iii) all the relevant facts were not considered, or not considered in a reasonable manner;

(iv) the officer concerned was not afforded a reasonable opportunity to answer the allegation;

(v)   the officer concerned could not reasonably be expected to have understood that the behaviour alleged would attract disciplinary action;

(vi) the sanction recommended is disproportionate to the underperformance or misconduct alleged.

Accordingly it is much more akin to a review as distinct from an appeal. Indeed clause 49 of the Code refers to the fact that 'an officer may seek a review of the disciplinary proceedings by the Board on the above grounds'. The word 'proceedings' seems to be deliberately used, ie it is the proceedings of the Board, not the procedures used or the sanction that is the subject of review.

Clause 57 deals with the matter of representation at the appeal hearing. Importantly clause 57 provides that 'the officer making an appeal is entitled, if he or she wishes, to make oral submissions to the Board either in person or through a serving civil servant of his or her choice, a whole-time official of the union holding recognition for his or her grade or such other person as the Board agrees may be present for that purpose'. The latter is interesting in that it seems to 'leave the door open' for legal representation. It is hard to reconcile this with clause 59 which provides that '[p]roceedings before the Board shall be informal'.

DISCIPLINARY REGULATIONS FOR AN GARDA SÍOCHÁNA

[5.07] New regulations for the disciplining of gardaí came into effect on 1 June 2007. The new streamlined code introduced new procedures to enable the Garda Commissioner to summarily dismiss a garda alleged to have brought the force into disrepute, abandoned duties, compromised the security of the State or unjustifiably infringed the rights of other persons. In addition, a four-member 'civilian management advisory team' was appointed in August 2006 to advise on implementing change options and addressing management and leadership challenges facing the Gardaí. The advisers were also mandated to promote a culture of performance management, succession planning, recruitment of civilians with specialist expertise, and improved training.[20]

The legal basis for the regulations is contained in s 123 of the Garda Síochána Act 2005. Garda Síochána (Discipline) Regulations 2007[21] sets out the Regulations. The Regulations are detailed, however, Sch 1 sets out the Acts or Conduct which constitute breaches of discipline. There are 30 of these in total, including neglect of duty, insubordination, deceit, soliciting a gratuity, abuse of authority etc. The Regulations, unlike those typical of private sector employments, provide for different procedures to be followed in the cases of minor, less serious breaches and serious breaches of discipline.

1. For minor breaches there should be informal resolution at local level.[22] Possible penalties here include advice, caution or warning.

2. More serious breaches are dealt with by regulations 14–21. Here a formal interview by a deciding officer, who is a member not below the rank of superintendent, takes place with the accused member. Sanctions include reduction in pay, warning and advice.

3. For alleged serious breaches of discipline Pt 3 of the Regulations apply. This provides for a formal investigation by a 'Board of Inquiry'[23] (the 'Board'). Serious breaches of discipline are defined as a breach of discipline which 'in the opinion of the Commissioner, may be subject to dismissal, the requirement to resign as an alternative to dismissal, reduction in rank or reduction in pay not exceeding four weeks' pay'. The Board is comprised of three persons who are appointed by the Commissioner. The Presiding Officer is selected from a panel nominated by the Minister each of whom must be a judge of the District Court or a practising barrister or solicitor with at least 10 years' experience. The purpose of the Board is to recommend disciplinary sanction; it is then up to the Commissioner within 14 days of the receipt of their report to decide on the appropriate disciplinary action.[24] This can include endorsing the decision of the Board or increasing the sanction. Here, the standard of proof required is on the balance of probabilities.[25] If the member is above the rank of inspector and the decision is to dismiss, to retire or resign as an alternative to dismissal or a reduction in rank, the Commissioner has to send a recommendation to that effect to the Minister for consideration by Government.[26] If after a decision by

---

20. The advisory team included Senator Maurice Hayes, Emer Daly (former director of strategic planning and risk management at Axa Insurance), Maurice Keane (former group chief executive at Bank of Ireland), Michael Flahive (Assistant Secretary at the Department of Justice, Equality and Law Reform and Dr Michael Mulreany (Assistant Director General at the Institute of Public Administration).
21. Garda Síochána (Discipline) Regulations 2007 (SI 214/2007).
22. Garda Síochána (Discipline) Regulations 2007 (SI 214/2007), reg 10.
23. Garda Síochána (Discipline) Regulations 2007 (SI 214/2007), reg 21(1).
24. Garda Síochána (Discipline) Regulations 2007 (SI 214/2007), reg 31.
25. Garda Síochána (Discipline) Regulations 2007 (SI 214/2007), reg 9.

the Commissioner the member is dissatisfied with his/her decision there is a right to appeal within seven days to an 'Appeal Board' comprising perhaps the Commissioner, a member of a representative association, or another member selected by the Commissioner where the member concerned is not a member of a representative association. The Chairman is appointed from a similar panel to the Presiding Officer panel.

A number of interesting features arise in this:

1. The seriousness by which the dismissal of a member is taken can be viewed from the fact that the whole process revolves around the Commissioner. It is clearly envisaged (presumably) that dismissal or serious sanction will be a rare event indeed.

2. The Commissioner must make an initial decision as to the seriousness of the matter. This could be seen to taint him in a somewhat prejudiced light from the outside, particularly if he decides to increase the recommended sanction from the Board of Inquiry.

3. The Commissioner may also be involved in the Appeal Board. It is hard to understand how this could function if the Commissioner has already decided to increase the recommended sanction from the Board of Inquiry.

4. It should be noted at all times that the dismissal and/or serious sanction of a member is the preserve of the Gardaí themselves. The civilians on the panel may only make a recommendation.

5. There appears to be somewhat of a contradiction in the contemplated sanctions for serious misconduct, in that it would seem entirely inappropriate to allow anyone the right to retire or resign (with all the pension rights intact) if it were contemplated that they may be guilty of serious misconduct.

The above serve to illustrate further the dichotomy that exists between the rules applicable to those in the private and public sectors.

Since the passing of the legislation there have been a number of dismissals. On 1 June 2010 the Minister for Justice brought three dismissals to Cabinet for approval. The first of those involved the dismissal of a garda for allegedly allowing members of a gang involved in criminal activities access to confidential garda files into their activities. The second of the dismissals was for alleged financial irregularities and the last for problems with business transactions the garda was involved in not connected with his work as a garda.

Representation

[5.08] Regulation 27(4)(e) provides that a member 'is entitled to be accompanied at the inquiry and to be represented by an official of that association, by another member of his or her choice or by a solicitor or barrister at the member's expense'. Unlike the

---

26.   Garda Síochána (Discipline) Regulations 2007 (SI 214/2007), reg 31(2)(b).

Industrial Relations Act 1990 (Code of Practice on Grievance and Disciplinary Procedures) (Declaration) Order 2000[27] which does not envisage legal representation at all, here members of the Garda Síochána are explicitly afforded that right by statute, albeit that it is restricted to a Board of Inquiry as per s 27(4)(e) or at an Appeal Board.[28] It is hard to reconcile why a member of the Gardaí should be afforded such a right yet ordinary members of society in most instances can be denied it.

DISCIPLINARY PROCEDURE IN THE HEALTH SERVICE EXECUTIVE (HSE)

[5.09] The HSE replaced the various health boards that represented the country geographically. Legislatively, this was done by the Health Act in 2004. The Act also repealed sections of the 1970 Health Act which dealt with the suspension and dismissal of permanent health board officers.[29] Subsequent to this, an agreement was reached with the IMPACT trade union for revisions to the disciplinary procedure to provide for protections not any less favourable than those enjoyed under the Health Act 1970 but modified to suit the new circumstances. It was in this context that a revised disciplinary procedure for employees of the HSE-EA and the health service unions was agreed. The procedure covers all HSE employees with some exceptions, they are:

1. Probationary employees[30] (note that in cases of allegations of serious misconduct being made against a probationary employee the matter will be investigated in accordance with stage 4 of the disciplinary procedure.

2. Employees on fixed term/specified purpose contracts whose employment is terminated by reason of the expiry date/cessor of the purpose of the contract.

3. Consultants covered by the Common Contract.

4. Medical doctors and dentists regarding complaints of professional misconduct and/or clinical capability which are addressed through a separate procedure.

5. General practitioners participating in the General Medical Services (GMS) Scheme and those specialising in substance abuse are covered by separate procedures outlined in their contract.

The disciplinary procedure

[5.10] Section 4 provides for a 'pre procedure'; this is informal counselling. After this, s 5 states that where the employee's conduct, attendance or work does not meet the required standards the matter will be dealt with through the disciplinary procedure. The procedure itself provides for four stages: an oral warning, a written warning, a final

---

27. Industrial Relations Act 1990 (Code of Practice on Grievance and Disciplinary Procedures) (Declaration) Order 2000 (SI 146/2000).
28. Garda Síochána (Discipline) Regulations 2007 (SI 214/2007), reg 36(2)(a).
29. The Health Act 2004 repealed the Health Act 1970, ss 22, 23 (i), (ii) (iii) and 24.
30. Appendix 1 details the procedure for probationary employees.

written warning and dismissal or action short of dismissal. Under stage 4 the decision-maker must be the relevant National Director.

Serious misconduct is also defined in stage 4 and includes such offences as theft, deliberate damage to property, fraud, gross negligence or dereliction of duties etc.

In handling matter of alleged serious misconduct there are various steps set out under the Code, not least:

1. Notifying the employee of the allegation.

2. Taking protective measures to ensure that no patient/client or employee is exposed to unacceptable risk. Such protective measures may include:

    (a)   reassigning the employee to other duties;

    (b)   providing an appropriate level of supervision;

3. putting the employee off duty with pay.

Notwithstanding that the views of the employee must be considered, the final decision rests with management.

In conducting the investigation, it must be conducted by a person(s) who is acceptable to both parties.[31]

Appendix 3 details the principles to be followed in carrying out an investigation. This includes the 'usual rights' to fair procedures and natural justice such as the right to have the matter dealt with expeditiously, to have copies of all documentation prior to and during the process, the right to representation, the right to call etc. Importantly, the investigation must be governed by predetermined terms of reference and must specify the timescale within which the investigation will be completed and that the 'scope of the investigation' is to be 'confined to deciding whether or not the allegation is upheld'.

Preliminary conclusions are to be formed based on the evidence given and the person adversely affected by those is allowed the opportunity to provide additional information or to challenge any aspect of the evidence.

Representation

[5.11] Appendix 2, which deals with how to conduct a disciplinary hearing requires, when the employee is being notified, that they be notified of the right to 'representation by a union representative or work colleague'. This would seem to rule out legal representation, at least at the disciplinary hearing.

However, Appendix 3 which deals with the conduct of the investigation is not as restrictive, merely stating that the 'employee against whom the allegation is made will be advised of the right to representation and given copies of all documentation prior to and during the investigation process'. It would seem incredible that one would be afforded legal representation at a preliminary investigation meeting yet not be afforded that at a potentially more serious disciplinary hearing.

---

31.   This again is something that practitioners operating in the private sector might find unusual. See **Ch 4** for a fuller discussion on this.

INVESTIGATIONS AND CIVIL SERVANTS

Revised Procedures for Suspension and Dismissal of Teachers Section 24(3) of the Education Act (1998)

[5.12] Section 24(3) of the Education Act 1998 provides for the suspension and dismissal of teachers by Boards of Management. Under the terms of the Social Partnership Agreement, *Towards 2016* the parties undertook to review and revise existing procedures and to agree new procedures. As the provisions of s 24 of the Education Act 1998 did not apply to teachers of a school established by a vocational education committee (VEC) sequential discussions took place in the vocational education sector on revisions to the procedures in that sector. Accordingly there are two department circulars that now deal with Teachers' Discipline and Dismissal.

1. Department circular 60/2009 Procedures Relating to Professional Competence and Disciplinary Matters – Principals and Teachers;

2. Department Circular (VEC) 59/2009 Procedures Relating to Professional Competence and Disciplinary Matters – Principals and Teachers;

Section 24(3) EDUCATION ACT 1998

DES CIRCULAR 59/2009		DES CIRCULAR 60/2009	
TEACHERS	SCHOOL PRINCIPALS	TEACHERS	SCHOOL PRINCIPALS
Prof. Competence Issues	Work, Conduct & Other Issues	Prof. Competence Issues	Work, Conduct & Other Issues

For the purposes of simplicity, this chapter distinguishes between Principals of all schools and teachers of all schools (including VECs).

It will examine Teachers Disciplinary matters and deals with Circulars 59/2009 which deals with VEC teachers and 60/2009 which deals with Teachers in all other schools and regards them together as by and large there is very little distinction between the two.

It will then go on to look at Principals in both VECs (circular 59/2009) and Principals of all other teaching establishments (Circular 60/2009) and again compare and contrast each circular and deal with them both in relation to s 24(3) of the Education Act 1998.

Teachers Discipline

[5.13] Department circular 59/2009 and 60/2009 sets out two separate and independent strands to be utilised in appropriate circumstances:

1. procedures relating to professional competence issues; and

2. procedures relating to work, conduct and matters other than professional competence.

The procedures apply to all teachers other than those teachers serving in a probationary capacity. In relation to teachers serving in a probationary capacity the previously existing probation arrangements continue to apply. The procedures are designed to deal solely with issues of employment and supersede all disciplinary procedures in existence prior to the agreement. However previously teachers were allowed appeal to patrons and this agreement is without prejudice to such appeals, where they are currently provided, pending any review of such appeals.

The essential elements of these procedures for dealing with disciplinary matters are that:

1.   they are deemed to be consistent, rational and fair;

2.   that the basis for disciplinary action is clear;

3.   that whatever course of action to be undertaken or any penalties that may apply are clearly outlined;

3.   an internal appeal mechanism must also be made available.

Such procedures serve a dual purpose in that they provide a framework which enables management to maintain satisfactory standards and teachers to have access to procedures whereby alleged failures to comply with these standards may be fairly and sensitively addressed.

Teachers are personally accountable for their individual work performance and behaviour. The onus is on the Principal to address any alleged problems informally with members of staff as soon as they arise, as early intervention at the appropriate level is always more desirable than having to go down the formal disciplinary route.

If the disciplinary procedure must be adopted, a teacher may be placed on leave with full pay pending an investigation, the outcome of an investigation or the outcome of a disciplinary hearing.

At all times these procedures will relate to the general principal of natural justice. There will be a presumption of innocence at all times.

A support service will be provided at both primary and post-primary levels where appropriate advice, training and assistance will be given to teaching staff and management.

Procedures relating to professional competence issues

[5.14] Every teacher is expected to maintain appropriate standards of teaching. If competence issues arise, a teacher is obliged to avail of all opportunities of assistance towards remediation. Often, professional competence issues are of a transient short-lived duration and may be quickly resolved.

If parental complaints relate to the professional competence of a teacher any issues will be initially addressed by the Principal in accordance with agreed complaint procedures. A number of stages will ensue – leading from informal to formal stages and if the matter is still not resolved, disciplinary action may need to be taken (up to and including dismissal).

It is at all times the right and duty of the Board of Management (BOM)/VEC (Vocational Education Committee) to act immediately in matters of serious misconduct – or in cases where there is a perceived threat to the health, safety and welfare of the student body.

Stage 1[32]

[5.15] The Principal and BOM are responsible for the guidance and direction of teachers. If concerns arise they will advise the teacher in question orally and furnish relevant documentation of the issue involved in addition to a copy of the outlined agreed procedures. The teacher will be expected to familiarize him/herself with the various stages of the procedures (and in the case of the VEC/EO (Education Officer)/CEO (Chief Executive Officer) advised of the various sanctions that may be invoked in the event of sustained underperformance). The Principal will discuss the underlying problem with the teacher and will advise the teacher of internal/external supports to include:

Employment Assistance Service;

Primary Professional Development Service;

Leadership Development for Schools (LDS);

Second Level Support Service (SLSS) and /or other support agencies.

Through informal dialogue transient professional competence issues should ordinarily be resolved within a three-month period – excluding holiday periods.

If the teacher refuses to engage positively with the process, the Principal will inform the teacher that the matter will be referred to the BOM or in the case of vocational schools referred to the CEO or EO in writing whereby a formal process will be initiated.

Stage 2

Initiation of the formal process

[5.16] The Principal will provide a written report of his/her concerns to the BOM/CEO/EO. A copy is sent to the teacher who has the opportunity to respond to the allegations within 10 school days of receipt of the report. The teacher will be invited to address the board. At this stage it is open to the teacher to invoke Stage 3 of these procedures within 10 school days of receipt of the report. Where the teacher adopts this course of action it is on the strict understanding that he/she cannot then seek to revert to any earlier stage of the process and that the Principal and BOM, CEO or EO may proceed to the next stage as appropriate.

If the teacher does not proceed to Stage 3, the BOM/CEO/EO will consider the report and the teacher's response to it. The teacher will be given the opportunity to address the BOM/CEO/EO.

---

32.   Outlined in the Education Act 1998, ss 22 and 23.

The board will then make a decision on how to proceed. This decision may involve the board or officer finding that:

- there are insufficient grounds to conclude that there is an issue of professional competence;

- there are sufficient grounds as to warrant the initiation of the formal process.

If sufficient grounds are found, the BOM/CEO/EO will request that the Principal define an improvement plan to discuss with the teacher outlining deficiencies, required improvement expected, range of support and training suggestions and timeframe to implement the above (three months excluding holiday periods – which may be extended by the Principal with the agreement of the BOM/CEO/EO/). All of the above will be put in writing to the teacher. The BOM/CEO/EO and Principal will support and facilitate the teacher at all times to carry out the requisite improvement plan. The Principal will furnish the BOM with a report of the outcome. If satisfied, the BOM /CEO/EO will write to the teacher to confirm the end of the formal process and the matter will be brought to a conclusion.

If not satisfied that the improvement plan has been adhered to, the Principal will outline in writing to the BOM/officer the reasons and the teacher will be afforded the opportunity to reply – orally and in writing. The BOM/CEO/EO, having given due consideration to the Principal's report and to the teacher's response thereto, will decide to draw the matter to a close or to modify the improvement plan or will agree that the teacher has not improved.

Stage 3

External review

[5.17] At this juncture, the Chief Inspector of the Department of Education will be contacted to review the teacher's work having been sent a report of the outcome by the BOM/CEO/EO. The teacher will be so informed by the BOM/officer in such instances. The request for a review should include details of the nature of the board's/officer's concerns, the supports offered to the teacher, the extent to which these supports were availed of by the teacher and the outcomes.

Before approving the review, the Chief Inspector (or his/her chosen advocate of the Inspectorate or a person with a particular expertise in a certain field) will satisfy himself/herself that the appropriate support has been offered to the teacher by the school and that, despite this, the teacher's work is still considered to be unsatisfactory. The review may entail several visits to the school in question by the Inspector's team to observe the teacher at work. The teacher will be expected to cooperate at all times. The teacher will be sent all documentation pertaining to the review by the BOM/CEO/EO. Where the teacher has availed of the option at Stage 2 to invoke Stage 3 the Chief Inspector will be aware of this before initiating the review. The Chief Inspector, according to s 13 of the Education Act 1998, is deemed to deal with the matter without prejudice. The Chief Inspector will assign as many personnel as is deemed necessary to conduct the review.

Any lack of cooperation by the teacher will be taken into account when the Inspector formulates his/her conclusions. The teacher may respond to the written report to the BOM/CEO/EO from the Inspector (within 10 school days) The VEC teachers respond within 15 school days. The matter will have concluded (the teacher will be informed within five school days) or will warrant further disciplinary action.

Stage 4

Hearing

[5.18] In accordance with the provisions of the VEC Amendment Act 2001, suspension and dismissal of staff are reserved functions. The following procedures – similar to all other schools will apply.

The teacher is given seven school day's notice and attends with his/her chosen trade union representative/colleague (max 2). Following the hearing, the BOM/CEO/EO will notify the teacher of its decision – and of any necessary disciplinary action – if required.

If it is decided to take disciplinary action, the BOM may avail of any of the following range of sanctions:

- final written censure;
- deferral of an increment;
- withdrawal of an increment or increments;
- suspension (for a limited period and/or specific purpose) with pay;
- suspension (for a limited period and/or specific purpose) without pay;
- dismissal.

If dismissal does not occur the BOM will review the case on an ongoing basis.

In the case of VEC teachers, suspension and/or dismissal are not an option at this juncture. Instead where disciplinary action is proposed, the case will be reviewed by the CEO/EO within a specified timeframe to consider whether further action is necessary.

The CEO/EO will act reasonably in all cases when deciding on the appropriate disciplinary action. The nature of the disciplinary action should be proportionate to the issue of professional competence.

If the CEO/EO considers that the matter requires to be referred to the VEC, as a reserved function, he/she shall do so. The teacher will be provided with an opportunity to attend at a meeting of a sub-committee of the VEC accompanied by his/her trade union representative/s or a colleague subject to an overall maximum of two.

The teacher will be given at least seven school days' notice of the meeting. The notice should state the purpose of the hearing and that fact that disciplinary action may be considered.

At the meeting the teacher will be given an opportunity to make his/her case in full and to challenge any evidence that is being relied upon for a decision.

Following the hearing the sub-committee of the VEC will make its report to the VEC. A copy of the report will be given to the teacher.

The VEC will consider the report of the sub-committee. The teacher will be provided with an opportunity to attend at a meeting of the VEC accompanied by his/her trade union representative/s or a colleague subject to an overall maximum of two.

The teacher will be given at least seven school days' notice of the meeting. The notice should state the purpose of the hearing and that fact that disciplinary action may be considered.

At the meeting the teacher will be given an opportunity to make his/her case in full and to challenge any evidence that is being relied upon for a decision.

Following the hearing the VEC shall make its judgment on the matter. In formulating its judgment the VEC will take account of the conclusions set out in the report of the Chief Inspector, the report of the sub-committee of the VEC, any other evidence and the teacher's representation (if any) thereon. The VEC may decide to:

- refer the matter to the CEO/EO;

- impose disciplinary action.

The VEC shall notify the teacher of its decision and any intended disciplinary action if that be the outcome of its deliberations. If it is decided to take disciplinary action, the following range of sanctions may be availed of:

- suspension (for a limited period and/or specific purpose) with pay;

- suspension (for a limited period and/or specific purpose) without pay;

- suspension in accordance with the Vocational Education Acts;

Where disciplinary action short of suspension in accordance with the Vocational Education Acts is proposed the case will be reviewed by the VEC within a specified time period to consider whether further disciplinary action, if any, is required.

The VEC will act reasonably in all cases when deciding on the appropriate disciplinary action. The nature of the disciplinary action should be proportionate to the issue of professional competence.

Stage 5

Appeal

[5.19] Any appeal will be heard by an independent appeal Panel appointed by the BOM/CEO/EO.

Notification to the Department of Education & Science and the Teaching Council

[5.20] The BOM, CEO or EO (as applicable) will inform the Department of Education & Science of the nature of the disciplinary action and will comply with any requirements of the Teaching Council in accordance with the provisions of s 37 of the Teaching Council Act 2001.

Disciplinary procedures for teachers in primary, voluntary secondary, and community and comprehensive schools and teachers employed in vocational educational committee schools

Work, conduct and matters other than professional competence

[5.21] This disciplinary procedure for teachers employed in primary, community and comprehensive and voluntary secondary schools as well as teachers employed in VECs was developed and agreed following discussions between the Department of Education & Science, school managerial bodies and recognised teachers' unions. It takes account of employment legislation and the Labour Relation Commission's Code of Practice on Disciplinary Procedures. It supersedes all existing local and national disciplinary procedures. Principals, teachers and boards of management/officers will be made aware of and be made fully conversant with this procedure and will adhere to its terms.

Bearing in mind that it is a matter for every individual teacher to maintain appropriate standards of work and conduct, and it is fully accepted that the majority of teachers discharge their duties in a competent and efficient manner, the onus is on the teacher to avail of all opportunities of assistance towards remediation of any issue that may arise. It must be borne in mind that issues are often transient in nature and may have their origin in areas of a personal or professional nature which are of relatively short time duration. Isolated issues or omissions of a minor nature will, where possible, be dealt with informally.

It follows that the approach to dealing with matters of work and conduct should involve a number of stages moving from informal stages to formal stages which may at the end of the process have recourse to disciplinary action (up to and including dismissal). Although disciplinary action will normally follow the progressive stages the procedure may be commenced by the school at any stage of the process if the alleged misconduct warrants such an approach.

Scope

[5.22] This procedure deals with work and conduct issues and any matters other than professional competence. It does not apply to any teacher engaged on a probationary capacity.

Allegations in respect of child abuse as defined in the Child Protection Guidelines for Primary and Post-Primary Schools are dealt with in the first instance under those guidelines.

Informal Stage

[5.23] Initially the Principal will undertake to resolve the matter informally with the teacher in question. He/she will discuss the unsatisfactory conduct with the teacher and inform him/her of the required improvements expected. The teacher will be given the opportunity to explain the reason for the conduct, which may be due to personal, health or domestic circumstances. Help and advice or guidance will be given as required. The teacher will also be informed that unless the necessary improvement is made the matter may proceed to the formal disciplinary procedure

Where a teacher's work or conduct does not meet the required standards despite informal intervention as set out above the matter will be dealt with under the following disciplinary procedure.

Stage 1:

Verbal warning

[5.24] If a formal disciplinary meeting is to occur the Principal shall give at least five school days' written notice. This notice should state the purpose of the meeting, outline the specific nature of the complaint and be accompanied by any supporting documentation. The teacher may bring a work colleague or a trade union representative to the meeting.

At the meeting the teacher will be afforded the opportunity to state his/her case, respond to any allegations made and challenge any evidence submitted. Having considered the response the Principal will decide on the appropriate action to be taken. Where it is decided that no action is warranted the teacher will be so informed in writing within five school days. If however disciplinary action is warranted, the Principal will inform the teacher that he/she is being given a verbal warning. This verbal warning will include an outline of what improvement is expected and a timescale for this improvement in conduct. The warning should inform the teacher that further disciplinary action may be considered if there is no sustained satisfactory improvement. The teacher will be advised of his/her right to appeal against the disciplinary action being taken and the appeal process should be explained.

A copy of the verbal warning will be retained on the personnel file by the Principal and a copy will be given to the teacher. The verbal warning will be active for a period of 6 months after which time it will cease subject to satisfactory noted improvement and it will be removed from the file.

There may however be occasions where the teacher's work or conduct is satisfactory throughout the period the warning is in force only to lapse very soon thereafter. Where such a pattern emerges and there is evidence of an undermining of the disciplinary process, the teacher's previous conduct and pattern of behaviour may be considered as a whole in a future disciplinary procedure.

Stage 2:

Written warning

[5.25] If the Principal perceives no improvement in the conduct of the teacher a further meeting will be called and a nominee of the BOM (or a senior officer nominated by the CEO) will be in attendance. The teacher will be given at least seven school days written notice of the meeting, stating the purpose of the meeting and the specific nature of the complaint together with any supporting documentation. The teacher concerned may be accompanied at any such meeting by his/her trade union representative(s) or colleague(s) subject to an overall maximum of two.

At the meeting the teacher should be given a clear statement of the areas where his or her conduct is perceived as unsatisfactory. He/she will be afforded the opportunity to state his/her case, respond to any allegations made and challenge any evidence submitted. Having considered the response the Principal and the BOM/CEO nominee will decide on the appropriate action to be taken. Where it is decided that no action is warranted the teacher will be so informed in writing within five school days. If however disciplinary action is warranted the teacher will be informed that he/she is being given a written warning. This written warning will include an outline of what improvement is expected and a timescale for this improvement in conduct. The warning should inform the teacher that further disciplinary action may be considered if there is no sustained satisfactory improvement. Again as in stage 1, the teacher will be advised of his/her right to appeal against the disciplinary action being taken and the appeal process should be outlined.

A copy of the written warning will be retained on the personnel file by the Principal/ VEC and a copy will be given to the teacher. The written warning will be active for a period not exceeding nine months and subject to a satisfactory improvement in conduct will cease to have effect following the expiry of the nine month period. At this point the record will be removed from the file.

Stage 3:

Final written warning

[5.26] If no perceived improvement is noted or there is an occurrence of a more serious offence another meeting will take place. A nominee of the board/chief executive officer will be present. The teacher will be given seven school days' notice and the letter will communicate the same information as above at stages 1& 2.

The meeting will go through the process as at stages 1& 2. Where it is decided that no action is warranted the teacher will be so informed in writing within five school days. If however disciplinary action is warranted the teacher will be informed that he/she is being given a final written warning. This final written warning will include an outline of what improvement is expected and a timescale for this improvement in conduct. The final written warning should inform the teacher that further disciplinary action may be considered if there is no sustained satisfactory improvement. Again as in stages 1 and 2, the teacher will be advised of his/her right to appeal against the disciplinary action being taken and the appeal process should be outlined.

A copy of the final written warning will be retained on the personnel file by the Principal/VEC and a copy will be given to the teacher. The final written warning will be active for a period not exceeding 12-months and subject to satisfactory service will cease to have effect following the expiry of the 12-month period. The record will be removed from the file after the 12-month period subject to satisfactory improvement during the period.

Stage 4:

[5.27] If the poor work or conduct continues and no improvement has been perceived or if the poor work/conduct issue is of a serious nature the Principal shall prepare a comprehensive report and forward it to the BOM/CEO/EO. A copy will be given to the teacher.

The BOM will consider the matter and will seek the views of the teacher in writing on the report prepared by the Principal. The BOM shall afford the teacher an opportunity to make a formal presentation of his/her case. He/she should be given at least ten school days' written notice of the meeting (seven days for VEC teachers). The notice should state the purpose of the meeting and the specific nature of the complaint and any supporting documentation will be furnished to the teacher. The teacher concerned may be accompanied at any such meeting by his/her trade union representative(s) or colleague(s) subject to a maximum of two. The teacher will be given an opportunity to respond and state his/her case fully and to challenge any evidence that is being relied upon for a decision and be given an opportunity to respond. Having considered the response the BOM/CEO will decide on the appropriate action to be taken. Where it is decided that no action is warranted the teacher will be so informed in writing within five school days. Where, following the hearing, it is decided that further disciplinary action is warranted the BOM may avail any of the following options:

- deferral of an increment;

- withdrawal of an increment or increments;

- demotion (loss of post of responsibility);

- other disciplinary action short of suspension or dismissal;

- suspension (for a limited period and/or specific purpose) with pay;

- suspension (for a limited period and/or specific purpose) without pay;

- dismissal.

The nature of the disciplinary action should be proportionate to the nature of the work or conduct issue that has resulted in the sanction being imposed and the board will be expected to act reasonably in all cases.

Where disciplinary action short of dismissal is proposed the case will be reviewed by the BOM within a specified time period to consider whether further disciplinary action, if any, is required.

In the case of VEC teaching staff, the CEO/EO shall notify the teacher of his/her decision and any intended disciplinary action if that be the outcome of his/her deliberations. If it is decided to take disciplinary action, the CEO/EO may avail of any of the following range of sanctions:

- final written censure;

- deferral of an increment;

- withdrawal of an increment or increments.

Where disciplinary action is proposed the case will be reviewed by the CEO/EO within a specified time period to consider whether further disciplinary action, if any, is required.

The CEO/EO will act reasonably in all cases when deciding on the appropriate disciplinary action. The nature of the disciplinary action should be proportionate to the work or conduct issue that has resulted in the sanction being imposed.

If the CEO/EO considers that the matter requires to be referred to the VEC, as a reserved function, he/she shall do so. The teacher will be provided with an opportunity to attend at a meeting of a sub-committee of the VEC accompanied by his/her trade union representative/s or a colleague subject to an overall maximum of two.

The teacher will be given at least seven school days' notice of the meeting. The notice should state the purpose of the hearing and that fact that disciplinary action may be considered.

At the meeting the teacher will be given an opportunity to make his/her case in full and to challenge any evidence that is being relied upon for a decision.

Following the hearing the sub-committee of the VEC will make their report to the VEC. A copy of the report will be given to the teacher.

The VEC will consider the report. The teacher will be provided with an opportunity to attend at a meeting of the VEC accompanied by his/her trade union representative/s or a colleague subject to an overall maximum of two.

The teacher will be given at least seven school days' notice of the meeting. The notice should state the purpose of the hearing and that fact that disciplinary action may be considered.

At the meeting the teacher will be given an opportunity to make his/her case in full and to challenge any evidence that is being relied upon for a decision.

Following the hearing the VEC shall make its judgment on the matter. In formulating its judgment the VEC will take account of the report of the sub-committee of the VEC, any other evidence and the teacher's representation (if any) thereon. The VEC may decide to:

- refer the matter to the CEO/EO;

- impose a disciplinary sanction.

The VEC shall notify the teacher of its decision and any intended disciplinary action if that be the outcome of its deliberations. If it is decided to take disciplinary action, the following range of sanctions may be availed of

- suspension (for a limited period and/or specific purpose) with pay;

- suspension (for a limited period and/or specific purpose) without pay;

- suspension in accordance with the terms of the Vocational Education Acts.

Where disciplinary action short of suspension in accordance with the terms of the Vocational Education Acts is proposed the case will be reviewed by the VEC within a specified time period to consider whether further disciplinary action, if any, is required.

The VEC will act reasonably in all cases when deciding on the appropriate disciplinary action. The nature of the disciplinary action should be proportionate to the work or conduct issue that has resulted in the sanction being imposed.

Gross Misconduct

[5.28] Where gross misconduct occurs or a threat to the health & safety to students or to other members of staff occurs a teacher may be dismissed without recourse to stages 1, 2 or 3 as outlined above.

The following are some examples of gross misconduct offences where stages 1–3 do not normally apply:

- theft;
- deliberate damage to school property;
- fraud or deliberate falsification of documents;
- gross negligence or dereliction of duties;
- refusal to comply with legitimate instructions resulting in serious consequences;
- serious or persistent incapacity to perform duties due to being under the influence of alcohol, un-prescribed drugs or misuse of prescribed medication;
- serious breach of health & safety rules;
- serious abuse/misuse of the school's property/equipment;
- serious breach of confidentiality;
- serious bullying, sexual harassment or harassment against an employee, student or other members of the school community;
- violent/disruptive behaviour;
- downloading/dissemination of pornographic material from the internet;
- circulation of offensive, obscene or indecent e-mails or text messages.

(Note: the above list is not exhaustive).

[5.29] For the purposes of this section gross misconduct may also relate to an act which took place or allegedly took place outside the school.

If there is an allegation of serious misconduct, the teacher may be suspended on full pay pending an investigation and the conclusion of any appeal process.

In the course of the investigation the teacher has the right to have the allegations brought to his/her attention and he/she has the right to respond to all allegations. If the investigation upholds a case of serious misconduct the normal consequence will be dismissal.

Stage 5

Appeal

[5.30] The teacher has the right to an appeal against any of the stages as set out above.

In the case of a sanction being imposed at stage 1 the appeal will be to a nominee of the BOM/CEO. In the case of a sanction being imposed at stage 2 or stage 3 the appeal will be heard by the BOM/CEO/EO. In the case of a sanction being imposed under stage 4 of the procedure an appeal will be to a Disciplinary Appeal Panel appointed by the BOM/VEC.

Notification to the Department of Education & Science and the Teaching Council

[5.31] The BOM will inform the Department of Education & Science of the nature of the disciplinary action and will comply with any requirements of the Teaching Council in accordance with the provisions of s 37 of the Teaching Council Act 2001.

Teachers Disciplinary Appeal Panel

[5.32] The BOM/VEC shall appoint a Teachers' Disciplinary Appeal Panel which shall comprise:

- an independent Chairperson from a Panel nominated by the Minister for Education & Science;

- a representative of the recognised management body;

- a nominee of the relevant teacher's union.

No member shall be appointed to the Panel to consider a case referred to the Panel who has had any prior interest in or dealings with the particular case in question.

Appeal process

[5.33] A teacher may seek a review of disciplinary proceedings by the Panel on one or more of the following grounds:

1. the provisions of the agreed procedures were not adhered to;
2. all the relevant facts were not ascertained;
3. all the relevant facts were not considered or not considered in a reasonable manner;
4. the teacher concerned was not afforded a reasonable opportunity to answer the allegation;
5. the teacher concerned could not reasonably be expected to have understood that the behaviour alleged would attract disciplinary action;
6. the sanction recommended is disproportionate to the underperformance or misconduct alleged.

The teacher who has been informed that disciplinary action is to be taken against him/her has 10 school days from receipt of notification to request that the disciplinary proceedings be reviewed by a Panel. If no request is received within 10 days the disciplinary action proposed will be implemented.

The following submissions must be made by the teacher in question before the Panel can review a case:

> a written statement by the teacher of the grounds on which the review is being sought, to be furnished to the Panel and the employer within 10 school days of the submission of the request for an appeal
>
> a written counter statement by the employer, to be submitted to the Panel and the teacher concerned within 10 school days of the receipt by the employer of the teacher's statement
>
> any other submission which the Panel may request from the teacher concerned or the appropriate authority, to be furnished in such form and within such time as the Panel may specify

The Panel may reject a request for a review of disciplinary proceedings if the request is not made within the prescribed timeframe or if the Panel considers that the case being brought by the teacher is frivolous, vexatious or without substance of foundation.

Where a request is rejected by the Panel the employer may proceed in accordance with the terms of this procedure as though the request had not been made.

Where the Panel has decided to review the disciplinary procedures having considered the submissions, it shall set a date for a hearing within 20 school days of receipt by the Panel of the request for an appeal.

The Panel may, at its sole discretion, invite any person to give evidence orally or in writing. The Panel shall consider any request from a party to the procedure to give evidence orally or in writing.

The teacher making the appeal is entitled to make oral submissions to the Panel either in person or through a serving teacher, a whole-time official of the union or other such person as the Panel agrees may be present for that purpose. The teacher, his/her representatives, the chairperson of the BOM/CEO, any nominee of the BOM/CEO, the Principal and any other person that the Panel allows are entitled to be present at such oral representations. These proceedings before the Panel shall be informal in nature.

Having taken all evidence into consideration the Panel shall issue its opinion as to whether grounds for review were applicable or not, within 10 working school days of the date of the hearing to the teacher, his/ her representative(s) and the Chairperson of the board.

If the Panel is of the opinion that such a case for review by the teacher was applicable the Panel has the discretion to recommend to the BOM/VEC/CEO that:

- no further action should be taken in the matter;

- the disciplinary action decided by the BOM/VEC or CEO should be amended in a specified manner; or

- the case should be re-considered by the BOM/VEC or CEO to remedy a specified deficiency in the disciplinary procedures (in which event the provisions of this Code shall continue to apply).

If the Panel is of the opinion that no case for review has been established, the disciplinary action will occur. The teacher and his/her representative will be notified in writing. Where no further action is to be taken the allegation will be deemed to have been withdrawn.

The final decision in respect of the Appeal Panel's recommendation rests with the BOM/VEC or CEO which shall set out in writing to all parties concerned the basis for its decision and the matter shall thereby conclude.

Procedures for Principals relating to their work, conduct and matters of professional competence in their role as principals

[5.34] Every Principal is personally accountable for his/her individual work performance and behaviour. Early intervention at the appropriate level to address perceived inappropriate behaviour is desirable for all parties concerned so as to minimise the risk of having to escalate sanctions as provided for in these procedures.

Where circumstances warrant, a Principal may be placed on administrative leave with full pay pending: a) an investigation; b) the outcome of an investigation; or c) the outcome of a disciplinary hearing.

At all times these procedures will relate to the general principal of natural justice. There will be a presumption of innocence at all times.

A support service will be provided at both primary and post-primary levels where appropriate advice, training and assistance will be afforded to school management and Principals in the formulation of improvement plans and their implementation where necessary. Principals may seek advice form relevant management bodies on issues relevant to the operation of these agreed procedures.

Procedures relating to professional competence issues for Principals in their role as teacher.[33]

[5.35] As is the norm with every profession, a Principal in his/her role as teacher is expected to maintain appropriate standards of teaching, of work and of conduct and to personally address such issues if and when they arise. If competence issues arise a Principal is obliged to avail of all opportunities of assistance towards remediation. Often, professional competence issues are of a transient short-lived duration and may be quickly resolved.

If parental complaints relate to the professional competence of a Principal in his/her role as teacher any issues will be initially addressed by the Chairperson of the BOM in accordance with agreed complaint procedures. The Chairperson will determine whether the complaint merits consideration and the parent will be informed of all stages and the final outcome of the process. A number of stages will ensue – leading from informal to formal stages and if the matter is still not resolved, disciplinary action may need to be taken (up to and including dismissal).

---

33. Circular 59/2009 does not deal with Principals in their role as Teacher working in VECs. This section therefore only applies to Principals in all other schools who perform teaching duties.

It is at all times the right and duty of the BOM to act immediately in matters of serious misconduct – or in cases where there is a perceived threat to the health, safety and welfare of the student body.

Stage 1[34]

Informal stage

[5.36] The BOM is responsible for the guidance and direction of all staff, including Principals. If concerns arise the Chairperson will discuss them informally with the Principal and an agreed course of action will be put in place to address the matter. The Principal will be advised about internal/external supports to include:

Employment Assistance Service;

Primary Professional Development Service;

Leadership Development for Schools (LDS);

Second Level Support Service (SLSS) and /or other support agencies.

Through informal dialogue transient professional competence issues should ordinarily be resolved within a three month period – excluding holiday periods.

If the Principal refuses to engage positively with the process the Chairperson will inform the Principal that the matter will be referred to the BOM in writing whereby a formal process will be initiated. A copy of the agreed procedures will be furnished to the Principal in order that he/she may familiarise themselves with the various stages that may ensue and the range of sanctions available to the board.

Stage 2

Initiation of the formal process

[5.37] A copy of the verbal warning will be retained on the personnel file by the EO/ designated officer and a copy will be given to the Principal. The verbal warning will be active for a period of six months and, subject to satisfactory service, will cease to have effect following the expiry of the six months period. The record will be removed from the file after the six months period subject to satisfactory improvement during the period.

There may however be occasions where a Principal's work or conduct is satisfactory throughout the period the warning is in force only to lapse very soon thereafter. Where such a pattern emerges, and there is evidence of an undermining of the disciplinary process, the Principal's previous conduct and pattern of behaviour may be considered as a whole in a future disciplinary procedure.

The Chairperson will provide a written report of his/her concerns to the BOM. Simultaneously a copy is sent to the Principal who has the opportunity to respond to the

---

34.   Outlined in the Education Act 1998, ss 22 and 23.

allegations within 10 school days of receipt of the report. The Principal will be invited to address the board. At this stage it is open to him/her to invoke Stage 3 of these procedures within 10 school days of receipt of the report. Where the Principal adopts this course of action it is on the strict understanding that he/she cannot then seek to revert to any earlier stage of the process and that BOM may proceed to the next stage as appropriate.

Alternatively, if the Principal does not proceed to Stage 3, the BOM will consider the Chairperson's report and the Principal's response to it. The Principal will be given the opportunity to address the BOM.

The board will then make a decision on how to proceed. This decision may involve the board finding that:

- there are insufficient grounds to conclude that there is an issue of professional competence;

- there are sufficient grounds as to warrant the initiation of the formal process.

If sufficient grounds are found, the BOM will request that the Chairperson define an improvement plan to discuss with the Principal in his/her role as teacher outlining deficiencies, required improvements expected, range of support and training suggestions and timeframe to implement the above (three months excluding holiday periods – which may be extended by the Chairperson with the agreement of the BOM). The Chairperson will be assisted in this regard by external mentors comprising of both retired and serving Principals and any persons with particular expertise in any given relevant field. The panel will meet with the Principal to discuss the implementation of the improvement plan. All of the above will be put in writing to the Principal. The BOM will support and facilitate the Principal at all times. The timeframe may be extended at the discretion of the Chairperson if required. The Chairperson will furnish the BOM with a report of the outcome. The Chairperson has the authority to seek the views of hi/her mentors at all stages involved in the improvement plan. If satisfied, the BOM will write to the Principal to confirm the end of the formal process and the matter will be brought to a conclusion.

If not satisfied that the improvement plan has been adhered to, the Chairperson will outline in writing to the board the reasons and the Principal will be afforded the opportunity to reply – orally and in writing. The BOM, having given due consideration to the Chairperson's report and to the Principal's response thereto, will decide to draw the matter to a close or to modify the improvement plan or will agree that Principal in his/her role as teacher has not improved.

Stage 3

External review

[5.38] At this juncture the Chief Inspector of the Department of Education will be contacted to review the Principal's work having been sent a report of the outcome by the BOM. The Principal will be so informed by the BOM in such instances. The request for a review should include details of the nature of the board's concerns, the supports offered to the Principal, the extent to which these supports were availed of by the Principal and the outcomes.

Before approving the review the Chief Inspector (or his/her chosen advocate of the Inspectorate or a person with a particular expertise in a certain field) will satisfy himself/herself that the appropriate support has been offered to the Principal by the school and that, despite this, the Principal's work is still considered to be unsatisfactory. The review may entail several visits to the school in question by the Inspector's team to observe the overall professional competence of the Principal at work. The Principal will be expected to cooperate at all times. The Principal will be sent all documentation pertaining to the review by the BOM. The BOM will provide the Principal with the opportunity to make a written response to the Chief Inspector's findings within 15 school days. Where the Principal has availed of the option at Stage 2 to invoke Stage 3 the Chief Inspector will be aware of this before initiating the review. The Chief Inspector, according to s 13 of the Education Act 1998, is deemed to deal with the matter without prejudice.

Any lack of cooperation by the Principal will be taken into account when the Inspector formulates his/her conclusions. The Principal may respond to the written report to the BOM from the Inspector (within 10 school days). The matter will have concluded (the teacher will be informed within five school days) or will warrant further disciplinary action.

Stage 4

Hearing

[5.39] The Principal is given seven school days' notice and attends with his/her chosen trade union representative/colleague (max 2). The notice should state the purpose of the hearing and the fact that disciplinary action may be considered. Following the hearing, the BOM will notify the Principal of its decision – and of any necessary disciplinary action – if required. In formulating its judgment the board will take into consideration the conclusions reached by the Chief Inspector, any other evidence presented in addition to the Principal's representations (if any).

If it is decided to take disciplinary action, the BOM may avail of any of the following range of sanctions:

- final written censure;

- deferral of an increment;

- withdrawal of an increment or increments;

- suspension (for a limited period and/or specific purpose) with pay;

- suspension (for a limited period and/or specific purpose) without pay;

- dismissal.

The Principal will be notified of its decisions and the outcome of its deliberations.

If dismissal does not occur the BOM will review the case on an ongoing basis in order to ascertain whether further action is required. It will act reasonably at all times.

Stage 5

Appeal

[5.40] The Principal may appeal any proposed action of the BOM. Any appeal will be heard by an independent appeal Panel appointed by the BOM.

Notification to the Department of Education & Science and the Teaching Council

[5.41] The BOM will inform the Department of Education & Science of the nature of the disciplinary action and will comply with any requirements of the Teaching Council in accordance with the provisions of s 37 of the Teaching Council Act 2001.

Disciplinary procedures for Principals in primary, voluntary, secondary, community, comprehensive, and Vocational Education Committee Schools

Work, conduct and professional competence

[5.42] This disciplinary procedure for Principals employed in primary, community, comprehensive and voluntary secondary schools as well as Principals in VECs was developed and agreed following discussions between the Department of Education & Science, school managerial bodies and recognised teachers' unions. It takes account of employment legislation and the Labour Relation Commission's Code of Practice on Disciplinary Procedures. It supersedes all existing local and national disciplinary procedures. Principals and boards of management will be made aware of and be made fully conversant with this procedure and will adhere to its terms.

Bearing in mind that it is a matter for every Principal to maintain appropriate standards of work and conduct, (which includes all aspects of the role of Principal – other than a teacher – as outlined in the Education Act 1998, s 23) and it is fully accepted that the majority of Principals discharge their duties in a competent and efficient manner in line with the best traditions of school leadership, the onus is on the Principal to avail of all opportunities of assistance towards remediation of any issue that may arise. It must be borne in mind that issues are often transient in nature and may have their origin in areas of a personal or professional nature which are of relatively short time duration. Isolated issues or omissions of a minor nature will, where possible, be dealt with informally.

It follows that the approach to dealing with matters of work and conduct should involve a number of stages moving from informal stages to formal stages which may at the end of the process have recourse to disciplinary action (up to and including dismissal). Although disciplinary action will normally follow the progressive stages the procedure may be commenced by the school at any stage of the process if the alleged misconduct warrants such an approach.

Scope

[5.43] The scope of these procedures includes all aspects of the role of Principal as outlined in the Education Act 1998 in addition to all other relevant Acts of the Oireachtas other than professional competence issues of Principals in their roles of teachers which was treated above as outlined in Circular 60/2009 – which excludes Principals in VECs.

Allegations in respect of child abuse as defined in the Child Protection Guidelines for primary and post-primary schools are dealt with in the first instance under those guidelines.

The Education Act 1998 provides that a Principal shall:

- have responsibility and contribute generally to the education and personal development of all students under his/her care;

- encourage learning, evaluate students regularly and report findings to students and parents;

- promote co-operation between the school and the community and carry out duties assigned by the BOM/CEO/VEC;

- be responsible and accountable for the day to day running of the school, as well as guiding all members of staff;

- provide leadership to all staff and students;

- be responsible of the creation of a school environment which is supportive of learning and which promotes professional development of teachers;

- set objectives for the school in consultation with the BOM/CEO. Teachers, parents and students and monitor those objectives;

- encourage all involved in the education of students and the achievement of the school objectives.

Informal Stage

[5.44] Initially the Chairperson/CEO/EO will undertake to resolve any problems relating to work or conduct informally with the Principal. He/she will discuss the unsatisfactory conduct and inform the Principal of the required improvements expected. The Principal will be given the opportunity to explain the reason for the conduct, which may be due to personal, health or domestic circumstances. Help and advice or guidance will be given (through internal and external support mechanisms) as required. The Principal will also be informed that unless the necessary improvement is made the matter may proceed to the formal disciplinary procedure.

Where a Principal's work or conduct does not meet the required standards despite informal intervention as set out above the matter will be dealt with under the following disciplinary procedure.

Stage 1:

Verbal warning

[5.45] If a formal disciplinary meeting is to occur the Principal shall receive at least five school days' written notice. This notice should state the purpose of the meeting, outline the specific nature of the complaint and be accompanied by any supporting documentation. The Principal may bring a work colleague or a trade union representative to the meeting.

At the meeting, the Principal will be afforded the opportunity to state his/her case, respond to any allegations made and challenge any evidence submitted. Having considered the response the Chairperson/EO/designated officer will decide on the appropriate action to be taken. Where it is decided that no action is warranted the Principal will be so informed in writing within five school days. If however disciplinary action is warranted, the Chairperson/EO/designated officer will inform the Principal that he/she is being given a verbal warning. This verbal warning will include an outline of what improvement is expected and a timescale for this improvement in conduct. The warning should inform the Principal that further disciplinary action may be considered if there is no sustained satisfactory improvement. The Principal will be advised of his/her right to appeal against the disciplinary action being taken and the appeal process should be explained.

A copy of the verbal warning will be retained on the personnel file by the Chairperson/EO/designated officer and a copy will be given to the Principal. The verbal warning will be active for a period of six months after which time it will cease subject to satisfactory noted improvement and it will be removed from the file.

There may however be occasions where a Principal's work or conduct is satisfactory throughout the period the warning is in force only to lapse very soon thereafter. Where such a pattern emerges and there is evidence of an undermining of the disciplinary process, the Principal's previous conduct and pattern of behaviour may be considered as a whole in a future disciplinary procedure.

Stage 2:

Written warning

[5.46] If the Chairperson perceives no improvement in the conduct of the Principal a further meeting will be called and a nominee of the BOM/EO/designated officer and a senior officer nominated by the CEO in the case of VECs will be in attendance. The Principal will be given at least seven school days written notice of the meeting, stating the purpose of the meeting and the specific nature of the complaint together with any supporting documentation. The Principal concerned may be accompanied at any such meeting by his/her trade union representative(s) or colleague(s) subject to an overall maximum of two.

At the meeting the Principal should be given a clear statement of the areas where his or her conduct is perceived as unsatisfactory. He/she will be afforded the opportunity to state his/her case, respond to any allegations made and challenge any evidence submitted. Having considered the response the Chairperson and the BOM nominee/EO and senior officer nominated by the CEO will decide on the appropriate action to be taken. Where it is decided that no action is warranted the Principal will be so informed in writing within five school days. If however disciplinary action is warranted the Principal will be informed that he/she is being given a written warning. This written warning will include an outline of what improvement is expected and a timescale for this improvement in conduct. The warning should inform the Principal that further disciplinary action may be considered if there is no sustained satisfactory improvement. Again as in stage 1, the Principal will be advised of his/her right to appeal against the disciplinary action being taken and the appeal process should be outlined.

A copy of the written warning will be retained on the Principal's personnel file by the Chairperson/CEO and a copy will be given to him/her. The written warning will be active for a period not exceeding nine months and subject to a satisfactory improvement in conduct will cease to have effect following the expiry of the nine month period. At this point the record will be removed from the file. Where the Principal's work soon lapses in to the former pattern and is undermining the disciplinary process this pattern of behaviour may be considered in a future disciplinary procedure.

Stage 3:

Final written warning

[5.47] If no perceived improvement is noted or there is an occurrence of a more serious offence another meeting will take place. A nominee of the board will be present. In VECs a senior officer will accompany the EO/designated officer. The Principal will be afforded seven school days' notice and the letter will communicate the same information as above at stages 1& 2.

The meeting will go through the process as at Stages 1& 2. Where it is decided that no action is warranted the Principal will be so informed in writing within five school days. If however disciplinary action is warranted the Principal will be informed that he/she is being given a final written warning. This final written warning will include an outline of what improvement is expected and a timescale for this improvement in conduct. The final written warning should inform the Principal that further disciplinary action may be considered if there is no sustained satisfactory improvement. Again, as in Stages 1 and 2, the Principal will be advised of his/her right to appeal against the disciplinary action being taken and the appeal process should be outlined.

A copy of the final written warning will be retained on the personnel file by the Chairperson/CEO and a copy will be given to the Principal. The final written warning will be active for a period not exceeding 12 months and subject to satisfactory service will cease to have effect following the expiry of the 12-month period. The record will be removed from the file after the 12-month period subject to satisfactory improvement during the period.

Stage 4:

[5.48] If the poor work or conduct continues and no improvement has been perceived or if the poor work/conduct issue is of a serious nature the Chairperson shall prepare a comprehensive report and forward it to the BOM/CEO. A copy will be given to the Principal.

The BOM will consider the matter and will seek the views of the Principal in writing on the report prepared by the Chairperson. The BOM shall afford the Principal an opportunity to make a formal presentation of his/her case. He/she should be given at least ten school days' written notice of the meeting. The notice should state the purpose of the meeting and the specific nature of the complaint and any supporting documentation will be furnished to the Principal. The Principal may be accompanied at any such meeting by his/her trade union representative(s) or colleague(s) subject to a maximum of two. The Principal will be given an opportunity to respond and state his/her case fully and to challenge any evidence that is being relied upon for a decision and be given an opportunity to respond. Having considered the response the BOM will decide on the appropriate action to be taken. Where it is decided that no action is warranted the Principal will be so informed in writing within five school days. Where, following the hearing, it is decided that further disciplinary action is warranted the BOM may avail any of the following options:

- deferral of an increment;
- withdrawal of an increment or increments;
- demotion (loss of Principal's allowance);
- other disciplinary action short of suspension or dismissal;
- suspension (for a limited period and/or specific purpose) with pay;
- suspension (for a limited period and/or specific purpose) without pay;
- dismissal.

The nature of the disciplinary action should be proportionate to the nature of the work or conduct issue that has resulted in the sanction being imposed and the BOM will be expected to act reasonably in all cases.

Where disciplinary action short of dismissal is proposed the case will be reviewed by the BOM within a specified time period to consider whether further disciplinary action, if any, is required.

The procedure for Principals of VECs varies somewhat to the above and is outlined as follows:

In accordance with the provisions of the Vocational Education Committee (Amendment) Act 2001 suspension and dismissal of staff are reserved functions of the VEC and Minister respectively. Consequently, the following procedures will apply.

If the CEO decides to proceed to a disciplinary process within his/her remit, the Principal will be provided with an opportunity to attend at a meeting with the CEO accompanied by his/her trade union representative/s or a colleague subject to an overall maximum of two.

The Principal will be given at least seven school days' notice of the meeting. The notice should state the purpose of the hearing and that disciplinary action may be considered.

At the meeting the Principal will be given an opportunity to make his/her case in full and to challenge any evidence that is being relied upon for a decision.

Following the hearing, the CEO will make his/her judgement on the matter. In formulating his/her judgement the CEO will take account of the report from the EO/ designated officer and nominee of the CEO and any other evidence and the Principal's representation (if any) thereon.

The CEO shall notify the Principal of his/her decision in the matter and if, in his/her view, disciplinary action is warranted.

The CEO shall notify the Principal of his/her decision and any intended disciplinary action, if that be the outcome of his/her deliberations. If it is decided to take disciplinary action, the CEO may avail of any of the following range of sanctions:

- final written censure;

- deferral of an increment;

- withdrawal of an increment or increments;

- demotion (loss of Principals allowance).

Where disciplinary action is proposed, the case will be reviewed by the CEO within a specified time period to consider whether further disciplinary action, if any, is required.

The CEO will act reasonably in all cases when deciding on the appropriate disciplinary action. The nature of the disciplinary action should be proportionate to the work or conduct issue that has resulted in the sanction being imposed.

If the CEO considers that the matter needs to be referred to the VEC, as a reserved function, he/she shall do so. The Principal will be provided with an opportunity to attend at a meeting of a sub-committee of the VEC accompanied by his/her trade union representative/s or a colleague subject to an overall maximum of two.

The Principal will be given at least seven school days' notice of the meeting. The notice should state the purpose of the hearing and that disciplinary action may be considered.

At the meeting the Principal will be given an opportunity to make his/her case in full and to challenge any evidence that is being relied upon for a decision.

Following the hearing, the sub-committee of the VEC will make a report to the VEC. A copy of the report will be given to the Principal.

The VEC will consider the report. The Principal will be provided with an opportunity to attend at a meeting of the VEC accompanied by his/her trade union representative/s or a colleague subject to an overall maximum of two.

The Principal will be given at least seven school days' notice of the meeting. The notice should state the purpose of the hearing and that disciplinary action may be considered.

At the meeting the Principal will be given an opportunity to make his/her case in full and to challenge any evidence that is being relied upon for a decision.

Following the hearing, the VEC shall make its judgement on the matter. In formulating its judgement the VEC will take account of the report of the sub-committee of the VEC, any other evidence and the Principal's representation (if any) thereon. The VEC may decide:

- to refer the matter to the CEO;

- to impose a disciplinary sanction.

In the event that the matter is referred to the CEO the procedures set out in para 4.1 above will apply.

The VEC shall notify the Principal of its decision and of any intended disciplinary action, if that be the outcome of its deliberations. If it is decided to take disciplinary action, the following range of sanctions may be availed of:

1. suspension (for a limited period and/or specific purpose) with pay;

2. suspension (for a limited period and/or specific purpose) without pay;

3. suspension in accordance with the terms of the Vocational Education Acts.

Where disciplinary action short of suspension, in accordance with the terms of the Vocational Education Acts is proposed, the case will be reviewed by the VEC within a specified time period to consider whether further disciplinary action, if any, is required.

The VEC will act reasonably in all cases when deciding on the appropriate disciplinary action. The nature of the disciplinary action should be proportionate to the work or conduct issue that has resulted in the sanction being imposed.

Gross Misconduct

[5.49] Where gross misconduct occurs or a threat to the health & safety to students or to other members of staff occurs a Principal may be dismissed without recourse to stages 1, 2 or 3 as outlined above.

The following are some examples of gross misconduct offences where stages 1–3 do not normally apply:

- theft;

- deliberate damage to school property;

- fraud or deliberate falsification of documents;

- gross negligence or dereliction of duties;

- refusal to comply with legitimate instructions resulting in serious consequences;

- serious or persistent incapacity to perform duties due to being under the influence of alcohol, un-prescribed drugs or misuse of prescribed medication;

- serious breach of health & safety rules;

- serious abuse/misuse of the school's property/equipment;

- serious breach of confidentiality;

- serious bullying, sexual harassment or harassment against an employee, student or other members of the school community;

- violent/disruptive behaviour;

- downloading/dissemination of pornographic material from the internet;

- Circulation of offensive, obscene or indecent e-mails or text messages.

(Note: the above list is not exhaustive).

For the purposes of this section gross misconduct may also relate to an act which took place or allegedly took place outside the school.

If there is an allegation of serious misconduct, the Principal may be suspended on full pay pending an investigation and the conclusion of any appeal process.

In the course of the investigation the Principal has the right to have the allegations brought to his/her attention and he/she has the right to respond to all allegations. If the investigation upholds a case of serious misconduct the normal consequence will be dismissal.

Stage 5

Appeal

[5.50] The Principal has the right to an appeal against any of the stages as set out above.
    In the case of a sanction being imposed at stage 1 the appeal will be to a nominee of the BOM/an officer nominated by the CEO. In the case of a sanction being imposed at Stage 2 or Stage 3 the appeal will be heard by the BOM/CEO. In the case of a sanction being imposed under stage 4 of the procedure an appeal will be to a disciplinary appeal Panel appointed by the BOM/VEC.

Notification to the Department of Education & Science and the Teaching Council

[5.51] The BOM will inform the Department of Education & Science of the nature of the disciplinary action and will comply with any requirements of the Teaching Council in accordance with the provisions of s 37 of the Teaching Council Act 2001.

Disciplinary Appeal Panel for Principal Teachers

[5.52] The BOM/VEC shall appoint a Disciplinary Appeal Panel which shall comprise:

- an independent Chairperson from a Panel nominated by the Minister for Education & Science;

- • a representative of the recognized management body;

- • a nominee of the relevant teacher's union.

No member shall be appointed to the Panel to consider a case referred to the Panel who has had any prior interest in or dealings with the particular case in question.

Appeal process

[5.53] A Principal may seek a review of disciplinary proceedings by the Panel on one or more of the following grounds:

7. the provisions of the agreed procedures were not adhered to;

8. all the relevant facts were not ascertained;

9. all the relevant facts were not considered or not considered in a reasonable manner;

10. the Principal was not afforded a reasonable opportunity to answer the allegation;

11. the Principal could not reasonably be expected to have understood that the behaviour alleged would attract disciplinary action;

12. the sanction recommended is disproportionate to the underperformance or misconduct alleged.[35]

A Principal who has been informed that disciplinary action is to be taken against him/her has 10 school days from receipt of notification to request that the disciplinary proceedings be reviewed by a Panel. If no request is received within 10 days the disciplinary action proposed will be implemented.

The following submissions must be made by the Principal in question before the Panel can review a case:

a written statement by the Principal outlining the grounds on which the review is being sought, to be furnished to the Panel and the employer within 10 school days of the submission of the request for an appeal;

a written counter statement by the employer, to be submitted to the Panel and the Principal within 10 school days of the receipt by the employer of the Principal's statement;

any other submission which the Panel may request from the Principal or the appropriate authority, to be furnished in such form and within such time as the Panel may specify.

The Panel may reject a request for a review of disciplinary proceedings if the request is not made within the prescribed timeframe or if the Panel considers that the case being brought by the Principal is frivolous, vexatious or without substance of foundation.

---

35. 'Towards 2016, Revised Procedures for Suspension and Dismissal of Teachers', VEC.

Where a request (for an appeal hearing) is rejected by the Panel the employer may proceed in accordance with the terms of this procedure as though the request had not been made.

Where the Panel has decided to review the disciplinary procedures having considered the submissions, it shall set a date for a hearing within 20 school days of receipt by the Panel of the request for an appeal.

The Panel may, at its sole discretion, invite any person to give evidence orally or in writing. The Panel shall consider any request from a party to the procedure to give evidence orally or in writing.

The Principal making the appeal is entitled to make oral submissions to the Panel either in person or through a serving teacher, a whole-time official of the union or other such person as the Panel agrees may be present for that purpose. The Principal, his/her representatives, the chairperson of the BOM/CEO/EO, any nominee of the BOM/VEC and any other person that the Panel allows are entitled to be present at such oral representations. These proceedings before the Panel shall be informal in nature.

Having taken all evidence into consideration the Panel shall issue its opinion as to whether grounds for review were applicable or not, within 10 working school days of the date of the hearing to the teacher, his/ her representative(s) and the Chairperson of the board.

If the Panel is of the opinion that such a case for review by the Principal was applicable the Panel has the discretion to recommend to the BOM/CEO or VEC as appropriate that:

- no further action should be taken in the matter;

- the disciplinary action decided by the BOM/ CEO or VEC as appropriate should be amended in a specified manner; or

- the case should be re-considered by the BOM/ CEO or VEC as appropriate to remedy a specified deficiency in the disciplinary procedures (in which event the provisions of this Code shall continue to apply).

If the Panel is of the opinion that no case for review has been established, the disciplinary action will occur. The Principal and his/her representative will be notified in writing of the basis for that decision. Where no further action is to be taken the allegation will be deemed to have been withdrawn.

The final decision in respect of the Appeal Panel's recommendation rests with the BOM /CEO or VEC as appropriate, which shall set out in writing to all parties concerned the basis for its decision and the matter shall thereby conclude.

Chapter 6

REDUNDANCY

STATUTORY DEFINITION OF REDUNDANCY

[6.01] The statutory definition of redundancy is outlined in the Redundancy Payments Act 1967, s 7(2) (as amended by s 4 of the Redundancy Payments Act 1971 and s 5 of the Redundancy Payments Act 2003). It provides that:

'An employee who is dismissed shall be taken to be dismissed by reason of redundancy if the dismissal is attributable wholly or mainly to:

(a)   the fact that his employer has ceased, or intends to cease to carry on that business in the place where the employee was so employed, or

(b)   the fact that the requirements of that business for employees to carry out work of a particular kind in the place where the employee was so employed have ceased or diminished or are expected to cease or diminish, or

(c)   the fact that their employer has decided to carry on the business with fewer or no employees, whether by requiring the work for which the employee had been employed (or had been doing before their dismissal) to be done by other employees or otherwise, or

(d)   the fact that their employer has decided that the work for which the employee had been employed (or had been doing before their dismissal) should henceforward be done in a different manner for which the employee is not sufficiently qualified or trained, or

(e)   the fact that their employer has decided that the work for which the employee had been employed (or had been doing before their dismissal) should henceforward be done by a person who is also capable of doing other work for which the employee is not sufficiently qualified or trained.'

It is noteworthy that the definition of what constitutes a redundancy is extremely broad.

ENTITLEMENT TO A REDUNDANCY PAYMENT

[6.02] There are certain criteria that must be met before employees are entitled to a redundancy payment. (This does not mean that they cannot be made redundant and genuinely so before this, it merely means that they are not entitled to a statutory payment):

(1)   they must have at least two year's continuous service (104 weeks);[1]

---

1.   Redundancy Payments Act 1967, s 7 as amended by Redundancy Payments Act 1971, Schedule, para 7.

(2) they must be in employment which is insurable for all benefits under the Social Welfare Consolidation Act 1993 or have been in such employment in the period of two years prior to their dismissal;[2]

(3) they must be over the age of 16;[3]

(4) they must have been made redundant as a result of a genuine redundancy situation.

Additionally employees if they meet the above criteria may be entitled to claim a redundancy payment by reason of lay-off or short-time working if such is imposed by their employer.[4]

Continuous service

[6.03] Employment will generally be regarded as continuous unless it has been terminated by the dismissal of the employee or where the employee voluntarily leaves their employment.[5]

Under Sch 3 of the Redundancy Payments Act 1967 and s 10(a) of the Redundancy Payments Act 1971 there has always been what is sometimes referred to as 'presumption of continuity of employment'. This has been greatly strengthened by s 12 of the Redundancy Payments Act 2003 in respect of redundancies notified/declared on or after 10 April 2005. Section 12(a) refers to a number of interruptions to an employee's service and states that continuity of employment is not broken by the matters referred to. These include:

(1) sickness;

(2) lay-off;

(3) holidays;

(4) service in the reserve defence forces of the State;

(5) leave, authorised by the employer (eg career break);

(6) adoptive leave;

(7) leave under maternity protection legislation;

---

2. Redundancy Payments Act 1967, s 4 as amended by Redundancy Payments Act 1971, Schedule, para 4.
3. Note that the Protection of Employees (Exceptional Collective Redundancies and Related Matters) Act 2007 repealed the Redundancy Payments Act 1979, s 5 thereby removing the previous upper age limit of 66.
4. Redundancy Payments Act 1967, s 11 as amended by Redundancy Payments Act 1971, s 19 and Redundancy Payments Act 1979, s 10.
5. Redundancy Payments Act 1967, Sch 3, para 3 as amended by Redundancy Payments Act 1971, s 19; Redundancy Payments Act 1979, ss 17, 23.

(8)   parental leave;

(9)   force majeure leave;

(10) carer's leave;

(11) absence from work because of a lock-out by the employer or because of participation by the employee in a strike.

Additionally para 5A of Sch 3 of the 1967 Act as inserted by s 19 of the 1971 Act provides that a dismissal by reason of redundancy before an employee has 104 weeks' service, followed by the re-employment of the employee within a 26-week period does not break continuity of service.

No reference is made to any time limit on periods of sick leave absence or absence due to lay-off for continuity of employment purposes, or indeed due to any other absences.

Workers on fixed-term/specified purpose contracts

[6.04] Fixed-term/specified purpose contracts arise where an employee is hired for a particular term/purpose. The Redundancy Payments Act 2003 safeguards the right to redundancy of a worker employed under a 'fixed-purpose' contract where the exact duration of the contract was incapable of being determined at the beginning and the contract is not renewed following the fulfilling of the purpose.[6]

Employment agencies

[6.05] Under the Redundancy Payments Act 2003 employees employed through employment agencies are covered for redundancy. Where the employment agency pays the wages of the employee, it is responsible for making the statutory redundancy payment.[7]

Employees commencing work abroad

[6.06] Under the Redundancy Payments Act 2003 employees who start work in a company abroad, work there for some time and are then transferred to the company or an associated company in the Republic of Ireland and work here for at least two years before being made redundant will have all of their service counted in calculating their statutory redundancy entitlements. The reverse is also the case, ie employees who start work here who are then posted abroad and subsequently return to Ireland and are then made redundant are given full credit for all their service for redundancy purposes.[8]

---

6.   Redundancy Payments Act 1967, s 9 as amended by Redundancy Payments Act 2003, s 6.
7.   Redundancy Payments Act 1967, s 2(1) as amended by Redundancy Payments Act 2003, s 3(c).
8.   Redundancy Payments Act 2003, s 8(b) inserts a new s (2A) after Redundancy Payments Act 1967, s 25(2).

Apprentices

[6.07] Redundancy payments will not be payable in any case where an employee is dismissed within one month after the end of his/her apprenticeship. If, however, an employer retains the services of an employee for more than a month after the completion of their apprenticeship, the period of apprenticeship will count in calculating any redundancy payments in respect of that employee in the future.

An apprentice whose employment terminates by reason of redundancy during the period of their apprenticeship will qualify for a redundancy lump sum payment if they meet the usual requirements for entitlement, ie are between the ages of 16 and 66 and have at least two years' service etc.[9]

Seasonal workers

[6.08] In the case of workers who are laid off for an average period of more than 12 weeks per year prior to redundancy, the provisions relating to lay-off will not apply until the end of that average period. In the case of a seasonal worker, therefore, there will normally be no question of redundancy until the usual commencement time of his seasonal work. If s/he is not then re-employed, the question of redundancy arises, but not until such time.

Insurable employment

[6.09] Employees must be in employment which is fully insurable for all benefits under the Social Welfare (Consolidation) Act 1993 but for the fact that the employment concerned is an excepted employment by virtue of paras 2, 4 or 5 of Pt II of the First Schedule to that Act.[10] This in effect means that employees will be entitled to a redundancy payment even where the employment is of a casual nature, where the employee is employed by a prescribed relative of the employed person, where the employment concerned is not the principal means of livelihood and where the employment is of 'inconsiderable extent'. The question of insurability is decided by the Department of Social and Family Affairs in accordance with the rules and appeals procedures provided for in the Social Welfare Acts.

Part-time workers

[6.10] The Redundancy Payments Act 2003 secured the rights of part-time workers to a statutory redundancy payment through amending insurability requirements for redundancy to bring them into line with the Social Welfare Acts and the Protection of Employees (Part-Time Work) Act 2001. This is in line with the provision of the 2001 Act that part-time employees cannot be treated in a less favourable manner than

---

9.   Redundancy Payments Act 1967, s 7(4).
10.   Redundancy Payments Act 1967, s 4 as amended by Redundancy Payments Act 2003, s 4.

comparable full-time employees in relation to conditions of employment. In particular, there is recognition for the rights of workers to statutory redundancy in:

- 'casual employment';[11]

- 'subsidiary employment', where a person depends on another employment for their livelihood;[12]

- 'employment of inconsiderable extent',[13] ie very low wage.

Aged over 16

[6.11] Employees to qualify for a redundancy payment must be over 16 years of age.

Genuine redundancy

[6.12] In general this means that the work no longer exists and the person is not replaced. The emphasis is on the job and not the person. This 'impersonal' requirement is endorsed by the amendment of s 7(2) of the 1967 Act by s 5 of the 2003 Act which inserts additional wording into the 1967 Act to reiterate this fact (also see **6.50**).

The right to a redundancy lump sum payment by Reason of lay-off or short-time (Form RP9)

[6.13] Lay-off and short-time are defined in s 11 of the 1967 Act as amended by s 10 of the 1979 Act.

A lay-off occurs where the services of an employee are not required because of lack of work to be carried out by that employee, once the employer gives notice to the employee beforehand that the break in employment is temporary in nature (Redundancy Form RP9 may be used for this purpose; see **6.81**). If an employer fails to give notice of lay-off, the door is then open to the employee to claim a statutory redundancy payment.

Short-time occurs when there is a reduction in the amount of work available, leading to a reduction in weekly earnings to less than half the normal weekly earnings or a reduction in the hours worked to less than half the normal weekly working hours. Here again employers must give notice that the short-time is of a temporary nature as failure to do so will leave open the possibility of claims for a redundancy payment from the affected employee(s).

Where an employee has been laid off or kept on short-time or a mixture of both takes place, either for four consecutive weeks or for a broken series of six weeks where all six weeks occur within a 13-week period, the employee may claim a redundancy payment.[14]

The employee must serve a written notice stating that they intend to claim redundancy by reason of lay-off or short-time (Form RP9 can be used for this purpose)

---

11. Social Welfare (Consolidation) Act 1993, Sch 1, Pt 2, para 2.
12. See Social Welfare (Consolidation) Act 1993, Sch 1, Pt 2, para 2.
13. See Social Welfare (Consolidation) Act 1993, Sch 1, Pt 2, para 5.
14. Redundancy Payments Act 1967, s 12(1)(a) as inserted by Redundancy Payments Act 1971, s 11.

or alternatively they must give notice in writing to their employer terminating their contract of employment (Form RP9 may also be used for this purpose).

Employees can wait longer than the periods mentioned to serve either of the notices. However, if the short-time or lay-off stops and if they do decide to claim, they must serve notice of their intention not later than four weeks after the lay-off or short-time ceases. After that, they are debarred from claiming a payment in respect of that particular period of lay-off or short-time.[15]

Redundancy by reason of lay-off and short-time and notice pay

[6.14] An employee who claims and receives a redundancy payment due to lay-off or short-time is deemed to have voluntarily left their employment and as such is not entitled to notice under the Minimum Notice and Terms of Employment Acts 1973 to 2001. In such cases it is the employee who is terminating the contract. Consequently they are not entitled to notice.[16]

Employer's right to give counter notice when redundancy by way of lay-off or short-time working is claimed

[6.15] Employers may also serve counter notice on an employee(s) claiming a redundancy payment by reason of short-time working or lay-off.[17] The counter notice must be given within seven days from the service of notice by the employee(s) on the employer claiming a redundancy payment and the employer must offer those affected not less than 13 weeks' unbroken employment starting within four weeks of the employee's/employees' serving notice. The counter notice by the employer must indicate that any claim for a redundancy payment by the employee(s) will be contested.[18] Again, redundancy form RP9 may be used for this purpose.

If, however, an unsatisfactory situation from the employee(s) point of view persists after the employer has given counter notice, with four more consecutive weeks of short-time or lay-off from their date of notice to claim redundancy, then the employee(s) become eligible for redundancy.[19]

Employees wishing to leave their employment before their notice of proposed dismissal expires

[6.16] Employees can give their employers notice in writing of their intention to terminate their contract of employment before their notice of redundancy expires, ie the date which is set out in redundancy form RP50 (see **6.82**). Part 1 of Form RP6 is used for this purpose (see **6.83**). Employers may however issue the employee with a counter-notice in writing, requesting them to withdraw their notice and to continue in

---

15.   Redundancy Payments Act 1967, s 12(1)(b) as inserted by Redundancy Payments Act 1971, s 11.
16.   See *Irish Country Meats Ltd v Duignan* M1164/94.
17.   Redundancy Payments Act 1967, s 13.
18.   Redundancy Payments Act 1967, s 13(1) and (2).
19.   Redundancy Payments Act 1967, s 13(3).

employment until the original date of notice expires. Employers should use form RP6 (Part 2 of the form). If the employee unreasonably refuses to comply with this counter-notice employers can then contest liability to pay a redundancy payment.[20]

Employers who agree to an employee's request to leave early can indicate their consent by using part 3 of form RP6. This involves the employer giving the employee consent to alter his proposed date of termination of employment so as to bring that new date within what is referred to as 'the obligatory period of notice'. The date of dismissal then becomes the date on which the employee's notice expires.[21]

DISENTITLEMENT TO A REDUNDANCY PAYMENT

[6.17] There are certain circumstances where an employee may, although they meet the criteria for a redundancy payment, not in fact be entitled to receive one.

Alternative work

[6.18] In certain circumstances an offer of alternative employment from their employer will bar an employee from a redundancy payment:[22]

(a) An employee whose contract is terminated and immediately renewed or who is immediately re-engaged will be taken not to have been dismissed nor will they be entitled to a redundancy payment if the provisions of the renewed or new contract do not differ from those of the previous contract and if the employee accepts.[23]

(b) An employer may give an offer in writing to an employee to have their contract renewed or to be re-engaged under a new contract on terms different from those of the previous contract. If the new or renewed contract takes effect within four weeks from the ending of the previous contract and the employee accepts it, they will not in these circumstances be taken to have been dismissed or be eligible for a redundancy payment.[24]

(c) If an employer offers an employee the opportunity to have their contract renewed or to be re-engaged under a new contract on terms which do not differ from those of their previous contract and if the renewal or re-engagement would take effect on the date of dismissal and the employee unreasonably refuses the offer, they will not be entitled to a redundancy payment.[25]

(d) An employee whose job is no longer available and who is offered alternative work by their employer may take the work for a trial period of not more than four weeks and then refuse the offer. In this instance the temporary acceptance

---

20. Redundancy Payments Act 1967, s 10 as amended by Redundancy Payments Act 1979, s 9.
21. Redundancy Payments Act 1967, s 10(3A) as inserted by Redundancy Payments Act 1979, s 9.
22. Redundancy Payments Act 1967, s 15 as amended by Redundancy Payments Act 1971, s 19.
23. Redundancy Payments Act 1967, s 15(1) as amended by Redundancy Payments Act 1971, s 19.
24. Redundancy Payments Act 1967, s 15(2) as inserted by Redundancy Payments Act 1971, s 19.
25. Redundancy Payments Act 1967, s 15(1) as amended by Redundancy Payments Act 1971, s 19.

shall not prejudice any plea by such employees that the refusal of the offer was reasonable.[26]

(e) An employee may also temporarily accept a substantial reduction in their remuneration or hours of work. If such reduction is not less than half their normal working hours or remuneration, eg a three- or four-day week, such temporary acceptance for a period not exceeding 52 weeks shall not be taken to be an acceptance by them of an offer of suitable employment and they will still be able to claim a redundancy payment.[27]

Employees who are entitled to a weekly payment and unreasonably refuse suitable employment offered or approved by FÁS 'shall be disqualified from receiving any further weekly payments'.[28]

Misconduct

[6.19] Section 14 of the 1967 Act provides that an employee shall not be entitled to a redundancy payment if they are dismissed by reason of their conduct and the employer is entitled to so dismiss them because of such conduct.

CALCULATION OF STATUTORY ENTITLEMENT

Calculation of a week's pay for purposes of the Act

[6.20] A week's pay for the purposes of the Act is defined as gross weekly wage plus average regular overtime plus benefits-in-kind.[29]

The total figure is then taken to be the weekly pay for redundancy calculation purposes. For calculation of a week's pay the legislation effectively defines two separate patterns of work. First, time-based workers, ie those workers whose pay does not vary in relation to the amount of work they do, and secondly, piece-rate workers, ie those workers whose pay depends on the amount of work they do.[30] However, there are also other circumstances that require careful consideration in calculating a week's pay such as when employees are job sharing, working part-time etc.

---

26. Redundancy Payments Act 1967, s 15(2A) as inserted by Redundancy Payments Act 1971, s 19.
27. Redundancy Payments Act 1967, s 15(2B) as inserted by Redundancy Payments Act 1971, s 11.
28. Redundancy Payments Act 1967, s 15(3) was entirely substituted by Redundancy Payments Act 1971, s 19(1), and its reference to the Employment Service altered to a reference to the National Manpower Service. The Labour Services Act 1987, s 18(4) made references to the National Manpower Service in any Act of the Oireachtas be construed as references to An Foras Aiseanna Saothair. Also the last four words of the section were substituted for the words 'a weekly payment for a period not exceeding six weeks' by Redundancy Payments Act 1971, s 17.
29. Redundancy Payments Act 1967, Sch 3 as amended by Redundancy Payments Act 1971, s 19.
30. Redundancy Payments Act 1967, Sch 3, paras 13 and 16 as amended by Redundancy Payments Act 1971, s 19.

Full-time employees on a fixed wage or salary

[6.21] This is the work pattern in most cases, ie a fixed wage or salary. Here the employee's wages do not vary in relation to the amount of work done. A week's pay in this instance means earnings for the normal weekly working hours at the date the employee was declared redundant, ie the date on which notice of proposed dismissal was given. This figure includes any regular bonus or allowance which does not vary in relation to the amount of work done along with any benefits-in-kind normally received by the employee.

Where an employee is normally expected to work overtime, their average weekly overtime earnings will be taken into account in determining their 'week's pay' for redundancy purposes. To establish the amount of overtime earnings applicable, add the total amount of overtime earnings in the period of 26 weeks ending 13 weeks before the date the employee was declared redundant and divide the amount by 26.

Piece-rate workers

[6.22] A piece-rate worker is defined as an employee whose pay depends on the amount of work they carry out, ie they are paid wholly or partly by piece rates, bonuses or commissions etc related to output. There is a special formula for calculating this amount, based on normal weekly working hours, as follows:

(a) The total number of ***hours*** worked by the employee in the 26-week period ending 13 weeks before the date of being declared redundant is calculated first. (Any week or weeks during the 26-week period, in which the employee did not work will not be taken into account and the most recent week or weeks counting backwards, before the 26-week period, will be taken into account instead.)

(b) Add up all the ***pay*** earned in this 26-week period. This should be adjusted to take into account any late changes in rates of pay which came into operation in the 13 weeks before the employee was declared redundant.

(c) The employee's average hourly rate of pay is then calculated by simply dividing the total pay as at (b) above by the total number of hours as at (a) above. Finally, establish the weekly pay by multiplying this average hourly rate by the number of normal weekly working hours of the employee at the date on which they were declared redundant (ie date of being given notice of redundancy).

Employees on short-time working

[6.23] The Redundancy Payments Act 2003 clarified this issue in respect of those on short-time working by providing that the gross wage for calculation of a redundancy lump sum is based on a full week's pay.[31]

---

31. Redundancy Payments Act 2003, s 11.

Where redundancy is claimed on the basis of lay-off or short-time (Form **RP9**), the date of termination of employment is taken to be the date that the employee applies for redundancy.

Job-sharers

[6.24] Where a person decides to job-share, their job-sharing pay rather than their previous full-time pay is used for redundancy calculation purposes.[32]

Employees on reduced working hours

[6.25] When a person is put on reduced working hours by their employer, eg a three-day week or a four-day week (as opposed to short-time which is a two-day week), the redundancy entitlement is calculated on the basis of a full week, provided the employee was put on reduced hours within 52 weeks before being made redundant. If they were made redundant after the first year of reduced working hours and it is clear that the employee fully accepted the reduced working hours as being their normal working week, then the employee is deemed to have accepted the reduced hours as their normal week. In this situation the gross pay for redundancy purposes is based on the reduced working hours.

On the other hand, if the employee never accepted the reduced working hours as their 'normal' hours and were constantly seeking to be put back on full time working, they could then be deemed not to have accepted their reduced hours 'as normal'. In these circumstances redundancy entitlement should be calculated at the full-time rate of pay.

Where an employee makes a request to be placed on reduced working hours, for their own reasons, and the employer agrees, the redundancy entitlement is automatically based on the reduced hours.[33]

Employees with no normal working hours

[6.26] In a case where an employee has no normal working hours their average weekly pay will be taken to be the average weekly pay including any bonus, pay allowance or commission over the period of 52 weeks during which they were working before the date on which they were declared redundant.[34]

Shift workers

[6.27] An employee who is employed on shift work and whose pay varies according to the shift on which they work will be taken to be an employee who is paid wholly or partly by piece rates.[35]

---

32.   Redundancy Payments Act 1967, s 15(2B) as inserted by Redundancy Payments Act 1979, s 11.
33.   Redundancy Payments Act 1967, s 15(2B) as inserted by Redundancy Payments Act 1979, s 11.
34.   Redundancy Payments Act 1967, Sch 3, para 20.
35.   Redundancy Payments Act 1967, Sch 3, para 19.

Minimum wage

[6.28] The minimum rates of pay laid down in the National Minimum Wage Act 2000 (as amended), should always be taken into account when calculating a statutory redundancy lump sum. The Department of Enterprise, Trade and Employment insists on evidence of payment of the full statutory redundancy entitlement to the employee, in accordance with the prevailing minimum rates of pay, before paying the 60% employer rebate.

Reckonable and non-reckonable service

[6.29] Even though an employee may have the requisite continuous service it does not necessarily hold that all that service will be reckonable for redundancy calculation purposes. The 2003 Act significantly altered the method of calculation of reckonable and non-reckonable service.

Non-reckonable service

[6.30] During the three-year period ending with the date of termination of employment for redundancies notified/declared on or after 10 April 2005 (being the date of coming into operation of s 12 of the Redundancy Payments Act 2003) the following are all non-reckonable for redundancy calculation purposes:[36]

(a) absence in excess of 52 consecutive weeks by reason of an occupational accident or disease within the meaning of the Social Welfare (Consolidation) Act 1993 – the first 52 weeks are therefore fully reckonable;

(b) absence in excess of 26 consecutive weeks by reason of any illness not referred to in subparagraph (a) – the first 26 weeks are therefore fully reckonable;

(c) absence by reason of lay-off by the employer;

(d) absence from work by reason of a strike in the business or industry in which the employee concerned is employed;

(e) carer's leave in excess of 65 days (see **6.36**).

Non-reckonable service for redundancy calculation purposes in respect of all redundancies from 10 April 2005 now applies only to the last three years of service. Before that date non-reckonable service did not exist as a concept. The exact wording used in s 12 is very clear:

> During, and only during the 3 year period ending with the date of termination of employment, none of the following absences shall be allowable as reckonable service ...

---

36. Redundancy Payments Act 1967, Sch 3, para 8 as inserted by Redundancy Payments Act 2003, s 11(b).

If a person has been employed, for example, for 10 years, there will be no non-reckonable service in respect of the first seven years – any non-reckonable service will only be included for the last three years.

This three-year rule does not apply to redundancies notified before the above date of 10 April 2005. In the case of such previous redundancies, therefore, non-reckonable periods of employment as above (a) to (e) are applicable to the entire employment history of the employee.

NOTE – While lay-off within the three-year period referred to above (ending on the date of termination of employment), is non-reckonable, absence due to short-time working is fully reckonable (for definition of short-time working, see **6.23**).

Reckonable service

[6.31] The following are regarded as reckonable service:[37]

(i) a week falling within a period of continuous employment during any part of which an employee is actually at work;

(ii) absence from work due to sickness, holidays or with their employer's permission (subject to the 52-week and 26-week rule (see (a) at **6.29** above));

(iii) absence from work because of a lock-out; or

(iv) periods of service where continuity is preserved in any case of redress by way of reinstatement or re-engagement under the Unfair Dismissals Acts 1977 to 2001.

The following allowable absences are specifically referred to in s 12 of the Redundancy Payments Act 2003 which came into operation on 10 April 2005 with respect to redundancies notified/declared as and from that date (maternity leave, adoptive leave, parental leave and carer's leave were already reckonable before that date):

(a) absence from work while on adoptive leave under the Adoptive Leave Act 1995 (as amended) – increased from 14 weeks to 16 weeks from 19 November 2004;

(b) absence from work while on additional maternity leave (maternity leave under the Maternity Protection Act 1994 was itself already allowable in the pre-10 April 2005 period), protective leave or natal care absence within the meaning of the Maternity Protection Act 1994 (amended by the Maternity Protection (Amendment) Act 2004);

(c) absence from work while on parental leave or force majeure leave within the meaning of the Parental Leave Act 1998;

(d) absence from work while on carer's leave within the meaning of the Carer's Leave Act 2001;

---

37. Redundancy Payments Act 1967, Sch 3, para 8A as inserted by Redundancy Payments Act 2003, s 11(b).

(e)   any absences not mentioned under (a) to (e) above but authorised by the employer, eg a career break.

Maternity leave and additional maternity leave for redundancy calculation purposes

[6.32] An employee cannot be given notice of redundancy while on maternity leave or additional maternity leave.[38] Thus the date of an employee's dismissal or termination of employment in a redundancy situation under the Redundancy Payments Acts 1967 to 2003 is deemed to be the date of the employee's expected return to work as notified to her employer (or his/her successor) under the maternity protection legislation.

Additional maternity leave of 16 weeks, protective leave or natal care absence within the meaning of the Maternity Protection Act 1994 and the Maternity Protection (Amendment) Act 2004 are all reckonable for redundancy calculation purposes in respect of redundancies notified/declared since 10 April 2005, being the date of the coming into operation of s 12 of the Redundancy Payments Act 2003.

Regarding employees declared redundant on or after 10 April 2005, there is no question of any maternity leave or additional maternity leave being non-reckonable in the period prior to the last three years of service, ending on the date of termination of employment. Thus, all periods of absence due to maternity or additional maternity leave arising before the last three years of employment are fully reckonable for such employees.

Parental leave for redundancy calculation purposes

[6.33] For statutory redundancy calculation purposes, parental leave, which at present is 14 weeks,[39] is already fully reckonable under the Parental Leave Act 1998. This has been reinforced under s 12 of the Redundancy Payments Act 2003 in respect of redundancies notified/declared since 10 April 2005, with specific provision being made whereby parental leave and force majeure leave[40] within the meaning of the Parental Leave Act 1998 are fully reckonable for statutory redundancy purposes.

Calculating 'excess days' in respect of redundancies notified/declared on or after 10 April 2005

[6.34] All 'excess' days are credited as a proportion of a year.[41] For example, 103 days give the employee an extra 28.22% of a year's service, on top of whatever number of full years they have worked for. The simple formula used in this situation for calculating the proportion of a year to be credited to the employee is 103 divided by 365 = .2822, or in percentage terms = 28.22%.

---

38.   Maternity Protection Act 1994, s 23 as amended by Maternity Protection (Amendment) Act 2004, s 15.

39.   Parental Leave Act 1998, s 6(1).

40.   See Parental Leave Act 1998, s 13.

41.   Redundancy Payments Act 2003, s 11.

Adoptive leave for redundancy calculation purposes

[6.35] Since 19 November 2004, 16 weeks of absence due to adoptive leave has been fully reckonable for redundancy calculation purposes, increased from 14 weeks before that date. As above, with respect to redundancies notified on or after 10 April 2005, any adoptive leave taken before the last three years of employment will be fully reckonable.

Carer's leave for redundancy calculation purposes

[6.36] Under the Carer's Leave Act 2001, there is a maximum period of reckonable service of 104 weeks in respect of any one care recipient.[42] Again, regarding all redundancies notified since 10 April 2005, the three-year rule of confining any non-reckonable service to the three years ending on the date of termination also applies to carer's leave. Before that three-year period, all carer's leave is fully reckonable.

Career break leave

[6.37] Under s 12(b) of the Redundancy Payments Act 2003 any absences outside of the usual type of absences due to maternity leave, additional maternity leave, parental leave, adoptive leave, carer's leave etc 'but authorised by the employer' are fully reckonable, even during the last three years of employment. The most common form of this type of leave would be a career break. Regarding such absences occurring before 10 April 2005, the position was that the first 13 weeks in any 52-week period were reckonable.

Employer's rebate

[6.38] All employers who comply with the legislation are entitled to a 60 per cent rebate following payment of a redundancy lump sum. Applications should be made to the Department of Enterprise, Trade and Employment using Form RP50, Pt B. This form can be submitted electronically to the Department through their website at http://www.entemp.ie.

Time limit for employer's rebate claim

[6.39] The time limit for making an employer's rebate claim to the Department of Enterprise, Trade and Employment is six months from the date of payment of the redundancy lump sum by the employer to the employee.

COLLECTIVE REDUNDANCIES

Legislation

[6.40] The Protection of Employment Act 1977 as amended by the Protection of Employment Order 1996 (SI 370/1996) and the Protection of Employment Regulations

---

42.   This was extended from 65 weeks to 104 weeks by the Social Welfare Reform of Pensions Act 2006, s 48.

2000 (SI 488/2000) stipulate the procedures to be followed before giving effect to collective redundancies. The purpose of the 1977–2000 Act is to place an onus on the employer, in the event of collective redundancies, to consult with employees and their representatives and to notify the Minister for Enterprise, Trade and Employment at least 30 days before any dismissals take effect.

Protection of Employment Act 1977

[6.41] The Protection on Employment Act 1977, brought Directive 75/129/EEC into law in Ireland,. The Act defines a collective redundancy in s 6(1) as amended by s 5 of SI 370/1996 as follows:

> where in any period of thirty consecutive days the number of such dismissals is;
>
> (a)   at least five in an establishment normally employing more than twenty and less than fifty employees;
>
> (b)   at least ten in an establishment normally employing at least fifty but less than one hundred employees;
>
> (c)   at least ten per cent of the number of employees in an establishment normally employing at least on hundred but less that three hundred employees; and
>
> (d)   at least thirty in an establishment normally employing three hundred or more employees.

The Protection of Employment Acts 1977–2000 does not apply to establishments employing less than 21 people.

The Directive applies to all employees with a contract for service. This means that all employees regardless of whether they are entitled to a redundancy payment or not count for the purposes of the above section.

Protection of Employment Order 1996

[6.42] The Protection of Employment Order 1996 (SI 370/1996) enacted the provisions of Directive 92/56/EEC into Irish law. The order added to the category of persons covered by the law on collective redundancies by providing that persons are deemed to be employees under the same deeming provisions contained in the Unfair Dismissals (Amendment) Act 1993, s 13. This means that agency workers are 'counted' for the purposes of the Act.

Protection of Employment Regulations 2000

[6.43] The Protection of Employment Regulations 2000 (SI 488/2000) amend the 1977 Act further by expanding on the definition of employee representative and providing that in the absence of same a person or persons should be chosen (under an arrangement put in place by the employer) by such employees as are affected from amongst their number to represent them in negotiations with the employer.[43]

Consultation

[6.44] Where collective redundancies arise, art 2(1) of EC Directive 98/59/EC imposes an obligation on employers to begin consultations with the workers' representatives 'in good time' in the case where they are 'contemplating collective redundancies'; such consultation must also be 'with a view to reaching agreement'.[44] This definition raises a number of queries for employers, such as what is the meaning of, inter alia, 'contemplating', 'in good time', and 'consult, with a view to reaching an agreement'. The ECJ case of *Junk v Kunhel*[45] clarified these.

In *Junk v Kunhel* the ECJ held that contemplating collective redundancies refers to a situation where an employer has drawn up a 'project' and to that end it corresponds with a situation in which no decision has yet been taken. By contrast the notification to a worker that his or her contract of employment has been terminated is the expression of a decision to sever the employment relationship. In this context the ECJ held that the terms used by the Community legislature indicate that the obligations to consult (and to notify) arise prior to any decision by an employer to terminate contracts of employment.

Furthermore the ECJ went on to hold that as consultation is provided for by the terms of art 2(2) of the Directive, 'with a view to reaching agreement', this imposes an obligation to negotiate. The ECJ concluded that the 'effectiveness of such an obligation would be compromised if an employer was entitled to terminate contracts of employment during the course of the procedure or even at the beginning thereof'. Accordingly a contract may only be terminated after the conclusion of the consultation procedure, ie after the employer has complied with the obligations set out in art 2.

Moreover consultations/negotiations should commence at the earliest opportunity but in any event at least 30 days before the first dismissal takes effect.

What this means for employers is:

- Consultations must start before any decision is made.

- Consultation in the context in which the Directive is written imposes an obligation to negotiate.

- No contracts can be terminated until after the consultation process has finished.

The 1977 Act defines 'employee representatives' as meaning a trade union, staff association or excepted body with which it has been the practice of the employer to conduct collective bargaining negotiations.[46] In the absence of a trade union, staff

---

43. Protection on Employment Act 1977, s 2(1) as inserted by Protection of Employment Regulations 2000 (SI 488/2000), reg 3.
44. EC Directive 98/59/EC, art 2(1) is transposed into Irish Law by Protection on Employment Act 1977, s 9(1) as amended by Protection of Employment Order 1996 (SI 370/1996) and Protection of Employment Regulations 2000 (SI 488/2000).
45. *Junk v Kunhel* (Case C–188/03).
46. Protection on Employment Act 1977, s 2(1) as amended by Protection of Employment Regulations 2000 (SI 488/2000), reg 3.

association or excepted body, the EC (Protection of Employment) Regulations 2000 requires an employer to put in place an arrangement whereby employees may nominate a person or persons to represent them in negotiations with their employer.

Consultations/negotiations with employee representatives must cover:[47]

(a) the possibility of avoiding the proposed redundancies; reducing the number of employees to be made redundant or the possibility of redeployment, or retraining of employees; and

(b) the basis on which it will be decided which particular employees will be made redundant.

Employers are obliged to give all information relevant to the proposed collective redundancies in writing to employee representatives, including the following:[48]

1. the reasons for the proposed redundancies;

2. the number, and descriptions or categories of employees whom it is proposed to make redundant;

3. the number of employees, and their description or categories, normally employed;

4. the period during which it is proposed to effect the proposed redundancies;

5. the criteria proposed for the selection of the workers to be made redundant; and

6. the method for calculating any redundancy payment other than those methods set out in the Redundancy Payments Acts 1967–1991.

Failure to consult

[6.45] Where an employer fails to engage in the consultation process, an employee, trade union, staff association, or excepted body may refer a complaint to a Rights Commissioner[49] within six months of the alleged contravention (in exceptional circumstances this period may be extended by a further six months). The decision of a rights commissioner may:

(a) declare that the complaint is, or as the case may be, is not well-founded;

(b) require the employer to comply with the provisions of the Act;

(c) require the employer to pay the employee compensation not exceeding four weeks' remuneration in respect of the employee's employment.

---

47. Protection on Employment Act 1977, s 9 as amended by the Protection of Employment Order 1996 (SI 370/1996) and Protection of Employment Regulations 2000 (SI 488/2000)

48. Protection on Employment Act 1977, s 10 as amended by Protection of Employment Order 1996 (SI 370/1996), art 9.

49. Protection of Employment Regulations 2000 (SI 488/2000), reg 6.

A Rights Commissioner recommendation may be appealed to the Employment Appeals Tribunal within six weeks of the date it is communicated to the relevant parties.[50] Failure to comply with the consultation process is also an offence under the Act. If prosecuted by the Minister for Enterprise, Trade and Employment, an employer may be liable on summary conviction to a fine not exceeding €1,904.61.[51]

Notification to the Minister

[6.46] In addition to the consultation procedures outlined, employers must notify the Minister for Enterprise, Trade and Employment in writing of the collective redundancy situation at the earliest opportunity and in any event at least 30 days before the first dismissal takes effect.[52] (See draft letter at **6.79**.)

Certain particulars must be specified in the notification including:

1. the name and address of the employer, indicating whether he or she is a sole trader, a partnership or a company;

2. the address of the establishment where the collective redundancies are proposed;

3. the total number of persons normally employed at that establishment;

4. the number and description or categories of employees whom it is proposed to make redundant;

5. the period during which the collective redundancies are proposed to be affected;

6. the reasons for the proposed redundancies;

7. the names and addresses of the employees' representatives consulted about the proposed redundancies;

8. the date on which those consultations commenced and the progress achieved to date of notification.

The Minister must also be supplied with a copy of all the information given to employee representatives.[53] Employers may be requested to enter into additional consultations with the Minister or an authorised officer in order to seek solutions to the problems posed by the proposed redundancies. Employee representatives must be given a copy of the information supplied to the Minister.[54] Where an employer fails to comply with the notification process, he or she is guilty of an offence and will be liable to a fine not exceeding €5,000.[55] While statutory notice due to employees may run concurrently with

---

50.   Protection of Employment Regulations 2000 (SI 488/2000), reg 6(4)(b).
51.   Protection of Employment Act 1977, s 11.
52.   Protection of Employment Regulations 2000 (SI 488/2000).
53.   Protection of Employment Act 1977, s 10(1).
54.   Protection of Employment Act 1977, s 12.
55.   Protection of Employment Act 1977, s 13 as amended by Protection of Employment Regulations 2000 (SI 488/2000), reg 5 and Protection of Employment (Exceptional Collective Redundancies and Related Matters) Act 2007, s 13.

the 30-day notice to the Minister, no redundancies can take effect during that time. Where collective redundancies are effected by an employer before the expiry of the 30-day period, the employer will be guilty of an offence and is liable to a fine not exceeding €250,000.[56]

Records

[6.47] An employer is obliged to keep all necessary records to show that the Act is being complied with. The records must be retained for at least three years.[57]

Information and Consultation Act 2006 and redundancies

[6.48] In addition to the requirements under the Protection of Employment Acts 1977–2000 to consult with employees 'with a view to agreement', there is also a requirement under the Information and Consultation Act to consult with employees (which may be with a view to agreement in some instances) on changes affecting their contract of employment. Failure to comply again leaves employers exposed to the possibility of fines.

REDUNDANCY AND UNFAIR DISMISSAL

(See also **3.61**.)

[6.49] Section 6(4)(c) of the Unfair Dismissals Act 1977 provides that a dismissal is not an unfair dismissal if it results wholly or mainly from the redundancy of the employee. Redundancy is therefore an absolute defence to a claim for unfair dismissal, provided the employee has been fairly selected for redundancy. It should be noted that the EAT is extremely vigilant in scrutinising unfair dismissal 'defence' claims on the basis of redundancy by employers and strict adherence by employers to the statutory definition of redundancy is required if a successful defence is to be mounted.

The redundancy must be genuine

[6.50] The first 'hurdle' that employers have to cross in defending an unfair dismissal claim relating to redundancy is that the redundancy was genuine. Employers will be put on strict proof of this fact and accordingly it is necessary to come prepared with facts and figures to prove that a redundancy existed. What will be required here is evidence that a redundancy situation existed; to prove this employers will need more than just a mere statement from a senior manager. Facts and figures will be required demonstrating

---

56. Protection of Employment Act 1977, s 14(2) as amended by Protection of Employees (Part-Time Work) Act 2001, s 21 and Protection of Employment (Exceptional Collective Redundancies and Related Matters) Act 2007, s 13.
57. Protection on Employment Act 1977, s 18.

such matters as for example a reduction in turnover, profit and loss figures, loss of customers etc and their direct effect on the company. Independent financial advice would also be helpful.

It is very clear that the Tribunal will scrutinise every case in order to determine whether a genuine redundancy exists. In *Lyons v Grangemore Landscapes Limited*[58] the claimant was employed by the respondent as a quantity surveyor. Arising out of financial difficulties the claimant was dismissed by reason of redundancy on 7 January 2008. After this the company employed an engineer in June 2008 to manage specific 'muck-shifting' jobs in Cork. This new employee had identical qualifications to the claimant. The claimant was not considered for this position. The main question considered by the Tribunal was whether the claimant's position was genuinely redundant? Whilst the Tribunal was significantly swayed by the fact that no consideration was given to the possibility of redeploying the claimant, emphasis was placed on the fact that the new employee, who had identical qualifications to the claimant, was employed 'within a few weeks' of the claimant's dismissal. All told the Tribunal was not satisfied that a genuine redundancy situation arose and was further satisfied that the claimant could have carried out the work of the new employee.

In *Cronin v Rachel Dalton Communications Limited*[59] the claimant held a senior position in the respondent's public relations (PR) agency. Problems began to develop regarding his performance which led to the employee receiving a verbal warning. As things deteriorated and the last of the employee's clients actually dispensed with the employee's services the employer decided to close his division. At the EAT hearing the employee produced an email from a consultant engaged by the employer which was sent to the employer prior to his dismissal stating that as the employer did not have adequate dismissal procedures in place to dismiss the employee fairly, but that redundancy may be a possibility. The EAT held that the dismissal by reason of redundancy was a sham used to circumvent the disciplinary procedure.

In *Ponisi v JVC Europe Ltd*[60] Mr Ponisi was the general manager for JVC in Ireland. Because of a downturn in the industry his employer decided to re-structure the company making his position redundant. The employer created a new role of sales manager for Ireland. Despite Mr Ponisi being consulted on and encouraged to apply for the post, he felt that the role was exactly the same as the one he held and refused to apply. The EAT, whilst accepting there was a need for redundancies in the company, determined that the role of sales manager was effectively the same position as general manager but at a much lower salary.

These cases demonstrate the necessity for a genuine redundancy situation to exist. To assist in this process it is necessary for a full a discussion on the need for redundancies to have initially occurred and notes should be available to assist at the Tribunal should they be required.

---

58. *Lyons v Grangemore Landscapes Limited* UD 541/2008.
59. *Cronin v Rachel Dalton Communications Limited* UD 1143/2008.
60. *Ponisi v JVC Europe Ltd* UD 949/08.

'Impersonality requirement'

[6.51] The second hurdle that employers have to cross is to prove that the redundancy, whilst being fair, did not relate to the person but the job or function. Whilst recognising the fact that the 1977 Act provides an absolute immunity to employers for unfair dismissal once the dismissal results 'wholly or mainly' from the redundancy of the employee, it is an essential feature of the redundancy that it is the function that is made redundant, not the employee, ie that there be an element of impersonality about the dismissal. In *Moloney v Decon & Sons Ltd*[61] one of the reasons given by the employer for the redundancy was the 'claimant's personality'. It was held not to be a valid redundancy. This impersonality requirement has been strengthened by s 5 of the Redundancy Payments Act 2003 which amends s 7(2) of the 1967 Act by making it clear that the selection of the employee for redundancy must be 'for one or more reasons not related to the employee concerned'. This points again to the fact that employers must be extremely vigilant and ensure that all redundancies are in fact redundancies.

'Reasonableness or otherwise of the conduct of the employer'

[6.52] The third 'hurdle' that must be crossed by employers is to prove that their conduct was reasonable when coming to the decision to make the person redundant. Prior to the enactment of the Unfair Dismissals (Amendment) Act 1993 it had been held in *Hickey v Eastern Health Board*[62] that the rules of natural justice do not apply where a dismissal results from redundancy. In this case the Supreme Court held that since the appellant had not been dismissed for any fault, or any failure to perform her duties properly, the rules of natural justice which are relevant to dismissal of a person for misconduct did not apply to her case.

However the 1993 Act provides that reasonableness of an employer's conduct is now an essential factor to be considered in the context of all dismissals, including redundancy dismissals.[63] It is clear now that the EAT will require that employers act reasonably in the context of redundancy dismissals.[64]

What is behaving reasonably?

[6.53] In behaving reasonably the sort of steps required from employers before moving to dismiss an employee or employees by reason of redundancy are the following:

ALTERNATIVES TO REDUNDANCY

[6.54] Employers, rather than move immediately to conclude that there should be redundancies, need to first of all consider the alternatives. Options such as short-time working, lay-off, early retirement, natural wastage, redeployment and alternative

---

61.   *Moloney v Decon & Sons Ltd* [1996] ELR 230.
62.   *Hickey v Eastern Health Board* [1991] 1 IR 208; [1990] ELR 177.
63.   Protection on Employment Act 1977, s 6(7) as inserted by the Unfair Dismissals (Amendment) Act 1993, s 5(g).
64.   See *Roche v Richmond Earthworks Ltd* UD 329/97.

working arrangements need to be thought through and the reasons as to why they may not be feasible documented so that the EAT or court can see at a future date that the employer did not simply opt for redundancy to the detriment of the employee. Also in unionised companies where redundancies are subject to collective bargaining the first step of the trade union is usually to reject the need for redundancies in total. The purpose of this is first of all to make the employer aware that they would prefer alternatives to their members losing their jobs, but in the alternative that any redundancy package will be difficult to negotiate and expensive. Once these negotiations begin it is vital that those acting on the employer's behalf present a unified voice and preparation on the alternatives to redundancy will help in this regard (see para **6.68** below on this issue).

There have been numerous interesting cases on this topic from the Tribunal, some of which are hard to rationalise. In *McGeehan v Park Developments*[65] there were eight claimants who were employed by the respondent as plasterers at various sites in the Dublin area. The employees were employed directly by the company with some having over 20 years of service. In 2006, with the construction sector booming, it was difficult to recruit direct labour and in January 2007, subcontracting began on a complex of 173 apartments. Due to the downturn in the economy the company had to reduce its workforce. The employees were made redundant and received statutory redundancy payment and payment in lieu of notice. At the time of the redundancy the company continued to engage subcontractors to complete work on other sites. The company argued that it had to make the employees redundant as they could not breach their contract with the subcontractors.

The Tribunal stated that the onus was on the company to establish that 'work was no longer being carried on at the workplace'. It stated that this was clearly not the case as the company had demand for plastering work long after the employees had been made redundant, specifically the work being carried out by the subcontractors.

The Tribunal noted that the company had given no consideration to temporary lay-off or short-time working options or to the option of re-negotiating the contracts with the subcontractors. The Tribunal found that the employees had been unfairly selected for redundancy and thus unfairly dismissed.

In this case the EAT noted that when considering redundancy the onus is on the company to establish that work is no longer being carried on at the 'workplace'. Equally they did find that no consideration was given to the alternatives to redundancy and whereas there is no actual legislative requirement providing that work is no longer being carried out at the 'workplace' it seems that the Tribunal have 'imposed' this requirement. This is not unusual, for example in *Sheehan and O'Brien v Vintners Federation of Ireland*[66] the Tribunal stated that the employer should have considered alternative suggestions to redundancy proffered by the employees. This again is an extra 'imposition' by the Tribunal.

It should be noted that redundancy in itself from an industrial relations perspective was traditionally seen as being outside the normal industrial relations rules of

---

65.   *McGeehan and others v Park Developments* UD 950/2008.
66.   *Sheehan and O'Brien v Vintners Federation of Ireland* UD 787/2007.

engagement. Equally the High Court in treating redundancy as a 'no fault' termination deem in the main that the rules of natural justice do not apply,[67] thus negating the requirement for considering alternatives etc. However the Tribunal, *per* the *Sheehan and O'Brien* case, takes a different view. To substantiate this view the Tribunal relies on s 6(7) of the Unfair Dismissals Act 1977 (as amended) which states that:

> In determining if a dismissal is an unfair dismissal, regard may be had, if the rights commissioner, the Tribunal or the Circuit Court, as the case may be, considers it appropriate to do so ... to the reasonableness or otherwise of the conduct (whether by act or omission) of the employer in relation to the dismissal.

Thus the term reasonableness has been extended to include 'considering all the alternatives'.

CONSULTATION

[6.55] Aside from the mandatory requirement to now consult/negotiate with an employee representative in a collective redundancy or where none is available the employee directly, employers should be aware that failure to consult can lead to a finding of unfair dismissal.[68] Thus, whilst strictly speaking (per *Hickey*)[69]employers may not be bound by the actual rules of natural justice, some sort of discussion and hearing either by notification or consultation and preferably the latter should take place prior to the decision being taken.

BREACHES OF THE COLLECTIVE REDUNDANCY LEGISLATION AND FAIRNESS

[6.56] A failure to consult with employee representatives does not of itself mean that a dismissal is unfair.[70] Similarly, consultation with trade unions does not preclude consultations with individuals.[71] Thus, in *Beaumont v Muintir na Tíre*,[72] the Tribunal stated that 'as a basic principle of natural justice and fairness, items as important as redundancy should be clearly discussed with the employee'. In *Mugford v Midland Bank plc* the EAT in the UK suggested three propositions for the guidance of employment tribunals in such circumstances:

(1) If there is no consultation with trade unions or individuals when redundancies are contemplated, a dismissal will normally be unfair, unless a reasonable employer would have concluded that consultation would be an utterly futile exercise.

(2) Consultation with a trade union does not of itself release the employer from an obligation to consult with individuals concerned.

---

67. *Nolan v Emo Oil* (2009) 20 ELR 122.
68. See *Trafford v Sharpe and Fisher (Building Supplies) Ltd* [1994] IRLR 325.
69. *Hickey v Eastern Health Board* [1991] 1 IR 208; [1990] ELR 177.
70. *Forman Construction Ltd v Kelly* [1977] IRLR 468.
71. *Walls Meat Co Ltd v Selby* [1989] ICR 60.
72. *Beaumont v Muintir na Tíre* UD 688/2004.

(3) It will be a question of fact and degree for the employment tribunal to consider whether such consultations as had taken place were so inadequate as to render a dismissal unfair. The lack of consultation by itself does not automatically lead to a finding of unfairness.

In this jurisdiction the Tribunal has deemed it relevant in a number of cases that the Protection of Employment Act 1977 has not been followed.[73]

Selection procedure (or criteria)?

[6.57] The final hurdle that employers have to cross is to prove that the person or persons were fairly selected for redundancy. In addition to exploring the alternatives to redundancy and then consulting with employees, employers are therefore also obliged to act reasonably in selecting those employees to be made redundant.

The first point to remember here is the impersonality requirement demanded by the legislation, ie it is the function that is made redundant not the employee. Thus where a redundancy situation occurs, those employees to be made redundant are those whose functions are redundant. Where there is a need to make several employees redundant from the same or similar functions then the employer has to select one or more employees from the body or group affected. In this instance the employer is under a general obligation to select fairly in accordance with s 6(3) of the 1977 Unfair Dismissals Act which provides as follows:

> Without prejudice to the generality of subsection (1) of this section, if an employee was dismissed due to redundancy, but the circumstances constituting the redundancy applied equally to one or more other employees in similar employment with the same employer who have not been dismissed and either;
>
> (a) the selection of the employee for dismissal resulted wholly or mainly from one or ore of the matters specified at subsection (2) of this section or another matter that would not be a ground justifying dismissal; or
>
> (b) he was selected for dismissal in contravention of a procedure (being a procedure has been agreed upon by or on behalf of the employer and by the employee or a trade union or an excepted body under the Trade Union Acts 1941 and 1971, representing him, or has been established by the custom and practice of the employment concerned) relating to redundancy and there were no special reasons justifying a departure form that procedure, the dismissal shall be deemed for the purposes of this Act, to be an Unfair Dismissal.

In summary what this means is that an employee can bring a claim for unfair dismissal if their selection for redundancy:

- is based on unfair reasons such as those prohibited by the 1977 Unfair Dismissals Act, ie trade union activity or membership of a trade union, pregnancy, colour, age, race, sexual orientation, membership of the travelling community; or

---

73. See *Dorian v Dundalk Golf Club* UD 237/1987.

- their selection is in contravention of an agreed procedure or custom and practice within the company and there was no special reason to depart from this procedure.

An agreed procedure exists where there is a formal arrangement between the employer and the employee(s) or trade union or an expected body under the Trade Union Acts which stipulates the selection procedure to be used in the event of a redundancy situation arising.

The agreement must be a formal one. Thus in *Browne v Consolidated Aluminium*[74] a comment by a senior manager to the effect that 'junior staff' would be selected for redundancy first was held not to be a formal agreement.

Once however a formal agreement exists, the selection criteria can only be changed if the employer can justify it. This does not mean that another criterion cannot be emphasised, but employers must demonstrate that it was reasonable to take this into account; see the UK case of *Tyrrell v Brooks Motors Ltd*.[75]

A formal arrangement need not be written down and employers have to be careful that one doesn't arise by virtue of custom and practice as the Tribunal in the absence of a formal procedure will look at the custom and practice within the company. In this instance though the onus rests with the employee to demonstrate that their selection for redundancy is in contravention of traditional custom and practice within the firm.

A single precedent will not be sufficient proof of this; the procedure must be well established, known and clear enough such that it would form an implied term of any agreed procedure.[76]

Once there is an agreed procedure which will arise formally or by custom and practice this can only be departed from where there is a special reason for doing so.[77] Custom and practice will vary between industries and sometimes across sites. In *Devlin and Leahy v McInerney Construction Ltd*[78] the Tribunal found that the respondent operated a 'last in first out' policy on a site-by-site basis and the policy had been objectively applied.

The Unfair Dismissals Acts allow an employer to depart from the formally agreed selection procedure or custom and practice where the employer shows a special reason for doing so. This is merely a defence. It does not prohibit an employee from taking a claim to the EAT citing unfair selection. What it allows though is an opportunity for employers to retain an employee whilst making another employee employed in similar circumstances redundant. The reasons have to be justifiable and reasonable. Thus selecting an employee because they were out sick has been held not to be a valid reason to justify a departure from LIFO.[79]

---

74. *Browne v Consolidated Aluminium* UD 729/1980.
75. *Tyrrell v Brooks Motors Ltd* UD 304/1981.
76. *Moloney v JLF Goodbody Ltd* UD 6/1978.
77. Unfair Dismissals Act 1977, s 6(3)(b).
78. *Devlin and Leahy v McInerney Construction Ltd* UD 726 and UD 727/2004.
79. *Foley v Mahon & McPhilips Ltd* UD 267/1979.

Choosing a selection procedure

[6.58] The first time redundancies are to be effected in an organisation requires some thought as any selection procedure that is adopted could set a precedent for future redundancies. As such any consequent alteration in the selection procedure for future redundancies could be deemed to be contrary to the previously agreed selection method and as a consequence held to be an unfair dismissal per s 6(3) of the Unfair Dismissals Acts 1977–2001.

As neither the redundancy legislation nor the unfair dismissal legislation sets out the criteria to be followed by employers in selecting employees to be made redundant, it is a matter of choice for individual employers. Employers must be aware that anything that is not a so-called 'voluntary redundancy' comes under close scrutiny by the EAT.

In *Boucher v Irish Productivity Centre*[80] the employer put forward various criteria to justify the redundancy of Mr Boucher based on skills, income earned, time, versatility and credit for research. The EAT found the selection to be unfair as the criteria were not shared with the claimant beforehand and thus he was denied the opportunity to make a constructive contribution to the selection process. From an employer's perspective the main points to take from *Boucher* are:

- the onus rests on the employer to justify the selection process;

- in the absence of agreement being reached with a trade union under the provisions of s 6(3)(b) of the 1977 Act the dismissals will be considered under s 6(1) of the same Act which deems all dismissals to be unfair unless there were substantial grounds justifying them;

- the existence of a general redundancy situation does not deny the individual employee the right to be fairly assessed for selection.

VOLUNTARY REDUNDANCY

[6.59] Because of the difficulties in agreeing a 'watertight' selection process many employers opt to offer voluntary redundancy. Voluntary redundancy occurs when an employer, faced with a situation which requires a reduced work-force, asks for volunteers for redundancy. The people who then volunteer for redundancy are, if they fulfil the normal criteria, eligible for statutory redundancy. Employers in this instance invariably pay an enhanced package to entice employees to avail/volunteer for the package. This has become the most popular way of reducing workforces in Ireland as it avoids issues such as having to force people out of their employment on a compulsory basis such as Last in First Out basis (so-called LIFO) or some other method. It also allows further flexibility in that employers can 'tailor' the package to suit particular groups. As for all redundancies the issue of impersonality arises and it is vital that one must bear in mind, regardless of the selection criteria, that there must be a genuine redundancy in the first instance.

---

80.   *Boucher v Irish Productivity Centre* [1990] ELR 205.

Invariably employers may 'tailor' their voluntary package to 'target' particular groups and in some instance this may involve offering generous early retirement packages to those aged 50 (or above). This has been widespread practice in the past. However, regard must by had to the equality aspects of such practices.

Such early retirement packages may involve some form of enhanced pension.

Pensions although not covered by the Employment Equality Acts 1998–2004 are covered instead by Pt VII of the Pensions Act 1990. (This legislation was extensively amended by the Social Welfare (Miscellaneous Provisions) Act 2004, which entered into force on 5 April 2004.) With effect from 5 April 2004, it is unlawful to discriminate directly or indirectly in relation to occupational pensions on any of the nine protected grounds (gender, marital status, family status, race, religion, age, disability, sexual orientation, or membership of the traveller community). All claims of discrimination in occupational pensions occurring on or after that date are made to the Equality Tribunal, which may refer to the Pensions Board if it so wishes for technical advice on pension matters.

That said, s 23(d) of the 2004 Equality Act allows an exception to 'provide different rates of severance to different employees or groups of employees, being rates based on or taking into account the period between the age of an employee on leaving employment and compulsory retirement age'. Given this it would seem that employers can validly offer the 'early retirement options' without being in breach of the 2004 Equality Act.

Another issue arises in voluntary packages where employers may seek to 'cap' the level of severance pay, for example at two years' pay or not greater than X number of weeks. 'Capping' severance has the effect of indirectly discriminating against those with longer service; arguably this is age-based discrimination and employers should be mindful of any such arrangements.

Collective agreements and redundancy selection

[6.60] Collective agreements generally arise where an employer recognises a trade union and engages in collective bargaining to negotiate agreements in relation to terms and conditions of employment, rates of pay, dispute resolution, redundancy terms, selection for redundancy etc.

Generally, collective agreements are not legally binding unless they have been registered with the Labour Court as provided for under s 25 of the Industrial Relations Act 1946 (Registered Employment Agreements) or have been expressly written into the contract of employment or deemed to be implied into the contract by custom and practice or acquiescence over time. Thus terms in collective agreements relating to redundancy (and other working conditions) can become an express or implied term of the contract of employment in some circumstances and can be binding on employees if they are not a member of the trade union who negotiated same.

The binding nature of unregistered agreements depends on the facts of each case. The consistent factor that must be present for such agreements to be binding is the intention to create legal relations. If an employee wishes to be excluded from the binding nature of such agreements then they must make this absolutely clear to the employer. In such circumstances it is probable that the collective agreement does not apply to such an individual. This can cause significant problems for trade unions. In circumstances where a trade union has a 'mandate' to negotiate on behalf of a group of employees and reaches an agreement on the terms and selection criteria for redundancy and say one or a small number object in such situations, the 'objecting individuals' cannot be bound by the majority.[81]

The question that arises is whether employees are bound by any collective decision taken on their behalf regarding redundancy?

In *Crosby & Rooney v Fuss Door Systems Limited*[82] the first named claimant had been employed for over seven years. On return from his annual leave he was informed by a colleague that his position had been made redundant. In a subsequent meeting with the managing director he was told that his position was to be made redundant due to the company experiencing financial difficulties. In the presence his trade union representative the claimant asked the managing director (MD) why he was being chosen and the MD asked him what his skills were and to sign some papers. The claimant refused and the MD asked him to leave the premises.

The second named claimant had been employed for over three years when he was called to a similar meeting with the MD. The trade union representative was not present and he asked why no one less senior than him was being let go? He then also signed some papers.

Arising out of all of the above it emerged that there had been an agreement between the employer and the union that in the case of redundancy that last in first out (LIFO) would apply. It was not applied to either of the claimants. The claimants also argued that they had been let go as their minimum entitlement was statutory redundancy whereas 12 other employees who had come to be employed after a takeover of another business had a collective agreement in place whereby they were entitled to statutory redundancy plus five weeks' pay for every year of service.

The EAT found that the two claimants had been unfairly dismissed. The failure by the respondents to consult with the union on the selection procedure constituted a breach of s 6(3)(b) of the Unfair Dismissals Acts as the last in first out procedure had not been complied with.

In *Geary v Board of Management Rushbrooke National School*[83] the employer was the Board of Management (BOM) of a primary school and the employee was a special needs assistant (SNA) in the school. This matter came before the Tribunal by way of an appeal from the Rights Commissioner. The employee commenced as an SNA in September 2002 under a 'child-specific contract' for specified purpose, providing for Pupil A. In 2003 she was assigned another pupil (Pupil B) and was working full time when she signed a second contract for specified purpose in October 2003.

In 2005 a review took place on behalf of the Department of Education and Science and it was recommended that the number of SNAs be reduced in the school from seven to five and that LIFO was to apply or if all the SNAs were employed subject to child-

---

81.   See *Goulding Chemicals v Bolger* [1977] IR 211.
82.   *Crosby & Rooney v Fuss Door Systems Limited* UD 294/2007.
83.   *Geary v Board of Management Rushbrooke National School* UD 931/2006.

specific contracts the SNA whose child was deemed to no longer need the service was to be made redundant.

Around 14 June 2005 the respondent was informed that Pupil B would no longer need the service and that Pupil A was to avail of the service only part time, and was to be catered for by another SNA so that the respondent's position was to be made redundant.

The respondent argued that an 'agreement' of 17 June 2005 negotiated between the Department of Education and Science and IMPACT which was signed by a senior industrial relations officer of the Labour Relations Commission (LRC) was breached when her position was made redundant in the manner it was. The Tribunal, in finding in favour of the BOM, stated that the BOM's decision to select the respondent employee on the basis that her pupil no longer needed the service was fair and reasonable in the circumstances. It deemed that the agreement from the LRC merely 'constituted a set of proposals and not an agreement' per se and therefore selecting the respondent for redundancy in breach of the conditions set out therein was not a breach of any agreement. They further found that the LRC agreement only became binding when it was accepted and circulated in Circular 0058/06 in June 2006 by the Department. Therefore, the BOM in following the direction of the Department in June 2005, although not in accord with the LRC paper of June 2005, was fair and reasonable as the LRC paper was not a binding collective agreement at that stage.

Each collective agreement will be different in both content and circumstance. Therefore each has to be examined in its own right. At a minimum there must be an intention for them to be legally binding.

'Last In, First Out' (LIFO)/compulsory redundancy

[6.61] Given the difficulties with arriving at an acceptable and perhaps agreeable selection method and the disadvantages that arise from a voluntary redundancy the 'traditional method' of LIFO is sometimes used. It is attractive in that it is generally agreeable to trade unions (in the absence of any voluntary package) and is perceived as fair by protecting longer serving employees. The robustness of this method has now been cast into doubt with the passing of the Equality Act 2004 and the inability to discriminate on age grounds.

Other methods of selection on a compulsory basis such as First in First Out (FIFO) run into the same trouble and selection methods that rely on other criteria such as work performance, attendance or cost as can be seen from *Boucher*[84] are notoriously difficult to enforce.

Selection by matrix

[6.62] Notwithstanding *Boucher*,[85] given the difficulties that many employers have faced with the voluntary, or last in first out schemes, both of which have considerable disadvantages from a HR and more particularly skill retention perspective, many employers now operate redundancy matrices. Typically these set out a number of factors

---

84. *Boucher v Irish Productivity Centre* [1990] ELR 205.
85. *Boucher v Irish Productivity Centre* [1990] ELR 205.

against which employees are measured and those with the 'worst' scores are selected. In general the Tribunal and the Labour Court approach such matrices sceptically. Thus in *Kerrie Mc Garvey v Intrium Justitia*[86] the Labour Court (on appeal from the Equality Tribunal) found that the redundancy matrix against which the claimant was measured was 'complex, opaque subjective and open to manipulation'. In *Dawson v Eir Imports Ltd*[87] the claimant was selected on the basis of competence. The Tribunal held that:

The criteria used in the absence of any other procedures were appropriate in the circumstances. The respondent was competent to make the assessment having regard to the small number of staff and his close contact with them. The principles of natural justice did not require the respondent to give the claimant details of his assessment and his not doing so resulted in no injustice.

In *Kirwan v Iona National Airways Ltd*[88] the claimant was selected for redundancy due to alleged low productivity. However this was never addressed with him and he was not advised that it may impact on his future. In *Bradley v Kilsheelan Technology International Ltd*[89] the Tribunal held that a secret ballot by staff on the selection criteria had deemed that selection criteria fair.

What we can take from all of the above is the following:

1.   If you are to use a selection matrix it must be absolutely transparent.

2.   It should be shared with all staff to be affected beforehand and comment sought on the fairness or otherwise of same.

3.   It should be as objective as possible; by this you should try and avoid subjective criteria as far as possible. This often causes a difficulty when employers come to consider previous performance ratings – which are often based on 'loose' competencies.

4.   Whereas you should absolutely share the selection criteria it is not absolutely necessary to share the results, although this would seem to be best practice and reduce any suggestion of bias.

Redundancy and a change of ownership

[6.63] Change of ownership of a business is dealt with under the Redundancy Payments Act 1967 and the European Communities (Protection of Employees on Transfer of Undertakings) Regulations 2003 (SI 131/2003).

Redundancy Payments Acts

[6.64] Under the 1967 Act, where there is a change of ownership in the business and the employee agrees to renew their contract of employment, redundancy doesn't arise and the employee's continuity of service is preserved.[90]

---

86.   *Kerrie Mc Garvey v Intrium Justitia* EDA 095.
87.   *Dawson v Eir Imports Ltd* UD 616/93.
88.   *Kirwan v Iona National Airways Ltd* UD 156/87.
89.   *Bradley v Kilsheelan Technology International Ltd* (2 June 2005, unreported), HC.
90.   Redundancy Payments Act 1967, s 15 as amended by Redundancy Payments Act 1971, s 19.

However, redundancy can arise where the employee, having accepted the renewed contract and having worked for a period of not more than four weeks with the new owner, then decides to leave.[91] The matter then falls to be considered by the Employment Appeals Tribunal who will concentrate on the reasonableness or otherwise of the employee's refusal.

Transfer of Undertakings Regulations

[6.65] (This issue is discussed in greater detail in Ch 9.) The European Communities (Protection of Employees on Transfer of Undertakings) Regulations 2003 preserve continuity of employment in the event of the transfer of a business or the merger of one business with another. The Regulations provide that the transfer of an undertaking does not give rise to the automatic dismissal of the employees employed in that undertaking.[92] The Regulations do provide though for dismissal for 'economic, technical or organisational reasons entailing changes in the workforce'.[93] If employees experience a substantial deterioration in working conditions such that they feel compelled to terminate their contract of employment the new employer is deemed responsible for that termination and will be liable for any redundancy payments that may arise.[94]

REFUSAL TO TRANSFER AND REDUNDANCY

[6.66] In Germany if an employee refuses to transfer to the new employer the employee remains employed by the old business. However in the UK the employee will be treated as if he has resigned.

The Irish courts got an opportunity to deal with this in the case of *Symantec v Leddy and Lyons*[95] The background to this is that in November 2006, Symantec transferred part of its business to Corporate Occupier Solutions (Ireland) Ltd. Leddy and Lyons were employed by Symantec at the time of the transfer of the business. Just under a year previously, Leddy and Lyons were informed about the proposed transfer. On 10 November 2006, both objected to the transfer and chose not to transfer even though the terms and conditions of their employment were to remain unchanged. They were also informed in advance that a failure to transfer would be treated as a resignation from their respective positions. The respondents contended that they had been dismissed by reason of redundancy and claimed to be entitled to redundancy payments under the Redundancy Payments Acts 1967–2007. They also claimed to be entitled to ex-gratia redundancy payments. The Tribunal found for the two men. In its view, 'in a transfer of undertaking, the employee is not obliged to accept the new employer'. The EAT adopted the position that the employees had a right to refuse to transfer, and that in refusing to

---

91. Redundancy Payments Act 1967, s 15(2A) as inserted by Redundancy Payments Act 1971, s 19.

92. European Communities (Protection of Employees on Transfer of Undertakings) Regulations 2003, reg 5(1).

93. European Communities (Protection of Employees on Transfer of Undertakings) Regulations 2003, reg 5(2).

94. European Communities (Protection of Employees on Transfer of Undertakings) Regulations 2003, reg 5(3).

95. *Symantec v Leddy and Lyons* (2009) IEHC 256.

transfer the employee would remain employed by the transferor (the German position). If the transferor had no alternative position to offer the employee, then the position would effectively be redundant and the transferor would be liable for any redundancy payment which may be payable.

The company appealed the decision to the High Court. They cited the decision of the ECJ in *Berg v Besselen*,[96] where it was pointed out that the Directive on the Transfer of Undertakings 'must be interpreted as meaning that after the date of transfer ... the transferor is discharged from all obligations arising under the contract of employment, or the employment relationship.' In the High Court ruling given on 28 May 2009, Edwards J stated: 'The fact that an employee objects to the transfer does not of itself have the effect of negating the transfer. It is just that an employee is not obliged to continue his employment relationship with the transferee.' The High Court therefore overturned the Tribunal's decision, holding that the refusal of an employee to transfer does not result in the employee being made redundant. Consequently the employee will not be entitled to any severance payment, statutory or otherwise (ie the UK approach). (At the time of writing this is under appeal to the Supreme Court.)

PRACTICAL CONSIDERATIONS

Notification timeline

[6.67] The first thing to do in trying to effect redundancies is to understand the process and what needs to be done. Column one deals with redundancies not falling within the collective redundancies legislation; this could be either a one-person redundancy or several redundancies which don't make the collective redundancy thresholds. Column two deals with those redundancies that fall within the collective redundancies legislation. This is a very brief and short guide to get you started. It should not be seen as definitive in any respect and advice should be taken beforehand.

Redundancies (not falling within the collective redundancy legislation)	**Collective Redundancies**
Phase 1. Preparation (Decision to effect redundancy(ies) already made)	**Phase 1. Preparation (Prior to any decision on redundancy(ies) being made)**
1. Determine that a genuine redundancy/ies exists, as you will be put on strict proof of this before an EAT. Set out clearly why the redundancy/ies are necessary, eg fall in sales, reduction in margin, loss of major customer(s), orders etc.	**1.** Determine that the redundancies are genuine as you will be put on strict proof of this before an EAT. Set out clearly why the redundancies are necessary, eg fall in sales, reduction in margin, loss of major customer(s), orders etc.
2. Determine on what grounds you are making the job(s) redundant having particular regard to the Redundancy Payments Act 1967, s7(2) (as amended by s 4 of the Redundancy Payments Act 1971 and s 5 of the 2003 Act).	**2.** Determine, if redundancies are to be effected, on what grounds the jobs are redundant having particular regard to the Redundancy Payments Act 1967, s 7(2) (as amended by s 4 of the Redundancy Payments Act 1971 and s 5 of the 2003 Act).

---

96.   *Berg v Besselen* [1998] ECR 2559.

Redundancies (not falling within the collective redundancy legislation)

3. Examine the alternatives to redundancy with other members of management (if appropriate) prior to talking to the employee(s) or their representative. Keep a detailed note of your thoughts in this regard.

4. Ensure all appropriate members of senior management partake in the above discussion and are fully briefed on the reasons why the redundancy/ies are necessary. This will ensure that if any of them are asked in the future they will be able to inform the person(s) of the reasons in a clear and concise manner. If there are no possible alternatives to redundancy, set out in writing the reasons why in the opinion of senior management none of these are possible and ensure they are kept in a safe place. This is important if any employee makes a claim under the Unfair Dismissals Act.

5. Prepare a spreadsheet with the proposed employee(s) name(s), start date(s), notice pay, and variations on the proposed package in advance of the redundancy. This will help crystallise thinking in respect of the financial considerations but also assist if consultations/negotiations are required.

Collective Redundancies

3. Examine the alternatives to redundancy with other members of management (if appropriate) prior to talking to the employees or their representatives. Keep a detailed note of your thoughts in this regard.

4. Ensure all appropriate members of senior management partake in the above discussion and are fully briefed on the reasons why the redundancies are necessary. This will ensure that if any of them are asked in the future that they will be able to inform the person(s) of the reasons in a clear and concise manner. If there are no possible alternatives to redundancy set out the reasons why in the opinion of senior management why none of these are possible in writing and ensure they are kept in a safe place. Not only is this important if any person claims unfair dismissal but it is also vitally important when the redundancy consultations/negotiations get under way. If all senior managers have been involved in the initial preparation and discussion on the alternatives then they are less likely to make mistakes and not contradict one another when the consultations/negotiations start.

5. On the basis that redundancies might occur, prepare a spreadsheet with the proposed employees' names, start dates, notice pay, and variations on the proposed package in advance of the redundancy. This will help crystallise thinking in respect of the financial considerations but also assist when consultations/negotiations begin on the redundancies proper. If every member of management is well prepared beforehand this will help prevent mishaps when the consultations/negotiations begin proper.

---

97.   See the Protection of Employment Act 1977, s 9.

98.   See the Protection of Employment Act 1977, s 10(2).

99.   The Protection of Employment (Exceptional Collective Redundancies and Related Matters) Act 2007 amended the Protection of Employment Act 1977, s 9 by substituting 'before the first notice of dismissal is given' for 'before the first dismissal takes effect', thus inserting the word notice. This was to comply with the ruling in *Junk v Kuhnel*.

Redundancies (not falling within the collective redundancy legislation)

6. Brief any tax, pension, social welfare, financial, outplacement, consultants that may be required or that you might propose offering. Also prepare to contact other local employers to determine whether they have vacancies arising or whether they would have interest in any displaced employee(s). Also make contact with any outside agencies that you may have to brief such as banks, IDA, PR companies. Whether you brief them before the actual announcement or later is a matter for careful consideration.

7. Determine the method of selection for redundancy, ie whether it will be voluntary, Last In First Out (LIFO) etc and set out the reasons in writing why the method selected is the most appropriate. Of help here is to conduct a careful analysis of the workforce beforehand in order to 'tailor' any package to those groups you may wish to see exit. Consideration needs however to be given to the employment equality legislation. Be mindful of any contractual agreements or company/union agreements which may refer to the method of selection to be used in the event of redundancies. Also be mindful of any contractual agreements or company union agreements that may refer to 'the ex gratia amount' to be paid in the event of redundancies or any previous precedent that might have to be followed. If selection is to be based on a matrix, examine same in detail and get input from other managers in order that an objective view can be taken.

Collective Redundancies

6. Brief any tax, pension, social welfare, financial, outplacement, consultants that may be required or that you might propose offering. Also prepare to contact other local employers to determine whether they have vacancies arising or whether they would have interest in any displaced employees (clearly they should not be notified at this juncture). Also make contact with any outside agencies that you may have to brief such as banks, IDA, PR companies. Whether you brief them before the actual announcement or later is a matter for careful consideration.

7. Determine the method of selection for redundancy, ie whether it will be voluntary, 'Last In, First Out' (LIFO) etc and set out the reasons in writing why the method selected is the most appropriate. Of help here is to conduct a careful analysis of the workforce beforehand in order to 'tailor' any package to those groups you may wish to see exit. Consideration needs however to be given to the employment equality legislation. Be mindful of any contractual agreements or company/union agreements which may refer to the method of selection to be used in the event of redundancies. Also be mindful of any contractual agreements or company union agreements that may refer to 'the ex gratia amount' to be paid in the event of redundancies or any previous precedent that might have to be followed. If selection is to be based on a matrix, examine same in detail and get input from other managers in order that an objective view can be taken.

Redundancies (not falling within the collective redundancy legislation)

Phase 2

Announcement/Consultation/Negotiation

8. Talk to the employee(s) to be affected and discuss in detail the alternatives to redundancy and the proposed selection method. If there is more than one redundancy and a matrix is to be used for selection purposes, issue this to them and ask for their opinion and comment. At all times stress that you are prepared to consider alternatives. Leave at least a week for employee(s)' discussions on this to occur and keep a detailed note of any such discussions.

Collective Redundancies

Phase 2

Announcement/Consultation/Negotiation

8. Notify your employees that you are contemplating redundancies and that you will be engaging in a negotiation/consultation procedure with their representatives over the coming 30 days.

The announcement should be well choreographed beforehand and the dates, times, methods of communication etc should be already documented and rehearsed. Remember to make contact with those who may not be present in work on the day of the announcement, such as those on sick leave, carers' leave, maternity leave, parental leave, etc. A question often arises as to what day to make the announcement. There are various thoughts on this! Some employers argue a Friday is the best day as it gives time for people to cool down over the weekend and talk the matter over with their family. Also 'press activity' is generally less coming into the weekend than it is earlier in the week. Others argue that mid-week is preferable in that it allows time for managers to reassure people once the announcement is made. Practically I think that if it is a complete closure then Friday is preferable; alternatively, I would advocate mid-week. A point to bear in mind here in unionised employments is whether you should 'tip' off the union that the announcement is forthcoming. Clearly good management practice, not to mention good manners, dictates that your own workforce and in particular those affected should know before any third parties. That said, trade unions do not like surprises and if one has to conclude an agreement with them then you will want to keep them 'on side' so to speak. What I have found to work in the past is, prior to the announcement, phone the employee representative(s) to alert them to the fact that a significant announcement will be made and that you will be in contact with them in due course to discuss the issue.

Redundancies (not falling within the collective redundancy legislation)	Collective Redundancies
9. Notify the person(s) to be made redundant personally.	**9.** In non-union companies arrange for an employee representative to be chosen to represent the employees. How this person is chosen is a matter for each employer to decide.
10. Notify the person(s) formally by completing Part A of the RP 50. Remember that the person(s) may also be entitled to notice pay so when issuing the RP50 it is advisable to inform the employee in writing that this notice also applies in respect of any notice entitlement due under the Minimum Notice and Terms of Employment Act 1973–2001 or their contract (whichever is the longer).	**10.** Formally notify the employee representative(s) of the fact that you are contemplating collective redundancies.
11. Be mindful of any contractual obligations to employees in respect of selection criteria and/or the 'ex gratia amount' to be paid to employees in the event of redundancy occurring.	**11.** Provide the employee representative(s) with the necessary information, ie reasons, numbers affected, categories, selection method, ex gratia proposals etc.[97] Bear in mind that these have to be given in writing, otherwise it is a breach of the Act – but they need only be given to the representatives, not the employees themselves[98]
12. During the period between completing Part A of the RP50 and the actual redundancy, talk to the person/those employees affected and reassure those not affected. The message to those staying needs to concentrate on the future and what it holds for them.	**12.** At the same time as you notify the employee representatives, notify the Minister for Enterprise Trade and Employment of the proposed redundancies at least 30 days in advance of the first *notice* of redundancy being issued[99] and send a copy of this note to the employee representative(s).
	13. After the announcement is made the negotiations will begin. This negotiation process is discussed in more detail below at 6.7.2.
Phase 3 Completion	**Phase 3 Completion**
13. On the day the person(s) is due to leave their employment, issue Part B of Form RP50. Get the person(s) to sign same along with a disclaimer. Pay any outstanding monies due and issue P45.	**14.** After the conclusion of the consultations/negotiations notify those effected by first of all talking to them personally and then notify them formally by completing Pt A of the RP 50. Remember most will also be entitled to notice pay so when completing the RP50 it is advisable to inform the employee in writing that this notice also applies in respect of any notice entitlement due under the Minimum Notice and Terms of Employment Act 1973–2001 or their contract (whichever is the longer).

Redundancies (not falling within the collective redundancy legislation)	**Collective Redundancies**
14. Apply to the Department of Enterprise, Trade and Employment (DETE) for the employer's rebate within six months of the employee receiving their redundancy lump sum. The composite redundancy form RP50 must be fully completed, signed by the employer and employee, and submitted. It should cover Notice of Redundancy, Confirmation of Receipt of Redundancy and Application for Employer's Rebate. Rebate claims can be submitted online at http://www.entemp.ie.	**15.** On the day the people are due to leave their employment, issue Pt B of Form RP50. Get them to sign same along with an appropriate disclaimer. Pay any outstanding monies due and issue P45s.
	16. Apply to the Department of Enterprise, Trade and Employment (DETE) for the employer's rebate within six months of the employee receiving their redundancy lump sum. The composite redundancy form RP50 must be fully completed, signed by the employer and employee, and submitted. It should cover Notice of Redundancy, Confirmation of Receipt of Redundancy and Application for Employer's Rebate. Rebate claims can be submitted online at http://www.entemp.ie.

Negotiations

[6.68] Most readers will associate negotiations with unionised employments. However, given the collective redundancies legislation (see **6.44**) and the *Junk v Kuhnel* case[100] all employers are obliged to consult with employee representatives and that must be with 'a view to reaching agreement'. Even in non-union companies and in the absence of a staff association or 'excepted body', employers have to put in place an arrangement whereby employees have to nominate a person or persons to represent them in negotiations with their employer. Given this latter requirement and the previously mentioned *Junk*[101] case, it is clear that regardless of whether employers want to negotiate on the actual need for redundancies the legislation and more lately case law obliges them to. Given that, those negotiations must cover:[102]

(a) the possibility of avoiding the proposed redundancies; reducing the number of employees to be made redundant or the possibility of redeployment, or retraining of employees; and

(b) the basis on which it will be decided which particular employees will be made redundant.

---

100. *Junk v Kuhnel* (Case C–188/03).
101. *Junk v Kuhnel* (Case C–188/03).
102. Unfair Dismissals Act 1977, s 9 as amended by Protection of Employment Order (SI 370/1996) and Protection of Employment Regulations 2000 (SI 488/2000).

It is also clear that the negotiations may not be limited merely to the amount of the lump sum. This is where the preparation stage mentioned above at **6.7** is vital. Although all negotiations vary as they are very much personality-driven by the employee representative(s) and/or the actual trade union(s), they tend to take a pattern as follows:

• Rejection of the need for the redundancies by the employee representative/trade union and exploration of the alternatives. The main point here is that the employee representative and/or the trade union cannot merely accept the need for redundancies from the outset as this weakens their position with the other employees/union members and also lets the employer know that any proposal in respect of an ex gratia payment will be difficult to negotiate and expensive.

• Once the alternatives have been explored and exhausted the next phase generally takes the form of negotiating on the ex gratia payments. Here it is usually the employer that will have to make the first offer (in practice it will often have been already made from the outset). Usually the employee representative will maintain a 'principled' position of rejecting the need for redundancies while negotiating on a without-prejudice basis on what form the ex gratia payment would take. As is usual in all negotiations but particularly so here, 'nothing is agreed until everything is agreed'. If the negotiations on the ex gratia amount cannot be agreed it may happen that the employer will have to try and progress the issue to try and conclude the negotiations. Remember in this instance the employee representative(s)/union(s) will be in no rush to finalise matters so the need to keep the impetus going rests with the employer. Often what may occur is that the employer is left with no alternative but to issue redundancy notices. The normal reaction from employee representative(s)/ union(s) is in turn to issue a strike notice; the compromise being that if the company lifts the redundancy notice then the employee representative(s)/trade union(s) lift the strike notice. In both union and non-union companies these negotiations may take some time and may involve the issue being referred to a third party such as the Labour Court or independent mediator.

Voluntary redundancy and negotiations

[6.69] The question often arises as to whether employers need to negotiate voluntary redundancy packages. After all it is merely voluntary and it is company money that will be expended to attract the right candidates and if people don't want to apply then they don't have to! That is a reasonable argument; however, once the redundancy is a collective redundancy employers are obliged to discuss the basis for the redundancies and the alternatives to same. Whilst this does not mean that the issue of any ex gratia payment has to be 'negotiated', in practice once 'consultations/negotiations' begin this will undoubtedly be a key topic. Additionally there are numerous Labour Court recommendations where the Labour Court has dealt with, recommended on and increased substantially 'voluntary' packages proposed by employers. In essence, how to present such packages and whether to negotiate on them or not is a matter for each individual company to decide upon.

Methods of calculating ex gratia redundancy payments

Statutory entitlement only

[6.70] This is all that employers are legally obliged to pay. For larger and in particular unionised companies it may prove difficult to only pay the statutory entitlement unless there are extenuating circumstances.

Weeks pay per year of service

[6.71] This is generally the most popular and widely used method. The number of weeks though varies greatly and is very dependent on industry norms, varying from two weeks per year of service to nine.

This formula suits employees with short service but can become extremely expensive for longer serving employees.

Lump sum payments

[6.72] This formula is most suitable where a smaller number of employees are being made redundant.

Multiples of statutory redundancy payments

[6.73] This is being used increasingly by employers as an equitable method of payment. It takes account of employee service but does not generally lead to very expensive payments.

Labour Court – What should be discussed

[6.74] Regardless of whether the redundancy is voluntary or not, the question arises as to what the Labour Court will deal with when presented with a problem. At one end of the scale is a claim by the employee representative(s)/union(s) that there is no need for the proposed redundancies and at the other is the more straightforward issue that the ex gratia payment is insufficient.

In answer the Labour Court will deal with whatever is put before them and more to the point with whatever employers let them deal with. The first question employers must deal with is whether the Labour Court should be empowered to deal with the 'fact' of redundancy, ie whether the employer's decision to effect redundancies is correct. From an employer's perspective the only topic for discussion at the Labour Court should be the ex gratia payment. Otherwise employers will be faced with the prospect of being 'second guessed' on their decision to effect redundancies by a third party. That said, the *Junk*[103] case and the collective redundancy legislation has seriously weakened the traditional position of employers not to allow the Labour Court to rule on the issue of the need for redundancies.

---

103. *Junk v Kunhel* (Case C–188/03).

Refusal to accept redundancy notice or RP50

[6.75] If an employee refuses to accept the RP50 employers are advised to send the notice to the employee's home address by registered post. Similarly if the employee will not accept Pt B of the RP50 this should be sent to the employee by registered post.

Draft severance letters

[6.76] The following is an example of wording to be used when providing employees with their severance pay in order to raise an estoppel if necessary.

Employer's letter

[6.77]

Please find enclosed form RP50 and a cheque in the amount of € _____ made up as follows:

Holidays _____

Payment in lieu of minimum notice _____

Statutory redundancy _____

Ex gratia severance payment[104] _____

Total _____

The ex gratia payment is being made in recognition of your long service with (company name) and, furthermore, is being paid to you in full and final settlement of all claims arising from the termination of your employment with (company name), both at common law and under all applicable enactments including the Redundancy Payments Acts 1967 to 2005, the Minimum Notice and Terms of Employment Acts 1973 to 2001, the Unfair Dismissals Acts 1977 to 2005, the Protection of Employees (Employers' Insolvency) Acts 1984 to 2001, the Organisation of Working Time Act 1997, the Payment of Wages Act 1991, the Terms of Employment (Information) Acts 1994 and 2001, the Maternity Protection Acts 1994–2004, the Adoptive Leave Acts 1995–2001, the Protection of Young Persons (Employment) Act 1996, the Parental Leave Act 1998–2011, the Protection for Persons Reporting Child Abuse Act 1998, the European Communities (Safeguarding of Employees' Rights on Transfer of Undertakings) Regulations 2003, the European Communities (Protection of Employment) Regulations 2000, the Carer's Leave Act 2001, the Equality Acts 1998 to 2004, Transnational Information and Consultation of Employees Act 1996, contractual and common law claims of any nature, type or kind whatsoever and howsoever arising from your former employment with the company and the termination thereof.

On a personal note I should like to wish you well for the future and thank you for your contribution to (company name).

---

104. Insert only if appropriate.

Employee's letter

[6.78]

I, _____ of _____ hereby accept

the sum of €_____. in full and final settlement of all claims arising from the

termination of my employment with (company name) both under statute and at common law.

I confirm that this document has been read over and explained to me, that I have had the benefit of independent legal advice prior to my signing and that I understand and accept the contents thereof.

Note: Estoppel is an equitable concept therefore no form of words can be guaranteed. Also employees must be made fully aware of what they are doing and what agreement they have entered into, the surest way of doing this is to insist they get independent legal advice, otherwise, the equitable doctrine of estoppel can be offset by other equitable doctrines, in particular undue influence.

Draft letter to Minister notifying collective redundancies

[6.79]

Dear Minister

I write to inform you that X… Company/Sole Trader/Partnership (as appropriate) located at …..will be making …..employees redundant from a total workforce of …with effect from…at our … premises. (in case premises is separate from the main office). Those affected come from the following categories (eg production operators, technicians, engineers, administration staff etc.) The reason for the redundancies is … (eg plant closure, plant rationalisation brought about by loss of major contract etc.)

The employees are represented by … trade union, or alternatively, we have entered into the process of selecting an employee representative in accordance with the EC (Protection of Employment) Regulations 2000 and … has duly been elected to represent the employees concerned. We have entered into the consultation process and this will be ongoing over the coming weeks.

The address of the employee representative(s) is ….

Yours Sincerely

Appeals

[6.80] The Employment Appeals Tribunal (EAT) deals with disputes relating to the Redundancy Payments Acts 1967–2003 (see **Ch 1**). Cases under the Redundancy Payments Acts may be appealed from the Tribunal to the High Court on a point of law.

Forms

RP9

[6.81]

3. RP9

 An Roinn Fiontar, Trádála agus Fostaíochta
Department of Enterprise, Trade and Employment

FORM RP9
LAY-OFF AND SHORT-TIME PROCEDURES

NOTES

An employer may use Part A overleaf of this form to notify an employee of temporary lay-off or temporary short-time (lay-off and short-time are defined at the end of this page).
An employee may use Part B overleaf of this form to notify his/her employer of intention to claim a redundancy lump sum payment in a lay-off or short-time situation.
An employer may use Part C overleaf of this form to give counter notice to an employee who claims payment of a redundancy lump sum in a lay-off/short-time situation.

EMPLOYER'S PAYE REGISTERED   ADDRESS OF EMPLOYEE
NUMBER   _____
1.   _____
2.   _____
     _____

Figures Letter

BUSINESS NAME AND ADDRESS OF
EMPLOYER

_____
_____
_____

SEX (TICK APPROPRIATE BOX)

MALE FEMALE

DESCRIPTION OF BUSINESS IN WHICH   DATE OF BIRTH OF EMPLOYEE
REDUNDANCY ARISES

Day Month Year

EMPLOYEE'S PERSONAL PUBLIC
SERVICE NUMBER (P.P.S.) NUMBER

DATE OF COMMENCEMENT OF
EMPLOYEE'S EMPLOYMENT

Figures Letter(s)

Day Month Year

EMPLOYEE'S SURNAME

ADDRESS OF PLACE OF EMPLOYMENT
_____
_____

EMPLOYEE'S FIRST NAME

DEFINITION OF LAY-OFF AND SHORT-TIME

A lay-off situation exists when an employer suspends an employee's employment because there is no work available, when the employer expects the cessation of work to be temporary and when the employer notifies the employee to this effect.

A short-time working situation exists when an employer, because he/she has less work available for an employee than is normal, reduces that employee's earnings to less than half the normal week's earnings or reduces the number of hours of work to less than half the normal weekly hours, when the employer expects this reduction to be temporary and when the employer notifies the employee to this effect.

PART A:
Notification to employee of TEMPORARY LAY OFF or TEMPORARY SHORT TIME
Notification in respect of this part need not be in writing
It is necessary to place you on

TEMPORARY LAY OFF ☐ TEMPORARY SHORT-TIME ☐
(Tick Appropriate Box)

as and from
Day Month Year
by reason
of_____
I expect the LAY OFF/SHORT TIME to be temporary.
Signature of Employer_____
Date:_____

PART B:
Notice of Intention to claim Redundancy Lump Sum Payment in a LAY-OFF/ SHORT-TIME situation

An employee who wishes to claim a redundancy lump sum because of lay-off/short-time must serve notice of intention to claim in writing within four weeks after lay-off/short-time ceases. In order to become entitled to claim a redundancy lump sum on foot of a period of lay-off, short-time or a mixture of both, that period must be at least four consecutive weeks or a broken series of six weeks where all six fall within a 13-week period. An employee who wishes to terminate his/her contract of employment by reason of lay-off or short-time must give his/her employer the notice required by his/her contract or if none is required, at least one week's notice.

An employee who claims and receives a redundancy payment in respect of lay-off or short-time is deemed to have voluntarily left his/her employment and therefore not entitled to notice under the Minimum Notice and Terms of Employment Acts 1973 to 2001.

To (Business Name of
Employer):_____

I give you notice of my intention to claim a redundancy lump sum in respect of
LAY-OFF/SHORT-TIME (delete whichever does not apply)

From To

Day Month Year Day Month Year
Signature of Employee_____ Date: _____

PART C:
Counter Notice to Employee's Notice of Intention to claim a Redundancy Lump Sum
Notification in respect of this part must be in writing and must be given to the employee within seven days of service of the employee's notice.
I contest any liability to pay you a Redundancy Lump Sum on the grounds that it is reasonable to expect that within four weeks of the date of service of your notice, namely,

(*Date of Service*)
Day Month Year
you will enter upon a period of employment of not less than thirteen weeks during which you will not be on lay-off or short-time any week.
Signature of Employer_____ Date: _____

Form RP50

[6.82]

(A) NOTIFICATION OF REDUNDANCY

See overleaf for instructions on how to complete this form and for terms and conditions

N.B. You may submit your claim online at the following web address: http://www.entemp.ie.

On-line claims are processed quicker as they are automatically validated and recorded on our system.

Claim No:
(office use only)

Employer PAYE No: *   Employee PPS No: *

Employer Registered Name: *   Employee Surname: *

Trading Name: (if different from above)   Employee First Name: *

Registered Address: *   Address: *
County: *   Post Code: County: *   Post Code:

Contact Name: *   Contact Telephone No: *

Contact Telephone No: *   Date of Birth: *

E-mail address: Gender: * ☐ Male ☐ Female

Date of Notice of Termination: *   Administrator Details (if applicable)

Proposed Date of Termination: *   Administrator PAYE No:

Payee Address: *   Company Name:
(if different from above)   Address:
County: *   Post Code: County: Post Code:

Employer Signature: *   Contact Name:

                                                    Contact Telephone No:

Role of Signee: *   E-mail Address:

(B) CLAIM FOR REDUNDANCY PAYMENT FROM THE SOCIAL INSURANCE FUND

EMPLOYER REBATE CLAIM   Please choose   EMPLOYEE LUMP
SUM CLAIM

Employment Address: (if different from above)	Date of Commencement of Employment: *
	Date of Termination of Employment: *
County: Post Code:	Is Employee a Director/Secretary/ Shareholder of this Company? * ☐ Yes ☐ No
Business Sector: *	Job Title: *
Weekly Hours: * PRSI Class: *	Reason for Redundancy: *
Gross Weekly Wage: *	Reason for Non-Payment (if appropriate):

See following page for Breaks in Service (if any)

Redundancy Payment Details

| No of Years Service: * | No of Weeks Due: * | Statutory Entitlement: * € | Rebate Amount due to Employer: * € |
| | | Amount Recd by Employee: * € | |

Rebate Claim Declaration   Lump Sum Claim Declaration

EMPLOYER/EMPLOYER   ADMINISTRATOR/EMPLOYER:
REPRESENTATIVE: *   I hereby certify that the above employer has
I hereby declare the above employee was   not paid the full statutory redundancy
dismissed by reason of redundancy, and   entitlement to the above employee, and
request payment of 60% of the statutory   payment should now be made to them from
amount paid to the employee.   the Social Insurance Fund.
Signed: Date: Signed: Date:
Role of Signee:

EMPLOYEE: *
I hereby certify that I have received
payment as outlined above from my
employer.
Signed: Date:

EMPLOYEE:
I certify that I have/have not (please indicate) received
payment as outlined above from my employer:
Signed: Date:

Breaks in Service

Start Date: **End Date:**   **Reason:**

Start Date: **End Date:**   **Reason:**

Start Date: **End Date:**   **Reason:**

Start Date: **End Date:**   **Reason:**

Start Date: **End Date:**   **Reason:**

Start Date: **End Date:**   **Reason:**

Start Date: **End Date:**   **Reason:**

Start Date: **End Date:**   **Reason:**

Start Date: **End Date:**   **Reason:**

Start Date: **End Date:**   **Reason:**

Start Date: **End Date:**   **Reason:**

Start Date: **End Date:**   **Reason:**

Start Date: **End Date:**   **Reason:**

Start Date: **End Date:**   **Reason:**

Start Date: **End Date:**   **Reason:**

Start Date: **End Date:**   **Reason:**

Start Date: **End Date:**   **Reason:**

Guide to Completing the Redundancy Form

Fields marked with * are mandatory fields and must be completed before submitting to the Department.

When do I
complete Part A?

When you wish to notify an employee of your intention to terminate their employment for reasons as stated in the Redundancy Payments Acts.

| When do I complete Part B? | When the employee is leaving and receiving their lump sum payment from you. |
| Why should I apply on-line? | Online applications are a speedier method of applying for Rebate or Lump sum payments and are processed. |

IMPORTANT NOTE: To establish a right to a Redundancy Payment, it may be necessary to refer to information from the Revenue Commissioners or other Government Departments. By signing this form, consent is given to the disclosure of such information for Redundancy purposes only. By signing, it is also certified that no other claim has been made in respect of the said employment details and that the claim is not awaiting a Decision from the Employment Appeals Tribunal.

OPERATION OF THE REDUNDANCY SCHEME & ENTITLEMENTS

What is Statutory Redundancy?	Statutory Redundancy is the minimum Lump Sum payment which an employer is obliged by law to pay all eligible redundant employees under the Redundancy Payments Acts 1967 to 2003.
What are the allowable Reasons for Redundancy?	Closure or relocation of Business, Rationalisation, (Fewer people required to do the work etc), Re-organisation of business, (Fewer required due to reduced product demand, Technological changes) Liquidation, Receivership, Bankruptcy, Death of Employer, Insolvency, End of Contract, Sale of Business. See our website at http://www.entemp.ie for complete list of reasons.
Who is eligible for Statutory Redundancy?	All employees must be between 16 and 66 years of age (Pension age), with more than two years (104 weeks) continuous service. If full time, must be in fully insurable employment. A genuine redundancy situation must exist.
What Notification is required?	A minimum of two weeks notice is required. For service of between 2 and 5 years – 2 weeks' notice, 5 and 10 years – 4 weeks' notice, 10 and 15 years – 6 weeks' notice, over 15 years – 8 weeks' notice.
How are Statutory Redundancy Entitlements calculated?	Two weeks pay for every years of service, together with a bonus week. Weekly pay is subject to a ceiling which is €600. The online redundancy calculator can be found at: http://www.entemp.ie
Who can claim a Rebate?	Any employer who pays the correct Statutory Redundancy Lump Sum Entitlement to an eligible employee.
What steps are required to claim a Rebate?	The composite redundancy form RP50 must be fully completed, signed by the Employer and Employee, and submitted. It should cover Notice of Redundancy, Confirmation of Receipt of Redundancy and Application for Employers Rebate and submitted within six months of the employee receiving their Lump Sum. Rebate Claims can be submitted online at http://www.entemp.ie
Who can claim a Lump Sum?	All eligible employees as above, where the employer fails to pay.
What steps are required to claim a Lump Sum?	The composite Redundancy Form RP50 must be completed, signed by the Employer, Employee, and where appropriate, the Administrator and submitted within one year of the Redundancy. If the Employer fails to pay, a case may be taken to the Employment Appeals Tribunal to establish entitlement to Statutory Redundancy. Lump Sum Claims can be submitted on-line at http://www.entemp.ie

What if the Employer is Insolvent?	If appointed, an administrator may apply to the Department on behalf of the Employee on-line at http://www.entemp.ie. If no appointment was made, an employee can make an application for Lump Sum payment directly to the Department by completing the Redundancy Form RP5O as above.
How do I calculate the Weekly Wage figure?	The Weekly Wage figure is calculated as the Gross Weekly Wage at date of Declaration Redundancy, together with average regular overtime, Bonuses and Benefit in Kind.
What happens if I have irregular / part-time work?	Total pay over a 26-week period, 13 weeks before the date of Declaration of Redundancy is divided by total hours worked in that period to get an average hourly rate of pay which is then multiplied by the normal weekly working hours.
What is meant by Breaks in Service?	All lay-off, absences due to long term ordinary illness and due to occupational injury or disease. Periods of Strike, etc. All reasons apply only on the last 3 years prior to redundancy. For a full list, please see our website at http://www.entemp.ie
(When) Do I need to supply Supplementary Information with this Claim?	When there is an Employment Appeals Tribunal Decision in favour of paying Statutory Redundancy.
Where can I get more information?	From Employment Rights Information Section, Department of Enterprise Trade & Employment, Davitt House, Adelaide Road, Dublin 2. Tel 631 3131. Lo-call (if outside 01 area) 1890 220222, Redundancy Payments Section, Davitt House, or our website at http://www.entemp.ie.

RP6

[6.83]

An Roinn Fiontar, Trádála agus Fostaíochta
Department of Enterprise, Trade and Employment

(Obligatory Period)

LEAVING BEFORE REDUNDANCY NOTICE EXPIRES

It may be that when you receive Form RP50 (Part A) – Notice of proposed dismissal for Redundancy – you might wish to leave your employment sooner than the date of termination notified to you, eg to take up alternative employment. If you decide to leave, there is a risk that you may lose any entitlement to redundancy payments unless you notify your employer in writing and also comply with the general conditions on the back of this form. You may use this form for writing to your employer.

If after receipt of this notice your employer objects to your leaving your employment and you leave notwithstanding, you may have to prove to the satisfaction of the Employment Appeals Tribunal that your grounds for leaving were reasonable.

PART 1:
NOTICE TO AN EMPLOYER BY AN EMPLOYEE TO TERMINATE EMPLOYMENT
(SECTION 10 OF THE REDUNDANCY PAYMENTS ACT 1967 AS AMENDED BY SECTION 9 OF THE REDUNDANCY PAYMENTS ACT 1979)

To..

....

....(Name and Address of Employer)

With reference to your Notice of Redundancy dated......................proposing to terminate my employment on......................(date of termination notified), I hereby give you notice of my intention to anticipate dismissal by leaving on........................(insert date on which you propose to leave). (Note *that the date on which you give this notice and the date on which it expires must be within the obligatory period of notice.* Your employer's consent may be necessary to ensure this, see Part 3 of this form).

Personal Public Service No:...........................

Signed..(Employee)

Date...

PART 2:
COUNTER-NOTICE BY EMPLOYER

To..

(Name of Employee)

I request you to withdraw your notice and to continue in my employment until the date on which my notice expires. If you do not withdraw your notice I will contest my liability to pay you a redundancy payment.

My reason for objection is...

....

Signed...

(Employer)

Date..

PART 3:

CONSENT BY EMPLOYER TO ALTER DATE OF HIS/HER DISMISSAL NOTICE SO AS TO BRING EMPLOYEE'S ANTICIPATORY NOTICE WITHIN THE OBLIGATORY PERIOD.

(SECTION 9 OF THE REDUNDANCY PAYMENTS ACT 1979)

I agree that the date of termination notified on my notice of proposed dismissal be altered to....................................so that the giving of employee's notice to anticipate dismissal and the expiration date of his/her anticipating notice shall be within the obligatory period of notice.

Signed..

(Employer)

Date..

EMPLOYEES PROPOSING TO ANTICIPATE THEIR REDUNDANCY NOTICE BY LEAVING SOONER THAN THE DATE OF TERMINATION NOTIFIED TO THEM ON FORM RP50 SHOULD READ THESE NOTES CAREFULLY BEFORE COMPLETING THE FORM OVERLEAF. (This is not a statutory form and it is open to you to use an alternative means of communication with your employer, provided it is in writing).

If you have been given Notice of proposed dismissal for Redundancy and you wish to leave your job sooner than the date you are to become redundant (as set out on the redundancy notice) you should, if you want to preserve your entitlement to redundancy payment, fill in form overleaf and send it or give it to your employer.

This must be done within (not before) your obligatory period of notice. Normally this period is the two weeks immediately before the date you are to become redundant but if you have been in the job for between 5 and 10 years, this period is extended to 4 weeks; if you have been in the job 10 to 15 years the period is 6 weeks and if you have been in the job more than 15 years the period is 8 weeks. If your contract of employment lays down a longer period of notice, this longer period is the obligatory period of notice in your case.

You may leave your job before the date specified in your redundancy notice and still preserve your redundancy entitlement only if the dates on which you give notice and on which you leave are within your obligatory period of notice as set out in the previous paragraph. Furthermore if your employer gives you a counter-notice in form similar to the 'counter-notice by employer' overleaf you will not be entitled to redundancy payment if you unreasonably refuse to comply with his request. (Any dispute on this matter may be referred to the Employment Appeals Tribunal).

If the date on which you wish to give notice is outside the obligatory period your employer may bring it within that period by agreement in writing to an alteration of the date of termination shown on his/her notice of dismissal (RP50 Part A) Part 1 of this form may be used for this purpose. You should obtain written agreement to alteration of termination date on employer's notice prior to giving your anticipation notice, and if your employer refuses to agree to such alteration you must wait until a date within the obligatory period before giving anticipatory notice.

NOTE FOR EMPLOYERS

If an employee under notice of redundancy leaves by his/her own decision before the date set out in his/her notice without complying with all of the conditions set out above, he/she may not be entitled to a lump sum under the Redundancy Payments Acts. Should you pay an employee a lump sum to which he/she is not entitled because he/she has not complied with the procedures outlined on this form, you will not get a rebate from the Department of Enterprise, Trade and Employment unless the Employment Appeals Tribunal decides otherwise.

If you agree to an employee leaving before the date set out in his/her notice of redundancy, though within his/her obligatory period of notice, you must attach completed form RP6, or whatever written notice you have received from him/her, to your claim for rebate, as evidence of compliance with these procedures, otherwise you will not be paid rebate.

If the date on which an employee wishes to give you anticipatory notice is outside the obligatory period you may (though you are not obliged to) bring it within such period by alteration of the termination date on your dismissal notice. Your agreement to do so must be in writing. Part 3 of this form may be used for this purpose.

If you do not agree to your employee's leaving before the date set out in his/her notice of redundancy, though within his/her obligatory period of notice, you should, before the expiration date of his/her anticipatory notice give him/her counter-notice in writing. Part 2 of this form may be used for that purpose.

The redundancy lump sum will be based on the period: date on which service commenced to date of actual termination.

Issued by the Department of Enterprise, Trade and Employment

Chapter 7

TAXATION OF LUMP SUM PAYMENTS

INTRODUCTION

[7.01] 'Pay' for tax purposes in general covers all payments made by employers to employees and company directors. All such payments are subject to PAYE unless they are exempt from tax or the Revenue Commissioners determine otherwise.

Lump sum payments in the event of redundancy or retirement do, however, qualify for special tax treatment and depending on the circumstances they may be exempt from tax altogether or may qualify for relief from tax. However, a lump sum paid under the terms of a contract of employment is taxable in full and does not qualify for exemption or relief. Settlements and awards made in employment cases are subject to an exemption from income tax in limited circumstances. These are dealt with in Part II of this chapter. Payment of legal fees in such instances can also be exempt from tax once certain conditions are adhered to. These are dealt with in Part III of this chapter.

PART I TAXATION OF LUMP SUMS (EXCLUDING SETTLEMENTS AND AWARDS PAYABLE IN EMPLOYMENT CASES)

LUMP SUM PAYMENTS EXEMPT FROM TAX

[7.02] The following lump sums are exempt from income tax:[1]

- statutory redundancy payments;

- payments made on account of injury or disability;

- payments for foreign service dependant on meeting certain conditions.

LUMP SUM PAYMENTS THAT QUALIFY FOR TAX RELIEF

[7.03] The following retirement and redundancy payments, although not entirely exempt from tax, qualify for some relief from tax:

- Salary paid in lieu of notice, on redundancy or retirement. Where the contract of employment provides for a payment of this kind on the termination of the contract, such payment is chargeable to income tax in the normal way without the benefit of the allowable exemptions and reliefs.

- Ex gratia payments – or as the Revenue calls them 'non-statutory redundancy payments'. This pertains to amounts payable over and above any statutory redundancy (for example, an employee receives a lump sum of €40,000 which

---

1. This is not an exhaustive list and 'other payments' may be eligible.

includes statutory redundancy of €10,000. Of the €40,000, €30,000 is subject to 'tax relief'. The statutory amount or €10,000 is exempt for tax purposes).

- All or part of ex gratia payments given in a non-cash form, eg car, house, renovations, holiday abroad, etc are taxable based on the equivalent cash value of the item received.

AVAILABLE TAX RELIEF

[7.04] The higher of the following will be exempt from tax the first time an employee is made redundant:

- Basic exemption (see **7.05**);

- Increased exemption (see **7.08**);

- Standard Capital Superannuation Benefit (SCSB, see **7.09**).

All of the above are subject to a limit of €200,000. This measure was introduced by the Government in the National Recovery Plan for 2011–2014 (see Finance Act 2011). Thus, any amounts over €200,000 are subject to income tax. Entitlements for an exemption against a lump sum payment are calculated on an individual basis for married couples, even if they are assessed for tax jointly.

Basic exemption

[7.05] The current basic exemption from tax is €10,160 plus €765 for each **full** year of service.

Career breaks

[7.06] Periods where a person is on a career break are not included for the purpose of determining a 'full year of service'. However, service before and after a career break may be added together.

Job sharers

[7.07] Employees who job share are credited with years' service as if they worked full-time.

PRACTICAL APPLICATION

Example

Jessica gets a lump sum of €15,000 when she leaves her employment after 9 years and 8 months' service. The basic exemption due to her is €17,045, ie [€10,160 plus (€765 x 9)]. There is therefore no tax due on the lump sum of €15,000 as it is under €17,045. The 8 months is ignored as it is each **full** year of service.

Increased exemption

[7.08] Employees who are not members of occupational pension schemes or who chose 'irrevocably' to give up their right to receive a lump sum from such a scheme can extend the basic exemption by €10,000. The entitlement for such employees is thus: the basic exemption of €10,160 plus €765 for each full year of service, plus a further €10,000. The only caveat is that the increased exemption can only be claimed providing the employee has not made any such claims in the previous 10 tax years.

Employees who are members of an occupational pension scheme have the increased exemption of €10,000 reduced by the amount of:

> any tax-free lump sum from the pension scheme to which they may be immediately entitled;

> or

> the present day value at the date of leaving employment of any tax-free lump sum which may be receivable from the pension scheme in the future.

If the lump sum from the pension scheme is more than €10,000 the employee is not due the increased exemption. If it is less than €10,000 they are due the increased exemption of €10,000 less the amount of the pension scheme entitlement.

PRACTICAL APPLICATION

Example 1

Jessica gets a lump sum of €20,000 when she leaves her employment after 10 years' service. She gets €12,000 from her pension scheme. She is only entitled to the basic exemption of €18,410, ie €10,160 + (€765 x 10). The €12,000 she received from her pension scheme means the increased exemption does not apply.

Example 2

Jessica gets a lump sum of €30,000 when she leaves her employment after 10 years. The present day value of her pension scheme entitlement at 65 years is €4,000. The exemption due to her is €23,810, ie (€10,160 + €6,000) plus (€765 x 10). The increased exemption of €10,000 is reduced by the amount paid from the pension scheme, ie €4,000.

Example 3

Jessica gets a lump sum of €30,000 when she leaves her employment of 15 years and 6 months. She is not a member of a pension scheme. The increased exemption due to her is €31,635 [(€10,160 + €10,000) + (€765 x 15)]. There is no tax due on her lump sum of €30,000 as it is under €31,635 and the increased exemption is claimed in full.

Standard Capital Superannuation Benefit (SCSB)

[7.09] This is a relief given for each year of service. The relief is equal to 1/15th of the average annual pay for the last three years of service to date of leaving, less any tax-free lump sum entitlement from the pension scheme. This generally benefits high earners and those with long service.

The formula for calculating the SCSB is:

$$A \times B - C/15$$

where:

A   is the average annual remuneration[2] for the last 36 months' service to date of termination;

B   is the number of complete years of service;

C   is the value of any tax-free lump sum received/receivable under an approved pension scheme.

If an employee has less than three years' paid service with an employer prior to their date of termination, the pay for the last 36 months of paid service is taken into account in arriving at the average for a year.

PRACTICAL APPLICATION

Example 1

Jessica commenced employment with Company A on 1 January 1991 and left on 31 January 2011, ie 20 full years' service. She received:

- a retirement lump sum of €65,000 (she had not been made redundant before or received any previous lump sums);

- a lump sum of €12,000 from an approved pension scheme.

Her pay including benefit-in-kind for the last 36 months to date of leaving was €100,000.

The amount of the lump sum, which is exempt from tax, is the higher of the following:

1. the basic exemption of €25,460, ie [€10,160 plus (€765 x 20 years)]; or

2. the increased exemption of €10,000 (not due in this case as the pension scheme lump sum of €12,000 is greater than €10,000); or

3. SCSB of €32,333 [(€100,000/3 x 20/15) – €12,000].

Jessica will get relief of €32,333 against her lump sum of €65,000. The taxable amount of her lump sum is therefore €32,667 (€65,000 – €32,333).

---

2.   Remuneration includes gross salary (before employee's contributions to an approved pension scheme), benefits-in-kind, less Revenue-agreed flat rate expenses.

Top slicing relief

[7.10] Whereas the aforementioned basic exemption, increased exemption and SCSB reduce the amount of the lump sum to be taxed, top slicing relief relates to the tax payable and ensures that an employee's lump sum is not taxed at a rate higher than their average rate of tax for the three years[3] prior to redundancy or retirement.

The formula for calculating this relief is:

- Taxable lump sum x (tax rate applied to lump sum) less average tax rate for previous three years.

For married couples the joint income of both spouses is taken into account in calculating the tax rate. This relief is claimed by the employee contacting the Revenue after the end of the tax year in which the payment is made.

PRACTICAL APPLICATION

Example 1

Jessica was made redundant on 30 November 2010. The taxable amount of her lump sum is €30,000, which is taxed at her marginal rate of 42%. Her average rate of tax for the prior three tax years was 38%.

Top slicing relief is:

€30,000 x (42% – 38%) = €600

The tax payable by Jessica will be reduced by €600.

Foreign Service Relief

[7.11] Redundancy or retirement lump sums may be exempt or partially exempt from tax where the employee has been on foreign service with the employer who is paying the lump sum, provided certain conditions are adhered to.

Subsequent claims

[7.12] The basic exemption and the SCSB are generally not available against any subsequent lump sum payments from different employers, ie they can only be given once against a lump sum from the same employer or associated employer.

TAXATION OF LUMP SUMS BY EMPLOYERS

[7.13] Employers are obliged to deduct PAYE on all of the lump sum less the basic exemption or SCSB. This can be done without prior approval from the Revenue. Employers should however apply to the Revenue well in advance of the payment date for

---

3.   With effect from 1 January 2005, the average rate of tax is calculated over the previous three years. Prior to this the average rate of tax was calculated over the previous five years.

any increased exemptions due to employees. If the Revenue has not granted approval at the time of payment for the increased exemption, tax must be deducted on the total lump sum less the basic exemption or SCSB. Employees may then apply afterwards to the Revenue before the end of four years from the date of payment to their Regional Revenue Office for the benefit of the increased exemption

Rate of tax on lump sums

[7.14] The taxable lump sum payment is regarded as part of an employee's total income and is taxed accordingly.

PRSI Contributions and the Universal Social Charge

[7.15] From 1 January 2011 the Health Levy and Income Levy were abolished and replaced by the Universal Social Charge (USC). The USC is due on the taxable part of the lump sum. There is no PRSI liability.

TIME LIMITS FOR CLAIMING TAX RELIEFS

[7.16] The time limit for claiming tax relief in respect of lump sum payments is four years from the end of the year in which the lump sum payment is treated as income.[4]

PART II TAXATION EXEMPTION FOR SETTLEMENTS AND AWARDS IN EMPLOYMENT CASES

INTRODUCTION

[7.17] In 2002 the Irish Revenue Commissioners began to tax awards to employees under the Employment Equality Act 1998, the Parental Leave Act 1998, the Adoptive Leave Act 1995 and the Maternity Protection Act 1994. This practice continued up until the enactment of the Finance Act 2004 which came into effect on 4 February 2004. Since then an exemption from income tax for compensation paid to an employee or former employee applies in limited circumstances.[5] Awards under the Unfair Dismissals Act are tax-exempt as the Tribunal deals with actual loss based on net figures. See **3.73**.

EXEMPTION

[7.18] The exemption only applies where:

(a) The settlement or award relates to 'a relevant act'; put simply, employment legislation which protects employees' rights and entitlements.

---

4.   Prior to 1 January 2005 the time limit was six years.

5.   Finance Act 2004, s 7 inserts the Taxes Consolidation Act 1997, s 192A.

(b) The compensation is paid in accordance with a recommendation, decision or determination of a Rights Commissioner, the Employment Appeals Tribunal, the Director of Equality Investigations, the Labour Court, the Circuit Court or the High Court.

(c) The payment is paid in accordance with a settlement arrived at under a mediation process provided for in legislation which contains provisions for protecting the rights of employees, in effect the Employment Equality Act.

(d) There is a written settlement between persons who are not connected[6] and which, if made by a relevant authority[7] would have been a bona fide claim and if it had not been settled is 'likely to have been the subject of a recommendation decision or determination by a Relevant Authority'. The amount of any settlement cannot exceed the maximum award possible under a relevant act dealing with employment law by a relevant authority (other than the Circuit Court or High Court).

(e) The compensation must not relate to loss of salaries or wages or arrears of salaries or wages.[8] Additionally payments referred to in ss 123(1) and 484(2)(a) of the TCA 1997 are excluded. These are payments which relate directly to retirement or removal from office. They are therefore taxable.

In summary, compensation, not including compensation for loss of earnings, arising out of such issues as harassment, bullying, maternity, Fixed Term Work Act claims or equality claims either under a formal decision, recommendation or determination by a 'relevant authority' or arising as a result of a settlement between parties, will be exempt from tax once it does not exceed the limits applicable under the legislation, the agreement is not between 'connected' persons and the settlement is set out in writing.

PRACTICAL ADVICE FOR EMPLOYERS

[7.19] Of primary importance is to ensure that the detailed particulars of any claim are available for inspection by the relevant authority.[9] In the absence of such detailed information as is set out below, the Revenue will likely treat the whole sum as loss of earnings and tax the full amount accordingly. Furthermore, the obligation to so tax rests with employers. To ensure that this does not arise employers should do the following:

1. Get the employee to set out their claim fully in writing (this is important as a 'statement of claim' must be produced for the Revenue Commissioners if they request it. In the event that it is unavailable then the settlement may be subject to tax).

---

6.   'Not connected' is defined in the Tax Consolidation Act 1997, s 10.
7.   The Taxes Consolidation Act 1997, s 192A(1) defines relevant authority as the Rights Commissioner, EAT, Labour Court, Director of Equality Investigations, Circuit Court or High Court
8.   Taxes Consolidation Act 1997, s 192A(5).
9.   Taxes Consolidation Act 1997, s 192A(4)(b).

2. Investigate the claim fully and take detailed notes.

3. Decide whether the claim is valid.

4. If it is determined as a valid claim, be satisfied as to whether the claim is one that is likely to succeed. Legal advice is appropriate at this stage and will assist in any discussions with the Revenue at a future date as the Revenue demand to know that the claim would have succeeded at the third party stage.

5. Determine what amount is reasonable to settle the matter. Remember that this cannot exceed any amount that would be awarded by a Rights Commissioner, the EAT, Labour Court or the Director of Equality Investigations.

6. Enter into a written settlement with the employee – again remember that the parties cannot be connected within the meaning of s 10 of the Tax Consolidation Act 1997 (which basically includes: an individual's husband or wife, or a relative, or the husband or wife of a relative, of the individual or of the individual's husband or wife, bodies corporate connected to the individual etc).

7. Set out clearly what proportion of the claim relates to compensation for the wrong committed and what proportion relates to loss of earnings (loss of earnings is taxable).

8. Copies of the agreement must be kept for a period of six years from the date of payment and these must be made available for inspection by the Revenue Commissioners.[10]

Structure of settlements

[7.20] From an employee's perspective it is beneficial to have the maximum amount due in any settlement categorised as compensation for the wrong committed rather than loss of earnings. The problem with this from an employer's perspective is that if the Revenue audit the document subsequently and dispute the structure of the settlement the Revenue will likely seek payment from the employer concerned, not the employee. Employers are therefore well advised to be careful in the structure of any such settlements and not to bend to employees' wishes to 'inflate' the amount due as compensation.

Employers should also be aware when settling so-called 'nuisance claims' where it is deemed more expedient to settle than to fight the case. In such instances employers generally settle for more than the case is worth to finalise matters and to 'move on' with business. However, any amount over and above what would be considered reasonable is liable to be taxed as loss of earnings. If this arises and it has not been already deducted from the agreed settlement the Revenue could seek repayment from employers.

---

10. Taxes Consolidation Act 1997, s 192A(4)(a)(iii).

PART III TAX TREATMENT OF LEGAL FEES IN EMPLOYMENT CASES

PAYMENT BY AN EMPLOYER OF LEGAL FEES IN DISCIPLINARY OR SIMILAR INVESTIGATION CASES WHERE EMPLOYMENT HAS NOT BEEN TERMINATED

[7.21] In Tax Briefing No 60[11] the Revenue Commissioners state that payment by an employer of legal fees incurred by an employee and/or director in relation to an investigation or disciplinary procedure instigated by the employer will not be subject to income tax provided the following conditions are met:

(a) the payment must be of fees 'due to a member of the legal profession' arising from representing the employee;

(b) the payment is in discharge of legal fees incurred solely in relation to the investigation/disciplinary procedure;

(c) the payment is made directly to the employee's and/or director's legal representative after the employer has seen the invoice issued to the employee; and

(d) if the investigation/disciplinary procedure results in a settlement, discharge by the employer of the legal fees must be a specific term of the settlement agreement.

Employers need to be aware of the above and be sure that if settling a case that the following steps are followed:

- the settlement agreement should contain a term that the legal fees will be paid;

- the agreement should state that they will be paid to the requisite legal representative;

- the payment should be made only upon receipt of an invoice issued to the employee.

PAYMENT BY AN EMPLOYER OF LEGAL FEES IN DISPUTES CONCERNING EMPLOYEES OR DIRECTORS WHERE EMPLOYMENT HAS BEEN TERMINATED

[7.22] The Revenue Commissioners take the view that payment of or contribution by an employer to an employee's/director's legal costs in relation to a dispute concerning the employer is payment which is assessable to income tax. In Tax Briefing No 52[12] the Revenue Commissioners set out the circumstances in which they would be prepared to

---

11. August 2005.
12. January 2003.

accept that income tax would not be payable by employees/directors in relation to such legal costs. These are:

    (a) when payment is made directly to the solicitor for the employee;

    (b) payment is in discharge of the solicitor's costs in connection with termination of employment only; and

    (c) the payment is specifically provided for in a settlement agreement or court order.

Again employers need to be aware of this and be sure when settling a case that the following steps are adhered to:

- The settlement agreement needs to provide for the payment of legal costs.

- The payment should be made directly to the solicitor representing the employee.

Summary

[7.23] Advice should be sought from the Revenue Commissioners if there is any doubt about the taxation of termination payments. The main point for employers to note is that if an employer fails to deduct or deducts too little tax the Revenue will be likely to hold them liable for the amount of income tax or PRSI not correctly withheld from the employee.

Chapter 8

WRONGFUL DISMISSAL AND THE EMPLOYMENT INJUNCTION

INTRODUCTION

[8.01] Wrongful dismissal is an action at common law for breach of contract. It is an alternative remedy to the statutory remedy of unfair dismissal. Applying the general law of contract the measure of damages is the sum which the employee would have earned but for the dismissal occurring. This in effect limits such claims to the duration of any notice period in the contract of employment. Accordingly such claims have never been as popular a remedy for dismissed employees as the statutory route. Another mitigating circumstance is the cost involved in taking a claim before the civil courts. However, for some higher earning executives with perhaps a longer notice period in their contract it is sometimes chosen in preference to the unfair dismissal route.

The action generally is for damages for wrongful dismissal and in limited and sometimes confusing circumstances (as will be explained below) an injunction preventing the dismissal of the employee or reinstatement of the employee, if the dismissal has already occurred.

WRONGFUL DISMISSAL AND UNFAIR DISMISSAL

[8.02] Where a Rights Commissioner has given a recommendation or the EAT has begun a hearing under the unfair dismissals legislation, the employee will not be entitled to recover damages at common law for wrongful dismissal in respect of the same dismissal.

Also where a hearing has begun in a civil court for damages for wrongful dismissal, the employee will not be entitled to redress for unfair dismissal in respect of the same dismissal.[1]

WRONGFUL DISMISSAL AND THE INDUSTRIAL RELATIONS ACTS

[8.03] An action for wrongful dismissal can also be processed through the Labour Court under the Industrial Relations Acts 1946–2004. Unlike under the Unfair Dismissals Act, an employee does not have to have one year's continuous service to qualify under this legislation. Employees have two options:

(1) Refer the case to a Rights Commissioner and then if necessary on appeal to the Labour Court. The Rights Commissioner's recommendation is not binding; however, if appealed to the Labour Court the Labour Court's recommendation is.

---

1.   The Unfair Dismissal Act 1977, s 15 as amended by the Unfair Dismissals (Amendment) Act 1993, s 10.

(2) Alternatively the employee can refer the case directly to the Labour Court under s 20 of the Industrial Relations Act 1969, in which case the employee is bound by the decision of the Labour Court but the employee is not.

There are no further appeals from the Labour Court under either section. In the first instance employers can decline to attend the Rights Commissioner and if they do, no further action can be taken by the employee under this section. In a 's 20' hearing there is no provision to decline to attend (although there is no obligation to attend) and as stated the decision is non-binding on the employer.

From a tactical perspective many employers will choose not to attend the Rights Commissioner. Hence this course of action generally leads to a referral under s 20. The issue with a s 20 hearing is that if an employer does not attend the chances of winning are reduced. On the other hand if an employer does attend they are perceived to be giving the hearing some credence. Ultimately the main issue with an unfavourable recommendation following a 's 20' hearing by the Labour Court may be the PR consequences both internally and externally. Tactically, therefore, some consideration needs to be given as to what to do when faced with such a claim.

Similar to the issues highlighted above in respect of dual claims for wrongful dismissal at common law and unfair dismissals, legislation limitations also apply to simultaneous proceedings being taken under the Industrial Relations Acts and the Unfair Dismissals Acts.

A claimant cannot refer a dispute in relation to a dismissal to a Rights Commissioner or to the Labour Court under the Industrial Relations Acts, if a Rights Commissioner's recommendation has been made or an Employment Appeals Tribunal hearing has begun under the Unfair Dismissals Acts in respect of the same dismissal.[2]

Furthermore, if a Rights Commissioner has issued a recommendation or the Labour Court has begun a hearing on a dismissal under the Industrial Relations Acts, the claimant 'will not be entitled to redress' under the Unfair Dismissals Acts in respect of the same dismissal.

Bear in mind that this does not mean that the employee cannot take a claim for unfair dismissal. It merely signifies that if the dismissal were held to be unfair, the employee would not be entitled to redress, ie reinstatement, re-engagement or compensation.[3]

THE EMPLOYMENT INJUNCTION

What is an injunction?

[8.04] An injunction is a remedy given by a court to protect a legal right as distinct from compensating for a breach of that legal right. The objective of the injunction is to maintain the status quo between the parties from the time of granting the injunction until the final disposal of the action.

---

2.   Unfair Dismissal Act 1977, s 8(10)(a) as amended by Unfair Dismissals (Amendment) Act 1993, s 7.
3.   Unfair Dismissal Act 1977, s 8(10)(b) as amended by Unfair Dismissals (Amendment) Act 1993, s 7.

Thus an injunction can be prohibitory in nature to restrain the party affected from carrying out certain actions, or mandatory in nature to ensure the party affected does a particular thing or things. The latter category encompasses the employment injunction.

An injunction is also temporary or interlocutory in nature in that it continues in force only until a further order is made or until the hearing of the action.

Injunctions can also be given on an interim or interlocutory basis. Interim injunctions are granted 'ex parte', ie with only one of the parties to the action present. As such they are only granted in cases of great urgency and generally only last a few days. Interlocutory injunctions are granted with both parties present and though also temporary in nature, last until the court makes some further order and in most cases until the trial of the action.

Principles applied by the courts on interlocutory injunction applications

[8.05] The case of *American Cyanamid Company v Ethicon Limited*[4] introduced a three-stage test for the court when considering whether to grant an interlocutory injunction. This test was adopted by the Supreme Court in Ireland in the case of *Campus Oil v the Minister for Energy*.[5] The three-stage test is:

1. ascertain whether there is a serious /fair issue to be tried;

2. ascertain whether damages would be an adequate remedy; and

3. ascertain where the balance of convenience lies – is it in granting or refusing the injunction?

Fair issue to be tried

[8.06] The employment injunction is in effect a mandatory injunction and the courts are reluctant to grant a mandatory injunction at the interlocutory stage. As such the 'normal test' that is usually applied, ie is there a serious/fair issue to be tried, is replaced with a much sterner test that there must be a *strong* case. This was re-emphasised by the Supreme Court in *Maha Lingam v Health Service Executive*[6] and reiterated by Clarke J in *Bergin v The Galway Clinic Doughiska Ltd.*[7] Thus in *Stoskus v Goode Concrete*[8] Irvine J held that the plaintiff had an 'arguable' and 'stateable' case, but on the facts before him he held that the plaintiff had not demonstrated a strong case and refused the injunction.

Damages an adequate remedy

[8.07] In the main the most a plaintiff can expect to recover in damages is the amount due by way of notice, thus one should assume that the amount of damages should be

---

4.   *American Cyanamid Company v Ethicon Limited* (1975) 1 AER 504.
5.   *Campus Oil v the Minister for Energy* (1983) 1 IR 88.
6.   *Maha Lingam v Health Service Executive* (2006) 17 ELR, 140.
7.   *Bergin v The Galway Clinic* [2007] IEHC 386.
8.   *Stoskus v Goode Concrete* (2007) IEHC 432.

easily computable in such cases and consequent upon such an assumption that an injunction to restrain dismissal should be exceptional or rare as damages should always be an adequate remedy. This line of reasoning does however overlook the fact that an employee will be deprived of their livelihood while waiting for the trial of the action. This was the factor that Costello J identified as being peculiar to the employment relationship in *Fennelly v Assicurazioni Generali SPA*[9] ('Fennelly'); here Costello J held that in view of the 'very special circumstances' before him he would require the plaintiff to be paid his salary and bonus under the terms of his contract until the trial of the action, hence the 'Fennelly order'. This case which has been followed by numerous others[10] demonstrates that the courts will not necessarily be bound by the *Campus Oil* guidelines when it comes to the adequacy of damages.

Notwithstanding the above and in considering whether damages are an adequate remedy the courts are also mindful of the damage that can be caused to an executive's reputation having been dismissed.

DAMAGE TO REPUTATION

[8.08] In *Howard v University College Cork*[11] O'Donovan J in granting an interlocutory injunction observed that there was no doubt that were the plaintiff to be removed, 'the public's perception would be that her role as head of department had been terminated because of misconduct of the kind that has been alleged against her.' In contrast in *Foley v Aer Lingus Group*[12] Carroll J held that damage to reputation is compensatable by an award of damages.

Balance of convenience

[8.09] The balance of convenience is a hard concept to grasp. Most employers generally feel that the balance of convenience will lie with them in not granting the injunction and the opposite applies for employees. In determining where the balance of convenience lies the court will consider the facts of the case and the relief sought. Thus in *Giblin v Irish Life and Permanent plc*[13] Laffoy J said that the balance of convenience had to be determined 'having regard to the precise form of relief sought by the plaintiff and will bear on the type of relief the Court is prepared to grant.' Thus there is a very wide discretion given to the court when determining where this lies. This indeed is problematic when one comes to advise either an employer or employee.

Undertaking as to damages

[8.10] In addition to the above in nearly all applications for an interlocutory injunction, the applicant will be required to give an undertaking as to damages. This in effect protects the position of the respondent by recognising that it would be unfair that a

---

9. *Fennelly v Assicurazioni Generali SPA* (1985) 3 ILTR 73.
10. See *Giblin v Irish Life and Permanent plc* (2010) IEHC 36.
11. *Howard v University College Cork* (2000) ELR 8.
12. *Foley v Aer Lingus Group* (2001) ELR 193.
13. *Giblin v Irish Life and Permanent plc* (2010) IEHC 36.

respondent who successfully defends an action at trial should suffer financial loss caused by the enforcement of the action.

In practice, however, there are very few plaintiffs who if called upon could in fact honour their undertaking, as in the main they would not be able to repay the salary received between the interlocutory and the date the of trial of the action. This in itself has been found not to be a 'determinative' factor in the application by Finnegan P in *Riordan v Minister for the Environment*.[14]

Non-application of Campus Oil

[8.11] The three-stage test set out in *Campus Oil* are not 'fixed in stone'! In *Cayne v Global Natural Resources Plc*[15] May LJ stated that 'a court must be very careful to apply the relevant passages from Lord Diplock's familiar speech in the *Cyanamid* case (on which *Campus Oil* relies) not as rules but only as guidelines.' This line of reasoning has been followed in this jurisdiction in *Reynolds v Malocco*[16] where Kelly J stated that the *Campus Oil* principles had 'a wide but not universal application'. In particular he went on to refer to contract of employment cases.

INTERLOCUTORY INJUNCTIONS IN EMPLOYMENT CASES – THEIR DEVELOPMENT

[8.12] The traditional view was that injunctions would not be granted to restrain breaches of contracts of employment. This is because the courts took the view that the employment relationship consisted of a contract of personal service and judges were reluctant to interfere. However, in more recent years the courts have demonstrated a willingness to entertain such claims and have granted injunctions where they have deemed there to exist 'special circumstances'.[17] The problem is that the courts have not been consistent in defining what constitutes these 'special circumstances'. Indeed in this regard there is significant variance in the decisions that have emanated from the courts to such an extent that Charleton J, in completing a paper in an extra-judicial capacity, observed that the case law cited to him in relation to applications for interlocutory employment injunctions seemed 'to be lacking in clarity'. This uncertainty makes it difficult to advise as to whether an employment injunction will be granted in any given case.[18]

What is clear, however, is that the courts are reluctant to compel an employer and employee to work together in circumstances where one or other no longer wishes to maintain the working relationship. The issue of trust and confidence between the parties is therefore crucial to whether or not the court will grant an injunction.

---

14. *Riordan v Minister for the Environment* (2004) IEHC 89.
15. *Cayne v Global Natural Resources plc* (1984) 1 All ER 225, 237.
16. *Reynolds v Malocco* (1999) 2 IR 203.
17. *Fennelly v Assicurazioni Generali Spa* (1985) 3 ILT 73 and *Shortt v Data Packaging Limited* (1994) ELR 251.
18. This is a view shared by Cox, Corbett and Ryan, *Employment Law in Ireland* (Clarus Press, 2009) 836.

In *Hill v Parsons and Co Ltd*[19] the Court of Appeal in the UK stated that as personal confidence between the parties continued to exist, one of the main grounds for refusing an injunction (that it is wrong to enforce a contract based on a confidential relationship in the absence of personal confidence) was not applicable. This line of thought was followed in Ireland in the case of *Fennelly v Assicurazioni Generali Spa and General Underwriting Agencies Ireland Ltd*[20] ('Fennelly') where the defendant purported to dismiss the plaintiff by reason of redundancy on the grounds of a large downturn in business. The plaintiff claimed that he was employed on a fixed term contract for a period of 12 years. Costello J stated that 'in view of the very special circumstances' pertaining he would order the defendant to pay the plaintiff's salary and bonus until the trial of the action. The plaintiff had argued successfully that he would be left without a salary to live on and that his circumstances would be nothing short of desperate. Costello J held that the balance of convenience was in Mr Fennelly's favour. This case stood as the only example in this jurisdiction of the exception to the rule against specific performance of contracts of employment until the case of *Shortt v Data Packaging Ltd*.[21] Mr Shortt was the managing director of Data Packaging and was informed by phone that due to a company restructuring he was to be made redundant. Later the same day he received a letter confirming that his employment was being terminated and that he was to vacate his office that evening. Mr Shortt claimed inter alia that the directors did not have the power to dismiss him and that his purported dismissal was a breach of fair procedures. Keane J was satisfied that damages would not be an adequate remedy and held that the balance of convenience was in favour of granting the injunction. This was despite Mr Shortt citing 'differences' between himself and his employers.

However, in the case of *John Keenan v Iarnrod Éireann*,[22] McMenamin J refused Iarnrod Éireann's Director of Human Resources, John Keenan's application for an interlocutory injunction to allow him to perform his duties ie to lift his suspension with pay and to prevent steps being taken to remove him. According to McMenamin J the level of controversy in the case where Mr Keenan had challenged the integrity of the company's Chief Executive and Chairman, as well as alleging a cover-up of substantial fraud, meant that there could not exist a relationship of trust and confidence between the parties.

It remains to be seen whether the employment injunction has reached its high water mark as there is now a marked reluctance on the courts behalf to grant same. The bar is continually being raised. One of the reasons for this is that employees continue to perceive a need for a speedy, robust and effective relief against their employer in the context of a deteriorating employment relationship. This is particularly so where there is a considerable delay in getting a case on before the Employment Appeals Tribunal.

However, the reality is that employment injunctions have traditionally been perceived as an important bargaining tool. The employee who successfully obtains such an order can approach negotiations in respect of the termination of his/her employment

19.   *Hill v Parsons and Co Ltd* (1972) Ch 305.
20.   *Hill v Parsons and Co Ltd* (1985) 3 ILTR 73.
21.   *Shortt v Data Packaging Ltd* (1994) ELR 251.
22.   *John Keenan v Iarnrod Éireann* (22 January 2010, unreported) HC.

from a position of considerable strength. This practical aspect is well recognised by the courts. Thus Clarke J stated in *Bergin v The Galway Clinic*[23] that:

> [I]t would be somewhat naïve not to surmise that a significant feature of the interlocutory hearing is concerned with both parties attempting to establish the most advantageous position from which to approach the frequently expected negotiations designed to lead to an agreed termination of the Contract of Employment concerned. The employee who has the benefit of an interlocutory injunction can approach such negotiations from a position of strength as can the employer who has successfully resisted an interlocutory application.

There are a number of common themes running through the High Court and Supreme Court judgments relating to employment injunctions. One is that there has been much judicial effort in analysing the specific legal parentage or yarn from which these equitable reliefs can be drawn. In the evolution of this area of law over the years, it is considered that the standard of proof required for a mandatory injunction is higher than that required for a prohibitory injunction.

A second theme is that very few cases where applications are made for an interlocutory injunction actually proceed to full hearing.[24] For practical reasons, the vast majority of cases are compromised between the parties prior to trial. An unhelpful by-product of this is that whilst there have been many applications for employment injunctions, there have been relatively few detailed judicial considerations in the area and therefore practitioners are left with an incomplete roadmap with which to guide their clients.

Whilst there is no doubt that such injunctions are becoming increasingly difficult to obtain, they are still available and employers need to be aware of the implications of such court orders and how to avoid the impact of same.

When are employment injunctions sought?[25]

[8.13] Employment injunctions most often arise in three main areas:

1. to restrain dismissal;

2. to intervene in the disciplinary process;

3. to enforce post-termination restrictive covenants.

1. Injunction to restrain dismissal

[8.14] Traditionally High Court judges took the view that, in normal circumstances, damages was not only an adequate remedy, but also that it was the appropriate remedy to an employment dispute. In those circumstances, where a breach of contract arose as a

---

23. *Bergin v The Galway Clinic* [2007] IEHC 386.
24. Again see the comments of Clarke J in *Bergin v The Galway Clinic* [2007] IEHC 386.
25. This section in the main is a re-print of a joint paper given by the author and Mr Killian O'Reilly (solicitor in O'Rourke Reid Solicitors) at the Legal Island annual review of employment law in late 2008.

result of a dismissal, the sole remedy was for a payment equivalent to the appropriate amount of notice due to the employee. This common law position exists quite apart from any statutory remedies that an aggrieved employee might have under the unfair dismissals or minimum notice legislation.

However, it is now more common for employees to have the benefit of well-drafted contracts of employment which often specify the basis upon which their employment can be terminated – ie incapacity, stated misbehaviour, redundancy etc. In those circumstances, employers may be required to comply with the rules of natural justice and fair procedures.

The Supreme Court considered this area in the case of *Sheehy v Ryan and Moriarty*.[26] Ms Sheehy was employed as a diocesan secretary for three successive bishops of Kildare and Leighlin. She did not have the benefit of a written contract of employment.

In the High Court, Ms Sheehy argued that her employment was permanent and pensionable and essentially that it could not be terminated until she reached retirement age. Carroll J held that Ms Sheehy's contract of employment (that is to say the mixture of express oral terms and implied terms which constituted her contract) was capable of being determined on reasonable notice. Importantly, the Supreme Court upheld that view.

Geoghogan J slightly qualified that by saying that 'it does depend on the contract but in the absence of clear terms to the contrary which are unambiguous and unequivocal, that is clearly the position'. Interestingly, the *Sheehy* case is one of the few cases which went to full trial and it is noteworthy that the plaintiff lost entirely.

Is seems likely that in the absence of a written contractual term specifying the basis upon which an employee may be dismissed, under common law an employer remains free to terminate on reasonable notice.

However, in cases where the applicant can demonstrate that the purported dismissal is in breach of fair procedures or natural and constitutional justice, the dismissal may be both unlawful and, indeed, ineffective. This was the position taken by Budd J in *Cassidy v Shannon Castle Banquets*.[27]

In the case of *Coffey v William Connolly and Sons Limited*[28] Edwards J concluded that the plaintiff was effectively looking for a mandatory interlocutory injunction on the basis that the plaintiff was arguing not so much that she had been wrongfully dismissed but rather that she had not been dismissed at all. He felt that it was indisputable that the plaintiff had raised a fair issue to be tried but found that whilst she had a stateable case, she had not gone far enough to show that she had a strong case that she was likely to succeed in her action.

Accordingly, while he did not grant an interlocutory injunction restraining the defendant employer from treating Ms Coffey as 'otherwise than continuing to be employed...' He did grant interlocutory injunctions restraining publication or announcement giving effect to the purported dismissal and restraining the appointment of any other person to the position held by Ms Coffey. The current position is that

---

26. *Sheehy v Ryan and Moriarty* [2008] IESC 14.
27. *Cassidy v Shannon Castle Banquets* [2000] ELR 248.
28. *Coffey v William Connolly and Sons Limited* [2007] IEHC 319.

applicants must be able to demonstrate that they have not only a fair case but that they have a *strong* case to be tried.

This position has been re-iterated in *Bergin v Galway Clinic Doughiska*,[29] also by Hedigan J in *Turner v O'Reilly*[30] and by McMenamin J in *John Keenan v Iarnrod Éireann*.[31] In *Keenan* whilst McMenamin J went on to say that Mr Keenan had 'crossed the threshold of a strong case' the facts were not like those in 'Maha Lingham' as the allegations made by the plaintiff 'were more radical'. Thus, even if one can prove a 'strong case' it does not necessarily mean that an injunction will be granted as every case will turn on its own facts.

2. Injuncting the disciplinary process

[8.15] As we have seen above, following the case of *Sheehy v Ryan*, in the absence of a helpful contractual provision, obtaining employment injunctions is likely to become more and more difficult unless the applicant is in a position to allege some form of misconduct against the employer. This has led to an increase in applications for the courts to become involved at an earlier stage before the dismissal, ie during the conduct of investigations or disciplinary proceedings.

At the outset, we must make a distinction between investigations which are focused on gathering facts as opposed to investigations which may make substantive findings. In simple terms, any investigation which is designed to gather evidence will not be required to adhere to the rules of natural justice and it will be extremely difficult for an applicant to successfully obtain an injunction at that stage.

In broad terms, the court will not intervene unless there is a fundamental flaw in the process which cannot be cured.

In the case of *Turner v O'Reilly*[32] the plaintiff was a legal executive who has worked for over 11 years with a firm of solicitors in Co Westmeath. She did not have the benefit of a formal written contract of employment and there was no formal disciplinary procedure in the firm. In February 2008, a dispute arose between her and her employer. Her employer handed her a letter which purported to dismiss her there and then and which required her resignation by the following Friday. She was directed to leave the office immediately. Importantly, no disciplinary action had been taken against the plaintiff at that stage.

Some days later, the employee received a letter from another solicitor in her employer's firm informing her that he had been delegated to conduct an inquiry into certain allegations of gross misconduct alleged against her and those allegations were set out in detail. Ms Turner was put on paid suspension and was invited to a disciplinary meeting. She was afforded the opportunity to have representation if she wished. A further letter was sent to her the following day setting out yet more allegations.

---

29. *Bergin v Galway Clinic Doughiska* [2007] IEHC 386, Clarke J.
30. *Turner v O'Reilly* [2006] IEHC 92, Hedigan J.
31. *John Keenan v Iarnrod Éireann* (unreported, 22 January 2010), HC, McMenamin J.
32. *Turner v O'Reilly* [2006] IEHC 92.

Hedigan J found that Ms Turner's application for an injunction was premature. He declined to injunct the disciplinary procedure even though the initial attempt to dismiss the plaintiff was 'entirely improper and made with no regard to fair procedures'.

Importantly, however, he stated 'I cannot make any assumptions that any investigation will not be a fair one'. He continued:

> '[I]t seems to me whilst the infirmities in the process on the 18th of February were tainted by unfairness, nothing so far has tainted the disciplinary investigation and I think it should be allowed to proceed to a conclusion. Following that conclusion, the plaintiff may take such proceedings as deemed appropriate if she considers the disciplinary proceedings were not fairly conducted. For the court to intervene at this stage, would, in my view, be premature.'

The application for interlocutory relief was refused. The *Turner* decision demonstrates the high threshold that an employee will need to cross if seeking to injunct the disciplinary process.

In the case of *Morgan v The Provost and Fellows of Trinity College Dublin*,[33] Kearns J in the High Court refused to restrain the application of the university disciplinary procedure.

Furthermore, in the cases of *Becker v Board of Management of St Dominic's School*,[34] and *Conway v Ireland*,[35] Clarke J refused to restrain the ongoing disciplinary procedures. There are of course investigative and disciplinary procedures which have been successfully injuncted.

In the case of *O'Sullivan v Mercy Hospital Cork Limited*[36] the initial investigative report made such unequivocal findings of fact against the plaintiff that Clarke J found that any further inquiry which the hospital proposed would be similarly tainted. He granted the interlocutory injunction but importantly did go on to state that if a further enquiry with an altered terms of reference were instituted, that that might withstand challenge.

A further example of a flawed investigation process occurred in the high profile case of *Fitzgibbon v Irish Nationwide Building Society.*[37] Ultimately, Clarke J found that the investigation which had been conducted up to that point by the defendant was inconsistent with its own procedural rules or indeed with the requirements of natural justice. He ordered that the plaintiff's suspension be lifted and the employer was restrained from proceeding with the proposed enquiry.

Importantly, whilst significant restrictions were placed on the type of enquiry that the defendant employer could undertake in the future (ie the managing director would have nothing to do with such a process), it is still clear that a further enquiry was not precluded as long as it was conducted in a lawful and fair manner.

---

33. *Morgan v The Provost and Fellows of Trinity College Dublin* [2003] 3 IR 158.
34. *Becker v Board of Management of St Dominic's School* [2007] IEHC 156.
35. *Conway v Ireland* (unreported, 12 April 2006) HC.
36. *O'Sullivan v Mercy Hospital Cork Limited* (3 June 2005, unreported), HC.
37. *Fitzgibbon v Irish Nationwide Building Society* (unreported, 18 November 2007), HC *ex tempore* judgment of Clarke J.

3. Post-termination restrictive covenants

[8.16] At the outset of the employment relationship, many employers take the precaution of including restrictive covenants in a prospective employee's contract of employment. These can take a number of forms but commonly seek to restrict various activities after the termination of the employment relationship.

Commonly, such restrictions include whom the employee can subsequently proceed to work for, the extent of the duties they can undertake and the type of clients/customers they can contact.

There is no common law basis for such restrictions and the courts have been reluctant to support them. Indeed, judges view them as a restraint on an individual's ability to earn a living and as anti-competitive.

If such clauses are to be capable of enforcement through the courts, restrictive covenants must be limited in subject matter, duration and geography. Furthermore, the employer must be able to point to some legitimate proprietary interest in the restriction and to some genuine commercial threat that the employee poses to the employer's enterprise.

If the restrictive trade clauses in a particular employee's contract are sufficiently well drafted and balanced, it is open to the former employer to seek injunctive relief to enforcing those clauses when the employment terminates.

Furthermore, a former employer may attempt to secure an injunction to prevent the release or publication of confidential information or trade secrets.

There are few reported decisions in this area. In the case of *Pulse Group v O' Reilly*[38] Clarke J held that while there were fair issues to be tried on the particular issues raised, he concluded that damages would be an adequate remedy for any wrong that might be established.

He went on to summarise the law in this area, including the relevant UK case of *Faccenda Chickens Limited v Fowler*.[39] He held that 'in the absence of an express term in a Contract of Employment, the only enduring obligation on the part of an employee after his employment has ceased is one which precludes the employee from disclosing a trade secret.'

The key point to note is that if a restrictive covenant is not correctly drafted and included in a written contract of employment, it will not be enforced by the courts.

WHEN WILL AN EMPLOYMENT INJUNCTION BE GRANTED?

[8.17] As can be seen, *Shortt*[40] demonstrated the willingness of the courts to consider the employment injunction where there are 'exceptional or special circumstances' at play. However it may be argued that the courts have not been consistent in defining what constitutes 'exceptional factors'. Such exceptional factors may arise in a variety of situations and as such the courts may potentially grant injunctions in a variety of

---

38.   *Pulse Group v O' Reilly* [2006] IEHC 50.
39.   *Faccenda Chickens Limited v Fowler* [1987] ICH 117.
40.   *Shortt v Data Packaging Limited* (1994) ELR 251.

situations. Roddy Horan SC in Issue 1 of the 2005 Employment Law Review neatly categorises these situations into five distinct areas.

1. Where the termination is in breach of contract

[8.18] These situations generally occur where the employee is dismissed in the absence of contractual notice or a contractual disciplinary process. The main case of note here is *Fennelly v Assicurazioni Generali Spa*[41] where Mr Fennelly argued he was on a 12-year fixed term contract. In this instance the court granted the injunction on the basis that there was a fair issue to be tried and that mutual trust and confidence still existed between employer and employee.

More recently an interim order restraining St Patrick's Athletic Football Club from dismissing its chief executive was granted by the High Court.[42] The Chief Executive Bernard O'Byrne, a former CEO of the Football Association of Ireland, claimed that he had a two-year contract and that it could be terminated only for gross misconduct or by mutual consent.

What is important here is the bond of mutual trust and confidence – where there is a breakdown of same it seems unlikely that an injunction will be granted on these grounds.

2. Where the dismissal is *ultra vires*

[8.19] This refers to a situation where the employer is for some reason not empowered to terminate the employees' contract. Thus in *Dudley O'Donnell v Chief State Solicitor*[43] there was an issue as to whether the Chief State Solicitor was empowered to terminate the plaintiff's employment since this power was, prima facie, reserved by statute to the Attorney General and the Minister for Justice. An interlocutory injunction was granted maintaining the plaintiff in his employment as a temporary solicitor pending trial. Also in the case of *Shortt*[44] which was one of the first employment law injunctions granted in the State, the injunction was granted on the basis that there was a fair issue to be tried as to whether the purported dismissal of the plaintiff (who was managing director) was in accordance with the company's Articles of Association.

3. Where the termination is in breach of fair procedures

[8.20] The constitution guarantees to the citizen basic fairness of procedures.[45] As such, prior to the dismissal of an employee it is necessary that the employee be given a fair hearing, allowed the right of representation, be presented with the evidence before him/her and be allowed to respond to same. However, an injunction for breach of fair

---

41.   *Fennelly v Assicurazioni Generali Spa* (1985) 3 ILT 73.
42.   *O'Byrne v Newtownheath Ltd trading as St Patrick's Athletic Football Club* (unreported, December 2005), HC.
43.   *Dudley O'Donnell v Chief State Solicitor* (2003) ELR 268.
44.   *Shortt v Data Packaging Limited* (1994) ELR 251..
45.   *Re Haughey* (1971) IR 217, 264

procedures will only be granted where the employer is alleging misconduct on behalf of the employee, as at common law an employer can terminate employment for any reason provided adequate notice is given.[46] Where the employee is dismissed for other reasons such as redundancy[47] (where the conduct of the employee is not in dispute) it is unlikely that an injunction will be granted on this ground only. Equally, even where there is a recognised breach of fair procedures this does not prevent an employer 'mending their hand', ie acknowledging the breach and undertaking to mend the breach. Thus in *Turner v O'Reilly*[48] even though there was a clear breach of procedures the employer was allowed to rectify matters.

4. Where the employee is asserting that there is an absence of grounds justifying dismissal

[8.21] This generally arises where there is an allegation by the employee that the employer has embarked on the dismissal in bad faith and/or that the dismissal is contrived. Most often this allegation occurs where the employer is trying to dismiss the employee by reason of redundancy and the employee is rejecting this as a 'cover up'. Redundancy is a purely statutory concept and does not discharge a contract of employment at common law. Given however that it is a full defence to a claim for unfair dismissal and as the issue of misconduct does not arise (which negates the need for fair procedures) it is not surprising that the court finds itself dealing with a significant number of cases with employees arguing that the redundancy was a smokescreen for an otherwise unfair dismissal. The problem is that there are various conflicting judgments in this jurisdiction where redundancy has been relied upon by employers to justify dismissal. In *Orr v Zomax*[49] Carroll J, in approving *Johnson v Unisys Limited*,[50] stated that 'the defendant gave notice in accordance with the plaintiff's contract plus an additional month' and 'as there was no allegation that notice was not adequate' and 'as the issue of misconduct did not arise' the injunctions requested had to be denied. Carroll J had also previously stated this view in *Sheehy v Ryan*.[51] However, where the defendant dismisses for a reason other than misconduct and the plaintiff alleges misconduct the court may find there is an arguable case for dismissal for misconduct in breach of natural justice and grant an injunction on that basis. Such a situation arose in *Moore v Xnet Informations Systems Ltd*.[52] Also there has been a UK case where the court granted an interlocutory injunction in a straight redundancy situation – *Anderson v Pringle Scotland Ltd*.[53]

---

46. See *Phelan v BIC (Ireland) Limited* (1997) ELR 208, *Hickey v Eastern Health Board* (1991) 1 IR 208 and *Orr v Zomax* (unreported, 25 March 2004), HC, Carroll J.
47. *Hickey v Eastern Health Board* (1991) 1 IR 208.
48. *Turner v O'Reilly* [2006] IEHC 92, Hedigan J.
49. *Orr v Zomax* [2004] IEHC 47, Carroll J.
50. *Johnson v Unisys Limited* (2001) 2 All ER 801.
51. *Sheehy v Ryan* [2005] IEHC 419.
52. *Moore v Xnet Informations Systems Ltd* (2001) ELR 193.
53. *Anderson v Pringle Scotland Ltd* (1998) IRLR 64.

5. Where the dismissal is in breach of a constitutional right

[8.22] In *Meskell v Coras Iompair Éireann*[54] the plaintiff was granted a declaration that his dismissal was a denial and violation of and an unlawful interference with his constitutional rights where the defendants were held to have attempted to coerce him into abandoning his constitutional right of disassociation from a trade union.

WHEN WILL AN INJUNCTION NOT BE GRANTED?

[8.23] There is a general reluctance on behalf of the courts to grant injunctions in redundancy based dismissals? In *O'Mahony v Examiner Publications (Cork) Limited, Thomas Crosbie Holdings Limited and Thomas Crosbie Printers Limited*[55] Laffoy J has, once again, emphasised this point.

In this case the Plaintiff had alleged (as is normal in such cases) that the company was attempting to effect a dismissal dressed up as a redundancy. In refusing the order, Laffoy J found that O'Mahony should have sought redress from the Employment Appeals Tribunal pursuant to the Unfair Dismissals Acts 1977–2007. This in effect restated the position Laffoy J had taken in her judgment in the case of *Nolan v Emo Oil Services*.[56]

PRACTICAL CONSIDERATIONS – PROCEEDINGS FOR INJUNCTIVE RELIEF

[8.24] From an employer's perspective it is vital that prior to dismissing an employee the possibility of the employee seeking an injunction to restrain the dismissal needs careful consideration. At a minimum the contract of employment needs careful scrutiny and in particular any reference to a contractual notice period.

In the event that an injunction is proceeded with, it is important to study the proceedings carefully to determine whether they are framed in such a way as to ensure that the plaintiff will also be entitled to redress for unfair dismissal in respect of the same dismissal.[57] This is generally standard practice for counsel. In the event of a settlement occurring it is important to ensure that it is in full and final settlement of all claims both under common law and statute, thus preventing the employee taking an additional claim to the EAT. At a minimum to avoid an application for injunctive relief:

(i)   Follow carefully the disciplinary process outlined in the contract of employment. Make sure this is consistent with the code of practice on grievance and disciplinary disputes.[58]

---

54.   *Meskell v Coras Iompair Éireann* (1973) IR 121.
55.   *O'Mahony v Examiner Publications* (5 November 2010, unreported) HC.
56.   *Nolan v Emo Oil Services* (2009) 20 ELR 122.
57.   The Unfair Dismissal Act 1977, s 15 as amended by the Unfair Dismissals (Amendment) Act 1993, s 10.
58.   SI 146/2000.

(ii) Allow fair procedures, both at the investigation and disciplinary hearing, and make a clear distinction between the investigation and disciplinary hearing including if practically possible appointing different persons to deal with each stage.

(iii) Consider independent third party investigation and disciplinary process if it is not possible to appoint separate personnel to each stage of the process.

(iv) Consider alternative dispute resolution mechanisms.

Interim injunctions

[8.25] Where an interim injunction is sought in great urgency, it is done on an 'ex parte' basis, ie with only one party present. This generally arises in an employment situation where an employer suspends an employee pending further investigation of some issue. The employee realising the seriousness of the situation then seeks an interim injunction restraining inter alia their dismissal.

When applying for the interim injunction on an ex parte basis the plaintiff's solicitor will have a plenary summons or civil bill as appropriate issued out of the Central Office of the High Court or Circuit Court (see **8.27**) for draft plenary summons) and a grounding affidavit (see **8.29**) sworn by the plaintiff containing all the information necessary to meet the criteria for granting an injunction including an undertaking as to damages.

Advance notice of making the application is normally given to the Central Office. This can be done outside normal court hours and if this is the case the approach is generally made by counsel. Whilst any judge of the High Court or Circuit Court can hear an application it is usual in the context of High Court proceedings to bring the application before one of the judges listed to hear either Chancery or judicial review matters. At the hearing the judge will be attended by a registrar and the solicitor for the plaintiff will hand in the original summons along with a certified copy of the grounding affidavit and the original exhibits.

If granted the interim order will usually be limited to apply for a period of a number of days and a return date will be fixed to be inserted into the notice of motion. It is usual for the plaintiff's solicitor to seek a direction from the court as to how the interim injunction is to be communicated to the defendant employer. More often than not it will be directed to be done by telephone and fax followed by a letter detailing the terms of the order made. As soon as possible afterwards the summons, motion, grounding affidavit and exhibits along with the interim order, if it has issued, will be served on the employer.

On the return date set out in the notice of motion (see **8.28**), the plaintiff's application becomes one for an interlocutory injunction in which the plaintiff seeks a continuation of the order pending the full trial of the action.

Interlocutory injunctions

[8.26] In circumstances that do not demand great urgency a plaintiff's solicitor will make an application for an interlocutory injunction as opposed to an interim injunction.

Here the plaintiff will have issued a plenary summons/civil bill along with a notice of motion and grounding affidavit setting out the basis for the injunction application, all of which are served on the defendant employer or their solicitor.

Plenary summons

[8.27]

20 No

THE HIGH COURT

BETWEEN

JOE BLOGGS

Plaintiff

-and-

AB COMPANY LIMITED

Defendant

PLENARY SUMMONS

To AB Company Limited
 the defendant
of (address)
This Plenary Summons is to require that within eight days after service thereof upon you (exclusive of the day of such service) you in person or by Solicitor do enter an Appearance in the Central Office, Four Courts, Dublin 7, in the above action' and TAKE NOTICE that in default of your so doing, the Plaintiff may proceed therein and judgment may be given in your absence.
By Order – THE HONOURABLE Mr Justice (insert name of Chief Justice)
Chief Justice of Ireland, the day of
Two Thousand and
NB This Summons is to be served within TWELVE calendar months from the date hereof, and, if renewed within six calendar months from the date of the last renewal, including the day of such date, and not afterwards.
The defendant may appear hereto by entering an Appearance either personally or by Solicitor at the Central Office, Four Courts, Dublin 7.

GENERAL ENDORSEMENT OF CLAIM

THE PLAINTIFF'S CLAIM IS FOR:
(Insert what the claim is for).
BARRISTER'S NAME
 Signed:_____
 Solicitors for the Plaintiff
 (Address)
 (Reference)
This Summons was issued by Joe Bloggs
whose addressed is
(Address)
This Summons was served by me at
on the Defendant
on day, the day of 20

Indorsed on the day of 20
Signed
Address

Notice of motion

[8.28]

20 No (Record No inserted here)

THE HIGH COURT

BETWEEN

Plaintiff

JOE BLOGGS

– and –

Defendant

AB COMPANY LIMITED

NOTICE OF MOTION

TAKE NOTICE that on the day of 20 at 11 o'clock in the forenoon or at the first available opportunity thereafter Counsel on behalf of the Plaintiff will make application to this Honourable Court sitting at the Four Courts, Inns Quay, Dublin 7 for the following relief:

1. An injunction restraining the Defendant, whether by itself or by its servants or agents from dismissing the Plaintiff (or whatever the case may be
2. An injunction restraining the Defendant from whether by itself or by its servants or agents from carrying out further or any disciplinary actions against the Plaintiff (or whatever the case may be).
3. Further or other relief
4. Costs.

WHICH SAID APPLICATION will be grounded on the proceedings already had herein, this Notice of Motion, the Affidavit of Joe Bloggs sworn on the day of 20 (a copy of which is served herewith), proof of service of the foregoing, such further evidence as may be produced, the nature of the case and the reasons to be offered.

Dated the day of 20 .
Signed:_____
( )

Solicitors for the Plaintiff
(Address)

To: The Registrar
High Court Central Office
Four Courts
Dublin 7.

And: Messrs.
Solicitors for the Defendant
(Address)

Grounding affidavit

[8.29]

20 No

THE HIGH COURT

BETWEEN

Plaintiff

JOE BLOGGS

– and –

Defendant

AB COMPANY LIMITED

AFFIDAVIT OF JOE BLOGGS

I, **Joe Bloggs**, of (Address) aged eighteen years and upwards, **MAKE OATH AND SAY** as follows:

1. I am an employee of AB Company Limited (the company) with Registered address at …
2. I have been employed with the company for 20 years, 6 months and 10 days.
3. I have the title of Director of Sales
4. I have held this position for the past five years being promoted to same on …
5. Without warning or notice to me I was summoned to a meeting to be held with the Managing Director of the company Mr … on ….at which he accused me of fraudulently withholding sensitive Sales information from the annual shareholders meeting.
6. Etc
7. In the circumstances therefore, I ask this Honourable Court for the relief's set out in the Notice of Motion together with such further and other relief's as may be appropriate in the circumstances and including an order for costs.
8. Finally, I can confirm that in the event of the said injunctive relief being granted, I am authorized on behalf of the Plaintiff to give the necessary undertaking as to damages.

SWORN by
this day of 20
At
in the City/County of
before me a Practising Solicitor/Commissioner for
Oaths and I know the Deponent
This Affidavit is file on (day of 20) on behalf of the Plaintiff by ( ) Solicitors, (Address)
Filed this day of 20…

Chapter 9

TRANSFER OF A BUSINESS

INTRODUCTION

[9.01] Employees' rights in the event of the transfer of a business or part of a business from one employer to another are protected by the European Communities (Protection of Employees on Transfer of Undertakings) Regulations 2003 (SI 131/2003) or the 'Transfer of Undertakings Regulations' as they are known.

These Regulations aim to protect the contractual rights of employees in respect of their employment in the event of the transfer to another employer of the business or part of the business in which they are employed. The Regulations provide that the rights and obligations of the original employer ('the transferor') arising from an employment contract existing at the date of a transfer shall, by reason of such transfer, be transferred to the new employer ('the transferee').[1] Furthermore, the transferee must continue to observe the terms and conditions agreed in any collective agreement on the same terms as were applicable to the transferor under that agreement until the date of termination or expiry of the agreement or the entry into force of another collective agreement.[2]

APPLICATION OF THE REGULATIONS

[9.02] Section 3(1) of the Regulations states that:

> 'These Regulations shall apply to any transfer of an undertaking, business, or part of an undertaking or business from one employer to another employer as a result of a legal transfer (including the assignment or forfeiture of a lease) or merger.'

Therefore for the Regulations to apply there must be a transfer, it must apply to an undertaking, business or part of a business, it must be from one employer to another and it must be as a result of a legal transfer or merger.

There must be a transfer

[9.03] The Regulations apply only in the event of a transfer. In most instances a transfer is readily identifiable. However, in some cases it may be difficult to ascertain and may occur without the parties to the transfer being aware that the transaction actually constitutes a transfer within the meaning of the Directive.

A transfer must however involve a change of employer, as if there is no change of employer then the Directive does not apply.[3] It is also the case that there must be a legal

---

1. European Communities (Protection of Employees on Transfer of Undertakings) Regulations 2003 (SI 131/2003), reg 4(1).
2. European Communities (Protection of Employees on Transfer of Undertakings) Regulations 2003 (SI 131/2003), reg 4(2).
3. European Communities (Protection of Employees on Transfer of Undertakings) Regulations 2003 (SI 131/2003), reg 3.

transfer from one undertaking to the next (this can involve the assignment or forfeiture or a lease or merger).

Spijkers[4] is one of the earliest cases to deal with the issue of a transfer and is still relevant today. Here Mr Spijkers worked for a company (Colaris) at their slaughterhouse. Colaris agreed to sell the slaughterhouse together with land, equipment and offices to Benedik CV on 27 December 1982. From that date Colaris ceased trading and no trading took place until 7 February 1983 when Benedik took over. As a result there was no goodwill in the business by the time Benedik resumed production. Equally Benedik did not commence an identical trade to Colaris, but a new trade which they started with all the previous employees of Colaris, with the exception of Mr Spijker and one other, who was too ill to work. Mr Spijkers claimed that there had been a transfer of an undertaking and that he should be both paid from 27 December 1982 and that Benedik should employ him. Advocate General Slynn made the following observation in his opinion:[5]

> It is clear that the overriding objective of the Directive is to protect workers in a business which is transferred. In deciding whether there has been a transfer ... all the circumstances have to be looked at. Technical rules are to be avoided ... the substance matter more than the form. The essential question is whether the transferee has obtained a business of an undertaking (or part thereof) which he can continue to operate. That at the time of the transfer is still active, that machinery is being used, customers supplied, workers employed and that all the physical assets and goodwill are sold are strong indications that a transfer ... has taken place. But these are not all necessary pre-requisites of a transfer in every case ... the fact that at the date of transfer trading has ceased or has substantially reduced does not prevent there being a transfer of a business if the wherewithal to carry on the business such as plant, building and employees are available and are transferred. Nor is the fact that goodwill or existing contracts are not transferred conclusive against there being a transfer.

Thus the court determined that in order for a business to come within the definition of transfer that the business must retain its 'identity'. To decide therefore if a transfer has taken place the court then set out the factors to be considered as follows:

> To decide whether these conditions are fulfilled it is necessary to take account of all the factual circumstances of the transaction in question including the type of undertaking or business in question, the transfer or otherwise of tangible assets such as buildings and stocks, the value of intangible assets at the date of transfer, whether the majority of the staff are taken over by the new employer, the transfer or otherwise of the circle of customers and the degree of similarity between activities before and after the transfer, and the duration or any interruption in those activities. It should remain clear however that each of these factors is only a part of the overall assessment which is required and therefore they cannot be examined independently of each other.[6]

---

4.   *Spijkers v Gebroeders Benedik Abbatoir CV* (Case C–24/85) (1986) ECR 1119.
5.   *Spijkers v Gebroeders Benedik Abbatoir CV* (Case C–24/85) (1986) ECR 1119.
6.   *Spijkers v Gebroeders Benedik Abbatoir CV* (Case C–24/85) (1986) ECR 1119.

Also of note in the *Spijkers* case is the relevance of having a 'gap' between employers. In the Spijkers case this was just over a month.

What we can take from this is that every transfer will be looked at on its own merits and for a transfer to occur the following will be assessed:

1. whether assets were transferred;

2. whether staff were tranferred;

3. whether customers were transferred;

4. whether the business is similar;

each of the above cannot be assessed independently.

Date of transfer

[9.04] Regulation 4(1) states that:

> The transferor's rights and obligations arising from a contract of employment existing on the date of a transfer shall, by reason of such transfer be transferred to the transferee'.

This in essence means that after the date of transfer the obligations all pass to the transferee and the transferor is 'off the hook', so to speak. However what determines the date of transfer?

The ECJ in *Astley v Celtec Ltd*[7] defined the date of transfer as:

> ... the date on which responsibility as employer for carrying on the business of the unit transferred moves from the transferor to the transferee. That date is a particular point in time, which cannot be postponed to another date at the will of the transferor or transferee.

Transfer within and outside the EU

[9.05] Once the transfer occurs within the EU the Directive and Regulations will apply. It may prove difficult for employees to enforce their rights in other jurisdictions; however, the Brussels Regulations[8] will apply, which provide for the enforcement of judgments in other jurisdictions in the various member states without the necessity for new litigation.

Whether a transfer outside to a non EEA/EU state comes within the ambit of the regulations has yet to be tested in this jurisdiction. However, it has been held in the UK that the Regulations, given that they have an international element and are concerned about protecting the rights of individuals, have the potential to apply to a transfer to a non-EU state.[9]

---

7.   *Astley v Celtec Ltd* (Case C–478/03) (2005) IRLR 647.
8.   Brussels Convention on Jurisdiction and the Enforcement of Judgements in Civil and Commercial Matters 1968.
9.   See the case of *Metal Industries Ltd V GMB* (2008) IRLR 187.

Closure of a business and resumption later

[9.06] *Spijkers* is also authority for the fact that where a transferor ceases his business and there is a gap in time before the transferee resumes the business, this does not prevent a transfer of an undertaking occurring. In *Spijker* Advocate General Slynn went on to observe that where:

> After the sale there is a gap before trading is resumed is a relevant fact but it is not conclusive against there being a transfer within the meaning of the Directive. The transferee may well want to spend time reorganizing or renovating the premises or equipment…the fact that the business is carried on in a different way is not conclusive against there being a transfer – new methods, new machinery, new types of customer are relevant factors but they do not of themselves prevent there being in reality a transfer of a business or undertaking.

A transfer can therefore occur in several ways:

Sale of shares

[9.07] The Transfer of Undertakings Regulations does not apply in a situation where there is a mere sale of shares. This is because shares in companies invariably change hands frequently and by various amounts all of which has no effect on employees. Even where it arises that a controlling interest in the company passes from one shareholder to another in practice this has no effect in law on the employees.

Sale of the assets and good will of business to a new employer

[9.08] In this instance the employees will be employed by a new person or company, and as there is a change of employer the Directive applies.

Transfer of ownership by operation of law or indirect means

[9.09] This arises where the ownership of a business changes on the happening of some event not requiring the specific agreement of the contracting parties. An example may be the surrendering of a lease or franchise. In this instance the Directive also applies. The case of *Daddy's Dance Hall*[10] demonstrated this as it was held that the Directive could apply where there was no change in the legal ownership of the business but a change in the person or body responsible for the management or day–to-day operation of the business. The background to this is that a Mr Tellerup was employed by a catering company which leased restaurants and bars from another company. Their lease was terminated and Daddy's Dance Hall was appointed to take over. Mr Tellerup was dismissed from the original company but prior to his notice terminating was taken on by Daddy's Dance Hall. However, he was subsequently dismissed by Daddy's Dance Hall and a dispute arose over his notice.

---

10. *Foreningen af Arbejdsledere i Danmark v Daddy's Dance Hall A/S* (Case 324/84) (1988) ECR 739.

It was held that the Directive applies to a situation where, after the termination of a lease, the owner of the undertaking leases it to a new lessee who continues to run the business. The court held:[11]

> It follows that when the lessee who has the capacity of proprietor of the undertaking at the termination of the lease loses this capacity and a third person acquires it under a new lease concluded with the owner, the resulting operation is capable of falling within the scope of the application of the Directive as defined in Article 1(1). The fact that in such case the transfer takes place in two phases in the sense that as a first step the undertaking is transferred back from the original lessee to the owner who then transfers it to the new lessee, does not exclude the applicability of the Directive as long as the economic entity retains its identity.

This approach was followed in *Landsorganisationen i Danmark v Ny Molle Kro*[12] and in *Berg and Busschers v Besselsen*[13] and has been followed in this jurisdiction by the Employment Appeals Tribunal in *Guidon v Hugh Farrington and Ushers Island Petrol Station*.[14] Here the claimant had been employed by Local Stores (Trading) Ltd trading as Seven – Eleven, which operated a branch in the petrol station. Seven – Eleven went into receivership and surrendered its lease on 14 June 1991 (a Friday). The claimant returned to work on Monday 17 June to be advised by a Mr Farrington who had taken over the shop that her employment was being terminated. The ECJ, having regard to the *Berg and Besselsen* case, determined that there had been a transfer of an undertaking of the Seven – Eleven Shop to Mr Farrington and that as the dismissal of the claimant was prohibited by the Directive as a result of a transfer, the dismissal of the claimant was unfair.

Another case of note in this regard is the case of *Redmond Stitching v Barton*.[15] Here the Dr Sophie Redmond Foundation leased a building from a local authority in the Netherlands to provide assistance to drug addicts. The local authority also provided funding for the project. The local authority ceased funding the Redmond Foundation and passed the funding to another foundation called the Sigma Foundation. The lease to the Redmond foundation also passed to Sigma as did the clients and some of the staff. Those displaced staff contended that a transfer of an undertaking applied within the meaning of the Directive. The ECJ held that the Directive applied and held inter alia that:

> The decisive criterion for establishing whether there is a transfer of an undertaking is whether the unit in question retains its identity after the transfer. In order to ascertain whether or not there is a transfer it is necessary to determine whether the functions performed are in fact carried out or resumed by the new legal entity with the same or similar activities'. They also went on to state that the Directive 'does not exclude non-profit making bodies' and that 'a transfer occurs where a public

---

11. *Foreningen af Arbejdsledere i Danmark v Daddy's Dance Hall A/S* (Case 324/84) (1988) ECR 739.
12. *Landsorganisationen i Danmark v Ny Molle Kro* (Case 287/86) (1987) ECR 5465.
13. *Berg and Busschers v Besselsen* (Joined cases 144 and 145/1987) (1988) ELR 98.
14. *Guidon v Hugh Farrington and Ushers Island Petrol Station* 1993 ELR 98.
15. *Redmond Stitching v Barton* (Case C–29/91) (1992) ECR I–3189.

body terminates a subsidy paid to one legal entity as a result of which the activities of that entity are terminated and transferred to another legal entity with similar terms'.

Undertakings or parts of undertakings

[9.10] The Regulations must apply to undertakings or parts of undertakings or to a business or part of a business. Undertakings are not defined in the Directive or the Irish Regulations. This naturally raises the question as to what an 'undertaking or part thereof' actually is. Basically it can be defined as a business or part of a business which is engaged in economic activity whether or not this is for profit-making purposes, ie the undertaking can be either public or private.[16]

As can be seen from the *Redmond Stitching v Barton* case[17] an undertaking can be a not-for-profit organisation. The Directive therefore has a very wide application.

Parts of undertaking or parts of business

[9.11] Whereas it is generally straightforward to recognise the transfer of a business, this may not be so when it comes to part of the business or undertaking. The ECJ in the case of *Schmidt Spar und Leibkasse der Fruheren amter Bordesholm*[18] provided guidelines on this issue. The background to this case is that Ms Schmidt was employed by the bank to carry out cleaning work. The bank decided to contract out this work to a contract cleaning firm. The question then arose as to whether the cleaning work constituted part of the undertaking of the bank. The bank claimed that the contract did not come within the scope of the Directive as it did not involve the transfer of an economic unit. The court held:

> The fact that the activity in question was performed prior to the transfer, by a single employee (is not sufficient) to preclude the application of the Directive.
>
> The decisive criterion for establishing whether there is a transfer … is whether the business in question retains its identity … the retention of that identity is indicated inter alia by the actual continuation or resumption by the new employer of the same or similar activities.

Who is covered?

[9.12] The Regulations cover certain categories of people.

Employees

[9.13] Employees are defined in SI 131/2003 as:

> a person of any age, who has entered into or works under (or, where the employment has ceased, entered into or worked under) a contract of employment

---

16.   See reg 3(3).
17.   *Redmond Stitching v Barton* (Case C–29/91) (1992) ECR I–3189.
18.   *Schmidt Spar und Leibkasse der Fruheren amter Bordesholm* (Case C–392/92) (1994) ECR I–1311.

and references, in relation to an employer, to an employee shall be construed as references to an employee employed by that employer; and for the purposes of these Regulations, a person holding office under, or in the service of, the State (including a civil servant within the meaning of the Civil Service Regulation Act 1956 (No 46 of 1956)) shall be deemed to be an employee employed by the State or Government, as the case may be, and an officer or servant of a harbour authority, health board or vocational education committee shall be deemed to be an employee employed by the authority, board or committee, as the case may be.

Employees are therefore anyone who enters into or works under a contract of employment. This definition covers those who work under a contract for service. Indeed this line of thought is in accordance with the decision given by the ECJ in *Botzen v Rotterdamasche Droodok Maatschappij BV*.[19] It also applies to those employed under a contract of apprenticeship and those agency workers covered by the Employment Agency Act 1971.[20]

Employers

[9.14] Employers are defined as those persons 'with whom the employee has entered into or for whom the employee works under (or, where the employment has ceased, entered into or worked under) a contract of employment'. In the case of agency workers the employer is deemed to be the person who pays the wages of the employee.

Employers do not have to be profit-making bodies and can also include public bodies.[21] In the case of *Henke v Gemeinde Schierke & Verwaltunsgemeinschaft 'Broken'*[22] the ECJ held that a local authority in Germany was an economic entity and therefore covered by the Directive (the Directive in this instance being the 1980 Transfer of Undertakings Directive (77/197/EEC) which has since been repealed).

Responsibility after the transfer

[9.15] In *Berg and Busschers v Besselsen*[23] the ECJ held that, where Member States have not determined that the transferor and the transferee shall be severally liable after the transfer, art 3(1) must be interpreted as meaning that, after the date of a transfer the transferor is, by virtue of the transfer alone, discharged from liability.

Thus where the Regulations and/or Directive are breached, liability falls on the transferee. In *Rotstart de Hertaing v J Benoidt SA (in liquidation)*[24] the ECJ held:

> Article 3(1) of the Directive is to be interpreted as meaning that the contracts of employment and employment relationships existing on the date of the transfer of an undertaking, between the transferor and the workers employed in the

19.   *Botzen v Rotterdamasche Droodok Maatschappij BV* (1986) 2 CMLR 50.
20.   European Communities (Protection of Employees on Transfer of Undertakings) Regulations 2003 (SI 131/2003), reg 3.
21.   European Communities (Protection of Employees on Transfer of Undertakings) Regulations 2003 (SI 131/2003), reg 3(3).
22.   *Henke v Gemeinde Schierke & Verwaltunsgemeinschaft 'Broken'* (1996) IRLR 701.
23.   *Berg and Busschers v Besselsen* (Joined cases 144 and 145/87) (1988) ECR 2559.
24.   *Rotstart de Hertaing v J Benoidt SA (in liquidation)* (Case C–305/94) (1996) ECR I–52927.

undertaking transferred, are automatically transferred from the transferor to the transferee by the mere fact of the transfer of the undertaking. ...

EMPLOYEES' RIGHTS

[9.16] As the purpose of the Directive is to protect employees' terms and conditions of employment in the event of a transfer occurring, the Directive is necessarily clear on the various rights it gives to employees.

Right to information and consultation

[9.17] Both the original and new employer are obliged to inform their respective employees' representatives of the date of the transfer, the reasons for the transfer and the legal, social and economic implications of the transfer. This must be done, where reasonably practicable, not later than 30 days before the transfer date, and in any event in good time before the transfer is carried out (or in the case of the transferee, in good time before the employees are directly affected by the transfer regarding conditions of employment).[25]

It should be noted that the right to information and consultation is limited.

Regulation 8(5) provides that:

> Where there are no employees' representatives in the undertaking or business of the transferor or, as the case may be, in the undertaking or business of the transferee, the transferor or the transferee, as may be appropriate, shall put in place a procedure whereby the employees may choose from among their number a person or persons to represent them (including by means of an election) for the purposes of this Regulation.

Regulation 8(6) provides:

> Where, notwithstanding paragraph (5), there are still no representatives of the employees in an undertaking or business concerned (through no fault of the employees), each of the employees concerned must be informed *in writing*, where reasonably practicable, not later than 30 days before the transfer and, in any event, in good time before the transfer, of the following:
>
> (a)   the date or proposed date of the transfer;
>
> (b)   the reasons for the transfer;
>
> (c)   the legal implications of the transfer for the employee and a summary of any relevant economic and social implications for that employee; and
>
> (d)   any measures envisaged in relation to the employees.

Therefore the right to information and consultation in the main must be given to employee representatives.

Where there are no representatives, the employers (either the transferor or transferee as appropriate) must arrange for the employees to choose representatives for this

---

25.   European Communities (Protection of Employees on Transfer of Undertakings) Regulations 2003 (SI 131/2003), reg 8.

purpose.[26] In the event that this is still not possible each of the employees concerned must be informed *in writing,* (note that this does not apply where there are employee representatives), where reasonably practicable, not later than 30 days before the transfer and, in any event, in good time before the transfer, of the date of the transfer, the reasons for the transfer, the legal implications of the transfer for the employees and a summary of any relevant economic and social implications for the employees and any measures envisaged in relation to the employees[27] (see draft letter at **9.39**).

In good time

[9.18] What does in good time mean? This matter was considered in the context of the EC Collective Redundancy Directive[28] by the UK High Court in the case of *Griffin v South West Water Services Ltd*[29] where the court went on to say, inter alia:

> I cannot see that the Article requires the employer to embark upon the process of consultation at any particular moment, much the less as soon as he can be said to have in mind that collective redundancies may occur. The essential point to my mind is that the consultation must be one where, if they wish to do so, the workers' representatives can make constructive proposals and have time in which to do so before the relevant dismissal notices are sent out.

Therefore, in good time seems to be defined as allowing the employees' representives sufficient time to make constructive proposals.

Employees' representatives

[9.19] The Regulations define employee representatives as a trade union, staff association or excepted body with which it has been the practice of the employees' employer to conduct collective bargaining negotiations, or in their absence a person or person chosen by such employees under an arrangement put in place by the employer to represent them in negotiations with the employer.[30] This is a much broader definition of employee representatives than typically the Labour Court have afforded in this jurisdiction, albeit that this may have changed with the decision of the Supreme Court in *Ryanair v Labour Court.*[31]

The status and function of the employees' representatives is protected across a transfer on the same terms and conditions and/or subject to any collective agreement between the employer and the representatives.[32]

---

26. European Communities (Protection of Employees on Transfer of Undertakings) Regulations 2003 (SI 131/2003), reg 8(5).
27. European Communities (Protection of Employees on Transfer of Undertakings) Regulations 2003 (SI 131/2003), reg 8(6).
28. EC Collective Redundancy Directive 75/129/EEC.
29. *Griffin v South West Water Services Ltd* (1995) IRLR 15.
30. European Communities (Protection of Employees on Transfer of Undertakings) Regulations 2003 (SI 131/2003), reg 2(1).
31. *Ryanair v The Labour Court* (2007) IESC 6.
32. European Communities (Protection of Employees on Transfer of Undertakings) Regulations 2003 (SI 131/2003), reg 7(1).

Details of any measures envisaged in relation to the employees must be discussed with the employees' representatives 'with a view to reaching an agreement'.[33] Bearing in mind the ECJ case of *Junk v Kuhnel*[34] this requires actual negotiations to take place (see **6.44**).

EXCEPTIONS TO PROTECTION OF RIGHTS IN THE EVENT OF A TRANSFER

[9.20] Not all rights are protected in the event of a transfer.

Pensions exception

[9.21] Employees' rights to old age, invalidity or survivors' benefits under supplementary company or inter-company pension schemes outside the Social Welfare Acts are not covered. In effect, such pension rights in place on the date of transfer do not transfer across to the new contract but are protected under the Pensions Acts 1990 to 2003 – where the relevant supplementary company pension scheme is an occupational pension scheme within the meaning of those acts (ie an approved pension scheme).

In relation to unapproved occupational pension schemes, the transferee (new employer) is required to 'protect' the rights of employees in such cases.[35]

Employer's insolvency

[9.22] Where the outgoing employer is subject to proceedings whereby they could be adjudicated bankrupt, or wound up (a company) for reasons of insolvency, by order of the High Court the 'transfer' obligations on the part of the employer do not apply.[36] Regulation 6 therefore excludes the transfer of an undertaking, business or part of an undertaking or business where the transferor is the subject of bankruptcy or insolvency proceedings. The High Court has confirmed this in *Re Castle Brand Ltd (in liquidation)* and in *Re the Companies Acts 1963–1983*.[37] The EAT has taken the view that a voluntary liquidation does not come within the exclusion of insolvent undertakings from the terms of the Regulations and Directive.

In *Kelly v Cavanagh Hiester Ltd (in liquidation) and Dubshad Ltd*[38] the Tribunal held:

> As the liquidation of Hiester Ltd was a voluntary liquidation the Tribunal holds that the ... Regulations, SI 306/1980 apply and in this instance there was a transfer

33.   European Communities (Protection of Employees on Transfer of Undertakings) Regulations 2003 (SI 131/2003), reg 8(4).
34.   *Junk v Kuhnel* Case C–188/03.
35.   European Communities (Protection of Employees on Transfer of Undertakings) Regulations 2003 (SI 131/2003), reg 4(3).
36.   European Communities (Protection of Employees on Transfer of Undertakings) Regulations 2003 (SI 131/2003), reg 6.
37.   *Re the Companies Acts 1963–1983* (unreported, 25 March 1995), HC Hamilton J.
38.   *Kelly v Cavanagh Hiester Ltd (in liquidation) and Dubshad Ltd* UD 222–224/96.

of the business to Mr Brian Cavanagh, when Hiester Ltd went into liquidation. Accordingly there was no break in the claimant's service'. Here the Tribunal relied on the ECJ decision of HBM Abels v Administrative Board of Bedrijfsvereniging Voor de Metaal- Industrie en de Electrotechnische Industrie.[39]

In the High Court case of *Mythen v Employment Appeals Tribunal*[40] Barrington J analysed the views of Advocate General Slynn in *Abels*[41] and took the view that the principle as outlined in *Abels* could only apply in an enforced liquidation of a bankrupt company, stating:[42]

> It follows that the reasons for not applying the directive to transfers of undertakings taking place in liquidation proceedings are not applicable to proceedings of this kind taking place at an earlier stage.

DISMISSALS

[9.23] An employee may not be dismissed by reason of the transfer of an undertaking.[43]

Dismissal by reason of the transfer

[9.24] In some instances it is not uncommon for the purchasers of a business to insist that they take over the business free from all employees. In an effort to circumvent the Directive this has led some employers to make all employees redundant prior to the transfer and to then sell the business after which the 'transferee' is free to do what he wishes with the business. In *P Bork International A/S (in liquidation) v Foreningen af Arbejdsledere i Danmark*[44] the ECJ held in a situation where the employees were dismissed and re-engaged by the 'new employer' immediately after the transfer that the workers must be considered as still employed in the undertaking on the date of the transfer with the consequent effect that the Regulations/Directive apply to them. The option therefore of making all employees redundant prior to the transfer and then selling the business 'employee free' is no longer a viable one for either the transferor or the transferee.

Having regard to the automatic transfer of liabilities to the transferee as referred to in *Rotsart de Hertaing v J Benoidt SA*[45] the only opportunity a transferee has of mitigating the cost of any subsequent, necessary restructuring costs is to negotiate effective indemnities from the transferor beforehand.

---

39. *Kelly v Cavanagh Hiester Ltd (in liquidation) and Dubshad Ltd* (1987) CMLR 406.
40. *Mythen v Employment Appeals Tribunal* (1990) ELR 1.
41. *Abels v The Administrative Board of the Bedrijfsvereniging voor de Metaal-industrie en de Electrotechnische Industrie* (Case 135/83) [1985] ECR 469.
42. *Mythen v Employment Appeals Tribunal* (1990) ELR 1, 10.
43. European Communities (Protection of Employees on Transfer of Undertakings) Regulations 2003 (SI 131/2003), reg 5(1).
44. *P Bork International A/S (in liquidation) v Foreningen af Arbejdsledere i Danmark* (1989) IRLR 41.
45. *Rotsart de Hertaing v J Benoidt SA* (1997) IRLR 127.

Dismissal for 'Economic, Technical or Organisational Reasons' (ETO)

[9.25] Regulation 5 of SI 131/2003 prohibits the termination of employment in the event of a transfer. This however is qualified by providing that 'nothing in this Regulation shall be construed as prohibiting dismissals for economic, technical or organisational reasons which entail changes in the workforce.'[46] In the main this may be interpreted as coming within the statutory definition of redundancy, ie valid redundancies that arise as a result of the transfer are allowable. In *Anderson v Dalkeith Engineering Ltd (1984)*[47] where a receiver had previously dismissed employees to make the company more viable to sell and where the new owners had subsequently re-hired some of those previously dismissed employees the EAT held that those not re-hired were not unfairly dismissed. The effect of this appears to be that if the transferor can show that in order to sell the business he had no option but to dismiss some or all of the workforce those dismissals will not be deemed unfair.

First, it is crucial to remember that this is merely a defence. It does not in itself provide a mechanism for reducing the size of a workforce. Secondly, it is vital that if seeking to rely on this defence the ETO reasons must entail 'changes in the workforce'. This will generally require an alteration to the numbers of people employed to perform particular tasks, not just a change in their terms and conditions.[48] In *Crawford v Swinton Insurance Brokers Ltd*[49] the EAT held that a 'change in workforce' could either be a change in the number of employees or a change where some person is engaged in a different occupation. The scope of the defence is therefore limited to the following:

- **The reasons for the defence only apply to the transferee**

  This may apply even if at the behest of the transferee he asks the transferor to dismiss, if it is clear at the time of that request that there is a defence for ETO reasons and it is also clear that it would be inevitable that after the transfer the employees' employment would be terminated.

- **There must be a change in the workforce**

  This cannot be limited to a change in terms and conditions. It seems there has to be an actual change in the workforce.

- **Dismissal can be for economic grounds**

  The economic grounds relate to the costs of running the business post the transfer and not prior to.

---

46.   European Communities (Protection of Employees on Transfer of Undertakings) Regulations 2003 (SI 131/2003), reg 5(2).
47.   *Anderson v Dalkeith Engineering Ltd* (1984) IRLR 429.
48.   See *Berriman v Delabole Slate Ltd* (1985) IRLR 3052, 213.
49.   *Crawford v Swinton Insurance Brokers Ltd* (1990) IRLR 42.

- **Dismissal can be for technical grounds**

  Equally technical grounds will only apply to dismissals post the transfer. These will relate to the skills necessary to carry out the job, the technical ability of the employees, and their abilities both physical and mental.

- **Dismissal can be for organisational grounds**

  This again will relate to the organisational needs of the business post transfer. It will consider the need for the business to organise itself in a particular way, whether geographically, departmentally, by product line etc.

Substantial change in working conditions

[9.26] If an employee's contract of employment is terminated because a transfer involves a substantial change in working conditions to the detriment of the employee, the employer concerned is regarded as having been responsible for the termination.[50] This clearly arises in the absence of the ETO defence. Therefore in order for employers to rely on the ETO defence they must be able to demonstrate that their decision was a bona fide decision to make the changes and that they consequently entailed changes in the workforce.

Thus where a transferee purchases a business or part of a business and this results in different terms and conditions, applying the ETO defence does not apply to the harmonisation of terms and conditions. Transferees are therefore left with the problem of trying to manage employees on different terms and conditions often doing the same or similar jobs. Options then only extend to either red circling employees or to improve all terms and conditions to the best available.

Indeed Regulation 9 does not help in this regard (see below also at **9.36**) This Regulation provides that any provision in an agreement which excludes or limits the application of any provision of the Regulations shall be void. Therefore if a provision in an agreement (even at the employee's consent becomes less favourable to an employee than a similar entitlement conferred by the Regulations, then the agreement is deemed to be modified so as not to be less favourable.[51] Regulation 9 also provides that nothing in the Regulations shall be construed as prohibiting the inclusion in an agreement of a provision more favourable to an employee than any provision in the Regulations.[52]

The transfer of a business and redundancy

[9.27] The question of what happens an employee who refuses to transfer has been dealt with extensively by the ECJ. In *Katiskas v Konstantinidis and Skreb*[53] the ECJ held that

---

50. European Communities (Protection of Employees on Transfer of Undertakings) Regulations 2003 (SI 131/2003), reg 5(3).

51. European Communities (Protection of Employees on Transfer of Undertakings) Regulations 2003 (SI 131/2003), reg 9(2).

52. European Communities (Protection of Employees on Transfer of Undertakings) Regulations 2003 (SI 131/2003), reg 9(3)

53. *Katiskas v Konstantinidis and Skreb* (1993) IRLR 179.

in the vent of a transfer, employees were entitled to object to the transfer and what happens to them then is a matter for each member state. In *Mikkelsen v Danmols Incentar A/S*[54] the ECJ stated:[55]

> The protection which the Directive is intended to guarantee is however redundant where the person concerned decides of his own accord not to continue the employment relationship with the new employer after the transfer. That is the case where the employee in question terminates the employment contract or employment relationship of his own free will with effect from the date of the transfer or where that contract or relationship is terminated with effect from the date of the transfer by virtue of an agreement voluntarily concluded between the worker and transferor or the transferee of the undertaking. In that situation Article 3(1) of the directive does not apply.

In *Merckz and Neuhuys v Ford Motor Company Belgium SA*[56] the ECJ stated:

> Article 3(1) of Directive 77/187 does not preclude an employee employed by the transferor at the date of the transfer of an undertaking from objecting to the transfer to the transferee of the contract of employment or the employment relationship. In such a case it is for the Member states to determine what the fate of the contract or employment relationship with the transferor should be.

In the case of *Symantec v Leddy and Lyons*[57] the Irish courts got an opportunity to address this issue. When Symantec sold part of its business to another company, Messrs Leddy and Lyons refused to transfer to the purchaser as was their right. The issue was whether the employees had been made redundant and whether they were entitled to their statutory redundancy payment.

The EAT held that in refusing to transfer the employees remained employed by the transferor. If Symantec had no alternative position to offer them, they would be made redundant and Symantec would be liable for that redundancy.

However on appeal the High Court overturned that decision and held that the refusal of an employee to transfer does not result in the employee being made redundant. As a result the employees were not entitled to any severance payment statutory or otherwise.[58] The High Court has in effect dealt with this in the same manner as it would be treated in the UK. The British Transfer of Undertakings Regulations provide that where an employee objects to a transfer, his contract with the transferor is at an end but he will not be treated as having been dismissed by the transferor.

Change of contractor/contracting out

[9.28] 'Contracting out' has long been a feature of Irish business life across all industries including milk collection in the dairy industry, boners in the meat industry, cleaners in practically every industry, canteen services, IT services etc. The question

---

54. *Mikkelsen v Danmols Incentar A/S* (1986) 1 CMLR 316.
55. *Mikkelsen v Danmols Incentar A/S* (1986) 1 CMLR 316, para 16.
56. *Merckz and Neuhuys v Ford Motor Company Belgium SA* (1996) IRLR 467.
57. *Symantec v Leddy and Lyons* (2009) IEHC 256.
58. At the time of writing this is on appeal to the Supreme Court.

that has bothered the courts in this jurisdiction and across the EU is what happens when a service that is contracted out changes from one contractor to another or what happens when an employer who carries out a service decides to contract that out to a separate service provider?

Throughout the mid-1990s the European Court of Justice (ECJ) took a very broad view on this issue. In the case of *Schmidt v Spar und Liehkasse der Fruheren Amter Bordesholm*,[59] as stated above Schmidt was employed to carry out the cleaning in a branch of a bank. The bank decided to contract out the work to a contract cleaning company which was already responsible for cleaning most of the other branches of the bank. Schmidt refused to transfer and claimed under the Directive. The ECJ in holding that the Regulations applied determined that 'where a business carried on its activities by virtue of a licence or contract, a successor acquired that licence or the contract to carry on that work. The ECJ inter alia based its decision on the fact that the cleaning work of the bank was part of the undertaking of the bank.

The ECJ now takes a more restrictive view of this issue. In the case of *Suzen v Zehnacker Gebaudereinigung Gmbh*[60] the court held that not every contract change is covered by the Regulations. Here the court claimed that:

> [T]he mere loss of a service contract to a competitor cannot by itself indicate the existence of a transfer within the meaning of the Directive. In those circumstances the service undertaking previously entrusted with the contract does not, on losing a customer, thereby cease fully to exist and a business or part of a business belonging to it cannot be considered to have been transferred to the new awardee of the contract.

The effect of this decision is that it is not sufficient that there is a transfer of a right to carry on a business; there must be a transfer of 'significant tangible or intangible assets' or a transfer of a 'major part' of the employees.

The *Suzen* decision caused considerable confusion when it first issued. Many commentators believed that the ECJ had overruled itself. However, in *Schmidt* the bank was clearly an economic entity and the cleaning of the bank was part of that entity. That part of the undertaking transferred to the outside cleaning company retained to do the cleaning work who then took over part of the economic entity and as such the employee was assigned to that part of the entity transferred with the work. In *Suzen* the cleaning work was already being done by an outside company and when the contract between them came to an end that contract was granted to a new service provider. Thus came the first distinction between contracting out part of your business and changing contractors.

This stricter test of what constitutes a transfer was reflected in the Directive[61] and indeed in reg 3 of the Irish 2003 Regulations, which provide that:

> 'transfer' means the transfer of an economic entity which retains its identity;

---

59.   *Schmidt v Spar und Liehkasse der Fruheren Amter Bordesholm* 1994 IRLR 302.
60.   *Suzen v Zehnacker Gebaudereinigung Gmb*h (Case C–13/95).
61.   Directive 2001/23/EC (12 March 2001).

> 'economic entity' means an organised grouping of resources which has the
> objective of pursuing an economic activity whether or not that activity is for profit
> or whether it is central or ancillary to another economic or administrative entity.

Thus there must be a transfer of an economic entity which retains its identity. In the case
of most transfers from one contractor to another this will not be the case but it may well
be the case where a company is contracting out part of its already existing economic
entity.

The *Suzen* definition has been applied in Ireland in the case of *Cannon v Noonan
Cleaning Limited and CPS Cleaning Services Limited*.[62] Here the EAT held that there
was no transfer of an undertaking when the contract for the cleaning of the Balbriggan
Garda Station was lost to CPS Cleaning Limited as no tangible assets and no employees
were transferred.

Also in *Power v St Paul's Nursing Home and T & M Cleaning Ltd*[63] the claimants
were employed as cleaners in St Paul's nursing home. The home decided to contract out
the cleaning duties in respect of which the claimants were employed and they were as a
result made redundant. St Paul's then entered into a contract with T & M Cleaning Ltd to
carry out the cleaning duties. Cleaning equipment and other ancillary minor assets were
transferred to T & M Cleaning Ltd. The EAT in holding that the Directive applied
stated:

> It is the opinion of this Tribunal that the Directive applies to these particular sets
> of circumstances and in fact it would be most artificial if it was held that the case
> was otherwise.

That said, the EAT appears to have changed the position it took in *Cannon v Noonan
Cleaning Ltd* in the decision of *Keenan v Professional Contract Services Ltd*.[64] The facts
are similar to *Noonan* in that Professional Contract Services Ltd took over a cleaning
contract from Grosvener Cleaning at Dublin City University. Here the Tribunal held
'that there was a transfer of an undertaking … which was accepted by the respondents'.
It seems in this latter case (a point that is not sufficiently set out in the reasoning of the
EAT) that there was some confusion as to whether the claimants actually wanted to
transfer.

Evidently one might adduce from the above that this issue is still very much one to
be considered per the facts in every single separate situation.

COMPLAINTS AND REMEDIES

[9.29] An employee (or his/her trade union/staff association or excepted body) may take
a complaint to a Rights Commissioner that an employer has contravened their
obligations to the employee under the Regulations.[65] This must be done within six

---

62. *Cannon v Noonan Cleaning Limited and CPS Cleaning Services Limited* 1998 ELR 212.
63. *Power v St Paul's Nursing Home and T & M Cleaning Ltd* (1998) ELR 212.
64. *Keenan v Professional Contract Services Ltd* UD 454/455/456/98.
65. European Communities (Protection of Employees on Transfer of Undertakings) Regulations
    2003 (SI 131/2003), reg 10.

months of the contravention alleged (or within a further six months where the Rights Commissioner is satisfied that exceptional circumstances prevented the complaint being presented within the first six months). The relevant complaint form is set out at **9.43**. Unlike the Unfair Dismissals legislation where a claimant may bring a claim before the Rights Commissioner or directly to the EAT, the Regulations provide that the complaint must be brought initially to the Rights Commissioner who will hold a hearing.

Employees can complain that there was a contravention of reg 8, ie the information and consultation requirements. In this instance they can be awarded up to four weeks' remuneration.[66] Bear in mind this is per employee so where there are a substantial number of employees this can amount to a significant sum.

In the event of any other contravention employees may be awarded up to two years' remuneration. Again this is per employee so the sums can be very sizeable.

A fine of up to €3,000 and possible imprisonment for up to 12 months on summary conviction can also be imposed where a person 'wilfully and corruptly makes any statement which is material and which he or she knows to be false.'[67] A breach of the Regulations could also give rise to a claim for constructive dismissal[68] and/or a referral under the Industrial Relations Act 1969–2004.

Appeals

[9.30] Appeals lie from a decision of the Rights Commissioner to the Employment Appeals Tribunal (a six-week time limit applies) and from the EAT to the High Court on a point of law only.[69]

Decisions of a Rights Commissioner and determinations (unless appealed) of the Tribunal are enforceable (by employee, trade union or Minister) in the Circuit Court.[70]

Injunctive relief

[9.31] Probably the most effective remedy for an employee is to seek and obtain an injunction preventing the transfer until their rights under reg 8 are adhered to. In *Maybury v Pump Services Ltd and Eldea Ltd*[71] the plaintiff successfully applied on an ex parte basis to the High Court to restrain his dismissal and to get both parties to the transfer to comply with their obligations under the Regulations against a background

---

66. European Communities (Protection of Employees on Transfer of Undertakings) Regulations 2003 (SI 131/2003), reg 10(5)(c)(i).
67. European Communities (Protection of Employees on Transfer of Undertakings) Regulations 2003 (SI 131/2003), reg 13(2).
68. See *Moran v Bloxham Stockbrokers* US 377/2002 where it was held that the employer was at fault in not outlining the terms of the transfer and in failing to guarantee that those terms were commensurate with the terms she enjoyed with the transferor.
69. European Communities (Protection of Employees on Transfer of Undertakings) Regulations 2003 (SI 131/2003), reg 12(2).
70. European Communities (Protection of Employees on Transfer of Undertakings) Regulations 2003 (SI 131/2003), reg 14(3).
71. *Maybury v Pump Services Ltd and Eldea Ltd* (unreported, 2 May 1990), HC.

where the transferee was unable to give the plaintiff any assurances about his continued employment. (The matter settled at the interlocutory stage.)

However, since then the UK High Court has refused to grant injunctive relief in *Betts v Brintel Helicopters Ltd; KLM ERA Helicopters (UK) Ltd*.[72] This concerned the loss of a contract to ferry offshore oil workers by helicopter to and from the oil rigs in the North Sea. The High Court in this instance held that the remedy was by way of an application to the Industrial Tribunal. Also in *Hyland Shipping Agencies*[73] the court refused a mandatory injunction directing the defendants to comply with their obligations under the Regulations to inform and consult.

PRACTICAL CONSIDERATIONS

[9.32] When faced with a situation where the Regulations apply there are a number of practical operational issues that the practitioner needs to carry out and there will undoubtedly be a number of usual questions that will arise.

Due diligence

[9.33] As part of the purchase of any business the transferee should carry out a comprehensive due diligence. The main focus of this is generally on the financial state of the company and is carried out by the purchaser's accountants. A wider due diligence by the transferee's solicitors will amongst other things focus on the employees' rights in the event of the Transfer of Undertakings Regulations being applicable and the necessary consequences of same.

Human Resources (HR) Audit

[9.34] Prior to the due diligence process evolving, a comprehensive audit of the 'target business' should be executed. This should involve preparing a list of all employees, their rates of pay, benefits and duration of service (the latter being necessary if redundancies are contemplated). This list should then be studied with consideration given to the possibility of each employee's future in the new company.

Similarly an audit of the transferee's business should be conducted to determine whether there will be a significant duplication of functions and a plan conceived as to how this might be dealt with going forward.

Indemnities and warranties

[9.35] As part of the due diligence process queries will be raised (and presumably answered) by the transferor, thereby securing representations from the transferor which may be relied upon in the future. As part of these queries transferees should ensure that they have received written confirmation from the transferor that they have complied with their obligations under reg 8 (Information and Consultation).

---

72.   *Betts v Brintel Helicopters Ltd; KLM ERA Helicopters (UK) Ltd* (1997) IRLR 361.
73.   *Hyland Shipping Agencies* (unreported, 2 February 1996), HC.

Notwithstanding this, transferees should also seek an indemnity from the transferor against any legal costs of having to defend themselves, where for example redundancies may need to be effected as a result of the transfer. Alternatively and more practically the costs of any redundancies should be determined and perhaps consideration given to providing for the cost of these in the purchase price. However, given the difficulties in measuring the cost of this at the time of the transfer it is not unusual for the transferee to seek some form of indemnity from the transferor. The transferor on the other hand will not wish to provide open-ended indemnities and/or warranties and these will likely fall to be negotiated between the contracting parties.

Can employees agree changes prior to or at the time of transfer?

[9.36] One must ask here, are the parties to an agreement free to reach agreement on something happening that the Regulation prohibits each of them doing individually? For example, both parties may agree on a variation of conditions of employment. This is not that clear.

What is clear is that it is not open to contract out of the Regulations and 'any provision or agreement, that seeks to limit the application of, to exclude, or which is inconsistent with the Regulations is void'.[74] In *Foreninger af Arbejdsledre i Danmark v Daddy's Dance Hall A/S*[75] the ECJ held that an employee cannot agree a change even where it may be advantageous to do so. Also in two separate UK cases[76] the House of Lords held that the employer is not in a position to negotiate with or agree changes with employees unless their contracts are validly terminated within the terms of the Directive and domestic Regulations prior to the transfer. That said these cases preceded Directive No 2001/23/EC and s 9(3) of the 2003 Regulations which provides that '[n]othing in these Regulations shall be construed as prohibiting the inclusion in an agreement of a provision more favourable to an employee than any provision of these Regulations'. This provision would appear therefore to override the aforementioned case law.

Picketing in the event of a transfer

[9.37] The issue here is whether the transfer of a trade dispute from the transferor to the transferee is protected by the Regulations. The ECJ held in *d'Urso v Ercole Marelli Elettromeccanica Generale Spa*[77] and *Rotsart de Hertaing v J Benoidt SA (in liquidation)*[78] that picketing by employees of a transferor directed against a transferee must be held to be valid and protected. In the event that the picket was against the transferor itself then the issue of the Regulations does not fall to be considered. In the one Irish case on this topic, *Westman Holdings Ltd v Mc Cormack*,[79] the High Court

---

74.   Regulation 9(1).
75.   *Foreninger af Arbejdsledre i Danmark v Daddy's Dance Hall A/S* (1988) IRLR 315.
76.   *Wilson v St Helens Borough Council and Meade and Baxendale v British Fuels Ltd* (1977) IRLR 505.
77.   *d'Urso v Ercole Marelli Elettromeccanica Generale Spa* (1992) IRLR 136.
78.   *Rotsart de Hertaing v J Benoidt SA (in liquidation)* (1997) IRLR 127.
79.   *Westman Holdings Ltd v Mc Cormack* (1992) 1 IR 151.

(upheld by the Supreme Court) granted an interlocutory injunction to the purchaser of a pub to restrain a picket placed by the employees of the former owners. In this instance the transferor had dismissed his employees and the transferee had failed to offer all the previously displaced workers alternative jobs. As none of the picketing employees had ever been employed by the plaintiff he successfully argued that he could not constitute their employer within the meaning of s 11(1) of the 1990 Industrial Relations Act. The case went no further and does seem to have been fought solely on the basis of the Industrial Relations Act as distinct from the Transfer of Undertakings Regulations.

Data Protection Issues

[9.38] An interesting issue arises once the transfer has been announced. Clearly, at this stage, the transferee will want to see exactly what the terms and conditions of employees are. Whilst much of this information may have been given during the due diligence it can only be given in general form as no specific details of an individuals terms and conditions of employment can be divulged without their consent. This equally prevails until such time as the actual transfer, unless the specific authority of the individual employees is provided. It is thus very important when dealing with these matters, either as a transferor or transferee, not to disclose any personal details that may infringe the Data Protection Acts 1998–2003.

Draft letter to employees in the event of a transfer where there are no employee representatives

[9.39]

Dear Employee, …….. Company Ltd

On behalf of the company I am writing to you as the company representative pursuant to section 8(6) of SI No 131 of 2003 to inform you that the company is being transferred to XYZ Ltd with effect from …/…/20…[80]

The reason for the transfer of the business is …[81]

It is envisaged that there shall be/shall not be[82] any legal, economic or social implications resulting from the transfer at the date of transfer. Your continuity of service will not be affected and XYZ Ltd will recognize all rights connected with or arising out of your contract of employment, including recognizing the existing collective agreement with …. Union.[83]

Yours faithfully,

For and on behalf of XYZ Ltd

---

80.   This date must be at least 30 days from the date of the letter.
81.   The company may give whatever the reasons are without divulging too much commercial detail.
82.   Whichever is the case.
83.   The latter only if appropriate.

Draft Transferor Letter

[9.40]

Dear [Insert name of employee],

The purpose of this letter is to formally notify you of the proposed transfer of your employment to (insert name of transferee) at midnight on (insert date of transfer).

For the purposes of Regulation 8 of the European Communities (Protection of Employees on Transfer of Undertakings) Regulations 2003, we are required to inform you of the following information not later than 30 days before the proposed transfer:

1   Date or proposed date of the transfer

(insert date of transfer)

2   Reasons for any transfer

(Insert the reasons for the transfer eg the business has been sold, a tender has been successful etc.)

3   Legal, economic and social implications for the transfer for the employees

Your employment with the Company will transfer to (insert name of transferee) with effect from midnight on (insert date).

All your rights and entitlements as an employee of the Company will transfer at midnight on said date and (insert name of transferee) is legally obliged to continue to employ you from that date.

From the date of transfer, your accrued service with the Company will be deemed to have been with (insert name of transferee) and you are entitled to the same (or no less favourable) terms and conditions of employment than those you enjoyed with the Company prior to the transfer.

4   Measures envisaged in relation to the employees

Further to our meeting with (insert name of transferee) on (insert date), you will be aware that they will only be in a position to identify and confirm whether any measures are envisaged in relation to your terms and conditions of employment once you have confirmed your intentions in relation to your contract of employment. Once you have confirmed your intentions to the Company and (insert name of transferee), then arrangements will be made for (insert name of transferee) to consult with you directly (if appropriate) in relation to those measures envisaged with a view to reaching agreement.

We would encourage you to raise any concerns or queries you have in this regard at the earliest possible date in order for the Company and/or (insert name of transferee) to address these issues.

Yours sincerely,

Draft Transferee Letter

[9.41]

Dear [insert employee name],

Further to you being made aware that (insert transferee name) have been successful in (their tender for/ have bought the business of, or whatever the circumstances are) ... with effect from [insert date of transfer], (Insert name of Transferee) is of the opinion that our impending takeover of this business is covered by the European Communities (Protection of Employees on Transfer of Undertakings) Regulations 2003, under which your employment will continue with no loss of seniority, entitlement or security which you currently have or enjoy with (insert name of Transferor). It is a requirement of the European Communities (Protection of Employees on Transfer of Undertakings) Regulations 2003 that we as the entity taking over the business maintain the continuity of employment of all existing employees.

In summary, therefore, we can assure that your employment will be continuous on the same terms and conditions of employment as are currently in place, thereby affording you the security that your service has earned under the legislation.

We can further assure you that we have received all your relevant employment details from (insert name of Transferor) so as to enable us to honour your current terms and conditions of employment.

We can appreciate that you may well have further queries regarding the impending takeover and how it will affect you. Any such queries can be directed to (insert name of contact person). We will endeavour to respond to all queries.

[9.42] Forms

Application to Rights Commissioner

[9.43]

APPLICATION TO RIGHTS COMMISSIONER

EUROPEAN COMMUNITIES (SAFEGUARDING OF EMPLOYEES RIGHTS ON TRANSFER OF UNDERTAKINGS) (AMENDMENT) REGULATIONS 2003.

(PLEASE USE BLOCK CAPITALS)

NAME:	NAME OF COMPANY OR EMPLOYER: (FULL LEGAL NAME, IF IN DOUBT CONSULT YOUR P60 OR P45)
ADDRESS:	ADDRESS:
TEL NO:	TEL NO:

NAME AND ADDRESS OF YOUR REPRESENTATIVE (IF ANY)

_____

_____

MY/OUR COMPLAINT IS THAT: _____

_____

_____

_____

_____

_____

_____

EMPLOYEE'S SIGNATURE: DATE:

PLEASE NOTE THAT A COPY OF THIS FORM WILL BE FORWARDED TO YOUR EMPLOYER.

Form T1–B

[9.44] Appeal of the Rights Commissioner's Recommendation to the Employment Appeals Tribunal.

FORM T1-B	**EMPLOYMENT APPEALS TRIBUNAL**	
Please read the notes supplied then complete this form in **BLOCK CAPITALS**. Please sign and date	**FOR OFFICIAL USE ONLY**	
	Case No/s:	

1. NOTICE OF APPEAL FROM RIGHTS COMMISSIONER'S RECOMMENDATION UNDER (Tick appropriate box or boxes)

	(i) Unfair Dismissals Acts 1977 to 2007
	(ii) Payment of Wages Act 1991
	(iii) Terms of Employment (Information) Acts 1994 and 2001
	(iv) Maternity Protection Act 1994 and 2004
	(v) Adoptive Leave Act 1995
	(vi) Protection of Young Persons (Employment) Act 1996
	(vii) Parental Leave Act 1998-2006
	(viii) Protections for Persons Reporting Child Abuse Act 1998
	(ix) European Communities (Protection of Employees on Transfer of Undertakings) Regulations 2003
	(x) European Communities (Protection of Employment) Regulations 2000
	(xi) Carer's Leave Act 2001
	(xii) Competition Act 2002
	(xiii) Consumer Protection Act 2007
	(xiv) Chemicals Act 2008
	Organisation of Working Time Act 1997 – Appeals as to holiday entitlement can be made to the Employment Appeals Tribunal along with another Act. Otherwise it must be appealed to the Labour Court

PLEASE STATE IF YOU ARE THE EMPLOYEE OR THE EMPLOYER:

2. IF EMPLOYEE:	**2. IF EMPLOYER:**
First Name:	Name/Company: ....
Surname:	Address: ....
Address:	....
....	....
Phone No:	Phone No: ....
Email Address::	Email Address:

3. WILL YOU HAVE A REPRESENTATIVE AT HEARING? (Trade Union Official, Solicitor, etc.) Yes ☐ No ☐	**3. WILL YOU HAVE A REPRESENTATIVE AT HEARING?** (Employer Representative, Solicitor, etc.) Yes ☐ No ☐
If yes, please give:	If yes, please give:
Name:	Name: ....
Address:	Address: ....
....	....
Phone No:	Phone No: ....

4. NAME AND ADDRESS OF PARTY AGAINST WHOM THE APPEAL IS BEING BROUGHT
Name: ....
Address: ....
....
Phone No: ....

PLEASE ADVISE THE TRIBUNAL SECRETARIAT OF ANY CHANGE OF ADDRESS.

5. Please enter the following dates (IF APPLICABLE)	Day	Month	Year
Date of Birth			
Employment Began			
Dismissal Notice Received			
Employment ended			

6. PAY (IF APPLICABLE)	€
Basic Weekly Pay	
Regular Bonus or Allowances	
Average Weekly Overtime	
Any other payments including payments in kind - specify	
Weekly Total Gross	
Net	

7. NAME OF RIGHTS COMMISSIONER

8. DATE AND REF. NO. OF DECISION/RECOMMENDATION TO WHICH THIS APPEAL APPLIES:
(Please enclose a copy of this decision/recommendation with your application)

9. TOWN OF EMPLOYMENT OR NEAREST TOWN:

10 THE REASONS FOR MY APPEAL ARE: (You can attach additional sheets if necessary)

A COPY OF THE RIGHTS COMMISSIONER'S RECOMMENDATION MUST BE FORWARDED WITH THIS FORM.

11. REMEDY SOUGHT (IF APPLICABLE):

IMPORTANT NOTE: INCOMPLETE FORMS WILL BE RETURNED AND MAY DELAY THE PROCESSING OF YOUR APPEAL

12. DECISIONS OF THE TRIBUNAL MAY BE PLACED ON THE TRIBUNAL'S WEBSITE
(Please refer to point (18) of Notes)

SIGNED: _____

DATE: _____

Please note that where the Tribunal processes a claim for hearing, all correspondence (*forms, letters, enclosures etc.*) received in this office will be copied to, and exchanged between, the parties to the claim.

PLEASE ADVISE THE TRIBUNAL SECRETARIAT (01-6313006) IF YOU REQUIRE ANY SPECIAL FACILITIES WHEN ATTENDING A TRIBUNAL HEARING.

Form T1B Notes

NOTICE OF APPEAL TO EMPLOYMENT APPEALS TRIBUNAL UNDER:

(i)	**UNFAIR DISMISSALS ACT 1977 TO 2007**
(ii)	**PAYMENT OF WAGES ACT 1991**
(iii)	**TERMS OF EMPLOYMENT (INFORMATION) ACT 1994 and 2001**
(iv)	**MATERNITY PROTECTION ACT 1994 AND 2004**
(v)	**ADOPTIVE LEAVE ACT 1995**
(vi)	**PROTECTION OF YOUNG PERSONS (EMPLOYMENT) ACT 1996**
(vii)	**PARENTAL LEAVE ACT 1998-2006**
(viii)	**PROTECTIONS FOR PERSONS REPORTING CHILD ABUSE ACT 1998**
(ix)	**EUROPEAN COMMUNITIES (PROTECTION OF EMPLOYEES ON TRANSFER OF UNDERTAKINGS) REGULATIONS 2003**
(x)	**EUROPEAN COMMUNITIES (PROTECTION OF EMPLOYMENT) REGULATIONS 2000**
(xi)	**CARER'S LEAVE ACT 2001**
(xii)	**COMPETITION ACT 2002**
(xiii)	**CONSUMER PROTECTION ACT 2007**
(xiv)	**CHEMICALS ACT 2008**

Organisation of Working Time Act 1997 – Appeals as to holiday entitlement can be made to the Employment Appeals Tribunal along with another Act. Otherwise it must be appealed to the Labour Court.

Notes for Persons Making Appeal

THIS FORM IS TO BE USED BY PERSONS WHO WISH TO APPEAL A RECOMMENDATION / DECISION OF A RIGHTS COMMISSIONER TO THE EMPLOYMENT APPEALS TRIBUNAL UNDER ONE OR MORE OF THE ABOVE ACTS

PART A – TIME LIMITS

<u>IMPORTANT</u>:   TIME LIMITS FOR PERSONS BRINGING AN APPEAL TO THE TRIBUNAL:

Note:
Appeals against a recommendation or Decision of a Rights Commissioner must be made to the Tribunal within a particular time-limit from the date the recommendation is communicated to you. The time limits for appeals under the various Acts are as follows:

UNFAIR DISMISSALS ACTS 1977 to 2007	Within 6 weeks to the Tribunal.
PAYMENT OF WAGES ACT 1991	Within 6 weeks to the Tribunal AND the other party
TERMS OF EMPLOYMENT (INFORMATION) ACT 1994 and 2001:	Within 6 weeks to the Tribunal.
MATERNITY PROTECTION ACT 1994 and 2004	Within 4 weeks to the Tribunal.
ADOPTIVE LEAVE ACT 1995	Within 4 weeks to the Tribunal.
PROTECTION OF YOUNG PERSONS (EMPLOYMENT) ACT 1996	Within 6 weeks to the Tribunal.
PARENTAL LEAVE ACT 1998-2006	Within 4 weeks to the Tribunal
PROTECTIONS FOR PERSONS REPORTING CHILD ABUSE ACT 1998	Within 6 weeks to the Tribunal
EUROPEAN COMMUNITIES (PROTECTION OF EMPLOYEES ON TRANSFER OF UNDERTAKINGS) REGULATIONS 2003	Within 6 weeks to the Tribunal
EUROPEAN COMMUNITIES (PROTECTION OF EMPLOYMENT) REGULATIONS, 2000	Within 6 weeks to the Tribunal
CARER'S LEAVE ACT 2001	Within 4 weeks to the Tribunal (This time limit may be extended for a further period not exceeding 6 weeks if the Tribunal considers it reasonable to do so having regard to all the circumstances)
COMPETITION ACT 2002	Within 6 weeks to the Tribunal
CONSUMER PROTECTION ACT 2007	Within 6 weeks to the Tribunal
CHEMICALS ACT 2008	Within 6 weeks to the Tribunal

PART B - NOTES

(1) **Box 1 - TICK APPROPRIATE BOX OR BOXES:**
Tick box or boxes representing the Act or Acts under which you are appealing .

(2) **Box 2 - NAME AND ADDRESS OF PARTY MAKING THE APPEAL:**
If you change your address after lodging this form, be sure to notify the Secretary, Employment Appeals Tribunal, Davitt House, 65A Adelaide Road, Dublin 2. In order to enhance the processing of applications we will use email, where applicable, to all parties at any stage in the processing of an appeal.

(3) **EMPLOYER'S FULL LEGAL NAME AND ADDRESS:**
Any Order made by the Tribunal may not be enforceable if incorrect information is given. For assistance, please consult your P45 or where appropriate, the Companies Registration Office (01-804 5200). The employer's Registered (PAYE) No. may be obtained from your P45, P60 and Tax Certificate P.6CL.

(4) **Box 3 - NAME, ADDRESS OF REPRESENTATIVE OF PARTY MAKING THIS APPEAL:**
It is not necessary to have representation before the Tribunal. However, if you have arranged for a representative to attend on your behalf at the Tribunal, notification of the hearing of your appeal will be sent to that person as well as to yourself.

(5) **Box 5 - DATES:**
Insert relevant dates

(6) **Box 6 - PAY:**
Basic Weekly Pay.
This means the basic pay before any deductions are made.

Average Weekly Overtime.
In unfair dismissal cases, overtime may be disregarded unless it is a normal feature of work. If it is a normal feature of work inasmuch as you are normally expected to work it, overtime pay is included in your normal weekly pay and overtime is included in normal weekly working hours.

Payments in Kind.
These would include the value of meals or board, use of company house, car or health insurance etc.

(7) **Box 7 - RIGHTS COMMISSIONER:**
Please fill in the name of the Rights Commissioner that heard your case

(8) **Box 8** – Please include the date the recommendation or decision was issued and the reference no. that appears on the signed decision. **Please enclose a copy of this decision with this form.**

(9) **Box 9** - In this box please give the name of the nearest town where you worked or the nearest town to this.

(10) **Box 10 - REASON FOR APPLICATION:**
Please give an outline of your case in the space provided. If you wish to provide further details, please attach any separate sheets to the form.

(11) **Box 11 – REMEDY SOUGHT**
Please state what remedy you are seeking

(12) **ACKNOWLEDGEMENT OF APPLICATION:**
If you do not get an acknowledgement of your application within a reasonable time you should contact the Secretary to the Tribunal by letter, telephone or email (details below).

(13) **HEARING OF CLAIM:**
Once you have received an acknowledgement, your case will be listed for hearing as soon as possible at the nearest town to your place of employment. You will get at least 2 weeks notice of a date for hearing.

(14) **ADJOURNMENTS:**
Adjournments may be granted only in **exceptional circumstances**. Otherwise, a case is expected to proceed at the time and place notified to the parties. When applications for adjournments are made, they may be made to any sitting Division of the Tribunal at any venue.

The following conditions should at least be met when applying for an adjournment. However, the existence of any one or all of these conditions should not be considered a guarantee for obtaining an adjournment.

o   Good cause should be shown as adjournments are only granted for very grave reasons.

o The application should be made at the earliest opportunity after receipt of the notice of hearing, save where the Tribunal for just cause dispenses with this requirement.

o The application should be made by a party or his representative appearing in person.

o Proof of consent from the other party or their representative may be required. The application can be made without consent but the Tribunal may require proof that consent was at least sought.

(15) **WITHDRAWAL OF APPLICATIONS:**
If you are seeking to withdraw your application, the Secretary to the Tribunal should be notified in writing as soon as possible.

(16) **COSTS:**
Frivolous or vexatious applications may lead to an award of costs against the applicant.

(17) **INFORMATION:**
For general information regarding employment rights please contact the National Employment Rights Authority (NERA) at Lo call No: 1890 80 80 90 or submit your query using their eform, which is located in the 'Contact Us' section of their website www.employmentrights.ie

(18) **DATA PROTECTION**
The Employment Appeals Tribunal holds data on all applications received. Data Protection is the safeguarding of the privacy rights of individuals in relation to the processing of personal data. The Data Protection Acts 1988 and 2003 confer rights on individuals as well as responsibilities on those persons processing personal data. Personal data, as covered by the Data Protection Acts, relates to the information on individuals and or sole traders only.

The Employment Appeals Tribunal provides copies of its decisions on its website. The decisions do not include the names of the parties (the name/s of the employee/s or the employer/s). The Data Protection Commissioner's web-site *www.dataprotection.ie* offers an explanation of the rights and responsibilities under the Data Protection Acts and information is also available from the Data Protection Commissioner's Office at Canal House, Station Road, Portarlington, Co. Laois; telephone number (057) 8684800.

(19) **USE OF INTERPRETERS**
The Tribunal does not provide a language interpreter service. However, if you feel that an interpreter is essential to the hearing of the claim, you can make an application before a sitting Division of the Tribunal. **Please Note: An application must be made at least two weeks in advance of the hearing date.**

NOTE
Please Detach Form from Notes and send to;

Secretary
Employment Appeals Tribunal
Davitt House
65A Adelaide Road
Dublin 2

Telephone: **(01) 631 3006**
1890 220222 Lo-Call service from outside (01) area
Website: www.eatribunal.ie
Email: eat@deti.ie

Form T–2

[9.45] This form is used to respond against a claim which has been lodged with the Employment Appeals Tribunal under the Transfer of Undertakings Regulations.

IN ORDER TO ACKNOWLEDGE RETURN RECEIPT OF THIS FORM YOU ARE ASKED TO SUPPLY, IF POSSIBLE, A DEDICATED EMAIL ADDRESS

Email Address:

Case No

EMPLOYMENT APPEALS TRIBUNAL

	(i)	Redundancy Payments Acts, 1967 to 2003
	(ii)	Minimum Notice and Terms of Employment Acts, 1973 to 2001
	(iii)	Unfair Dismissals Acts, 1977 to 2001
	(iv)	Protection of Employees (Employers' Insolvency Acts, 1984 to 2001
	(v)	Organisation of Working Time Act, 1997

NOTICE OF APPEARANCE

by a party against whom a claim has been lodged under the legislation ticked above _____

by _____

against _____

N.B. If employer's name is different from above, please give employer's correct legal name.

Do you have a representative acting for you?   Yes _____   No _____

If Yes, please give name and address:

Do you dispute the claim/s being made   Yes _____   No _____

If Yes, please state the claim/s at no.'s (i) to (v) above being made:

_____

P.T.O.

Please set out the reasons in the space provided below:

(Note: While you should try to set out your case as fully as possible, you will not be necessarily confined to what is given on this form at the hearing.)

DECISIONS OF THE TRIBUNAL MAY BE PLACED ON THE TRIBUNAL'S WEBSITE
(Please refer to point (7) of Notes)

Signed: _____

Date: _____

Chapter 10

DISMISSAL AND EMPLOYER INSOLVENCY

INTRODUCTION

[10.01] Under the Companies Act 1963, s 214 a company is deemed insolvent if it is proven inter alia that it is unable to pay its debts, and in determining whether it is unable to pay its debts the court has to have regard to the contingent and prospective liabilities of the company. If a company is unable to pay its debts and is thus insolvent, this has significant consequences for employees. In many instances such employees will not be able to avail of the normal rights available to employees in solvent companies (such as their rights under the Transfer of Undertakings Regulations).[1] Notwithstanding this, there are a number of protections for such employees.

Firstly, employees are preferred creditors both under the Bankruptcy Act 1988 and the Companies Act 1963 (as amended). Secondly, certain employee rights are protected by the Insolvency Payments Scheme as provided for in the Protection of Employees (Employers' Insolvency) Acts 1984–2004 (as amended).[2]

Employees preferential debts include wages during the four months to the winding up to a maximum of €3,174, all accrued holiday and sick pay, minimum notice pay, statutory redundancy lump sums, compensation awarded by the EAT in respect of Unfair Dismissal claims and contributions, both employer and employee deducted from employees in respect of any pension schemes.[3]

This, however, is often not of much use to employees as the company being wound up has to have sufficient assets to discharge the debts owed and fixed assets are often subject to mortgages or other such fixed charges which rank in preference to preferential creditors. Hence the remainder of this chapter focuses on the Insolvency Acts.

Prior to studying same, it is useful to consider the effect of insolvency on the contract of employment.

Effects of various types of insolvency on the Employment Contract

[10.02] A company or an employer becomes insolvent when liabilities exceed assets.[4] Whilst insolvency has significant and grave implications for the employment contract, the nature of the insolvency generally determines the fate of a person's employment and whilst employees are provided some protection by virtue of being preferred creditors[5] and having recourse to the Protection of Employees (Employers Insolvency) Act 1984, often it is too late for employees to retrieve anything substantial following a wind up.

---

1. Transfer of Undertakings Regulations (SI 131/2003).
2. Protection of Employees (Employers' Insolvency) Act 1984 (Amendment Order 1988 (SI 48/1988; and European Communities (Protection of Employees (Employers' Insolvency)) Regulations 2005 (SI 630/2005).
3. Companies Act 1963, s 285 as amended; Bankruptcy Act 1988, s 6
4. Companies Act 1963, s 214 details the circumstances in which a company is insolvent.
5. Bankruptcy Act 1988 and Companies Act 1963 (as amended).

Equally albeit that employees have preferential creditor status, protection in this regard only extends to the employee where there are sufficient assets to discharge the debts owed. The key issues for employees when faced with an insolvency are generally their right to redundancy pay, their right to notice pay, their right to payment of outstanding wages and holiday pay and their right to information and consultation in the event of collective redundancies.

Bankruptcy

[10.03] Bankruptcy arises where the property or assets of an individual who is unable or unwilling to pay their debts is transferred by an order of the court to a trustee to be sold. A person can be declared bankrupt following a petition being issued and the High Court declaring them a bankrupt. In the alternative, a person can declare themselves bankrupt where they are unable to pay their debts and their estate is sufficient to produce at least €1,900.

Once a person is adjudicated bankrupt, that property becomes vested in the official assignee.[6] The obligations of the official assignee are similar to those of a liquidator of a company. In the case of *re Collins*,[7] it was deemed that rights arising under an employment contract are not regarded as proprietary for bankruptcy purposes. Where an employment contract is silent (as most are) on what is to occur in the event of a bankruptcy arising, the effect of same on the employment contract is unclear. This might either frustrate the contract or give rise to a claim for unfair dismissal, although in practice given that the person is bankrupt it is generally not worthwhile pursuing either option. The employee must then rest on the facts of the actual case and pending same, bankruptcy may either bring the contract to an end by operation of law, frustrate the contract, or constitute an unfair dismissal.

Voluntary Liquidation

[10.04] A voluntary liquidation can either arise on the virtue of:

1.   A creditor's voluntary winding up; or

2.   A member's voluntary winding up.

In both instances the company will usually be deemed to be dissolved on the expiration of three months after the Registrar of Companies registers the account of the winding up which has been submitted to him by the appointed liquidator. If an employee's contract is terminated at the same time as the resolution for voluntarily winding up the company is passed it will give rise to a case for wrongful dismissal as the employer will be deemed to have committed a repudiatory breach of the employment contract.[8] Where the employee agrees to work subsequent to the resolution being passed, their position is less clear. Thus, in *re Forster v Schumann*[9] the court stated that the passing of the resolution

---

6.   Bankruptcy Act 1988, s 44(1).
7.   *Re Collins* 1925 CH 536.
8.   *Reigate v Union Manufacturing Company Limited* (1918) 1 KB 592 at 606.
9.   *Re Forster v Schumann* (1) 7 19 lr 240.

had the same effect as the making of the winding up order. However, it is not always clear that this is the case.[10]

Compulsory Liquidation

[10.05] A compulsory liquidation is made by order of the High Court. In *Donnelly v Gleeson*,[11] Hamilton J held that 'an order for the winding up of a company is notice of discharge to all persons in the employment of the company'. Importantly, Hamilton J also went on refuse an order to have the date of dismissal deemed to be at the date the petition for winding up the company was presented. The Companies Act 1963, s 220 provides that the date of dismissal is the date of the presentation of the petition and this was actually brought to Hamilton J's attention in the case. However, he took the more practical view that if he were to adhere to the said section that this would run contrary to the employees' rights to notice. Employee's rights in the event of a compulsory winding up can be divided between those who are dismissed at the time of the order and those who continue working after the date of the order:

(i) *Employees dismissed at the date of the order*

In this event employees may be entitled to claim damages for wrongful dismissal, breach of contract and breach of statutory rights. In respect of the latter it is clear that such employees have the statutory right to Minimum Notice pay.

(ii) *Employees who work post the order*

In this instance a number of possibilities arise:

(a) Employees could be deemed to be merely working their notice.

(b) The liquidator can waive the notice of discharge and the employees original contracts are deemed to continue.[12] This will normally be specific, in that the liquidator will specifically notify the employees that their contracts are discharged. However it can also arise by implication. Thus in *Dodd v Local Stores (Trading) Ltd*[13] the liquidator did not inform the employees at his appointment but subsequently terminated all contracts without notice. The employees pursued claims under the Minimum Notice and Terms of Employment Act 1973, the Tribunal held that the notice of discharge normally implicit in the making of the winding up order had been waived by the liquidator. This does not mean that a short delay between the winding up order and the appointment of the liquidator will be sufficient to argue successfully that the notice of discharge is waived.[14]

---

10. See Forde, *Employment Law* (2nd ed, Thomsons Round Hall, 2002) 242.
11. *Donnelly v Gleeson* (1985) 4 JISLL 109.
12. *Re Collins* (1925) Ch 536.
13. *Dodd v Local Stores (Trading) Ltd* (1992) ELR 61.
14. *Donnelly v Gleeson* (1985) 4 JISLL 109.

(c)   The original contract is terminated by the petition and a new contract comes into existence. *In Donnelly v Gleeson,*[15] Hamilton J indicated that a specific request by the liquidator was necessary to form such a contract and in *Irish Shipping Ltd v Byrne and the Minister for Labour*[16] the court refused to imply new contracts in circumstances where the official liquidator had retained the employees for four months after the notice of discharge. Also in the *Irish Shipping* case the liquidator successfully argued that the employees were not entitled to their minimum notice as they had been re-employed after their dismissal for longer than their notice period and therefore had suffered no loss.

Provisional Liquidation

[10.06] In some instances, the court appoints a provisional liquidator. The purpose of this is to safeguard the assets of the company before an orderly winding up. The appointment of a provisional liquidator does not discharge a contract of employment.[17]

Receivership

[10.07] A receiver is appointed to a company to realise assets and or manage the affairs of the company in the hope that the debts outstanding to the debenture holder, which appointed the receiver, can be met. The duties of a receiver are normally set out in the instrument under the terms of which they are appointed. A notice of appointment of receiver (**Form E8**) must be filed with the Companies Registration Office within seven days of appointment and must also be published in Iris Oifigiúil and in at least one daily newspaper circulating in the district where the registered office of the company is situated. Where a receiver is appointed there is no change in the identity of the employer: thus the appointment does not operate to terminate or change the contract of employment.[18]

This may be different, however, where the appointment of a receiver runs contrary to retaining the services of an employees. This will generally arise where a receiver in effect carries out the role of the Managing Director or CEO. In such instances it could be argued that the employment is terminated or that a repudiatory breach of contract has occurred. Each case will of course be considered on its own merits, thus if the receiver intends to fully control the company it may well give rise to the termination but if the receiver intends to exercise control lightly or remotely this may not be the case.

In some instances a receiver can be appointed by the court. When this occurs, the receiver does not act as an agent of the company.[19] There is some debate about what impact this has on the contract of employment. Traditionally, it was thought this would be similar to the appointment of a liquidator and thus the contract of employment would

---

15.   *Donnelly v Gleeson* (1985) JISLL 109.
16.   *Irish Shipping Ltd v Byrne and the Minister for Labour* (1987) IR 468.
17.   *Donnelly v Gleeson* (1985) 4 JISLL 109.
18.   *Re B Johnson & Co (Builders) Ltd* (1955) Ch 534.
19.   *Moss Steamship Company Ltd v Whinney* (1912) AC 254.

terminate. However, the court in Australia has refused to adhere to this view.[20] As such, the matter remains somewhat in flux.

Examinership

[10.08] The Companies (Amendment) Act 1990 introduced the concept of examinership. This allows a company which is unable or unlikely to be able to pay its debts to apply to the court for protection for a period of time during which no winding up order can be made.[21] As the company continues in existence, the appointment of an examiner has no effect on the employment contract.

PURPOSE OF THE INSOLVENCY ACT

[10.09] The Act provides for payment of certain outstanding entitlements relating to the pay of an employee where employment has been terminated because of an employer's insolvency. These payments are made from the Social Insurance Fund. This fund was initially called the Redundancy and Employers Insolvency Fund but was renamed the Social Insurance Fund in accordance with the provisions of the Social Welfare Act 1990.[22]

INSOLVENCY LEGISLATION

[10.10] An employer is regarded as being insolvent where:[23]

1.   the employer has been adjudicated bankrupt;

2.   the employer petitioned for arrangement or has executed a deed of arrangement within the meaning of s 4 of the Deeds of Arrangements Act 1887;

3.   the employer has died and the estate, being insolvent, is being administered in accordance with the rules set out in Pt 1 of the First Schedule to the Succession Act 1965;

4.   the employer is a company and is ordered to be wound up compulsorily, ie is in liquidation;

5.   the employer is a company and is being voluntarily wound up;

6.   the employer is a company and either a receiver is appointed on behalf of the holder of any debenture secured by a floating charge or possession is taken by or on behalf of the holders of any debentures secured by a floating charge of any property of the company comprised in or subject to the charge;

---

20.   *Sipad Holding DDPO v Popovic* (1996) 3(1) DULJ 15, 33.
21.   Companies Act 1990, s 2.
22.   No 5 of 1990.
23.   Protection of Employees (Employers' Insolvency) Act 1984, s 4 as amended.

7.   the employer is a company registered under the Industrial and Provident Societies Acts 1893 to 1978.

The important point to note here is that it is not sufficient for employees to prove that their entitlements remains unpaid, they must prove that their employer has become insolvent.

Date of insolvency

[10.11] Dependent on the definition of insolvency, the date at which an employer is adjudged insolvent varies. The chart below sets out an easy reference point for each variation.

Insolvency Type	Date Effective
1. Where the employer has been adjudicated bankrupt	Date of adjudication
2. Where the employer petitioned for arrangement or has executed a deed of arrangement within the meaning of s 4 of the Deeds of Arrangements Act 1887	Date on which the petition was filed
3. Where the employer has died and the estate, being insolvent, is being administered in accordance with the rules set out in Part 1 of the First Schedule to the Succession Act 1965	Date of death
4. Where the company is ordered to be wound up compulsorily, ie is in liquidation	Mostly the date of the appointment of the provisional liquidator[24]
5. Where the company is being voluntarily wound up	Date of passing of the resolution for voluntarily winding the company up
6. Where either a receiver is appointed on behalf of the holder of a debenture secured by a floating charge or possession is taken by or on behalf of the holders of any debentures secured by a floating charge of any property of the company comprised in or subject to the charge	Date of appointment of the receiver or date possession is taken by or on behalf of the debenture holder
7. Where the company is a company registered under the Industrial and Provident Societies Acts 1893 to 1978	Date of appointment of liquidator or receiver

WHAT EMPLOYEES ARE COVERED?

[10.12] Employees are defined as those who have entered into or work under (or, in the case of a contract which has been terminated, worked under) a contract with an employer, whether the contract is for manual labour, clerical work or otherwise, is expressed or implied, oral or in writing, and whether it is a contract of service or apprenticeship or otherwise, and 'employer' and any reference to employment shall be construed accordingly.[25]

---

24.   See the Companies Act 1963, s 285.
25.   Protection of Employees (Employers' Insolvency) Act 1984, s 1.

All employees must be in employment which is insurable for all benefits under the Social Welfare Acts (ie generally those employees who pay full PRSI), must be between 16 and 66 years of age or, if over 66 years, in employment which, but for their age, would be insurable for all benefits under the Social Welfare Acts.[26]

EMPLOYEE ENTITLEMENTS

[10.13] An employee (known as the applicant) may apply to the Minister on the prescribed form (see **10.30** below) and the Minister shall pay the debts owed subject to certain limits.

Prerequisites for a valid claim

[10.14] Prior to paying any debt the Minister must be satisfied that:

- the applicant is an employee as defined within the scope of the Acts;
- the employer has become insolvent;
- the date of the insolvency is not prior to 22 October 1983;
- on the relevant date (see **10.11**) the applicant was entitled to be paid the whole or part of any debt.

Relevant date

[10.15] The relevant date is assessed as when:[27]

(a) If the debt is an amount, damages or fine resulting from a successful unfair dismissals or equality claim, the relevant date is the date on which:

- the employer became insolvent;
- a relevant recommendation, determination, decision, award or order of the court is made, whichever is the later.

(b) Any other debt, the relevant date is the date on which:

- the employer became insolvent;
- the employee's employment was terminated (whichever the employee shall decide as regards the debt);
- in any other case the date on which the employer became insolvent.

What debts are recoverable?[28]
[10.16]

1. Arrears of normal weekly remuneration – subject to a maximum of eight weeks to which the employee was entitled over the relevant period. (The relevant

---

26. Protection of Employees (Employers' Insolvency) Act 1984 (Amendment Order) Order 1988, art 8.
27. Protection of Employees (Employers' Insolvency) Act 1984, s 6(9)(a).
28. Protection of Employees (Employers' Insolvency) Act 1984, s 6(20).

period is defined as the period of 18 months immediately preceding the relevant date. Normal weekly remuneration is defined at point **10.17**.)

2. Sick pay – any arrears due in respect of a period or periods not exceeding a total of eight weeks under a sick pay scheme which forms part of an employee's contract of employment. These payments are only for periods during which the employee was unable to fulfil the contract due to ill health and to sick pay to which the employee became entitled during the relevant period. The amount payable is limited to the difference between any disability or injury benefit in addition to any pay-related benefit payable under the Social Welfare Acts and normal weekly remuneration.

3. Holiday pay – holiday pay is defined as:

    •   pay taken in respect of a holiday actually taken; or

    •   any holiday pay which had accrued at the date of termination of the contract of employment.

4. Payment in lieu of statutory notice entitlement under the Minimum Notice and Terms of Employment Act 1973 or an award by the Employment Appeals Tribunal under that Act.

5. Any amount which an employer is required to pay by virtue of a determination by the Employment Appeals Tribunal, a recommendation of a Rights Commissioner or an order by the Circuit Court under the Unfair Dismissals Act 1977, Maternity Protection Act 1994, Adoptive Leave Act 1995 and the Parental Leave Acts 1998–2006, provided that such determination, recommendation or order was made not earlier than 18 months prior to the date of insolvency of the employer, or after the date of insolvency.

6. Any amount which an employer is required to pay under an Employment Regulation Order within the meaning of Pt IV of the Industrial Relations Act 1946 (as amended by the Industrial Relations Act 1990).

7. Any amount which an employer is required to pay under the Employment Equality Acts 1998–2004 by virtue of a:

    (i)   decision by an Equality Officer;

    (ii)   mediated settlement by an Equality Officer;

    (iii)   determination by the Labour Court;

    (iv)   civil court award or order.

8. Any arrears of wages, sick pay, holiday pay or damages at common law for wrongful dismissal awarded by a court.

9. Any amount which an employer is required to pay by virtue of a decision, determination, award or order under the National Minimum Wage Act 2000.

10. Any arrears of pension contributions.

11. Deductions such as union dues, VHI/BUPA etc, life assurance, etc, made from wages by agreement and not paid over to the relevant authority.

12. Awards under the Terms of Employment Information Act 1994 (s 6(2)(a)(xv)).

13. Awards under the Protection of Young Persons (Employment) Act 1996 (s 6(2)(a)(xvi)).

14. Awards under the Protection for Persons Reporting Child Abuse Act 1998 (s 6(2)(a)(xviii)).

15. Awards under the European Communities (Protection of Employment) Regulations 2000 (s 6(2)(a)(xx)).

16. Organisation of Working Time Act 1992 (s 6(2)(a)(xviii)).

17. Protection of Employees (Part-Time Work) Act 2001 (s 6(2)(a)(xix)).

18. Competition Act 2002 (s 6(2)(a)(xxiii)).

19. Protection of Employees (Fixed-Term Work) Act 2003 (s 6(2)(a)(xx)).

20. TUPE (s 6(2)(a)(xxii)).

21. Industrial Relations (Miscellaneous Provisions) Act 2004 (s 6(2)(a)(xxv)).

21. Employment Permits Act 2006 (s 6(2)(a)(xxvi)).

Definition of normal weekly remuneration

A. TIME-BASED EMPLOYEES

[10.17] Section 6(9) of the Protection of Employees' (Employers' Insolvency) Act 1984 defines 'normal weekly remuneration' as having the same meaning assigned to it as in Sch 3 to the Redundancy Payments Act 1967 (see also **6.20**). This defines normal weekly remuneration as an employee's earnings for a normal working week. This includes any regular bonus or allowance which does not vary in relation to the amount of work done. Additionally any payment in kind normally received by an employee, eg complimentary canteen, subsidies etc must be taken into account.

Overtime pay is calculated by calculating the total amount of overtime earnings in the period of 26 weeks which ended 13 weeks before the date of termination of the employee's employment and dividing that amount by 26. This is then multiplied by the number of weeks for which overtime is outstanding. The total number of weeks payable may not exceed eight. Where normal weekly remuneration and overtime are outstanding for the same period, the amounts outstanding for each week should be combined and the total number of weeks payable may also not exceed eight.

B. Employees whose Normal Weekly Remuneration varies in relation to Work Done and Employees with a Shift Premium

[10.18] These are employees whose normal weekly remuneration varies in proportion to the amount of work carried out. This could arise by virtue of bonuses, commission, piece rates etc.

Normal weekly remuneration is calculated as follows:

(i)   Calculate the total number of hours worked by the employee in the 26-week period ending 13 weeks before the date on which the employee's employment was terminated. Any week or weeks during the 26-week period in which the employee did not work will not be taken into account, but the most recent week or weeks counting backwards, before the 26-week period can be substituted in lieu of these weeks. Additionally, if the employee worked with different employers during this 26-week period these weeks can be taken into account if the change in employer did not affect the continuity of employment.

(ii) The pay to be taken into account will be the pay for all the hours worked during the 26-week period including any variations in the rate of pay which became operative during the 13 weeks before the employment was terminated.

(iii) The employee's average hourly rate of pay is calculated by dividing the total pay at (ii) by the total hours as at (i). The weekly pay is then calculated by multiplying this average hourly rate by the number of normal weekly working hours of the employee concerned at the date on which employment was terminated.

C. Employees with no Normal Working Hours

[10.19] Employees who have no normal working hours have their remuneration including bonuses, etc averaged over the last 52 weeks worked, to determine their normal weekly wage.

PAYMENT[29]

[10.20] A payment will only be made on various conditions:

•   The amount payable to an employee in respect of any debt which may be calculated with regard to remuneration cannot exceed €600.00 per week, with effect from 1 January 2005 (€507.90 prior to that date).[30]

•   The date on which a recommendation, decision, determination, award or court order was made and which is the subject of a claim under the Acts must not be earlier than 18 months prior to the date of insolvency of the employer concerned.

---

29.   Protection of Employees (Employers' Insolvency) Act 1984, s 6(4)(c).
30.   SI 696/2004.

- Arrears of normal wages, deductions for union dues, VHI/BUPA, etc, sick pay and holiday pay are limited to a maximum total of eight weeks which arose in the period of 18 months prior to the date of insolvency of the employer concerned. Where an employee's employment has been terminated as a result of the employer's insolvency, the date of termination will apply.

- No payments shall be made in respect of awards arising under the Unfair Dismissals Act, the Employment Equality Act or any such recommendations, decisions, determinations or court orders, unless any appeal proceedings have been determined or withdrawn, or the period of time for bringing an appeal has expired.

- An application for arrears due under an Employment Regulation Order cannot be paid unless proceedings have been instituted against the employer concerned for an offence under s 45(1) of the Industrial Relations Act 1946.

- The amount payable for damages at common law awarded by a civil court for wrongful dismissal is subject to a maximum of 104 weeks' wages.

- Legal costs are excluded from all court awards.

EMPLOYER INSOLVENCY IN PRACTICE

[10.21] The Protection of Employers' Insolvency (Forms and Procedure) Regulations 2005 (SI 682/2005), reg (1) provide the statutory forms which must be used to make a claim under the Act. Once the forms are completed the employee gives the form to the 'relevant officer' which is the person appointed in connection with the insolvency (eg receiver, liquidator, etc). If there is no relevant officer the Minister may appoint one – Protection of Employees (Employers' Insolvency) Act 1984, s 1(1).

Employee forms

[10.22] **Form EIP1** (reproduced below at **10.30**). In the case of a claim for outstanding wages, sick pay, holiday pay or minimum notice entitlements, an employee should complete Form EIP1.[31]

Form EIP4 (reproduced below at **10.31**). In the case of a claim arising under the Employment Equality Acts 1998–2004, the Unfair Dismissals Acts 1977–2001, Court Awards for Unfair or Wrongful Dismissal, Awards under the Maternity Protection Acts 1994–2004, Adoptive Leave Act 1995, Parental Leave Act 1998, National Minimum Wage Act 2000 and Statutory Minimum Wages under an Employment Regulation Order (the exception being pension scheme contributions) under the Insolvency Payments Scheme, an employee should complete Form EIP4.[32]

---

31. SI 197/2003.
32. Protection of Employees (Employers' Insolvency) (Forms and Procedure) Regulations 2003 (SI 682/2005).

The completed application form(s) should be forwarded to the insolvent employer's representative, usually a liquidator or receiver.

Employer forms

[10.23] Form EIP3 and Form EIP6 (reproduced below at **10.32** and **10.33**). The 'relevant officer' (ie the employer's representative) after examining the employee's claim form (either EIP1 or EIP4) has to certify the amount which appears to be owed to the employee. This certification is given on Form EIP3 in the case of outstanding entitlements other than pension scheme contributions, (in the case of pension entitlements Form EIP6 is used). The completed Forms EIP3, or EIP6 as appropriate, together with the original copies of the employees' applications (Forms EIP1 and EIP4) should be forwarded to the Insolvency Payments Section of the Department of Enterprise, Trade and Employment.

The Minister, upon receipt of the application, will pay the monies owing to the 'relevant officer' unless there are some exceptional reasons for making the payment directly to the applicant. When the payment is made by the relevant officer to the employee the relevant officer has to inform the Minister in writing that the payment has been made and detail any deductions made in respect of income tax, PRSI etc. The latter deductions have to be forwarded to the Revenue Commissioners.

The Minister may also by notice in writing require the employer to furnish him with the relevant information including records kept pursuant to the Organisation of Working Time Act 1997.[33]

Payment of unpaid contributions to pension schemes[34]

[10.24] There is provision in the Acts for the payment of unpaid contributions to an occupational pension scheme which forms part of the contract of employment. 'Relevant contributions' are defined in s 7(2) of the Act as those which both the employer and the employee were liable to pay in respect of the employee's occupational pension scheme during the year prior to the date of insolvency of the employer. An employee's contribution is only payable when that sum has been deducted from the employee's pay but was not paid over to the trustees/administrators of the occupational pension scheme. The amount payable in respect of an unpaid employer contribution is the lesser of:

(a) the balance of the employer's contributions remaining unpaid for the period of 12 months ending on the day prior to the date of the employer's insolvency; or[35]

(b) the amount certified by an actuary to be necessary for the purpose of meeting the liability of the scheme on dissolution to pay the benefits provided by the scheme. This only applies where the pension scheme provides for such a liability.

---

33. Protection of Employees (Employers' Insolvency) Act 1984, s 8.
34. Protection of Employees (Employers' Insolvency) Act 1984, s 7(4).
35. Protection of Employees (Employers' Insolvency) (Forms and Procedure) Regulations 2005 (SI 682/2005).

Forms

[10.25] The Protection of Employees (Employers Insolvency) Occupational Pension Scheme) (Forms and Procedure) Regulations 1990 (SI 121/1990) were repealed and replaced by the 2005 regulation. These now provide the statutory forms for making such claims. Where an application is submitted for payment of outstanding employer's contributions, the application must be accompanied by an actuarial certificate which must be obtained by the insolvent employer's representative. Form E1P7 is used for this purpose.

Form EIP6. This is the form to be used in the case of an application for payment of amounts deducted from pay of an employee is respect of their contributions to the scheme which were not paid into the scheme and unpaid contributions of an employer on his own account to an occupational pension scheme. Part I of the form should be completed by the trustees/administrators of the scheme or by a person competent to act on behalf of the scheme. The form should then be forwarded to the insolvent employer's representative (usually the liquidator or receiver) who is responsible for completing Pt II of the form and forwarding it to the Department.

Form EIP7 (reproduced below at **10.34**). This is the Actuarial Certificate, which must be completed by the actuary. This must accompany the EIP6 when a claim in respect of unpaid pension scheme contributions is being made. A copy of the Trust Deed should also be attached. The actuary must sign the form and give details of their professional qualification in addition to their business name and address.

The copy of the scheme submitted with the application should include full current details of the scheme, eg names and addresses of trustees and administrators, contribution rates and benefit entitlements, etc.

Employers' representatives are obliged to notify the Insolvency Payments Section of the Department of Enterprise, Trade and Employment in writing of the making of the payment to the employees as soon as the payments are made. The notification should also specify the amounts (if any) deducted in respect of income tax, PRSI, pension contributions or otherwise.

The Department will pay fees from the Social Insurance Fund to employers' representatives/relevant officers (liquidators, receivers, etc) for the processing of applications under the Act. The fees are payable on a per capita basis for each former employee of an employer.

Transfer to the Minister of certain rights and remedies

[10.26] Section 10 of the 1984 Act specifies that where a payment is made from the Social Insurance Fund in respect of any debt payable under the Acts to an employee, or in the case of pension contributions, any amount paid into the assets of an occupational pension scheme, the rights and remedies of the employees concerned or the applicants in the case of pension contributions in respect of that debt which the employee may have under the Companies Act 1963 (as amended), the Bankruptcy Act 1988, will be transferred to the Minister for Enterprise, Trade and Employment. This signifies that:

- any claim by the Minister against the assets of an insolvent employer ranks as priority over any other preferential claim of the employees concerned; and

- that in the final winding-up proceedings in liquidations, receiverships, bankruptcies, etc, the Minister becomes a preferential creditor against the assets of the employer in respect of the amount paid, subject to certain statutory limits as provided for under the Companies Acts and bankruptcy legislation.

This signifies that the insolvent employer's debt is not eliminated by the Insolvency Act but merely transfers from the employer to the Social Insurance Fund.

Complaints to the Employment Appeals Tribunal

[10.27] Complaints can be made to the Employment Appeals Tribunal by a person:[36]

- to whom the Minister has failed to make a payment; or
- who alleges that any payment made by the Minister is less than an amount which should have been paid.[37]

However, complaints (under this Act) can only be made for the following debts:

- remuneration;
- monies due under a sick pay scheme;
- holiday pay; or
- outstanding occupational pension scheme contributions.

Complaints must be made to the Employment Appeals Tribunal within six weeks of the notification of the Minister's decision to the applicant. The Tribunal, at its discretion, may extend the period for making an appeal in certain circumstances. If the Tribunal finds that the Minister is liable, a declaration shall be made to that effect and the declaration shall specify the amount of the payment.

Forms

Form T1C (reproduced at **10.35**) can be used for making an appeal to the Employment Appeals Tribunal by employees and trustees in the case of pension funds if the Minister for Enterprise Trade and Employment has:

1. refused to pay an amount applied for; or
2. reduced an amount applied for.

Appeals

The decision of the Tribunal on any matter referred to it under the Acts is final and conclusive, except that any person dissatisfied with the decision may appeal to the High Court on a question of law.[38]

---

36.   Protection of Employees (Employers' Insolvency) Act 1984, s 9.
37.   Protection of Employees (Employers' Insolvency) (Forms and Procedure) Regulations 2005 (SI 682/2005). Protection of Employees (Employers' Insolvency) Act 1984, s 9.
38.   Protection of Employees (Employers' Insolvency) Act 1984, s 9(5).

Minister's right to refuse an application

[10.28] Section 6(8) of the 1984 Act gives a right to the Minister to refuse an application where he is satisfied that there has been a prior agreement between the employer and employee that 'the whole or any part of the debt would be the subject of an application' where at the time of the agreement the employer had the means to pay all or part of the debt.

Offences

[10.29] Proceedings for an offence may only be instituted with the consent of the Minister.[39] All forms used under the Acts are statutory forms. Proceedings may be taken against any person who, in relation to a claim/application under the Acts, makes a false statement or produces or furnishes false documentation or refuses or neglects to provide required information etc.[40] Such person shall be liable on summary conviction to a fine not exceeding €634.87.

If an offence is committed by a body corporate, both the company and certain officers may also be liable.

---

39.   Protection of Employees (Employers' Insolvency) Act 1984, s 14.
40.   Protection of Employees (Employers' Insolvency) Act 1984, s 15.

Forms

EIP1[41]

[10.30]

FORM EIP1

An Roinn Fiontar, Trádála agus Nuálaíochta
Department of Enterprise, Trade and Innovation

INSOLVENCY PAYMENTS SCHEME

PROTECTION OF EMPLOYEES (EMPLOYERS' INSOLVENCY) ACTS 1984–2004

APPLICATION BY EMPLOYEE FOR PAYMENT OF • WAGES • HOLIDAY PAY • MINIMUM NOTICE • SICK PAY

FORM EIP1: GUIDANCE NOTES

1. An employer is regarded as insolvent for the purposes of the Acts if in liquidation, receivership, adjudicated bankrupt, etc.

2. When completed, this Form should be returned to the Relevant Officer (the Liquidator, Receiver, etc.).

3. The maximum period for which arrears are normally payable is 8 weeks. A statutory weekly limit applies to the amount of any entitlement based on pay.

4. Payments made under the Insolvency Payments Scheme are generally subject to Income Tax and Pay-Related Social Insurance deductions. Deductions will be made, where appropriate, by the Relevant Officer.

5. In relation to a claim for overtime, bonus or commission, please give both the actual amount due and average amount, calculated in accordance with Schedule 3 of the Redundancy Payments Act 1967. If rates given in Part 4 and Part 5 of the Form differ, please explain the difference.

6. Deductions for union dues, medical insurance (e.g., VHI, BUPA), etc. which were made from gross wages and not paid to the appropriate body should be inserted in Part 4.

7. In the case of sick pay, payment will not exceed the difference between any social welfare benefit payable and gross weekly pay.

PLEASE NOTE THAT FAILURE TO COMPLETE THE FORM FULLY MAY RESULT IN DELAY IN MAKING A PAYMENT.

---

41. Protection of Employees (Employers Insolvency) (Forms and Procedure) (Amendment) Regulations 2003 (SI 197/2003).

Insolvency Payments Section	
Department of Enterprise, Trade and Innovation	Phone: (01) 6312121
Davitt House	Fax: (01) 6313217
65a Adelaide Road	Lo-call: 1890 220 222
Dublin 2	Web: www.entemp.ie

Part 1   *Employee Details*

Please complete in Block Capitals.

	Figures								Letters	
Employee's PPS No.										

Employee's surname

Employee's first name

Employee's address

Employee's date of birth [   ] Day [   ] Month [   ] Year

Class of Insurance

Please attach copy of P45 if available.

Part 2   Employer Details

Business name of employer

Employer's address

Type of business

Part 3   Employment Details

Occupation

Date of commencement of employment [   ] Day [   ] Month [   ] Year

Date of termination of employment [   ] Day [   ] Month [   ] Year

Gross pay [€   ] Week or [€   ] Month

317

Number of days and hours normally worked per week		Days		Hours

	Director	Secretary	Shareholder
f you were a Director, Secretary or Shareholder of the Company, please indicate as appropriate.			

Part 4   Arrears of Wages

If application is for arrears of pay, overtime, bonus or commission payments, please give details in the spaces provided (See Note 5 in Guidance Notes). If application involves dishonoured or "bounced" pay cheques, please attach cheques.

Type (wages, bonus, overtime, etc.)	From Day	Month	Year	To Day	Month	Year	Number of weeks/days	Gross weekly pay/bonus/ overtime	Amount Due (Actual)
								€	€
								€	€
								€	€
								€	€

Average (if required – see Note 5)   € _____

Total arrears of pay claimed   € _____

Deductions from pay

Type (e.g., Union subscription, VHI, BUPA, etc.)	Day	From Month	Year	Day	To Month	Year	Number of weeks	Weekly Deduction	Amount Due
								€	€
								€	€

Total arrears of deductions claimed   € _____

Part 5   Arrears of Holiday Pay

Claim period for which holidays are owed	From Day	Month	Year	To Day	Month	Year	Total number of weeks due (incl public holidays)

Annual leave entitlement   [ ] Number of days

Annual leave taken in the claim period above   [ ] Number of days

Public holidays due   [ ] Number of days

Gross pay   € _____ Week/Month (please specify)

Arrears of holiday pay claimed	€

Part 6   Minimum Notice

No. of weeks' statutory notice due (or awarded by Employment Appeals Tribunal)*	€

Gross pay	€	Week/Month (please specify)

Total amount of minimum notice claimed	€

*If claim is in respect of an Employment Appeals Tribunal Award, please attach copy of the Tribunal Award and complete the following:

	Day	Month	Year
Date of Employment Appeals Tribunal Award			

Reference number of Award	

Part 7   Arrears due under a Company Sick Pay Scheme

Period to which claim relates	From		To		Total number of weeks due (incl. public holidays due)
	Day Year	Mont h	Day Year	Month	

Weekly amount of Social Welfare Benefit	€

Total amount of Social Welfare Benefit payable during the period	€

Weekly payment by employer under sick pay scheme (exclusive of Social Welfare payment)	€

Gross pay	€	Week/Month *(please specify)*

Total arrears of sick pay claimed	€

I apply for payment due to me under the Protection of Employees (Employers' Insolvency) Acts 1984–2004 and declare that I have made no other applications in respect of the amounts shown above. I am aware that my rights and remedies against my employer in respect of these amounts will be transferred to the Minister for Enterprise, Trade and Innovation when payment has been made.

I also declare in respect of the amounts claimed above that I have made no appeal in respect of these amounts and I am not aware, to the best of my knowledge, that these amounts are the subject of an appeal by someone else.

Signature: _____   Date: _____

LEGAL PROCEEDINGS MAY BE TAKEN AGAINST ANYONE MAKING A FALSE STATEMENT ON THIS FORM

Form EIP4[42]

[10.31]

FORM EIP4

An Roinn Fiontar, Trádála agus Nuálaíochta
Department of Enterprise, Trade and Innovation

INSOLVENCY PAYMENTS SCHEME

PROTECTION OF EMPLOYEES (EMPLOYERS' INSOLVENCY) ACTS 1984–2004
APPLICATION BY EMPLOYEE FOR PAYMENT UNDER THE INSOLVENCY PAYMENTS SCHEME FOR ENTITLEMENTS DUE UNDER:

• Unfair Dismissals Act 1997 • Common Law in respect of Unfair or Wrongful Dismissal • Employment Equality Act 1998 • National Minimum Wage Act 2000 • Maternity Protection Act 1994 • Adoptive Leave Act 1995 • Parental Leave Act 1998 • Payment of Wages Act 1991 • Terms of Employment (Information) Act 1994 • Protection of Young Persons (Employment) Act 1996 • Organisation of Working Time Act 1997 • Protections for Persons Reporting Child Abuse Act 1998 • European Communities (Protection of Employment) Regulations 2000 • Protection of Employees (Part-Time Work) Act 2001 • Competition Act 2002 • Protection of Employees (Fixed-Term Work) Act 2003 • European Communities (Protection of Employees on Transfer of Undertakings) Regulations 2003 • Industrial Relations Acts 1946, 1969 and 1990 (Registered Employment Agreements or Employment Regulation Orders) • Industrial Relations (Miscellaneous Provisions) Act 2004 (concerning victimisation awards)

---

42.   Protection of Employees (Employers Insolvency) (Forms and Procedure) (Amendment) Regulations 2003 (SI 197/2003).

FORM EIP4: GUIDANCE NOTES

1. An employer is regarded as insolvent for the purposes of the Acts if in Liquidation, Receivership, adjudicated bankrupt, etc.

2. When completed, this Form should be returned to the Relevant Officer (the Receiver, Liquidator, etc).

3. A copy of the relevant supporting document, e.g., Determination, Order, Decision, etc., should be enclosed with this form when submitting a claim.

4. In completing Part 5 of this Form, please note the following:

   - Employment Regulation Order – A claim under this part is payable only where proceedings have been instituted against the employer under Section 45(1) of the Industrial Relations Act 1946 for the amount concerned.

   - Registered Employment Agreement – A claim under this part is payable only where proceedings have been instituted against the employer under Section 54(1) of the Industrial Relations Act 1990 for the amount concerned, or the Labour Court has made an order under Section 32(1)(b) of the Industrial Relations Act 1946 or Section 10(1)(b) of the Industrial Relations Act 1969.

   - National Minimum Wage – A claim under this part is only payable where proceedings have been instituted against the employer under Section 35 of the National Minimum Wage Act 2000 for the amount concerned or a Rights Commissioner has made a decision under Section 26 of the National Minimum Wage Act 2000, or the Labour Court has made a determination under Section 29 of the National Minimum Wage Act 2000.

Insolvency Payments Section	
Department of Enterprise, Trade and Innovation	Phone: (01) 6312121
Davitt House	Fax: (01) 6313217
65a Adelaide Road	Lo-call: 1890 220 222
Dublin 2	Web: www.entemp.ie

Part 1   Employee Details

Please complete in Block Capitals

	Figures								Letters
Employee's PPS No.									

Employee's surname	

Employee's first name	

Employee's address	

Employee's date of birth		Day		Month		Year

Class of insurance

Please attach copy
of P45 if available

Part 2   *Employer Details*

Business name of
employer

Employer's address

Type of business

Part 3   *Employment Details*

Occupation

Date of commencement of employment		Day		Month		Year

Date of termination of employment		Day		Month		Year

Gross pay	e	Week or		e	Month

No. of days and hours normally worked per week		Days		Hours

	Director	Secretary	Shareholder
If you were a Director, Secretary or Shareholder of the Company, please indicate as appropriate.			

Part 4   *Claims for Entitlements awarded under Other Acts*
Please tick appropriate box and attach copy of award, decision, etc.

Unfair Dismissals Act 1977 or Court Award in respect of Unfair or Wrongful Dismissal ☐

Employment Equality Act 1998 ☐

Maternity Protection Act 1994 ☐

Adoptive Leave Act 1995 ☐

Parental Leave Act 1998 ☐

Payment of Wages Act 1991* ☐

Terms of Employment (Information) Act 1994* ☐

Protection of Young Persons (Employment) Act 1996* ☐

Organisation of Working Time Act 1997* ☐

Protections for Persons Reporting Child Abuse Act 1998* ☐

European Communities (Protection of Employment) Regulations 2000* ☐

Protection of Employees (Part-Time Work) Act 2001* ☐

Competition Act 2002* ☐

Protection of Employees (Fixed-Term Work) Act 2003* ☐

European Communities (Protection of Employees on Transfer of Undertakings) Regulations 2003* ☐

Industrial Relations (Miscellaneous Provisions Act) 2004* ☐

Type of Award (e.g., decision/ determination)	Day	Date of Award month	Year	Amount	Reference Number of Award, etc.	Has an appeal been lodged? Yes/No

*Applies to insolvencies occurring from 8 October 2005

Part 5   Statutory Minimum Wage under an Employment Regulation Order, Registered Employment Agreement* or Minimum Wage under the National Minimum Wage Act 2000

Before completing this Section, see Note 4 of Guidance Notes.

Please tick appropriate box and attach copy of award, decision, etc.

Employment Regulation Order ☐

Registered Employment Agreement ☐

National Minimum Wage Act 2000 ☐

Title of Employment
Regulation Order/
Registered Employment
Agreement (where
applicable)

If claim relates to an
decision of a Rights
Commissioner or a
determination/order of
the Labour Court, please
give reference number

or

If proceedings have been
instituted against the
employer, please give
details.

Period in respect of which the claim is being made		From			To	
	Day	Month	Year	Day	Month	Year

Total Number of
Weeks

Gross Weekly Pay   €

Total Claimed   €

*Applies to insolvencies occurring from 8 October 2005

I apply for payment due to me under the Protection of Employees (Employers' Insolvency) Acts 1984–2004) and declare that I have made no other applications in respect of the amounts shown above. I am aware that my rights and remedies against my employer in respect of these amounts will be transferred to the Minister for Enterprise, Trade and Innovation when payment has been made. I also declare in respect of the amounts claimed above that I have made no appeal in respect of these amounts and I am not aware, to the best of my knowledge, that these amounts are the subject of appeal by someone else.

Signature: _____   Date: _____

LEGAL PROCEEDINGS MAY BE TAKEN AGAINST ANYONE MAKING A FALSE
STATEMENT ON THIS FORM

FORM EIP3[43]

[10.32]

An Roinn Fiontar, Trádála agus Nuálaíochta
Department of Enterprise, Trade and Innovation

INSOLVENCY PAYMENTS SCHEME

**PROTECTION OF EMPLOYEES (EMPLOYERS' INSOLVENCY) ACTS 1984–2004
APPLICATION BY A RELEVANT OFFICER FOR FUNDS IN RESPECT OF
EMPLOYEE CLAIMS**

• Arrears of Wages • Holiday Pay • Sick Pay • Minimum Notice Entitlements/Awards • Unfair Dismissals Act 1997 • Common Law in respect of Unfair or Wrongful Dismissal • Employment Equality Act 1998 • National Minimum Wage Act 2000 • Maternity Protection Act 1994 • Adoptive Leave Act 1995 • Parental Leave Act 1998 • Payment of Wages Act 1991 • Terms of Employment (Information) Act 1994 • Protection of Young Persons (Employment) Act 1996 • Organisation of Working Time Act 1997 • Protections for Persons Reporting Child Abuse Act 1998 • European Communities (Protection of Employment) Regulations 2000 • Protection of Employees (Part-Time Work) Act 2001 • Competition Act 2002 • Protection of Employees (Fixed-Term Work) Act 2003 • European Communities (Protection of Employees on Transfer of Undertakings) Regulations 2003 • Industrial Relations Acts 1946, 1969 and 1990 (Registered Employment Agreements or Employment Regulation Orders) • Industrial Relations (Miscellaneous Provisions) Act 2004 (concerning victimisation awards).

FORM EIP3: GUIDANCE NOTES

1. When making an initial claim to the Insolvency Payments Section on behalf of the former employees of an insolvent employer, please attach copies of the following documentation:

    (a) Notice of appointment of Liquidator/Receiver

    (b) Statement of Affairs/Accounts

2. Initial claims for each employee should be accompanied by a copy of the employee's P45 or written confirmation of his/her class of insurance.

**PLEASE NOTE THAT FAILURE TO COMPLETE THE FORM FULLY MAY RESULT
IN DELAY IN MAKING THE PAYMENT.**

DETAILS OF INSOLVENT EMPLOYER

Employer's PAYE registered No.									

Business name of employer	

---

43. Protection of Employees (Employers Insolvency) (Forms and Procedure) (Amendment) Regulations 2003 (SI 197/2003).

Business address

Nature of Business

Names of Directors and
Company Secretary

PPS No.

%
Shareholding

Figures

Letters

Date of insolvency

Day   Month   Year

Type of insolvency

RELEVANT OFFICER CERTIFICATE

Name of relevant officer

Name of company

Business address

Telephone No.

Relevant Officer Tax No.

Please attach a schedule of employee entitlements. The Annex attached shows the format required. Please ensure that your schedule is clearly headed by the company name and PAYE No.

Number of pages of Annex attached

Declaration

To the Minister for Enterprise, Trade and Innovation:

In connection with the provisions of the Protection of Employees (Employers' Insolvency) Acts 1984–2004, I have accepted and certify, based on the best information available to me, the entitlement of the employees as shown on the attached schedule. I have made no other application in respect of these entitlements. I understand that it may be necessary for you to refer information on the entitlements to the Revenue Commissioners and/or to other Government Departments. I hereby give my consent to the disclosure of such information as is in my possession. I also agree to make available to you such records as may be required for examination. I undertake to distribute the appropriate amounts to the employees concerned from the funds received pursuant to this application. Copies of employee claims are on the relevant forms are attached.

I declare that the company is insolvent and that there are no funds available from which the entitlements claimed on the attached schedule can be paid.

The instrument of payment should be drawn in favour of (Relevant Officer)

Address

Signature of Relevant Officer

Date

Insolvency Payments Section	Tel:	(01) 6312121
Department of Enterprise, Trade and Innovation	Fax:	(01) 6313217
Davitt House	Lo-call:	1890 220 222
65a Adelaide Road	Web:	www.entemp.ie
Dublin 2		

Form EIP3 – Annex   Schedule of Employee Entitlements

Business Name of Employer   PAYE No

327

Employee's Name	PPS No.	Total Arrears of Wages	Deductions (Union dues, VHI/ BUPA, etc)	Total Arrears of Holiday Pay	Total Arrears of Sick Pay	Total Minimum Notice	Award under other legislation covered by the Scheme	Total of Columns (c) to (h)
(a)	(b)	(c)	(d)	(e)	(f)	(g)	(h)	
1.								
2.								
3.								
4.								
5.								
6.								
7.								
8.								
9.								
10.								
11.								
12.								
13.								

Form EIP6[44]

[10.33]

Form EIP6

 An Roinn Fiontar, Trádála agus Nuálaíochta
Department of Enterprise, Trade and Innovation

INSOLVENCY PAYMENTS SCHEME

PROTECTION OF EMPLOYEES (EMPLOYERS' INSOLVENCY) ACTS 1984–2004

APPLICATION FOR PAYMENT OF UNPAID CONTRIBUTIONS TO OCCUPATIONAL
PENSION SCHEME OR PERSONAL SAVINGS RETIREMENT ACCOUNT (PRSA)

FORM EIP6: GUIDANCE NOTES

1.	Part 1 of this form and the Schedule should be completed by a trustee, administrator or other person competent to act on behalf of the occupational pension scheme or PRSA provider, as appropriate.
2.	Part 2 of this form should be completed by the Relevant Officer (liquidator, receiver, etc.). A breakdown of the unpaid contributions in respect of the 12 months prior to the date of insolvency should be attached.
3.	Where a claim is being made for unpaid contributions payable into a relevant occupational pension scheme on an employer's own account, an actuarial certificate (Form EIP7) should be obtained by the Relevant Officer and attached to the claim.
4.	Details of the occupational pension scheme (e.g., a Trust Deed, Deed of Adherence) or PRSA should accompany this application if not already forwarded.
5.	The date of insolvency for the purpose of payments under the Insolvency Payments Scheme is defined in Section 4 of the Protection of Employees (Employers' Insolvency) Acts 1984- 2004.

Insolvency Payments Section

Department of Enterprise, Trade and Innovation	Tel: (01) 6312121
Davitt House	Fax: (01) 6313217
65a Adelaide Road	Lo-call: 1890 220 222

LEGAL PROCEEDINGS MAY BE TAKEN AGAINST ANYONE MAKING A FALSE
STATEMENT ON THIS FORM

---

44. Protection of Employees (Employers' Insolvency) (Occupational Pension Scheme) (Forms and Procedure) Regulations 1990 (SI 121/1990).

PART 1   TO BE COMPLETED BY A PERSON COMPETENT TO ACT FOR
           OCCUPATIONAL PENSION SCHEME OR PRSA PROVIDER

To:

NAME OF RELEVANT OFFICER

I am/We are authorised to act on
behalf of/in relation to:

DESCRIPTION OF OCCUPATIONAL PENSION SCHEME OR PRSA

NAME OF INSOLVENT EMPLOYER

In respect of employee(s) of:

TYPE OF SCHEME (IF PRSA, PLEASE INSERT "PRSA")

I/We certify that in respect of the occupational pension scheme or PSRA in operation <u>within the 12 months prior to the date of the insolvency</u>, the contributions payable were as follows: -

Total amount of contributions (where applicable) payable on the employer's own account in respect of the 12 months prior to the date of insolvency

e

Total amount of contributions payable by the employee(s) in respect of the 12 months prior to the date

e

I/We apply for payment from the Social Insurance Fund, in accordance with the terms of the Protection of Employees (Employers' Insolvency) Acts 1984 to 2004, of any relevant unpaid contributions to the occupational pension scheme or PRSA(s) in respect of the twelve months prior to the insolvency of the employer.

I/We declare that any money received by me/us as a result of this application will be paid into the resources of the occupational pension scheme or PRSA(s).

I/We understand that where payment is made from the Fund in respect of the contributions, any rights and remedies in respect of those contributions belonging to the persons competent to act in respect of the scheme shall become rights and remedies of the Minister for Enterprise, Trade & Innovation.

Signature _____

Date _____

Designation (Trustee/Administrator, PRSA Provider, etc.)

_____

Name(s)

| | | | | | | | | | | | | | | | | | | | | | | | | | | | | | | | |

| | | | | | | | | | | | | | | | | | | | | | | | | | | | | | | |

Address

| | | | | | | | | | | | | | | | | | | | | | | | | | | | |

| | | | | | | | | | | | | | | | | | | | | | | | | | | | |

| | | | | | | | | | | | | | | | | | | | | | | | | | | | |

PART 2   TO BE COMPLETED BY THE RELEVANT OFFICER

Employer's PAYE registered No.

| | | | | | | | | |
Figures   Letter

Business name of insolvent employer

| | | | | | | | | | | | | | | | | | | | | | | | | | | | |

Business address

| | | | | | | | | | | | | | | | | | - | | | |

| | | | | | | | | | | | | | | | | | | | | | | |

| | | | | | | | | | | | | | | | | | | | | | | |

| | | | | | | | | | | | | | | | | | | | | | | |

Type of Business

Date of Insolvency			Type of Insolvency
Day	Month	Year	

I have examined the amounts certified in Part 1 of this form and in the attached schedule. I certify, based on the best information available to me, that the amount of contributions which were not paid into the occupational pension scheme or PRSA(s) in respect of the 12 months prior to the date of insolvency is: -

Amount of unpaid contributions by the employer on his/her own account (where applicable): -   e

Amount deducted from the employees' pay in respect of contributions but which was not paid into the scheme or PRSA(s): -   e

To: The Minister for Enterprise, Trade & Innovation, Davitt House, 65A Adelaide Road, Dublin

If sickness/disability formed part of the scheme, please tick   here and state element of contribution

331

If life assurance formed part of the scheme, please tick here ☐ and state element of contribution

An Actuarial Certificate (Form EIP7 – See Guidance Note 3): Is attached ☐ Is not attached ☐ (Please tick appropriate box)

To: The Minister for Enterprise, Trade & Innovation, Davitt House, 65A Adelaide Road, Dublin 2.

In accordance with the provisions of the Protection of Employees (Employer's Insolvency) Acts 1984 to 2004, I have accepted, based on the best information available to me, the amounts outstanding to the occupational pension scheme or PRSA(s) as shown in this application. I confirm that all employees concerned were insurable at the date of termination of employment for all benefits under the Social Welfare (Consolidation) Act 1993 in accordance with Section 3 of the Protection of Employees (Employers' Insolvency) Acts 1984–2004. I understand that it may be necessary for you to verify information on the application with other Government Departments. I hereby give my consent to the disclosure of such information as may be necessary. I also agree to make available to you such records as may be required for examination. I undertake to pay to the applicant for payment, into the occupational pension scheme or PRSAs concerned, the funds received pursuant to this application.

Name of Relevant Officer

Address

Signature of Relevant Officer_____ Date _____ Telephone_____

SCHEDULE

DESCRIPTION OF OCCUPATIONAL PENSION SCHEME OR
PRSA

(Attach additional sheets to this schedule if necessary)

Name of Employee *(Please insert "D" after the names of any employees who were directors of the company.)*	PPS No.	Period of unpaid contributions in respect of relevant period*		Total unpaid contributions in respect of relevant period* €
		FROM	TO	

*Relevant period is the twelve months prior to date of insolvency

Total

FORM EIP7[45]

[10.34]
FORM EIP7

An Roinn Fiontar, Trádála agus Nuálaíochta
Department of Enterprise, Trade and Innovation

INSOLVENCY PAYMENTS SCHEME

PROTECTION OF EMPLOYEES (EMPLOYERS' INSOLVENCY) ACTS 1984–2004

OCCUPATIONAL PENSION SCHEME ACTUARIAL CERTIFICATE

PLEASE NOTE:
This certificate should accompany Form EIP 6 when a claim in respect of relevant unpaid pension scheme contributions payable on an employer's own account is being made under the Insolvency Payments Scheme.

DESCRIPTION OF OCCUPATIONAL PENSION SCHEME	
BUSINESS NAME AND ADDRESS OF INSOLVENT EMPLOYER	DATE OF INSOLVENCY
	Day Month Year

I certify, in accordance with Section 7 (3) (b) of the Protection of Employees (Employers' Insolvency) Acts 1984 – 2004 that the amount necessary for the purposes of meeting the liability to pay the benefits provided by the scheme on dissolution in respect of the employees is:

€

SIGNATURE OF ACTUARY	DATE

PROFESSIONAL QUALIFICATION

---

45.   Protection of Employees (Employers' Insolvency) (Occupational Pension Scheme) (Forms and Procedure) Regulations 1990 (SI 121/1990).

BUSINESS NAME AND ADDRESS OF ACTUARY

T1–C

[10.35]

Form T1-C

<table>
<tr><td colspan="2">For Official Use:</td></tr>
<tr><td>Case No:</td><td></td></tr>
</table>

NOTICE OF APPEAL TO THE EMPLOYMENT APPEALS TRIBUNAL
UNDER THE PROTECTION OF EMPLOYEES (EMPLOYERS' INSOLVENCY) ACTS, 1984 TO 2001

(THIS FORM MUST BE COMPLETED IN BLOCK CAPITALS)   NOTE: Please read notes overleaf before completing this form

1. EMPLOYEE DETAILS:

Surname:
First Name:
Address:
Telephone No:
Occupation:
R.S.I. No.:

2. NAME AND ADDRESS OF EMPLOYER:

Telephone No:

3. TYPE OF APPEAL:
   (Tick ✓ relevant box)

Arrears of Wages	☐
Arrears of Holiday Pay	☐
Arrears of Sick Pay	☐
Pension Contributions	☐

4. APPEAL DETAILS:

PERIOD OVER WHICH CLAIM AROSE							
	Day	Month	Year		Day	Month	Year
From				To			
From				To			
Date of Birth:							
Date of termination of employment:							
Date informed of Minister's decision:							

5. TOWN OR NEAREST TOWN TO PLACE OF EMPLOYMENT:

6. NORMAL WEEKLY PAY:

	€
Basic Weekly Pay	
Regular Bonus or Allowance	
Average Weekly Overtime	
Any other payments including: payments in kind - specify	
Weekly Total	

7. NAME AND ADDRESS OF REPRESENTATIVE (UNION OFFICIAL ETC.) OF PERSON MAKING THE COMPLAINT

Telephone No:

8. THE GROUNDS OF MY APPEAL ARE:
   (Please attach copy of Minister's decision)

Signed:
Date:

Send this form to: The Secretary
                   Employment Appeals Tribunal
                   Davitt House,
                   65A, Adelaide Road, Dublin 2
Telephone: (01) 631 2121
              1890 220222 LoCall from outside (01) area

NOTES FOR PERSONS COMPLETING THIS FORM

1. A Guide to the Acts is available on request from the Information Unit of the Department of Enterprise, Trade and Employment.

2. Employees and trustees, in the case of pension contributions, may only complete this form if the Minister for Enterprise, Trade and Employment has:

    a) Refused to pay an amount applied for, or
    b) Reduced an amount applied for

AND

the claim was in respect of arrears of wages, arrears of sick pay, arrears of holiday pay or unpaid pension contributions.

3. Complaints to the Tribunal must be made within six weeks from the date on which the Minister's decision on your application was communicated to you.

    The Tribunal has discretion to extend this time limit.

NOTES ON COMPLETING THIS FORM:

BOX 1: If you change your address after lodging this form, inform the Tribunal immediately.

BOX 3 A trustee of a pension scheme may only make a complaint to the Tribunal in respect of arrears of unpaid contributions.

BOX 4: The period over which the claim arose is the period over which you were, for example, entitled to holidays and in respect of which you have not been paid.

BOX 6: A guide to the calculation of normal weekly pay is set out in the Guide to the Acts. Basic pay means gross pay before deductions. Average overtime, bonuses and allowances are calculated by obtaining gross payment for the 26 week period which is immediately prior to 13 weeks before the date of termination of the employee's employment and dividing this figure by 26 to obtain the average.

BOX 7: Only complete this box if you have consulted the representative beforehand and he/she is willing to attend the Tribunal hearing. Notification of the hearing will be sent to them also.

BOX 8: If you do not have sufficient space to set out your grounds of appeal, continue them on a sheet of paper and attach to this form.

Caution: The Tribunal may award costs against a party who has acted frivolously or vexatiously in the matter of an appeal.

Chapter 11

DISCRIMINATORY DISMISSAL AND DISMISSAL AND THE EMPLOYMENT EQUALITY LEGISLATION

INTRODUCTION

[11.01] The legislation governing dismissal on equality grounds is founded on several EU Directives. The main Irish legislation is the 1998 Employment Equality Act and the 2004 Equality Act.

Section 8(6)(c) of the 1998 Act provides that an employer shall be taken to have discriminated against an employee in relation to conditions of employment, if the employee is afforded less favourable terms, on any of the discriminatory grounds, outlined in the Act in respect of, inter alia, dismissal and disciplinary measures.

Claims for dismissal arising under the Acts generally arise on the basis of constructive dismissal where the employee contends that they were left with no alternative but to resign because of the employer's discriminatory conduct but can clearly also arise on the basis of straightforward dismissal.

Legislation

[11.02] The Equality Act 2004 implements the provisions of the amended Gender Equal Treatment Framework, Framework Employment Directive and Race Directive, ie:

> (Council Directive 2002/73/EC of 23 September 2002 amending Council Directive 76/207/EC on the implementation of the principle of equal treatment for men and women as regards access to employment, vocational training and promotion and working conditions [2002] OJL2 69/15; Council Directive 2000/78/EC of 27 November 2000 establishing a general framework for equal treatment in employment and occupation [2000] OJ L 303/16 Council Directive 2000/43/EC of 29 June 2000 implementing the principle of equal treatment between persons irrespective of racial or ethnic origin [2000] OJ L180/22).

These Directives take precedence over Irish law and as such Irish law needs to be read and interpreted with due regard to the provisions of these Directives.

Additionally, quite apart from any statutory or common law rights, the Irish Constitution allows an aggrieved employee to seek redress under its terms. Whilst the Constitution does not provide any specific prohibition on sex discrimination or dismissal as a result of same, Article 40.3 provides for certain personal rights as follows:

(i)   The State guarantees in its laws to respect and as far as practicable by its laws to defend and vindicate the personal rights of the citizen

(ii)   The State shall in particular by its laws protect as best it may from unjust attach and in the case of the injustice done, vindicate the life, person, good name, and property rights of every citizen.

In *Ryan v Attorney General*[1] Kenny J held that there existed a number of unspecified rights in addition to those specifically mentioned in Article 40.3 which included the right to bodily integrity. In *Murtagh Properties v Cleary*[2] Kenny J held that the framers of the Constitution intended that men and women were to be regarded as equal and concluded that a rule that sought to prevent an employer employing men or women on the ground of sex only was prohibited by the Constitution.

EMPLOYMENT EQUALITY ACTS 1998 AND 2004

Purpose

[11.03] The purpose of the Employment Equality Act 1998 and the Equality Act 2004[3] is to promote equality in the workplace, prohibit discrimination, prohibit harassment and sexual harassment, prohibit victimisation in the event that a person pursues a claim, allow positive action measures to ensure full equality in practice and to require appropriate measures for people with disabilities in relation to access, participation in and training in employment.

Extent

[11.04] As well as prohibiting discriminatory dismissal the Acts cover other aspects of employment including the prevention of discrimination in advertising, in access to employment, in vocational training, in respect of terms and conditions of employment, in collective agreements etc.[4]

Application

[11.05] The Acts apply to all full-time, part-time and temporary employees, including those in both the public and private sectors,[5] those employed in vocational training bodies,[6] employment agencies,[7] trade unions and professional and trade bodies.[8] The Acts also apply to those who are self-employed, involved in partnerships[9] and those people employed in another person's home.[10]

Equally the legislation encompasses those workers protected under the Protection of Employees (Fixed-term Work) Act 2003 and the Protection of Employees (Part-Time Work) Act 2001.

---

1.   *Ryan v Attorney General* [1965] IR 294.
2.   *Murtagh Properties v Cleary* [1972] IR 330.
3.   Employment Equality Act 1998 & Equality Act 2004.
4.   Employment Equality Act 1998, ss 8, 9, 10 and 12 as amended by Equality Act 2004.
5.   Employment Equality Act 1998, s 2 as amended by Equality Act 2004, s 3.
6.   Employment Equality Act 1998, s 12 as amended by Equality Act 2004, s 6.
7.   Employment Equality Act 1998, s 11.
8.   Employment Equality Act 1998, s 13.
9.   Employment Equality Act 1998, s 13A as inserted by Equality Act 2004, s 7.
10.   Equality Act 2004, s 3.

PROHIBITION OF DISCRIMINATION

[11.06] Discrimination and dismissal arising out of that discrimination is prohibited on nine specific grounds.[11] This is unlike the previous 1977 Employment Equality Act (which was repealed by the 1998 Act) which only prohibited discrimination on grounds of sex and marital status.[12]

Gender

[11.07] It is prohibited to discriminate against a man, a woman or a transsexual person under s 6(2)(a) of the 1998 Act. (Specific protection is provided for pregnant employees and in relation to maternity leave.)

In *Boyle v Ely Property Group*[13] where the company had previously told the complainant that they needed a man to do her job, where they had said that they needed someone who could 'handle themselves' and someone who would get 'physical' and where she had been dismissed following the appointment of new employee, the equality officer found that the dismissal had occurred in circumstances amounting to discrimination on the grounds of gender.

In *A Worker v Mid Western Health Board*[14] the Labour Court determined that to establish discrimination on gender grounds, a complainant must show:

- less favourable treatment; and that

- such treatment arose from the sex of the complainant.

Therefore it is not sufficient just to show that the complainant was treated differently, the treatment must also be less favourable and arise because of their sex.

Marital status

[11.08] Section 2 of the 1998 Act defines marital status as referring to single, married, separated, divorced or widowed persons. The 1998 Act for the first time included single persons in the definition of marital status. The issue of extending benefits such as health insurance to employees' dependents is dealt with by s 34(1)(b) of the 1998 Act which provides that it is not unlawful for an employer to provide a benefit to a person as a member of an employee's family which includes certain persons – whilst at the same time excluding others – who are not included in the definition of 'member of the family' in the Employment Equality Acts 1998–2004.[15]

---

11.   Employment Equality Act 1998, s 6 as amended by Equality Act 2004, s 4.
12.   At the time of the Bill the opposition attempted to get the government to widen the discriminatory grounds to include the grounds of political opinion and trade union membership.
13.   *Boyle v Ely Property Group* DEC–E2009–013.
14.   *A Worker v Mid Western Health Board* (1996) ELR 72.
15.   See *Geraldine McGrane v The Department of Finance & the Department of Foreign Affairs* DEC–E2005– 011.

Family status

[11.09] Family status is defined as a person who has responsibility for someone else under the age of 18. This necessarily includes a parent of a person under 18 years or the resident primary carer or a parent of a person with a disability.

This issue most usually arises where people fail to secure a job or promotion as a result of having a child and there are very few dismissal related cases.

In *An Employee v An Employer*[16] a female employee had been employed until she resigned upon marriage in 1972. She subsequently worked with the employer from time to time on a temporary basis and eventually applied for a permanent position, which she was unsuccessful in securing. The recruitment manager informed her that the reason she was unsuccessful in her application was due to her inflexibility with regard to her domestic situation; at this stage she was separated and had two children. She claimed she was discriminated against because of her sex and/or marital status. The equality officer upheld her complaint stating that 'the status of male candidates or female candidates who did not have the same childcare responsibilities would not have been similarly perceived by the employer as irreconcilable with the capacity to give a commitment to a permanent career position'.

In the case of *Morgan v Bank of Ireland Group*[17] the complainant argued that she had been discriminated against in relation to her application for part-time work because it was over five years from her original application to the date that she would have been able to start work in a job sharing position. The equality officer found that there discrimination on grounds of family status as the respondent had failed at all three stages in justifying the delay making the part-time position available. However, the Labour Court held that: 'it would be manifestly unreasonable to hold that an employer must provide a woman with a facility to job-share in every case in which such a facility is requested and such a result could not have been intended. It is self evident that such facilities can only be made available within the exigencies of the business'.

Higgins v TSB[18] concerned the same issue, ie whether the complainant had been discriminated against in respect of her four applications for part-time working (both permanent part-time and alternative working pattern scheme). In this case the complainant was able to compare her application (under the alternative work pattern scheme) to a male colleague in the same department. The equality officer held that she had been discriminated against but on the gender ground.

Sexual orientation

[11.10] Section 6(2)(d) of the 1998 Act prohibits discrimination on the basis of sexual orientation. This includes discrimination against gay, lesbian, bisexual or heterosexual persons. Further it has been held that discrimination against transsexuals constitutes discrimination on the grounds of sex.[19]

---

16.   *An Employee v An Employer* (1995) ELR 139.
17.   *Morgan v Bank of Ireland Group* DEC–E2008–029.
18.   *Higgins v TSB* Dec–E2010–084.
19.   See *P v S and Cornwall County Council* (1996) IRLR 347 and *Chessington World of Adventures Ltd v Reed* (1998) IRLR 56.

In *A Worker v Brookfield Leisure Ltd*[20] the claimant was dismissed from her job following an allegation, which she denied, that she had been seen kissing another woman in the changing rooms of the leisure centre. She claimed she was dismissed because of her sexual orientation. The Labour Court dismissed the claim on the basis that a man would have suffered the same treatment for a similar display of his sexual orientation. This decision has since been overruled.

However in the case of *A Construction Worker v A Construction Company*[21] the Equality Tribunal upheld the complaint of a general operative who complained that he had been subjected to sexual harassment on the grounds of his sexual orientation. He had worked with the respondent from June 1996 until April 2006 and alleged he have been treated in a discriminatory manner and victimised when his conditions of employment were changed, when he was placed on sick leave and ultimately made redundant. The respondent accepted that some of the incidents took place but denied that the sick leave or redundancy represented less favourable treatment on the basis of his sexual orientation or that he was adversely treated because of his complaints.

Religion

[11.11] Section 6(2)(e) of the 1998 Act prohibits discrimination on the basis of religion. This includes having a different religious belief, a different religious background, a different religious outlook or no religious belief or outlook.

In *Sheeran v Office of Public Works*[22] (a case under the Equal Status Act 2000) the claimant, a humanist, objected to hearing the angelus bell sounded from a chapel in Dublin Castle. Whilst he had no objection to a bell ringing by religious groups he felt it was inappropriate for public property to be used. The equality officer held that the claimant had not established a prima facia case of discrimination in that the complainant had not shown that the respondent treated some religious groups less favourably than others nor that 'the ringing of the angelus bell represents anything other than a minimal intervention into his own lack of religious belief'. Consistently the issue that arises is whether the claimant has been treated 'less favourably' than others.

Age

[11.12] Section 6(2)(f) prohibits discrimination on grounds of age. The 2004 Act amended the 1998 Act by inserting a new sub-s (2A) after sub-s (2) of s 6. This section applies to all ages above the maximum age at which a person is statutorily obliged to attend school (presently 16) but an employer may set a minimum age not exceeding 18 years for recruitment to a post.[23] There is no upper limit on what age a person must be in order to take a claim. Section 6(3)(d) of the 1998 Act amended s 2 of the 1977 Unfair Dismissals Act to remove this.

---

20.   *A Worker v Brookfield Leisure Ltd* (1994) ELR 79.
21.   *A Construction Worker v A Construction Company* DEC–E2008–048.
22.   *Sheeran v Office of Public Works* DEC–S2004/015.
23.   Employment Equality Act 1998, s 6(3)(b).

The first age-related dismissal case was *A Firm of Solicitors v A Worker*[24] where the Labour Court found that the worker's dismissal resulted from the employer's decision to employ a younger person. Also in *Kerrigan v Peter Owens Advertising and Marketing Ltd*[25] the EAT held that selection for redundancy on the grounds of age constituted an unfair dismissal.

The significant difference between discriminary treatment based on age and that based on other factors, such as disability, religion etc, is that art 6[26] presents a set of specific circumstances where age based discrimination may be justified, such as Member States taking action designed to achieve a legitimate employment policy. This has given rise to significant difficulties both at EU level and in this jurisdiction.

Retirement

[11.13] Article 6 of the Framework Employment Directive provides that:

> 1. Notwithstanding Article 2(2), Member States may provide that differences of treatment on grounds of age shall not constitute discrimination, if, within the context of national law, they are objectively and reasonably justified by a legitimate aim, including legitimate employment policy, labour market and vocational training objectives, and if the means of achieving that aim are appropriate and necessary.

> 2. Notwithstanding Article 2(2), Member States may provide that the fixing for occupational social security schemes of ages for admission or entitlement to retirement or invalidity benefits, including the fixing under those schemes of different ages for employees or groups or categories of employees and the use in the context of such schemes or age criteria in actuarial calculations, does not constitute discrimination on the grounds of age, provided this does not result in discrimination of the grounds of sex.

The Directive therefore allows member states (not employers) to provide different treatment in art 6(1). There is also a reference to retirement ages in the non-binding recital 14:

> (14) This Directive shall be without prejudice to national provisions laying down retirement ages.

The above was transposed into Irish law by s 34(4) of the Act which provides that:

> Without prejudice to subsection (3), it shall not constitute discrimination on the age ground to fix different ages for retirement (whether voluntarily or compulsorily) of employees or any class of employees.

What is clear and unusual about s 34(4) is that it does not set a retirement age nor is it even referred to. What it does do though is unconditionally exempts retirement ages from the scope of the legislation. Whether s 34(4) properly transposes the intentions of

---

24.   *A Firm of Solicitors v A Worker* (2002) ELR 124.
25.   *Kerrigan v Peter Owens Advertising and Marketing Ltd* UD 31/97.
26.   Council Directive 2000/78/EC of 22 November 2000, art 6 establishing a general framework for equal treatment in employment and occupation [2003] OJ L303/16.

the Directive regarding retirement ages is the matter of some debate. Thus in *Calor Teoranta v McCarthy*[27] the Labour Court suggested that the section might not be compatible with EU law. Equally on appeal to the High Court Clarke J[28] questioned whether the section properly interpreted in light of the Directive provides in all cases an immunity in respect of a discrimination claim where someone retires at contractual retirement age.

The High Court had previously considered the question of a compulsory retirement age set at 60 in the case of *Donnelly v The Minister for Justice, Equality and Law Reform and the Garda Commissioner.*[29] McKechnie J in his judgment gives careful consideration to the provisions of the Directive. In this regard he goes on to say:

> With regard to compliance with Directive 2000/78/EC, firstly although the Regulation by setting up a system of mandatory retirement, is *prima facie* direct discrimination, it can be said that the overall aim of the scheme is a legitimate one. In particular, given the particular structure on an Garda Síochana ... the aims of ensuring motivation and dynamism through increased prospect of promotion, the creation of the most useful pool of candidates possible for appointment to the position of Commissioner, are both rational and legitimate.

He also went on to address the issue of whether the measure was proportionate by stating that the procedure 'serves to temper the severity of what would otherwise be an absolute retirement age; thereby rendering it, in my opinion, proportionate. It cannot therefore be entirely equated with a blanket policy type position.'

He also stated:

> I know of no other employment position where this is possible, a member can retire after 30 years of service with a full pension at age 50. Thus, in addition to the financial package, which in this case is significant ... a member's retirement is such that the prospect of a second career is very much open.

He concludes by saying:

> I must say that comments as to the legitimacy of the measure utilized in this case, as is usual, turn wholly on the specific facts of the case and such comments should not be taken as supporting the general legitimacy of all mandatory retirement or appointment ages. As noted, national measures relating to compulsory retirement ages are not excluded from consideration under Directive 2000/78/EC. Any discrimination with regards to age must, as put by that Directive, serve a legitimate aim or purpose and the means taken to achieve that purpose must be appropriate and should go no further than is necessary, ie they should be proportionate.

This judgment of Mc Kechnie J can be contrasted with that of Hedigan J in *McCarthy v The Health Service Executive.*[30] Here Ms McCarthy had challenged her retirement at the

---

27.   *Calor Teoranta v McCarthy* 2008–EDA–089.
28.   *Calor Teoranta v McCarthy* [2009] IEHC 139.
29.   *Donnelly v The Minister for Justice, Equality and Law Reform and the Garda Commissioner* [2008] IEHC 7, HC, (2008) 3521P.
30.   *McCarthy v The Health Service Executive* (2010) ELR 165.

age of 65 from the HSE. She specifically argued that any she had not been issued with a contract of employment detailing her retirement age and that any attempt to make her retire was discriminatory. Hedigan J found against her on both.[31]

In the case of *Fitzgerald v HSE*[32] the complainant claimed that she was discriminated against on the grounds of age on the basis that two male comparators were offered extensions to their contracts post the age of 65 whereas she was not. The equality officer took the view that in circumstances where the two male comparators were granted the extension that she could not have been discriminated on grounds of age. He did however go on to hold that she was subjected to discrimination on grounds of gender.

ECJ case law

[11.14] *Mangold v Helm*[33] was the first European case to consider the terms of the Directive and particularly art 6. The case concerned offering fixed term contracts to older workers. Whilst the ECJ found that the aims identified by the German court were legitimate, ie to encourage employers to recruit older workers the court found that they were not proportionate. In particular the court said that as a fixed-term contract deprived an older worker of all employment protection merely because of their age that this was not proportionate.

Palacios de la Villas v Cortefiel Servicios SA[34] examined the legality of compulsory retirement ages. Here the Court of Justice held that mandatory retirement ages in Spanish collective agreements could be justified as an appropriate and necessary way of achieving the legitimate aim of regulating the national labour market. Whilst mandatory retirement ages were ultimately upheld in the case, the judgment makes it clear that they are not always lawful but must be found on the facts as having been an appropriate and necessary way of achieving a legitimate aim. This decision was followed in the *Age Concern* case[35] (also known as the *Heyday* case). Here the question arose as to whether the UK retirement age of 65 could be justified in accordance with art 6(1) of the Directive as a proportionate way of achieving a legitimate aim. The Advocate General held that a national mandatory retirement age could be justified so long a s legitimate aim related to employment and social policy was being pursued that was a:

> … proportionate means to achieve a legitimate social policy objective related to employment policy, the labour market or vocational training.

Petersen v Berufungsausschuss fur den Bezirk Westfalen-Lippe[36] concerned the dental board's refusal to allow the plaintiff practice as a panel dentist after the age of 68 in the German public health sector. This was said to be justified on three grounds:

1.   to protect public health, regarding the competence of dentists;

---

31.   This at the time of writing is under appeal.
32.   *Fitzgerald v HSE* DEC–E2010–120.
33.   *Mangold v Helm* (Case C–144/04).
34.   *Palacios de la Villas v Cortefiel Servicios SA* (Case C–411/05).
35.   *Age Concern England Secretary of State for Business, Enterprise and Regulatory Reform* (Case C–388/07), [2009] WLR (D) 82.
36.   *Petersen v Berufungsausschuss fur den Bezirk Westfalen-Lippe* (Case C–341/08).

2.   to ensure a redistribution of employment opportunities between employees of different ages where jobs are limited; and

3.   to ensure a financial balance in the German health system.

Whereas as the court accepted the latter two as valid, they rejected the first and pointed out that it took no account of the individual capacity of the person concerned and there was no mention of any evidence of a general or specific nature to justify the assumption in the specific case.

In *Rosenbladt v Oellerking Gebäudereinigungs mbH*[37] Mrs Rosenbladt was a part-time cleaner who had worked in an army barracks for 39 years. A collective agreement covered the cleaning industry, a part of which allowed for compulsory retirement when workers reached the age of 65 or when they became entitled to a pension. Mrs Rosenbladt wanted to stay on past the age of 65 in her part-time job. The ECJ held that the law permitting compulsory retirement did not beach the prohibition on age discrimination in the EU Equal Treatment Framework Directive. The ECJ noted that the provision in question was the result of an agreement negotiated between employees and employers' representatives exercising their right to collective bargaining. By guaranteeing employees stability of employment and in the long term foreseeable retirement, while offering employers flexibility in managing their staff, the automatic termination clauses reflected a balance between diverging but legitimate interests.

What we can take from all of the above is the following:

1.   Every case will turn on its own merits.

2.   Whereas we now have two very different interpretations by the High Court in relation to the Directive it does not seem that s 34(4) provides a complete exemption in relation to a contractual retirement age.

3.   That does not mean that as an employer you should not set a fixed retirement age. If you want to you must have a clear justification as to why you want to set it.

4.   If you do wish to set a mandatory retirement age it would be wise to justify it on social policy grounds (if possible), ie any age discrimination must serve a legitimate aim or purpose.

5.   Aims such as ensuring motivation and dynamism through increased prospect of promotion, the creation of the most useful pool of candidates possible for appointment could be deemed legitimate.

Even if there is a legitimate purpose the aims taken to achieve it must be proportionate.

---

37.   *Rosenbladt v Oellerking Gebäudereinigungs mbH* (Case C–45/09).

Disability

[11.15] There is no definition of disability in the Framework Employment Directive. The ECJ has ruled that 'sickness itself is not enough to qualify as a disability', for the purpose of the Directive.[38]

Disability is defined in s 2 of the act as:

(a)   the total or partial absence of a person's bodily or mental functions, including the absence of a part of a person's body;

(b)   the presence in the body of organisms causing, or likely to cause, chronic disease or illness;

(c)   the malfunction, malformation or disfigurement of a part of a person's body;

(d)   a condition or malfunction which results in a person learning differently from a person without the condition or malfunction; or

(e)   a condition, illness or disease which affects a person's thought processes, perception of reality, emotions or judgment or which results in disturbed behaviour;

and shall be taken to include a disability which exists at present, or which previously existed but no longer exists, or which may exist in the future or which is imputed to a person;

What is not a disability?

[11.16] Despite the clear statement by the ECJ that 'sickness itself is not enough to qualify as a disability', the Labour Court stated in *Customer Perception Ltd v Leydon*[39] that the Irish definition does not require a certain severity of impairment or of functional limitation. This statement would seem to set a very broad definition. That said, there are a number of helpful judgments as to what is not a disability, thus an ankle injury was held not to be a disability where a light cage fell on an employee's ankle and punctured her skin;[40] similarly a one-day illness which cleared up quickly did not satisfy the test.[41]

An interesting case arose in *Moloney v M J Clarke & Sons Ltd*.[42] Here the complainant was profoundly deaf (which clearly amounts to a disability); however he did not complain about this per se but rather about 'psychological scarring.' The equality officer stated that:

I find that no explanation on how psychological scarring is a disability as defined under the Acts was provided to the Tribunal. Further more, no report from a recognised mental health professional to confirm such a diagnosis was produced in evidence…it is therefore the case that no diagnosis of a 'condition, illness or disease' was provided to the Tribunal to show that he complainant was disabled within the meaning of s 2(e) of the Acts.

---

38.   See *Navas v Eurest Colectividades SA* (Case C–13/05).

39.   *Customer Perception Ltd v Leydon* ED 02/1 (12 Dec 2003).

40.   *Colgan v Boots Ireland*–DEC–E201–008.

41.   *O'Rourke v JJ Red Holding Limited t/a Dublin City Hotel* DEC–2010–046.

42.   *Moloney v M J Clarke & Sons Ltd* DEC–E2010–140.

Finally in the case of *A Worker v A Food Manufacturer*[43] non-descript sickness certificates were deemed not to constitute a disability under the Acts.

What constitutes a disability?

[11.17] Notwithstanding the above, through case law 'disability' has been defined broadly to include a range of medical conditions including people with physical, intellectual, cognitive, learning and emotional disabilities.[44] Alcoholism has also been held to be a disability even if the person is in recovery.[45]

The first disability-related dismissal was *A Computer Component Company v A Worker*[46] where the employer terminated the worker's employment because she suffered from epilepsy. Epilepsy was held to constitute a disability under the Act and the worker was awarded €19,046.07.

In *A Health and Fitness Club v A Worker*[47] the Labour Court held that an employee who suffered from anorexia and bulimia suffered a disability as defined under the 1998 Act. As the employer in this instance made no effort to obtain a prognosis of the complainant's condition and reached a conclusion on same without the benefit of any form of professional advice or assessment of the risks associated with her condition and as they did not discuss the situation with her before taking a decision on her future, her dismissal was deemed to be contrary to the Act and she was awarded €13,000 in compensation. In *Woods v Euro Route Logistics*[48] the respondent company relied on the fact that the complainant left on medical advice. The equality officer was satisfied that the respondent had considered the complainant's disability as an impediment to his continued employment and found that he was terminated because of his asthma. The equality officer cited with approval the case of *A Government Department v An Employee*[49] where the Labour Court stated that:

> [T]he requirement to establish that there was no discrimination whatsoever means that the Court must be alert to the possibility that a person with a disability may suffer discrimination not because they suffer from a disability per se, but they are perceived, because of their disability to be less capable or less dependable than a person without a disability. The Court must always be alert to the possibility of unconscious or inadvertent discrimination and mere denial of a discriminatory motive in the absence of independent corroboration, must by approached with caution.

The above highlights the necessity for employers in dealing with disability cases to ensure that they seek the best possible independent medical advice in relation to the employee's condition before moving to terminate their employment.

---

43. *A Worker v A Food Manufacturer* DEC–E2010–187.
44. See *A Company v A Worker* ED/04/13 DETERMINATION NO 051 where obsessive compulsive disorder (OCD) was held to be a disability.
45. See *An Employee v A Government Department Equality Officer* DEC–E2005/034.
46. *A Computer Component Company v A Worker* (2002) ELR 124.
47. *A Health and Fitness Club v A Worker* ED/02/59 DETERMINATION NO 037.
48. *Woods v Euro Route Logistics* DEC–E2010.
49. *A Government Department v An Employee* ADE/05/19.

Awareness of disability

[11.18] In *A Company v A Worker*[50] the Labour Court held that for an employer to be able to respond to a disability it is essential that they are aware of the fact that there is a disability in existence and that there is a problem with work as a consequence.

Capability

[11.19] Section 16 of the 1998 Act provides that an employer is not required to recruit, retain, train or promote a person who will not or is not available to carry out the duties of a position or who will not accept the conditions under which the duties attached to a post are to be performed or who is not fully competent to carry out the duties concerned. This section was amended by s 9 of the 2004 Act and also applies to employment agencies and other bodies covered by s 13, ie employers' organisations, trade union and professional bodies.

The section provides a complete defence to a claim of discrimination on the disability ground if the employer can prove they formed a bona fide belief that the complainant was not fully capable of performing the duties for which they were employed. Employers are obliged, however, to make adequate enquiries to establish the full factual position in relation to an employee's capacity. This would mean in practice ensuring that there are up-to-date medical reports including an independent opinion of a medical specialist. In *Humphrey's v Westwood Fitness Club*[51] the court stated:

> [T]he nature and extent of the enquiries which an employer should make will depend on the circumstances of each case. At a minimum, however, an employer should ensure that he or she is in full possession of all the material facts concerning the employee's condition and that the employee is given fair notice that the question of his or her dismissal for incapacity is being considered. The employee must also be allowed an opportunity to influence the employer's decision.

The court went on to state that any investigation should follow a two-stage approach. At the first stage the employer should familiarise themselves with all the relevant medical data either from the employee's doctor or independently. The second stage would be to consider what, if any, special treatment or facilities may be available by the employer such that the employee could become fully capable. The cost of such special treatment or facilities must also be considered.

This line of reasoning was also followed in the case of *A Health and Fitness Club v A Worker*.[52] The case which is widely reported upon involved the dismissal of a child care assistant in a crèche. The respondent believed that her conditions of anorexia and bulimia rendered her unsuitable to work in a child care facility. The Labour Court in

---

50.   *A Company v A Worker* ED/04/13 DETERMINATION NO. 051.
51.   *Humphrey's v Westwood Fitness Club* (2004) ELR 296 300.
52.   *A Health and Fitness Club v A Worker* EE/DO/37.

their decision had to consider s 16 of the Act and put forward a two-stage approach for considering reasonable accommodation. The court stated:

> This section, on which the respondent relies can provide a completed defence to a claim of discrimination on the disability ground if it can be shown that the employer formed the bona fide belief that eh complainant is not fully capable, within the meaning of the section, of performing the duties for which they are employed. However, before coming to that view the employer would normally be required to make adequate enquiries so as to establish fully the factual position in relation to the employee's capacity.

The nature and extent of the enquiries which an employer should make will depend on the circumstances of each case. At a minimum, however, an employer should ensure that or she is in full possession of all the material facts concerning the employee's condition and that the employee is given fair notice that the question of his or her dismissal for incapacity is being considered. The employee must also be allowed an opportunity to influence the employer's decision.

In practical terms this will normally require a two-stage enquiry, which looks firstly at the factual position concerning the employee's capability including the degree of impairment arising from the disability and its likely duration. This would involve looking at the medical evidence available to the employer either from the employee's doctors or obtained independently.

Secondly, if it is apparent that the employee is not fully capable s 16(3) of the Act requires the employer to consider what if any special treatment or facilities may be available by which the employee can become fully capable. The section requires that the cost of such special treatment or facilities must also be considered. Here, what constitutes nominal cost will depend on the size of the organization and its financial resources,

Finally, such an enquiry could only be regarded as adequate if the employee concerned is all a full opportunity to participate at each level and is allowed to present medical evidence and submissions'

In summary what the Labour Court is saying is that prior to dismissing any employee on the grounds of capability employers must:

1.   get the employee independently medically examined;

2.   in the event that the employee is medically unfit for work then you must consider what special treatment or facilities may be available by which the employee can become fully capable; and

3.   the employee concerned must be allowed to fully participate at each level – this would include discussing what special treatment or facilities may be available and discussing any medical reports and offering such counter reports as may be available to them.

Whilst that can all be taken from the above the case of *Mr A v A Government Department*[53] seems to add a fourth point to those above and that is that employers need

---

53.   *Mr A v A Government Department* DEC–2008–023.

to take a proactive approach. In the instance case the court found the employer failed to pursue the assessment of the complainant's situation and an exploration or reasonable accommodation in a proactive fashion.

So not only must employers consider all options but they must be proactive in doing so! Of particular importance in all of the above is that all of the information and enquiries need to be shared with the employee and they should be allowed to present 'relevant medical evidence and submissions.' (Note the decision in *An Applicant v A County Council*[54] where the respondent is criticised for not allowing the complainant the opportunity to comment on medical evidence.) In practice this often gives rise to acrimonious exchanges as invariably the company's medical practitioner may be saying one thing whilst the employee's says another. The best advice in this area is to ensure that the employee is referred to an occupational health specialist in the first instance and secondly if there is debate between a specialist hired by the company and one instructed by the employee it may be necessary to get a third opinion. Of note here is the decision in *Ryan v Dublin Airport Authority*[55] where it states that:

> [I]t is not the place of the Tribunal to assess contradictory medical opinions as I don't prefer one opinion over another. Rather, it is for me to consider whether the respondent has satisfied the test in *A Health and Fitness Club v A Worker*.

Disability and reasonable accommodation

[11.20] The Framework Directive imposes an obligation on employers to take appropriate measures to enable a person with a disability to have access to employment to participate or advance in employment, or to undergo training unless the measures would impose a disproportionate burden.

Section 16(3)(a) of the 1998 Act states that:

> For the purposes of this Act a person who has a disability is fully competent to undertake and fully capable of undertaking, any duties if the person would be so fully competent and capable on reasonable accommodation (in this subsection referred to as 'appropriate measures') being provided by the person's employer.

In keeping with the Framework Directive the section provides that 'appropriate measures 'should not 'impose a disproportionate burden on the employer'.

In *A Company v A Worker*[56] the Labour Court confirmed this by stating:

> Article 5 of Directive 2000/78 of the 27th of November 2000 establishing a general framework for equal treatment in employment and occupations, it imposes a positive duty on employers to take appropriate measures, where needed in a particular case, to enable a person with a disability to have access to, participate in, or advance in employment. A similar requirement is now incorporated in section 16(3) of the Act as amended.

54.　*An Applicant v A County Council* DEC–E2010–054.
55.　*Ryan v Dublin Airport Authority* DEC–E2010–059.
56.　*A Company v A Worker* ADE/09/21.

Appropriate measures as defined in s 16(4) as:

'appropriate measures' in relation to a person with a disability—

(a)   means effective and practical measures, where needed in a particular case, to adapt the employer's place of business to the disability concerned.

(b)   without prejudice to the generality of paragraph (a), includes the adaptation of premises and equipment, patterns of working time, distribution of tasks or the provision of training and integration resources, but

(c)   does not include any treatment, facility or thing that the person might ordinarily or reasonably provide for himself or herself.

In *An Employer and A Worker*[57] the Labour Court defined this as an objective test to be determined by what is reasonable and one which must have regard to all the circumstances of the case. Here the court went on to say that special treatment could mean:

(i)   considering adjusting the person's hours, allowing them to work from home, allowing them to undertake certain tasks which others doing similar tasks would be expected to perform;

(ii)   affording the person with a disability more favourable treatment that one without a disability.

In the case of *Bus Éireann v Mr C*[58] the court took the view that the failure of the company to consider possible alternative positions despite the court agreeing that Mr C was unfit for his present position was a 'failure to fulfil the duty imposed by s 16(1)(b) of the Act'.

In *Noel Flynn V Emerald Facilities Services*[59] the equality officer found that the complainant was covered by the disability ground in that he suffered from alcoholism; however the officer was also satisfied that the complainant never stated this to the respondent or asked for reasonable accommodation to be granted. In those circumstances the equality officer found that the facts had not been established upon which the complainant could rely in asserting that he suffered a discriminatory dismissal and his complaint failed.

Phased return to work

[11.21] In *A Worker (Mr O) v An Employer No 1*[60] the Labour Court considered the issue of whether an employer should be obliged to provide an employee with a 'phased return to work' and whether the failure to allow them to return to work on such a basis (as advised by their doctor) constituted a failure to accommodate their needs by providing a special treatment or facilities in accordance with the Employment Equality Act. The Labour Court held that the decision of the company not to provide a phased return to

---

57.   EAA 0413 15 November 2004.
58.   *Bus Éireann v Mr C* ADE/07/EDA 08111.
59.   *Noel Flynn V Emerald Facilities Services* DEC–E2009–065.
60.   *A Worker (Mr O) v An Employer No 1* (2005) ELR 113.

work meant the employee in effect could not return to work and that this was discriminatory (see also **3.43**).

Disproportionate burden

[11.22] What constitutes a disproportionate burden on employers is a matter to be determined from the facts of each case[61] but there are few decisions. In *Patrick Kennedy v Stresslite Tanks Ltd & Stresslite Floors Ltd*[62] it was held that leaving a person on the books of the company once their sick pay had expired would not have placed a disproportionate burden on the company. Also in *O'Sullivan and Siemens Business Services Ltd*[63] the equality officer held that the provision of an assessment test in an electronic format could not in any sense be considered as imposing a disproportionate burden.

Race

[11.23] Section 6(2)(h) of the 1998 Act defines race as being differences 'in race, colour, nationality or ethnic or national origins'.

Race

[11.24] The definition of race contained in s 6 of the Act is broader than that contained in the Directive in that nationality is expressly included in the Irish definition whereas it is not in the Directive. Thus the Act provides significantly greater scope to claims of discrimination as a complainant does not have to show a different ethnic or racial origin to prove less favourable treatment. This 'broad' definition can be seen in many decisions; thus in the case of *A Manager of an English Language School v An Institute of Technology*[64] the equality officer found that calling the complainant a 'Fiery Latin' fell within the definition of harassment on grounds of race.

Ethnic origin

[11.25] The question of what constitutes ethnic origins has been the subject of some case law but not in this jurisdiction. The Court of Appeal in *Dawkins v Department of the Environment*[65] deemed that Rastafarians were not a separate 'racial group' within the ethnic group of the Afro–Caribbean community. In *Mandla v Lee*[66] the House of Lords stated that a group may be defined by reference to its 'ethnic origins' if it constitutes a separate and distinct community by virtue of characteristics which are commonly associated with common racial origin and is a term 'appreciably wider than strictly racial or biological'.

---

61. See *A Health and Fitness Club v A Worker* (EE/DO/37).
62. *Patrick Kennedy v Stresslite Tanks Ltd & Stresslite Floors Ltd* DEC–E2009–078.
63. *O'Sullivan and Siemens Business Services Ltd* DEC–E2006–058.
64. *A Manager of an English Language School v An Institute of Technology* DUC–2007–019.
65. *Dawkins v Department of the Environment* (1993) IRLR 284.
66. *Mandla v Lee* (1983) IRLR 209.

In this jurisdiction the general approach which is adopted in considering cases of racial discrimination was that laid down by the House of Lords in *Glasgow City Council v Zafar*.[67] This case was subsequently adopted in this jurisdiction by Quirk J in *Davis v Dublin Institute of Technology*.[68] In *Zafar*[69] Lord Browne-Wilkinson pointed out that where there is a difference in treatment and a difference in race there is prima facie evidence of discrimination and it is for the respondent to provide a non-discriminatory explanation.

The views of the Labour Court in *Campbell Catering v Rasaq*[70] should also be noted. The court said:

> It is clear that many non-national workers encounter special difficulties in employment arising from a lack of knowledge concerning statutory and contractual employment rights together with differences of language and culture. In the case of disciplinary proceedings, employers have a positive duty to ensure that all workers fully understand what is alleged against them, the gravity of the alleged misconduct and their right to mount a full defence, including the right to representation. Special measures may be necessary in the case of non-national workers to ensure that this obligation is fulfilled and that the accused worker fully appreciates the gravity of the situation and is given appropriate facilities and guidance in making a defence. In such cases, applying the same procedural standards to a non-national worker as would be applied to an Irish National could amount to the application of the same rules to different situations and this could in itself amount to discrimination.

This case points to the necessity for employers not only to be procedurally correct in dealing with such an issue but to ensure that every case is treated individually.

Membership of the Traveller Community

[11.26] Section 6(2)(i) of the 1998 Act prohibits discrimination on the basis that a person is a member of the travelling community. What little case law there is on this topic is confined to breaches of the Equal Status Act 2000 which prohibits discrimination in the provision of goods and services.

SEXUAL HARASSMENT AND HARASSMENT

[11.27] A new s 14A was inserted into the 1998 Act by s 8 of the Equality Act 2004. This was necessary to reflect the common approach taken in the directives to the treatment of harassment on any of the discriminatory grounds. Consequently the separate provisions of the 1998 Act in respect of sexual harassment (s 23) and harassment (s 32) have been repealed by virtue of ss 14 and 21 of the 2004 Act.

---

67.   *Glasgow City Council v Zafar* [1998] 2 All ER 953.
68.   *Davis v Dublin Institute of Technology* (23 June 2000, unreported) HC.
69.   *Glasgow City Council v Zafar* [1998] 2 All ER 953.
70.   *Campbell Catering v Rasaq* ED/02/52 DETERMINATION No 048.

Definition of harassment and sexual harassment

[11.28] Section 23 of the 1998 Act defined sexual harassment very broadly. No attempt is made to do so in the 2004 Act. The 1998 Act relied mostly for its definition on the European Commission's Code of Practice on measures to combat sexual harassment[71] and the Department of Justice, Equality and Law Reform's Code of Practice on Measures to Protect the Dignity of Women and Men at Work.[72] Drawing from the Department's Code of Practice which was given statutory effect by SI No 78 of 2002, harassment and sexual harassment can broadly be defined as follows:

- harassment is any form of unwanted conduct related to any of the discriminatory grounds;

- sexual harassment is any form of unwanted verbal, non–verbal or physical conduct of a sexual nature.

In *Health Board v BC and the Labour Court*[73] Costello J stated that sexual harassment is a term which, while it is in general use, 'has no well-established legal definition'. He then went on to quote the definition of sexual harassment as provided for in the employer's handbook and further commented that the definition as set out reflected 'well the connotation of the phrase as it is used in everyday life in this country today'. That definition was:

Sexual harassment is defined as 'unsolicited, unreciprocated behaviour of a sexual nature to which the recipient objects or could not reasonably be expected to consent and may include:

- unwanted physical contact;

- lewd or suggestive behaviour whether verbal or physical;

- sexually derogatory statements or sexually discriminatory remarks;

- the display of pornographic or sexually explicit material in the workplace'.

In both sexual harassment and harassment it is conduct which has the purpose or effect of violating a person's dignity and creating an intimidating, hostile, degrading, humiliating or offensive environment for the person and in both instances the unwanted conduct may include acts, requests, spoken words, gestures or the production, display or circulation of written words, pictures or other material.

Sexual harassment or harassment of an employee is discrimination by the employer. It is a defence for an employer to prove that they took reasonably practicable steps to prevent the person harassing or sexually harassing the victim or (where relevant) prevent

---

71. (1992) OJ C49/1.
72. Similar but in addition to these codes of practice, the Health and Safety Authority has also published a Code of Practice on Workplace Bullying and the Labour Relations Commission has published a Code of Practice on Bullying in the Workplace.
73. *Health Board v BC and the Labour Court* (1994) ELR 27.

the employee from being treated differently in the workplace or in the course of employment (and to reverse its effects if it has occurred).

Essential characteristics of sexual harassment and harassment

[11.29] The essential characteristic of sexual harassment is that it is unwanted by the recipient. This can arise even where there is a consensual relationship between adults. In *A Company v A Worker*[74] the Labour Court stated that a sexual relationship between consenting adults does not imply that that consent is unlimited as regards either time or its duration or what acts may take place between the parties.

Furthermore, the person who carries out the harassing does not have to be an employee of the company.[75] Indeed one of the largest awards ever made in Ireland for sexual harassment was handed down by the *Circuit Court in Atkinson v Carty*.[76] Damages amounting to €137,500 (with a deduction of 25% for contributory negligence) were awarded to Ms Atkinson, a legal accountant who had experienced serious sexual harassment from an independent contractor to the firm in which she was employed over a period of seven or eight years. The high level of the award is indicative of the seriousness with which the courts approach this issue.[77]

Sexual harassment can also take place outside the workplace, as in (*A Limited Company v One Female Employee*),[78] or at a company social event (*O'N v An Insurance Company*).[79]

Defence to sexual harassment and harassment (reasonably practicable steps)

[11.30] Section 14A(2) of the 1998 Act provides a defence for employers if they can prove that they took such steps as were reasonably practicable to prevent the person from 'harassing or sexually harassing the victim or any class of persons which includes the victim or to prevent the victim from being treated differently as a result of the harassment occurring.'

Equally s 15 which deals with vicarious liability provides a defence for employers where they 'took such steps as were reasonably practicable to prevent the employee—

    (a)   from doing that act, or

    (b)   from doing in the course of his or her employment acts of that description'.[80]

---

74.   *A Company v A Worker* EE03/1991.
75.   Employment Equality Act 1998, s 14A(a)(iii) as inserted by Equality Act 2004, s 8.
76.   *Circuit Court in Atkinson v Carty* (2005) ELR 1.
77.   See also *A Company v A Worker* EE03/1991.
78.   *A limited Company v One Female Employee* EE10/1998.
79.   *O'N v An Insurance Company* DEC–E2004–052.
80.   Equally this was a new section inserted in the 1998 Act to fill a major lacuna in the 1977 Act. This section renders an employer liable for the acts of employers done in the course of their employment whether the acts are done with the employer's knowledge or consent or not. Similar to s 14A an employer can avoid liability by taking reasonably practicable steps.

Reasonably practicable steps would include the following:

Grievance procedure

[11.31] As a bare minimum every employer needs to have a basic grievance procedure. This is necessary to ensure that the employee knows where to direct their complaint, what they will expect to happen arising from the complaint, the procedure for carrying out the investigation and what will happen when the investigation ends. It will also ensure that the issue is brought to the employer's attention and they have an opportunity to deal with it in a speedy, professional and confidential manner. Of course there are practical problems in small companies or where the alleged harasser is the person's boss. Where such a procedure is in place and has been brought to the employee's attention they are obliged to use it. In one instance the Labour Court determined that the claimant had produced no evidence determining that she had complained that she was being harassed and as such her claim failed.[81]

Adopt codes of practice into a detailed policy

[11.32] The fact that an employer may have a basic grievance procedure and has informed employees of it may not be sufficient to successfully defend an action, except perhaps in the smallest of employments and probably even there, will not be deemed satisfactory. Regard must be given to the existing codes of practice in this area and these must be adopted and/or incorporated into existing policies and procedures. As there are no fewer than three relevant codes of practice in the area of harassment this can get complicated. These are:

- the Equality Authority's 'Code of Practice on Sexual Harassment and Harassment at Work';

- the Labour Relations Commission's Code of Practice on 'Procedures for Addressing Bullying in the Workplace';

- the Health and Safety Authority's Code of Practice on 'Workplace Bullying'.

Note: as bullying is seen primarily as a health and safety issue, employers will be required to consult with employees and/or their representatives when developing policies. It is also necessary to provide training.

As a result of these 'codes' employers are now operating within the context of a legal and quasi-legal framework, which requires the development of policies to prevent workplace bullying, sexual harassment and harassment, ie employers now need to:

- in respect of sexual harassment, harassment and bullying develop written prevention policies, which set out procedures (both informal and formal) for handling complaints and managing investigations;

---

81.   DEE 2/1988.

- apply health and safety principles and identify if there are bullying hazards in particular workplaces, assess the risks presented by these hazards and put in place prevention/control measures;

- ensure the policies are communicated effectively and that employees are also trained in them.

The Health and Safety Authorities' Code is, according to its chairperson,[82] 'admissible in evidence in cases taken on the issue'.[83] The HSA code has a 'semi legal status'.[84] Whilst this means that not abiding by the code is not of itself an offence, failure to observe it may be admissible in evidence in any proceedings brought under the Act. It is clear therefore that where an employer fails to develop and implement the above policies and a claim arises it will be difficult to defend any such action. In *An Employee v An Employer*[85] the respondent company did not have any policy in place to deal with sexual harassment at the time of the harassment. This was held against them. More instructive perhaps are the equality officer's comments in relation to the policy that the respondent company had put in place by the time of the hearing, where she states:

> I am not satisfied as to the adequacy of the one page document (which also deals with bullying) in terms of preventing sexual harassment from occurring in the workplace and in the event that it does occur in providing an appropriate procedure for dealing with a complaint. (see also *EH v A Named Company Trading as A Cab Company Dublin* below).

Also in the case of *A Female Employee v A Recruitment Company*[86] the employer in this instance had no policy in place. Despite this they sought to rely on s 15. In the circumstances the equality officer held that where the employer did not have a proper policy in place and presented no evidence that it had taken any steps that were reasonably practicable to prevent sexual harassment, the company could not avail of the defence.

It is evident therefore that not only must appropriate policies be put in place for a defence to be mounted but they need to be detailed and clear. Also it does seem from various decisions that any policy on bullying should be documented separately.[87]

Communicate and train employees on company policies

[11.33] It is not sufficient to merely adopt these codes. Employers need to make employees aware of them, both at an employee's induction into the workforce and at regular intervals thereafter. It is no defence to have policies in place if employees are not made aware of them and regular training sessions not provided. In the case of *Jacqui*

---

82. Kate Hayes in 'Industrial Relations News' (IRN 11/04/2002).
83. The Code was given legal effect by SI 78/2002.
84. HSA Director Tom Beegan (IRN 11/04/2002).
85. *An Employee v An Employer* DEC–E 2003–027 30/6/03.
86. *A Female Employee v A Recruitment Company* DEC–E2008–015.
87. See *An Employee v An Employer* DEC–E 2003–027 30/6/03.

McCarthy (claimant) v Dublin Corporation (respondent)[88] the equality officer in finding the respondent vicariously liable stated:

> [I]n relation to an employer's vicarious liability for the discriminatory actions of its employees and agents, the existence of a policy on harassment or equality is not sufficient to prevent discrimination without clearly bringing the provisions of the policy to the attention of staff and creating a consciousness on all employees and agents as to what constitutes discrimination.

Also, if the policy is not adhered to, this will be detrimental to any employer's case and will be taken into consideration by the equality officer in their decision.[89]

But if it is this will be seen in a good light, thus in *A Manager of an English Language School v An Institute of Technology* the equality officer found that because the equal opportunities policy was well established and properly applied that the employer was entitled to a defence under s 15.

The case of *A Worker v An Engineering Company*[90] points to the need to communicate the policy. Here the complainant, a British national, claimed that he had been subjected to constant harassment because of his nationality. He never made any complaint to his employer but stated that this was because his own supervisor was involved in the harassment. Whilst the defendant had a policy, the equality officer found that they could not invoke the defence under the Act as they were unable to show how their policy had been disseminated amongst staff.

Carry out any Investigation in an impartial, fair, confidential and as speedy a manner as possible

[11.34] It is also vital that the employer carry out investigations into alleged complaints in a fair, speedy and impartial manner. Any such investigation should be carried out in accordance with the rules of natural and constitutional justice. In *An Employer v An Employee*[91] the equality officer made reference to the fact that the respondent failed to interview people properly, take appropriate statements, maintain confidentiality, make any clear findings in relation to whether sexual harassment had occurred, communicate such findings to the complainant and take any disciplinary action against the perpetrator. All of these are clearly factors that employers should be aware of when carrying out such investigations.

Additionally, where because of the size of the company, the number of people involved, or where the proposed investigator comes with some degree of partiality[92] it is not possible to carry out a truly independent investigation, companies should consider hiring an external independent person to do the investigation. The Labour Court in a number of decisions has referred to this in a favourable light.[93]

---

88.   *Jacqui McCarthy (claimant) v Dublin Corporation* EE 2000/45 (10 May 2001).
89.   *A Named Female Employee v A Named Respondent* DEC–E2003/001.
90.   *A Worker v An Engineering Company* DUC–2008–03.
91.   *An Employer v An Employee* DEC–E 2003–027 30/6/03.
92.   See *Athlone Institute of Technology v SIPTU*, Recommendation No 17013, CD/01/498.
93.   See *Bank of Ireland v A Worker Recommendation* No 17014 CD/01/474.

COMPENSATION FOR HARASSMENT

[11.35] Compensation for harassment tends to be higher than normal. Thus *Atkinson v Carty*[94] saw the largest ever award made for sexual harassment. Also in the case of *EH v A Named Company Trading as a Cab Company Dublin*[95] the employer was found to have subjected the complainant to offensive and humiliating pictures. Additionally she also experienced laxatives being placed in a kettle which she used. There was no policy in place. In finding that the company was liable for sexual harassment and deeming that to be of a 'grossly offensive nature', the Equality Tribunal awarded the maximum compensation of two years' remuneration and directed the company to put in place a policy to prevent sexual harassment in accordance with the Code of Practice.

Finally in the case of *A Construction Worker v A Construction Company*[96] €14,700 was awarded for discrimination (loss of earnings), a further €10,000 for distress and the effects of the sexual harassment he had suffered and €25,000 for the effects of victimisation.

VICTIMISATION

[11.36] It is unlawful for an employer to penalise an employee for taking action to support their rights as provided for in the Employment Equality Acts 1998–2004. Victimisation is defined in s 74 of the 1998 Act as amended by s 29 of the 2004 Act. Victimisation occurs where the dismissal or other adverse treatment of an employee is a reaction by the employer to:

(a)   a complaint of discrimination made by the employee to the employer,

(b)   any proceedings by a complainant,

(c)   an employee having represented or otherwise supported a complainant,

(d)   the work of an employee having been compared with that of another employee for any of the purposes of these Acts or any enactment repealed by these Acts,

(e)   an employee having been witness in any proceedings under these Acts or any such repealed enactment;

(f)   an employee having opposed by lawful means an act which is unlawful under these Acts or any such repealed enactment, or

(g)   an employee having given notice or an intention to take any of the actions mentioned in the preceding paragraphs.

In *A Complainant v A Department Store*[97] the equality officer emphasised that 'victimisation' was a matter that must be considered 'very seriously' and that 'significant compensation' should be awarded to successful complainants. Also in

94.   *Atkinson v Carty* (2005) ELR 1.
95.   *EH v A Named Company Trading as a Cab Company Dublin* DEC–E2006–026.
96.   *A Construction Worker v A Construction Company* DEC–E2008–048.
97.   *A Complainant v A Department Store* DEC–E2002/017.

Dublin City Council v McCarthy[98] the Labour Court stated that 'the victimisation of a person for having in good faith taken a claim under the equality legislation is very serious as it could have the impact of undermining the effectiveness of the legislation and is completely unacceptable'. The court in this instance awarded €25,000.

Similar to harassment, compensation for claims of victimisation generally appear to be more generous than those for discrimination. Thus in *A Named Employee v Tesco Ireland*[99] the complainant's claim of discrimination on grounds of race was unsuccessful. However, €8,000 was awarded for victimisation where the company had interviewed the complainant for a post that had already been filled. Also in *A Female Employee v A Candle Production Company*[100] the complainant was awarded €7,000 for discrimination and €10,000 for victimization. Also in *O'Brien v Compute Scope Limited*[101] €5,000 was awarded for discrimination and twice that for victimisation.

VICTIMISATION POST DISMISSAL

[11.37] In *Catherine Connerty v Caffrey Transport Limited*[102] the complainant was previously employed with the respondent company. After she left she alleged that two prospective employers had received bad references about her from her former employer. Specific mention was made of the equality case that she had taken against them. The equality officer, whilst finding that she had failed to establish a prima facie claim of discriminatory treatment on grounds of gender, marital status and family status did determine that she had been victimised by her former employer by them making reference to her equality claim and other employment claims she had brought against them. She was awarded €15,000 compensation for the stress caused as a result of the victimisation.

VICARIOUS LIABILITY

[11.38] Section 15 deals with vicarious liability. This section renders an employer liable for the acts of employers done in the course of their employment whether the acts are done with the employer's knowledge or consent or not. Similar to s 14A an employer can avoid liability by taking reasonably practicable steps. (For a discussion on reasonably practicable steps see **11.5.3.**)

PRACTICAL CONSIDERATIONS

[11.39] The initial practical consideration for employers when faced with a claim under the Acts is to understand what institutions will deal with the claim and what the process entails. Even though many practitioners will be used to dealing with the Labour Court

---

98. *Dublin City Council v McCarthy* EDA 2/2002.
99. *A Named Employee v Tesco Ireland* DEC–E2006–031.
100. *A Female Employee v A Candle Production Company* DEC–E2006–035.
101. *O'Brien v Compute Scope Limited* DEC–E2006–030.
102. *Catherine Connerty v Caffrey Transport Limited* DEC–E2008–018.

their role in dealing with equality issues is somewhat different to the one carried out in industrial relations cases, bound as they are by the legislation that governs this area. (For an explanation of the Equality Tribunal and the Labour Court see **Ch 1.**)

Referral forms

[11.40] Complainants refer their complaints on a Form EE1 (reproduced below at **11.55**). This form sets out the broad claim of the complainant. It can be amended at the hearing. Thus in the case of *Professor Kevin James v Cork Institute of Technology*[103] the equality officer went on to say:

> I accept the submission on behalf of the respondent that the Form EE1 was only intended to set out, in broad outline, the nature of the complaint. If it is permissible in court proceedings to amend pleadings, where the justice of the case requires it, then[104] a fortiori, it should be permissible to amend a claim as set out in a form such as the EE1, so long as the general nature of the complaint (in this case discrimination on the grounds of sexual orientation) remains the same. What is in issue here is the furnishing of further and better particulars, although, it must be said, in the context of an expanded period of time.

Also in the case of *Mary Higgins v TSB* the initial complaint referred by the complainant was that of indirect discrimination. The equality officer held that despite this that she was entitled to address issues of direct discrimination. In this regard she goes on to say:

> In EE5/1988 the Equality Officer addressed an argument made by the respondent that as the complainant had only made allegations in respect of direct discrimination she, the Equality Officer, was precluded from looking at indirect discrimination. The Equality Officer accepted the arguments as valid and did not address indirect discrimination. In that regard, and all others, the Labour Court upheld her decision in Determination DEE190. In Siobhan Long and the Labour Court, Mairead Blackhall and Power Supermarkets Ltd Trading as Quinnsworth, 1990 No 58 Judicial Review the High Court ordered that the decisions of the Equality Officer and the Labour Court in so far as the Equality Officer had no jurisdiction to consider the applicant's allegation under the provisions relating to indirect discrimination, were null and void and it ordered that the matter be remitted to the Equality Officer for reconsideration in that regard. On that basis I am satisfied that I have jurisdiction to address direct discrimination even where the only case initially referred by the complainant relates to indirect discrimination.

Defending a claim

[11.41] The Equality Tribunal, the Labour Court and the Circuit Court all have roles in relation to claims of discrimination and dismissal arising as a result of that discrimination. All claims (except for gender discrimination claims) must be referred in

---

103. *Professor Kevin James v Cork Institute of Technology* DEC–E2010–076.
104. Note there is a spelling error in the decision which I have amended here.

the first instance to the Equality Tribunal. (Gender discrimination claims have the option of going to the Circuit Court).[105]

Employee's right to certain information.

[11.42] Section 76 of the 1998 Act allows any person who believes that they may have experienced discrimination to write to the person who may have discriminated against them asking for certain information which will assist in deciding whether to refer a claim.

There is no obligation on employers to reply to such requests but should the claim proceed an equality officer may draw such inferences as seem appropriate from the failure to respond or from responding with inaccurate, misleading or inadequate information. For these reasons it is always advisable to respond to such requests. Employees are requested to use a standard form of questionnaire. The Employment Equality Act 1998 (Section 76 – Right to Information) Regulations 1999[106] set out the forms that must be used. Form EE1 is used for the initial complaint by the complainant. Form EE2 also known as a request for information form is used by the complainant to seek additional information and Form EE3 is used by the respondent to reply to the former (reproduced at **11.54** below).

Time limits

[11.43] Once a complaint of discrimination has been received employers should immediately check the date on which it was made. A complaint of discrimination or harassment must be made within the six-month time limit from the last act of discrimination.[107] The date of receipt of the referral form, and not the date of posting, is the date of referral of a claim to the Director.[108]

The six-month time limit can be extended up to 12 months by the Director 'for reasonable cause'. This aspect was examined in detail by the *Labour Court in Cementation Skanska v Carroll*[109] (a case under the Organisation of Working Time Act 1997. This Act also allows for an extension of time based on 'reasonable cause'). Here the court held that it was for the claimant to show 'that there were reasons which both explain the delay and afford an excuse for the delay'.[110] The court further noted that even where 'reasonable cause' was shown it should still consider whether it was appropriate in the circumstances to grant an extension of time.

---

105. Employment Equality Act 1998, s 77(3).

106. Employment Equality Act 1998 (Section 76 – Right to Information) Regulations 1999 (SI 321/ 1999).

107. Employment Equality Act 1998, s 77(5) as amended by Equality Act 2004, s 32(b).

108. See *A Named Female Employee v A Named Respondent* DEC–E2003–001.

109. *Labour Court in Cementation Skanska v Carroll* DWT 38/2003.

110. Citing Costello J in *O'Donnell v Dun Laoghaire Corporation* (1991) ILRM 301, 315, a case which concerned whether there were 'good reasons' for extending the time under Rules of the Superior Courts 1986, Ord 84, r 21.

This line of reasoning was followed in the *Department of Finance v IMPACT*[111] where the Labour Court said that in considering if reasonable cause exists, it was for the applicant to show that there were reasons which both explain the delay and which afford an excuse for it. The court also went on to state that the explanation must be reasonable, not absurd or irrational and that this should be decided by applying common sense and accepted standards of reasonableness. The standard is an objective one but it must be applied to the facts known to the applicants at the material time.

Thus whilst it is not specifically stated in the Act it does seem that even if a complainant demonstrates reasonable cause, the court should then go on to consider if there are any compensating factors which might make it unjust to extend the time limit. These factors could include:

- the length of the delay;

- any prejudice which might have been suffered by the respondent as a result of the delay;

- whether the complainant was culpable in the delay.

What is also clear from the above is that the bar to be overcome is much lower than that expected from claimants under the Unfair Dismissals Act where 'exceptional circumstances' is the test.

ACCRUAL OF A CAUSE OF ACTION

[11.44] In the case of *Professor Kevin James v Cork Institute of Technology*[112] the equality officer confirmed that a cause of action does not accrue when the complainant discovers its existence but rather when the requisite elements existed. The Equality Officer went on to state:

> I accept the respondent's contention that a cause of action does not accrue when the complainant discovers its existence. In this, I am guided by the recent Labour Court case where the Chairman pointed out 'had the Oireachtas intended to provide a discoverability test it could easily have made such a provision.' ... in that case the Court held that a cause of action accrues at the time when all the requisite elements of the action existed whether or not the plaintiff knew of their existence.

The Equality Tribunal

STEP 1. MEDIATION

[11.45] The Director of the Equality Tribunal (the Director) can at any stage – but only with the consent of both parties – appoint an equality mediation officer.[113] A case will not be referred for mediation if there is an objection from either party. Mediation occurs in private.[114] Where a case is referred to mediation but it has not been solved, the

---

111. *Department of Finance v IMPACT* EET2/2004.
112. *Professor Kevin James v Cork Institute of Technology* DEC–E2010–076.
113. Employment Equality Act 1998, s 78 as amended by Equality Act 2004, ss 34 and 46.
114. Employment Equality Act 1998, s 78(4).

equality mediation officer 'shall issue a note to that effect to the complainant and the respondent'.[115] Where this notice has been issued and if within 28 days of the issue of that notice the complainant makes an application for the resumption of the case then the case can resume.[116] Note that it is only the complainant that can make the application for a resumption of the case. In *A Male Complainant v A Bar and Restaurant*[117] the equality officer confirmed that jurisdiction to re-open an investigation, following an attempt to resolve the dispute at mediation, depended on an application being made within the specified time limit and that the Act did not leave him with any discretion in the matter.

Section 91 of the 1998 Act as amended by ss 39 and 46 of the 2004 Act provides for the enforcement by order of the Circuit Court of a mediated settlement. Applications are made by way of originating Motion on Notice.[118]

In December 2002, the Director published a report entitled 'Developments in Alternative Dispute Resolution', the purpose of which is to demystify the mediation process by 'identifying key developments in equality mediation'. Most of the staff employed in this area have completed accredited training from the Mediation Institute of Ireland.

For employers the question as to whether to attend mediation is an important one. The main benefit in doing so is that the dispute can be resolved in private with a trained negotiator and the process is less time-consuming than a full investigation and/or further hearing by the Labour Court. Also if an employer's case is in any way weak it may be possible to settle for a smaller compensatory amount than perhaps if the case proceeded further.

STEP 2. INVESTIGATION

[11.46] If either party does object to mediation or if the process of mediation is unsuccessful, the case will be referred to an equality officer for investigation.[119] The equality officer will issue a determination which again is enforceable through the Circuit Court.[120] (Form 4 reproduced at **11.56** below can be used for this purpose.)

BURDEN OF PROOF

[11.47] A new s 85A was inserted into the 1998 Act to give effect to Council Directive 97/80/EC revoking the European Communities (Burden of Proof in Gender Discrimination Cases) Regulations 2001 (SI 337/2001) in so far as they relate to any proceedings under the 1998 Act.

---

115. Employment Equality Act 1998, s 78(6) as amended by Equality Act 2004, s 34.
116. Employment Equality Act 1998, s 78(7) as amended by Equality Act 2004, s 34.
117. *A Male Complainant v A Bar and Restaurant* DEC–E 2003–005.
118. See Circuit Court Rules (Employment Equality Act 1998) 2004 (SI 880/2004).
119. Employment Equality Act 1998, s 79 as amended by Equality Act 2004, ss 35 and 46.
120. Employment Equality Act 1998, s 91 and Circuit Court Rules (Employment Equality Act 1998) 2004 (SI 880/2004).

Section 85A(1) provides as follows:

> Where in any proceedings facts are established by or on behalf of a complainant from which it may be presumed that there has been discrimination in relation to him or her, it is for the respondent to prove the contrary.

In the *Southern Health Board v Mitchell*[121] the Labour Court went on to consider the extent of the evidential burden which a claimant must discharge before a prima facie case of discrimination can be made out. They laid down a two-step test:

- The first requirement is that the claimant must establish facts from which it may be presumed that the principle of equal treatment has not been applied to them. This indicates that a claimant must prove on the balance of probabilities the primary facts on which they rely in seeking to raise a presumption of unlawful discrimination.

- It is only if these primary facts are established to the satisfaction of the court, and they are regarded by the court as being of sufficient significance to raise a presumption of discrimination that the onus shifts to the respondent to prove that there is no infringement of the principle of equal treatment.

In the case of *Melbury Development v Arturs Valpetters*[122] the Labour Court whilst examining the circumstances in which the probative burden of proof operates held that:

> Section 85A of the Acts provides for the allocation of the probative burden in cases within its ambit. This requires that the Complainant must first establish facts from which discrimination may be inferred. What those facts are will vary from case to case and there is no closed category of facts which can be relied upon. All that is required is that they be of sufficient significance to raise a presumption of discrimination. However they must be established as facts on credible evidence. Mere speculation or assertions, unsupported by evidence, cannot be elevated to a factual basis upon which an inference of discrimination can be drawn. Section 85A places the burden of establishing the primary facts fairly and squarely on the Complainant and the language of this provision admits of no exceptions to that evidential rule.

The issue of the burden of proof was also considered at length by the Labour Court in *ICON Clinical Research v Djemma Tsourova*.[123] In this case counsel for the respondent submitted that the complainant must prove every aspect of her case and that it is not permissible for the court to apply a shifting burden other than in cases of alleged discrimination on the gender ground. The court rejected this argument by inter alia relying on s 85A.

The Circuit Court (gender discrimination cases)

[11.48] A complainant who is alleging discrimination on the gender ground can take a claim to the Circuit Court instead of to the Director of the Equality Tribunal.[124] This

---

121. *Southern Health Board v Mitchell* (2001) ELR 201.
122. *Melbury Development v Arturs Valpetters* EDA 0917.
123. *ICON Clinical Research v Djemma Tsourova* Labour Court (Case 04/2) Determination No 054.
124. Employment Equality Act 1998, s 77(3) as amended by Equality Act 2004, ss 32 and 46.

provision follows the European Court of Justice decision in *Marshall v Southampton Area Health Authority (No 2)*[125] where the court held that a cap on the potential award for sex discrimination was inconsistent with the right to an effective judicial process pursuant to art 6 of the Equal Treatment Directive. Thus, where gender discrimination cases are referred to the Circuit Court there is no ceiling on the award that may be made by the court. Section 82(3) of the 1998 Act allows that the award may exceed the normal civil jurisdiction of the Circuit Court.

An action in the Circuit Court is commenced by the issue and service of an Employment Law Civil Bill (Form 1) (Reproduced at **11.57** below). A defence to the proceedings is made on Form 2 (both reproduced at **11.58** below).

Remedies

The Labour Court and the Director of the Equality Tribunal

[11.49] Where a discriminatory dismissal has occurred and the equality officer or the Labour Court finds in favour of the complainant, the following orders can be made:

- an order for compensation for the effects of discrimination of up to a maximum of two year's pay.[126] This is regardless of whether or not there was discrimination on more than one ground;

- an order for re-instatement or re-engagement with or without an order for compensation.

Section 82(1)(c) of the 1998 Act makes it clear that compensation can be given not just for the loss of earnings suffered as a result of discriminatory dismissal but also 'for the effects of acts of discrimination or victimisation'. This section clarified the practice that had been in place before the 1998 Act where the equality officers and the Labour Court had taken it upon themselves under the Employment Equality Act 1977 to award compensation for hurt feelings even though there was no statutory basis for them to do so. This is unlike the position that prevails under the unfair dismissals legislation where claimants have to prove actual loss and demonstrate that they have attempted to mitigate that loss.

The Circuit Court

[11.50] There is no limit to the amount of compensation that may be ordered by the Circuit Court for discriminatory dismissal on gender grounds.[127]

Appeals

[11.51] Decisions of the Director (including decisions on time limits and striking out of the claim) may be appealed to the Labour Court not later than 42 days from the date of a

---

125. *Marshall v Southampton Area Health Authority (No 2)* (1993) ECR I–4367.
126. Employment Equality Act 1998, s 82(4).
127. Employment Equality Act 1998, s 82(3)(d).

decision,[128] not the date when it was received by the party wishing to appeal.[129] The date of the decision is to be included in the calculation.[130]

Where a determination is made by the Labour Court on an appeal, either party may appeal to the High Court on a point of law.[131]

Costs

[11.52] In general, costs are not awarded. Costs in respect of travelling and other expenses (except expenses of representatives) can be awarded where a person obstructs or impedes the investigation or appeal.[132]

Forms

Form EE1

[11.53]

Form EE1. EMPLOYMENT EQUALITY ACTS

COMPLAINT TO THE EQUALITY TRIBUNAL OF DISCRIMINATION RELATING TO EMPLOYMENT.

Before you begin to fill the form please read the notes supplied in a separate document.

There are 9 sections to be completed on this form.

Start of form.

Section 1 of 9. Your details.

Please enter your details below.

Name: . . . . .

Address: . . . . .

Phone Number: . . . . .

Email Address: . . . . .

Important: If your address changes, you must let the Tribunal know. Otherwise you may miss important letters from the Tribunal, including the date of any hearing, which will be sent by post unless otherwise requested, and the complaint could be decided in your absence or even dismissed.

End of Section 1.

Section 2 of 9. Your representative.

Do you have a representative, please answer Yes below and put in their name and contact details. If not, please answer No.

---

128. Employment Equality Act 1998, s 83(1).
129. See *Hegarty v Labour Court* (1999) 3 IR 603.
130. See *Byrne v Minaguchi* EDA4/2003 and *Dunnes Stores v Boylan* EDA5/2003.
131. Employment Equality Act 1998, s 90(1).
132. Employment Equality Act 1998, s 99A as inserted by Equality Act 2004, s 41.

Do you have a representative?   . . . . .

Name: . . . . .

Address: . . . . .

Phone Number:. . . . .

Fax Number: . . . . .

Email Address: . . . . .

You can bring your case by yourself but, if you wish you can be represented by a lawyer, support organisation or support person. You will have to pay any costs involved as the Tribunal cannot award costs.

End of Section 2.

Section 3 of 9. Who you are complaining about.

Please enter details of the person, organisation or company you are complaining about below.

Name: . . . . .

Address: . . . . .

Phone Number: . . . . .

Fax Number: . . . . .

Email Address: . . . . .

End of Section 3.

Section 4 of 9. Grounds for discrimination.

Please indicate below which of the 9 grounds you say you have been discriminated against. Answer Yes or No to each choice. You may choose more than one.

Gender: . . . . .

Marital Status: . . . . .

Family Status: . . . . .

Sexual Orientation: . . . . .

Religion: . . . . .

Age: . . . . .

Disability: . . . . .

Race: . . . . .

Membership of the Traveller Community: . . . . .

End of Section 4.

Section 5 of 9. Reasons you were treated unlawfully.

Please indicate which of the following 11 reasons do you say the respondent treated you unlawfully. Answer Yes or No to each choice. You may choose more than one reason.

Getting a job: . . . . .

Promoting me:

Giving me training: . . . . .

Conditions of employment: . . . . .

Dismissing me for Discriminatory Reasons: . . . . .

Harassing me:. . . . .

Sexually harassing me: . . . . .

Victimising me: . . . . .

Dismissing me because I oppose discrimination: . . . . .

Failing to give me reasonable accommodation for a disability: . . . . .

Other: . . . . .

End of Section 5.

Section 6 of 9. Equal pay claims.

If you are claiming equal pay with someone else, please answer Yes and put in their name below. Otherwise, please answer No.

Are you claiming equal pay with someone else?   . . . . .

If Yes please provide the name of the person with whom you are claiming equal pay:

This person is know as the "comparator".

End of Section 6.

Section 7 of 9. Collective agreement claims.

If you are claiming a collective agreement contains discriminatory provisions, please answer Yes, provide a copy of the agreement and mark the sections you think are discriminatory. Otherwise, please answer No.

Are you claiming a collective agreement contains discriminatory provisions?

End of Section 7.

Section 8 of 9. Details of complaint (other than equal pay).

Last date of discrimination: . . . . .

Date you left your job or were dismissed: . . . . .

Please set out briefly in your own words what happened, when it happened and where it happened. You may use a separate sheet if required (a short description is sufficient as you will be asked at a later date to provide a more detailed submission): . . . . .

End of Section 8.

Section 9 of 9. Related complaints.

Please state details of any related complaints:

If you have made a complaint about the same issue to the Labour Court, The Labour Relations Commission or the Employment Appeals Tribunal, please attach details and the current status of that claim.

End of Section 9.

Please sign and enter the date.

Sign here:

Date:

End of Form.

Please return the completed and signed form to:

The Equality Tribunal,

3 Clonmel Street,

Dublin 2.

Telephone 014774100.

Lo Call   1890344424.

Information on Data Protection

The Equality Tribunal will treat all information submitted in accordance with the purposes registered under the Data Protection Acts 1998 to 2003.

Official use only

This part of the form is for official use only. Please do not fill this part in.

Received Stamp

Case Ref Number

End of official part of form.

Form EE2

[11.54]

Employment Equality Acts, 1998 to 2004

Section 76: "Right to information"
Complainant's request for information from the respondent

Explanatory note:
The Employment Equality Acts 1998 to 2004 provide at section 76 that :

- where a person thinks they may have been discriminated against, or treated in any other way which is unlawful under the Employment Equality Acts,

- that person (the "complainant") may, if they so wish,

- write to the person or organisation whom they think may have treated them unlawfully, (the "respondent")

- asking for relevant information to help them in deciding whether they should refer a case to the Equality Tribunal or to help them in formulating and presenting their case.

This Form EE.2 contains the form prescribed by law[1] for a complainant to use in asking for this information.

Some types of information are excluded. According to Section 76, information is "relevant" if it is:

➢ information about the respondent's reasons for doing, or omitting to do, anything relevant

➢ information about any relevant practices or procedures of the respondent

➢ information (other than confidential information, or information about the scale or financial resources of the employer's business) about the remuneration or treatment of other persons who are in a comparable position to the complainant,

➢ any other information which is not confidential, and which it is reasonable for the complainant to ask for in the circumstances.
Confidential information means *"any information which relates to a particular individual, which can be identified as so relating, and to the disclosure of which that individual does not agree."*

The respondent can reply using Form EE.3, which is prescribed by law for this purpose. (The respondent is not obliged to reply. Section 81 of the Acts provides that if they do not reply, or if their replies are false or misleading, this may be taken

---

[1] See *Employment Equality Act 1998 (Section 76 – Right to Information) Regulations, 1999*, Statutory Instrument no 321 of 1999. Character references are excluded, and special provisions apply to requests for information about interviews by the Civil Service Commissioners, Local Appointments Commissioners, Defence Forces or Garda Siochana: see section 76.

Page 1 of 5

into account in deciding the case.)

Employment Equality Acts 1998 and 2004, section 76
Questionnaire of the Complainant

Name and address of person to be questioned (the Respondent):	To... of.. ....
Name and address of Complainant:	1. I.. of.. ....
Delete the circumstances which do not apply to your complaint.	consider that you may have: (a) discriminated against me; (b) dismissed or otherwise penalised me in circumstances amounting to victimisation; (c) failed to provide equal remuneration to me as required by an equal remuneration term; (d) failed to provide equal treatment to me as required by an equality clause under my contract of employment; contrary to the provisions of the Employment Equality Acts, 1998 to 2004.
Indicate the discriminatory ground(s) which you consider to apply to your complaint. (Tick where appropriate).	2. Gender ( ) Marital Status ( ) Family Status ( ) Sexual Orientation ( ) Religion ( ) Age ( ) Disability ( ) Race ( ) Traveller Community Ground ( ).

Form EE.2

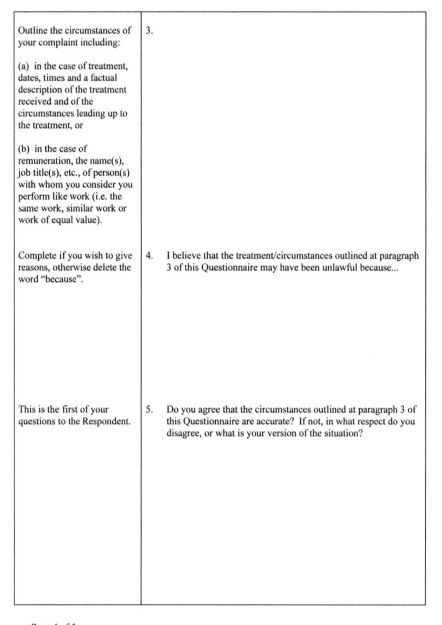

Outline the circumstances of your complaint including: (a) in the case of treatment, dates, times and a factual description of the treatment received and of the circumstances leading up to the treatment, or (b) in the case of remuneration, the name(s), job title(s), etc., of person(s) with whom you consider you perform like work (i.e. the same work, similar work or work of equal value).	3.
Complete if you wish to give reasons, otherwise delete the word "because".	4. I believe that the treatment/circumstances outlined at paragraph 3 of this Questionnaire may have been unlawful because...
This is the first of your questions to the Respondent.	5. Do you agree that the circumstances outlined at paragraph 3 of this Questionnaire are accurate? If not, in what respect do you disagree, or what is your version of the situation?

Page 4 of 5

Form EE.2

This is the second of your questions to the Respondent.	6.	Do you accept that your treatment of me, or the rate of remuneration afforded to me, was unlawful, contrary to the provisions of the Employment Equality Acts, 1998 to 2004? If not: (a) Why not? (b) For what reason did I receive the treatment/remuneration which is the subject of my complaint?
Enter here any other questions you wish to ask including any request for other non-confidential material information in respect of other persons who are in a comparable position to you or information which it is reasonable for you to require in the context of your case.	7.	
Address to which reply should be sent, if not the same as that at paragraph 1 of this Questionnaire.	8.	Signature of Complainant .... Date..

Note
If there is not sufficient space to request information, please use additional page(s) and sign and date each of them.

Form EE3

[11.55]

Form EE.3

Employment Equality Acts, 1998 to 2004

Reply to a request for information

<u>Explanatory note:</u>

- The <u>Employment Equality Acts 1998 to 2004</u> provide at section 76 that:
- where a person thinks they may have been discriminated against, or treated in any other way which is unlawful under the Employment Equality Acts,
- that person (the "complainant") may
- write to the person or organisation whom they think may have treated them unlawfully, (the "respondent")
- asking for relevant information to help in deciding whether they should refer a case to the Equality Tribunal or to help in formulating and presenting a case.

- Form EE.2 contains the form prescribed by law for a complainant to use in asking for such information.

- **This Form EE.3 is prescribed by law[1] as the form for a respondent to use in replying to a request for information.**

- The respondent is not obliged to reply to a request for information.

- However, section 81 of the Employment Equality Acts provides that if they do not reply, or if their replies are false or misleading, this may be taken into account in deciding the case.

- Some types of information are excluded. According to Section 76, information is relevant if it is:

- information about the respondent's reasons for doing, or omitting to do, anything relevant
- information about any relevant practices or procedures of the respondent
- information (other than confidential information, or information about the scale or financial resources of the employer's business) about the remuneration or treatment of other persons who are in a comparable position to the complainant,
- any other information which is not confidential, and which it is reasonable for the complainant to ask for in the circumstances.

Confidential information means *"any information which relates to a particular individual, which can be identified as so relating, and to the disclosure of which that individual does not agree."*

---

[1] See *Employment Equality Act 1998 (Section 76 – Right to Information) Regulations, 1999,* Statutory Instrument no 321 of 1999.

Page 1 of 4

Form EE.3

Employment Equality Acts 1998 and 2004 – Section 76
Reply by the Respondent

Name and address of Complainant:	To.. of ....
Name and address of Respondent:	1 . I... of .... hereby acknowledge receipt of the Questionnaire signed by you and dated................................
Delete sentence at (a) or (b) as appropriate and, if (a) is deleted, complete (b).	2 . (a) I agree that the statement/circumstances outlined in paragraph 3 of the Questionnaire is/are accurate. (b) I disagree with the statement/circumstances outlined in paragraph 3 of the Questionnaire in that.....

Delete sentence at (a) or (b) as appropriate and, if (a) is deleted, complete one or more of the sentences at (b) (i) and (b) (ii).	3 . (a)	I accept that my treatment of you, or the rate of remuneration afforded to you, was unlawful, contrary to the provisions of the Employment Equality Acts, 1998 to 2004.
	(b)	I dispute that my treatment of you, or the rate of remuneration afforded to you, was unlawful, contrary to the provisions of the Employment Equality Acts, 1998 to 2004:
	(i)	My reasons for disputing are....
	(ii)	The reasons why you received the treatment accorded to you or the rate of remuneration afforded to you are as follows....

Form EE.3

Replies to the questions in paragraph 7 of the Questionnaire should be entered here.	4 .
Delete this entire sentence if you have answered all of the questions in the Questionnaire.	5 . I have deleted (in whole or in part) the paragraph(s) numbered .... above, because I am unable / unwilling (delete as appropriate) to reply to those questions for the following reasons- Signature of Respondent .... Date ....

Notes

If there is not sufficient space to enter a reply, please use additional page(s) and sign and date each of them.

If a Respondent fails to provide the information sought by the Complainant, or the information provided is false or misleading or is otherwise not such as the Complainant might reasonably require in accordance with the appropriate provisions of the Employment Equality Acts 1998 to 2004, the Director of the Equality Tribunal, the Labour Court or the Circuit Court may draw such inferences as seem appropriate in the circumstances.

Page 4 of 4

381

Form 4 Circuit Court Motion on Notice

[11.56]

(AN CHUIRT CHUARDA)
THE CIRCUIT COURT

(INSERT CIRCUIT) **CIRCUIT**   **COUNTY OF** *(INSERT COUNTY)*

BETWEEN/

(INSERT NAME OF RESPONDENT)

Respondent

AND

(INSERT NAME OF APPELLANT)

Appellant

NOTICE OF MOTION

TAKE NOTICE that on the (*insert date*) at (*insert time*) in the forenoon or on the first opportunity thereafter, application will be made to this Honourable Court sitting at (*insert address*) by way of Appeal against the determination of the Employment Appeals Tribunal dated (*insert date*) and written communication which was received by the Appellant herein on the (*insert date*) under Reference Number (*insert reference number*) upholding the claim of the Claimant maintained pursuant to the provisions of the above cited enactments.

AND TAKE NOTICE that the Appellant will rely on the following grounds:-

(*Insert particulars*)

1. The Tribunal erred in law and in fact in finding that the Claimant's dismissal lacked proper procedure and was contrary to natural justice.
2. Without prejudice to the foregoing the Tribunal's award in the amount of (*insert amount of award*) as compensation under the Unfair Dismissals Act 1977-2001 takes no account of the contribution of the Claimant to his dismissal nor does the said amount take into account the fact that the Claimant failed to mitigate his loss in this regard.
3. Such further or other grounds as may arise at or be put forward at the hearing of the said Appeal.
4. The following documents are in accordance with the requirement of the Rules of the Circuit Court annexed hereto:-

   a) A copy of the original Notice of Appeal to the Tribunal
   b) A copy of the Notice of Appearance
   c) A copy of the determination of the Tribunal
   d) Copy of the original letter from the Tribunal notifying the making of communication of the said determination
   e) A copy of the particulars provided by either party at the Tribunal – N/A

Dated this   day of   , 20

Signed: _____

        (*Insert Solicitor name*)
        Solicitors for the Appellant
        (*Insert address*)

To: The County Registrar
        Circuit Court
        (*Insert address*)

And: (*Insert name*)
Representative for the Claimant
(*Insert address*)

And: The Secretary
        Employment Appeals Tribunal
        65A Adelaide Road
        Dublin 2

(*INSERT CIRCUIT*) CIRCUIT

(AN CHUIRT CHUARDA)

THE CIRCUIT COURT

COUNTY OF (*INSERT COUNTY*)

BETWEEN/

(*INSERT NAME OF RESPONDENT*)

<u>Respondent</u>

AND

(*INSERT NAME OF APPELLANT*)

<u>Appellant</u>

<u>NOTICE OF MOTION</u>

Form 1 Circuit Court Employment Law Civil Bill

[11.57]

AN CHUIRT CHUARDA
(THE CIRCUIT COURT)

(*insert circuit*) **Circuit**   **County of** (*insert county*)

IN THE MATTER OF
THE EMPLOYMENT EQUALITY ACT 1998-2004

BETWEEN/

(*Insert name of Plaintiff*)
                                        PLAINTIFF

-AND-

(*Insert name of Defendant*)
                                        DEFENDANT

EMPLOYMENT LAW CIVIL BILL

You are hereby required within ten days after the service of this Civil Bill upon you to enter or cause to be entered with the County Registrar at his office at the Courthouse, (*insert location*) an Appearance to answer the claim of (*Insert name of Plaintiff*) of (*insert address*), the Plaintiff herein, as indorsed hereon.

AND TAKE NOTICE that, unless you do enter an Appearance you will be held to have admitted the said claim, and the Plaintiff may proceed therein and judgment may be given against you in your absence without further notice.

AND FURTHER TAKE NOTICE that, if you intend to defend the proceeding on any grounds, you must not only enter an Appearance as aforesaid, but also within ten days after Appearance deliver a Statement in writing showing the nature and grounds of your Defence.

The Appearance and Defence may be entered by posting the same to the said Office and by giving copies thereof to the Plaintiffs, or his/their Solicitor, by post.

Dated the   day of   , 20 .

Signed: _____

(*Insert name*)
Solicitors for the Plaintiff,
(*Insert address*).

To: (*Insert Name and address of Defendant*)

INDORSEMENT OF CLAIM

1. The Plaintiff is a (*Insert occupation*) with (*Insert Defendant name*) and resides at (*Insert address of Plaintiff*).

2. The Defendant is a (*insert type of business of Defendant*) having its registered address at (*Insert address*).

3. On or about (*Insert date*) the Plaintiff was employed as a (*Insert occupation*) under a Contract of Employment by the Defendant. The Plaintiff was successful in the position as (*Insert occupation*) and faithfully and diligently performed her duties for the Defendant.

4. It was an express or alternatively an implied term of the Plaintiff's Contract of Employment that she would be provided with a safe place of work, safe and competent staff including management, a safe system of work and a workplace free from discrimination on grounds of her gender.

5. The Plaintiff was subjected to sexual harassment, harassment, bullying and discrimination on the grounds of gender and family status by the Defendant, their servants or agents and the Defendant has been in breach of the Plaintiff's terms of employment as set out above.

6. The Defendant, their servants or agents failed to deal adequately or at all with the said treatment to which the Plaintiff was subjected by the Defendant, their servants or agents about which the Defendant knew or ought to have known.

7. The less favourable treatment and discrimination to which the Plaintiff was subjected culminated in the termination of the Plaintiff's employment on the (*Insert date*). The less favourable treatment was direct discrimination on grounds of gender and/or family status.

8. The less favourable and discriminatory treatment was in breach of the Plaintiff's Contract of Employment and the Defendant's Policies and Procedures and was in breach of the Plaintiff's entitlements pursuant to the Employment Equality Act 1998, as amended and in particular Sections 6, and 8 thereof.

PARTICULARS OF UNLAWFUL DISCRIMINATION/BASIS OF JURISDICTION

(Insert detailed particulars of unlawful discrimination)

The above instances are examples of the harassment and discriminatory treatment suffered by the Plaintiff. The Plaintiff reserves the right to adduce further examples.

10. The behaviour by the Defendant, its servants or agents described above towards the Plaintiff has had profoundly negative psychological and physical effects on the Plaintiff and has gravely damaged the reputation and career of the Plaintiff. By reason

of the foregoing behaviour the Plaintiff has been caused offence, stress, personal injury, anxiety, embarrassment, loss, damage and upset.

11. Council Directive 76/207 or 2002/73/ EEC on the implementation of the principle of equal treatment for men and women as regards access to employment, vocational training and promotion and working conditions is implemented in Ireland by way of the Employment Equality Act 1998 as amended. This provides inter alia that an employer, its servants or agents shall not discriminate against or harass an employee on the gender ground including dismissal.

12. The less favourable treatment and harassment of the Plaintiff and the termination of the Plaintiff's employment by the Defendant was in breach of the Plaintiff's contract of employment and was in breach of the Plaintiff entitlement's pursuant to the Employment Equality Act 1998 as amended by the Equality Act 2004 and in particular sections 6,8 and 14A thereof. This unfavourable and discriminatory treatment was also in breach of the Maternity Protection Act 1994 and Council Directive 92/85EC (the Pregnant Workers Directive).

13. At all times the less favourable treatment and harassment to which the Plaintiff was subjected by the Defendant, its servants or agents, which treatment culminated in the termination of the Plaintiffs employment, was as a direct result of the Plaintiff's gender.

14. Further the Plaintiffs treatment was in breach of the Safety, Health and Welfare at Work Act 2005 and Regulations thereto.

15. The last act complained of occurred on the (*Insert date*), on which date the Defendant dismissed the Plaintiff.

   AND THE PLAINTIFF CLAIMS: Damages for breach of Contract and/or breach of duty including breach of statutory duty and/or orders pursuant to Section 82(3) of the Employment Equality Act 1998 as amended, which damages are not limited by the normal jurisdictional limits of this Honourable Court, such further or other relief as to this Honourable Court shall deem meet, including an extension of time to commence proceedings if required, interest pursuant to Statute, and the costs of these proceedings.

*(**Insert name of Barrister**)*

(Insert Name)
Solicitors for the Plaintiff,
(Insert address).

AN CHUIRT CHUARDA
(THE CIRCUIT COURT)

(*insert circuit*) Circuit   County of (*insert county*)

IN THE MATTER OF
THE EMPLOYMENT EQUALITY ACT 1998-2004

BETWEEN/

(*Insert name of Plaintiff*)

PLAINTIFF

-AND-

(*Insert name of Defendant*)

DEFENDANT

EMPLOYMENT LAW CIVIL BILL

Form 2 Defence to Circuit Court Civil Bill

[11.58]

Record No.

AN CHUIRT CHUARDA
(THE CIRCUIT COURT)

(*insert circuit*) Circuit   County of (*insert county*)

IN THE MATTER OF
THE EMPLOYMENT EQUALITY ACT 1998-2004

BETWEEN/

(Insert name of Plaintiff)

PLAINTIFF

-AND-

(Insert name of Defendant)

DEFENDANT

DEFENCE

DELIVERED ON THE   DAY OF   20   BY   , SOLICITORS FOR
THE DEFENDANT HEREIN.

1.   The Plaintiff is put on proof of her employment as a   with the
        Defendant and that she was successful in that position and that she completed her
        duties diligently and faithfully.

2.   The Plaintiff is put on proof of the express or alternatively the implied terms of her
        contract of employment.

3.   It is denied that the Plaintiff was subjected to sexual harassment, harassment,
        bullying, discrimination on the grounds of gender and family status by the
        Defendant their servants or agents and it is denied that the Defendants have been in
        breach of the Plaintiff's terms of employment as alleged.

4.　　　It is denied that the Defendants failed to deal adequately or at all with the alleged treatment and any such treatment is denied.

5.　　　It is denied that the Plaintiff was less favourably treated by the Defendants and/or discriminated against and/or that such treatment culminated in the termination of the Plaintiff's employment on the 　　　　　.

6.　　　It is denied that the Plaintiff was less favourably treated, discriminated against or that the Defendant was in breach of the Plaintiff's alleged Contract of Employment and/or that the Defendants were in breach of policies or procedures or in breach of statutory duty as alleged or at all.

7.　　　The particulars of unlawful discrimination are denied as if hereunder set forth and individually traversed seriatum.

8.　　　The Defendants will rely on the fact that the Plaintiff was made redundant in .

9.　　　It is denied that the Plaintiff has suffered psychological, physical effects or that the Plaintiff's career or reputation have been damaged.

10.　　　It is denied that the Plaintiff has suffered offence, stress, personal injury, anxiety, embarrassment, loss and damage or upset.

11.　　　It is denied that the Plaintiff was in breach of the matters set out in paragraphs 11,12, 13, and 14.

12.　　　It is denied that the Plaintiff was dismissed on the 　　　　, but was in fact made redundant.

13.　　　The Plaintiff is not entitled to the relief claimed.

BL

Signed:　　_____

　　　　　Solicitors for the Defendant

To:　　　The County Registrar
　　　　　Circuit Court Office

To:　　　Solicitors for the Plaintiff

INDEX